"Jon is the great gaming librarian, the dramaturg of *D&D*. He is always my first call when I'm researching anything related to the history of tabletop gaming. If he doesn't know, most likely no one else does, and this book is no exception. With it, Jon sets straight the 'canon' of the tragic history of how *Dungeons & Dragons* and TSR were ripped from the very grasp of the man who dreamed them up."

—**Joe Manganiello**, actor, producer, *Dungeons & Dragons* ambassador, and writer/game designer for Wizards of the Coast/Hasbro

"Like an intrepid adventurer, Jon Peterson delves deep into the labyrinth of TSR's checkered history and the controversies surrounding *Dungeons & Dragons*. His broad knowledge of the subject and impeccable research allow you to share in his discoveries, with a focus on the colorful characters who were swept up in the *D&D* phenomenon and transformed by their experiences. Along the way, he uncovers many of the elements that led to the company's demise, including nepotism, hubris, poor management decisions, and unfulfilled promises. It's a compelling story."

—**Mike Carr**, TSR game designer, editor, writer, and executive (1976–1983)

"I thought I knew well the story of the meteoric rise of *Dungeons & Dragons*. Jon Peterson proves me half wrong as he reveals the labyrinth beneath the castle that Gygax and Arneson built. This book is the essential history of the personal perils, business pitfalls, and legal combats risked in the creation of the world's first roleplaying game."

—**Sam Witwer**, actor, Dungeon Master, part-time Sith

"While we were busy exploring the *Tomb of Horrors* in the 1980s, little did we know that the creators of *Dungeons & Dragons* were on a real-world adventure of their own—filled with tricks, traps, treasure hoards, and illusions—that nearly resulted in the dreaded Total Party Kill. *Game Wizards* is a gripping read and the definitive account of their quest."

—**Ray Winninger**, Executive Producer of *Dungeons & Dragons*, Wizards of the Coast

T0407255

"Every great empire needs a legendary historian. For *Dungeons & Dragons*, the foremost authority is unquestionably and without a doubt Jon Peterson. After tireless research and interviews, Jon now brings us the most harrowing quest ever to happen in *D&D*—and it's anything but fantasy. Jon meticulously documents the true story of the triumphant rise of the timeless tabletop game, and its even more utterly fascinating and heartbreakingly dramatic demise. This real life saga will be a page turner for hardcore tabletop gamers, but the mind-blowing events that Jon documents will absolutely captivate any reader."

—**Adam F. Goldberg**, TV showrunner, writer–producer, Half-elf Ranger proficient in bows and short swords

Game Wizards

Game Histories

edited by Henry Lowood and Raiford Guins

Game Wizards

The Epic Battle for *Dungeons & Dragons*

Jon Peterson

The MIT Press
Cambridge, Massachusetts
London, England

© 2021 Massachusetts Institute of Technology

All rights reserved. No part of this book may be reproduced in any form by any electronic or mechanical means (including photocopying, recording, or information storage and retrieval) without permission in writing from the publisher.

The MIT Press would like to thank the anonymous peer reviewers who provided comments on drafts of this book. The generous work of academic experts is essential for establishing the authority and quality of our publications. We acknowledge with gratitude the contributions of these otherwise uncredited readers.

This book was set in Stone Serif and Stone Sans by Westchester Publishing Services. Printed and bound in the United States of America.

Library of Congress Cataloging-in-Publication Data

Names: Peterson, Jon, author.
Title: Game wizards : the epic battle for Dungeons & Dragons /
   Jon Peterson.
Other titles: Dungeons and Dragons
Description: Cambridge, Massachusetts : The MIT Press, [2021] |
   Series: Game histories | Includes bibliographical references and index.
Identifiers: LCCN 2020047264 | ISBN 9780262542951 (Paperback)
Subjects: LCSH: Dungeons and Dragons (Game)--History. | TSR, Inc.--History.
   | Gygax, Gary. | Arneson, Dave, 1947–2009.
Classification: LCC GV1469.6 .P483 2021 | DDC 793.93--dc23
LC record available at https://lccn.loc.gov/2020047264

10 9 8 7 6 5 4 3 2

"No inventor can be a man of business, you know."

—*Little Dorrit*

Contents

Series Foreword

What might histories of games tell us not only about the games themselves but also about the people who play and design them? We think that the most interesting answers to this question will have two characteristics. First, the authors of game histories who tell us the most about games will ask big questions. For example, how do game play and design change? In what ways is such change inflected by societal, cultural, and other factors? How do games change when they move from one cultural or historical context to another? These kinds of questions forge connections to other areas of game studies, as well as to history, cultural studies, and technology studies.

The second characteristic we seek in "game-changing" histories is a wide-ranging mix of qualities partially described by terms such as *diversity, inclusiveness*, and *irony*. Histories with these qualities deliver interplay of intentions, users, technologies, materials, places, and markets. Asking big questions and answering them in creative and astute ways strikes us as the best way to reach the goal of not an isolated, general history of games but rather of a body of game histories that will connect game studies to scholarship in a wide array of fields. The first step, of course, is producing those histories.

Game Histories is a series of books that we hope will provide a home—or maybe a launch pad—for the growing international research community whose interest in game history rightly exceeds the celebratory and descriptive. In a line, the aim of the series is to help actualize critical historical study of games. Books in this series will exhibit acute attention to historiography and historical methodologies, while the series as a whole will encompass the wide-ranging subject matter we consider crucial for the relevance of historical game studies. We envisage an active series with output that will reshape how electronic and other kinds of games are understood, taught, and researched, as well as broaden the appeal of games for the allied fields such as history of computing, history of science and technology, design history, design culture, material culture studies, cultural and social history, media history, new media studies, and science and technology studies.

The Game Histories series will welcome but not be limited to contributions in the following areas:

- Multidisciplinary methodological and theoretical approaches to the historical study of games.
- Social and cultural histories of play, people, places, and institutions of gaming.
- Epochal and contextual studies of significant periods influential to and formative of games and game history.
- Historical biography of key actors instrumental in game design, development, technology, and industry.
- Games and legal history.
- Global political economy and the games industry (including indie games).
- Histories of technologies pertinent to the study of games.
- Histories of the intersections of games and other media, including such topics as game art, games and cinema, and games and literature.
- Game preservation, exhibition, and documentation, including the place of museums, libraries, and collectors in preparing game history.
- Material histories of game artifacts and ephemera.

Henry Lowood, Stanford University

Raiford Guins, Indiana University Bloomington

Preface

The very first edition of *Dungeons & Dragons* credits two people on its cover: E. Gary Gygax (1938–2008) and David L. Arneson (1947–2009). As the game appeared well within living memory, and quickly found its place in popular culture, it should be straightforward to say what exactly those two people had to do with its creation and popularization. With the half-century anniversary of *D&D*'s 1974 release approaching, this pen-and-paper tabletop game is, to the surprise of nearly everyone, more popular and influential than ever, which makes its genesis a subject of growing interest. But sometimes, circumstances conspire to make even recent history difficult to recover.

Part of the problem is that the events leading up to the publication of *D&D* did not seem especially momentous at the time. The process involved only a handful of people working within an esoteric hobby, which left little by way of paperwork and few memorable moments. It is hard to imagine a project less obviously destined for mainstream success than *D&D*—and the shock of its triumph did more to disturb its historical record than clarify it. Gygax and Arneson had a falling out a few years after the game's release, and their scuffle over money and credit kicked up dust that obscures the key historical particulars to this day.

This book is the story of how *D&D* rose from its humble origins to become a pop culture phenomenon, and what that remarkable journey did to the people who made it. It does not focus on the innovations in game design of *D&D*, nor does it dwell on questions of who invented which concepts—except in so far as those details became part of the public or legal dispute over the game, which in a few cases they did. Readers interested in game system evolution are directed to my book *Playing at the World*, which was the starting point for much of the research here. Apart from the brief overview of the development process of *D&D* in part I, there remains nothing more than to reaffirm the sentiments expressed at the beginning of *Playing at the World*: that Gygax and Arneson were co-creators of *D&D*, in at least the crucial sense that Gygax would never have worked toward such a game without the inspiration of Arneson's vision, and Arneson would never have realized the publication of such a game without the structure that Gygax provided for it.

When Gygax began to see signs that *D&D* would cross over into the mainstream, he famously compared his company TSR to a low-level character in *D&D* that would gain experience over the years and eventually level up to rival the likes of Milton Bradley or Parker Brothers. He saw business from the perspective of an adventurer progressing to endlessly greater heights of power, and he played that adventurer as if it were his own personal *D&D* character. His embattled years running TSR tick off with something of the regularity of game turns, made up of phases: like the summer gaming conventions, effectively the combat phase of each turn; or the winter upkeep phase of shareholder meetings and fiscal reports. The battle for *D&D* was perhaps most like a game of *Diplomacy* (1959), where a succession of warring powers form and dissolve alliances as they seek to conquer World War I–era Europe—and like in any *Diplomacy* game, there are "stabs," moments of betrayal where alliances collapse. The narrative from part II forward thus follows that yearly turn structure, loosely, and hopefully not too intrusively.

As the annals progress, this story depicts the flow of events as it appeared to people at the time and, whenever possible, as they described it contemporaneously. This is not to say that people always understood matters perfectly as they happened, but what they expressed had dramatic consequences for TSR and *D&D*. This story thus pays close attention to gossip, not for the sake of its accuracy but rather for the role it played in shaping the perceptions of the broader hobby community. Within each chapter, we will endeavor to see things as they looked at the time, and to remain ignorant of the future—foreshadowing is reserved only for those events of prophetic moment that require a spotlight. Sometimes you have to know how a game ends to fully appreciate its opening moves.

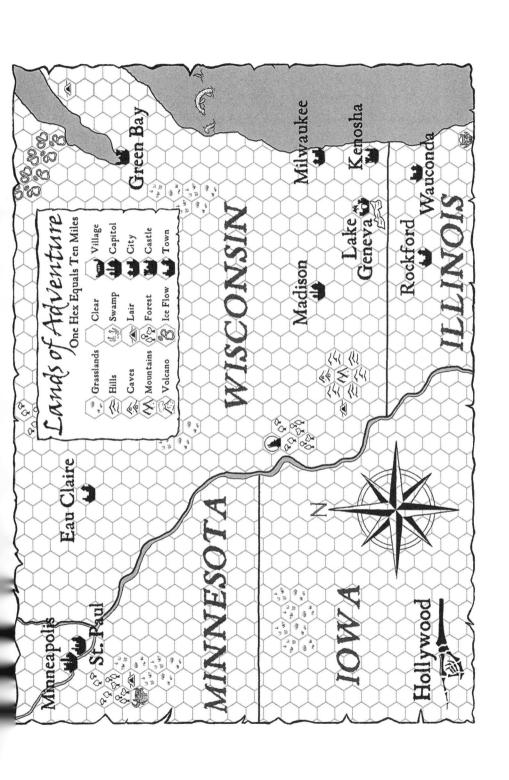

I From a Club to a Company

In the fall of 1985, Ernest Gary Gygax was the most famous and powerful figure in hobby gaming. He was President and Chairman of the Board of TSR, Inc., the company that published *Dungeons & Dragons*, and when the game took American popular culture by storm in the early 1980s, his star rose with it. As an author and executive, Gygax had steered the development of *D&D* for the last decade. The success of *D&D* had brought him into the realm of mainstream celebrity: his bearded face, adorned with thick glasses, had been featured on newsstands in slicks like *People* magazine, and *60 Minutes* had interviewed him for a September episode. His name and his game seemed inseparable.

October 22 was a Tuesday, and another day was wrapping up at TSR corporate headquarters on Sheridan Springs Road in Lake Geneva, Wisconsin, a workplace that then housed around a hundred employees—but had been built for many more. Gygax's final appointment was a board meeting just after the close of business, one that had been hurriedly called the day before. The meeting started late, at quarter past five. Of the company's six board members, five were present: two of the independent directors, James Huber and Wesley Sommer, and then the three principal shareholders: Gygax, Brian Blume, and Kevin Blume. The Blume family was Gygax's longest-standing business partner, having provided essential capital when the company was formed. Gygax was surprised to find both of the Blume brothers in attendance. Though they held a substantial stake in the company, they had kept some distance from TSR after leaving their management positions in prior reorganizations.

Everyone knew this was going to be a tense meeting. Despite the success of *D&D*, TSR faced significant financial challenges at the time. The board agonized over the company's turbulent negotiations with its primary creditor, the American National Bank, before moving on to the ostensible purpose of the meeting: a discussion regarding TSR's royalty payments to authors. In recent internal memos, Gygax had insisted that the company allow its employees, himself especially, to retain all copyrights and trademarks for works authored rather than assigning them to TSR, as well as receiving a royalty boost; in the eyes of other directors, this would violate existing contracts. The company needed to hold on to every penny it could if it were to remain viable. Gygax, for his part, felt that his contribution was undervalued.

During the heated disputes that followed, Gygax mused that the easiest way for him to secure a better agreement with the company would be to resign and negotiate a new contract as a freelancer. It was of course preposterous for a majority shareholder to suggest their own resignation, but Gygax found the room coldly receptive to this course of action. Sommer openly suggested that it would be in the best interests of the company and the shareholders for Gygax to go, and called for him to step down. Gygax was quick to point out that, with his majority control of the stock, the board was powerless to make such demands: he could simply call a shareholder meeting, replace the entire board with allies, and reinstate himself as president.

Or could he? The presence of the two Blume brothers was disconcerting. Gygax turned to the board secretary, Willard Martens, to ask if his personal stake as chairman relative to the other shareholders had changed recently. At first, Martens replied only that Lorraine Williams had exercised her option for fifty shares in TSR. Williams had joined the company in April as vice president of administration; her options alone could not endanger Gygax's majority.

"Have there been any other changes?" Gygax further inquired.

Martens only then volunteered, "Brian Blume exercised his option for seven hundred shares."

Realization set in. Gary Gygax said simply, "I see."

What did Gygax see, in that moment? He saw enough shares in play that he stood to lose control of TSR, a company he had founded and transformed into a global brand. But he surely also saw something even more dear at stake: that he might lose control of *Dungeons & Dragons*.

Opening Moves

To understand what the loss of TSR and *Dungeons & Dragons* must have meant to Gygax, we have to appreciate just how far he had come. His was not the sort of overnight success blundered into serendipitously: it was a grueling and precarious climb from virtually nothing to worldwide acclaim. A dozen years earlier, in the summer of 1973, Gary Gygax had first resolved to found a new imprint to publish game rules in his sleepy hometown of Lake Geneva, Wisconsin. Much of the firm's capital, staffing, and ideas came from a local game club, the Lake Geneva Tactical Studies Association—then a group of ten or fifteen people, some who commuted from nearby towns to play—so the company took the name Tactical Studies Rules, or TSR. At the time, Gygax already had in hand the promising set of rules TSR would market as *Dungeons & Dragons*.

But it would be a mistake to suppose that Gygax back then intended to create something we would recognize as an entrepreneurial start-up. No one who knew the market for games as intimately as Gygax would aspire to make a living off the sorts of rules he intended to publish. The best outcome he could hope for would be to popularize his work among a small but dedicated community of hobbyists and not lose money. But the release of *D&D* would set off a singular, nearly miraculous, chain of events, forging a TSR that Gygax could never have anticipated. Over the course of a tumultuous decade, filled with challenges and triumphs, *D&D* would steadily elevate TSR into a successful medium-sized business. It might seem that the establishment of a medium-sized business requires no supernatural intervention—but only if you overlook the sort of business it was.

There were people who made a living off of games in the early 1970s, of course. Nineteenth-century institutions like Milton Bradley and Parker Brothers sold games to the multitudes in multitudinous quantities. At a price point below $10, *Monopoly* alone then traded about two million copies a year for Parker Brothers—for a lifetime total of perhaps seventy million sold as the 1935 game neared its fortieth birthday—and it was just the most prominent of a rotating cast of faddish children's board games sold by the tens of millions annually. Tactical Studies Rules was not founded to make games with such broad appeal, though: instead, it would publish wargame rules. The commercial market for wargames was effectively created by one company, Avalon Hill, which in the 1970s was one of only a handful of wargaming firms with sufficient revenue to maintain a modest full-time staff.

The story of Avalon Hill handily illustrates the prospects awaiting entrepreneurs in the wargaming space. With the support of one partner, Charles S. Roberts self-financed his first board game *Tactics* in 1954 under an imprint he then called Avalon Games, so named after his home town of Avalon, Maryland. At the time, there was nothing on the market quite like *Tactics*: it was a two-player conflict simulation of modern military forces which effectively opened up a new genre of American board gaming. It was a deep, serious game, too complicated for young children, aimed squarely at people looking to learn more about military command than one could glean from 1950s titles in the vein of *Risk* or *Stratego*. It took Roberts four years to move the 1,800 or so copies of *Tactics* he warehoused in his garage, during which time he held down a job in advertising. But the opportunity he uncovered selling *Tactics* inspired him to incorporate in 1958 as the Avalon Hill Game Company, which recruited a small staff and managed to sell around 125,000 units of games a year up through 1963, most of them closely following the principles of the original *Tactics*. More than a fifth of those sales would be copies of *Gettysburg*, the company's bestselling re-creation of that famous historical battle; a revised edition of *Tactics* sold 82,000 copies over that same interval.

Innovative game design did not translate into business acumen, however, and a debt crisis at the end of 1963 forced Roberts to sell to a creditor: specifically, his printer, Eric Dott of Monarch Services, who discovered how to make Avalon Hill's business sustainable. Dott kept on some key personnel, such as game designer Tom Shaw, but Roberts found himself ousted from the firm he started, just shy of a decade after he published his first game. Whatever object lesson we might learn about the fate of innovators from Roberts's personal rise and fall, the reincarnated Avalon Hill remained a stable business for decades to come, the steady bulwark of a modest wargame industry. In the early 1970s, the entire product line of Avalon Hill sold around 200,000 boxed games annually, with each retailing between $7 and $9—a fraction of the market share enjoyed by a Parker Brothers, but enough to support some few livelihoods. By then, wargaming boasted a market large enough to support a prominent rival: Simulation Publications, Inc. (SPI) rose to challenge Avalon Hill by releasing a stream of games through its popular magazine *Strategy & Tactics*.

But Gygax hadn't founded TSR to make games quite like those, either. Avalon Hill and SPI sold board games, featuring colorful terrain maps, cardboard counters to represent troops, and dice to resolve combat as described in a rulebook. That was not TSR's plan. What Gygax initially aspired to sell were not "games" as such but instead "rules" for playing games—hence the "rules" in "Tactical Studies Rules." Open any board game box and throw away the board, the pieces, the dice, the cards, and seize that flimsy, stapled rulebook on the bottom. That is what TSR proposed to market to consumers: just the instructions on how to play a game with components that were sold separately. That may not sound like something anyone would pay for, and in general it was not. But a tiny niche hobby interested in such rules existed among wargamers who collected toy soldiers, or military "miniatures" as they called them. The primary inspiration for these games came from H. G. Wells, the esteemed science-fiction author, who published a slim book called *Little Wars* in 1913 to instruct the world in playing wargames with such miniatures, the sort that a middle-class British household of his day likely had lying around the nursery. Unsurprisingly, collectors, painters, and manufacturers of toy soldiers became strong champions of this new form of popular entertainment. A handful of other authors since the days of Wells had sold books that further developed his idea to teach novices how to deploy toy soldiers as tools for simulating conflict in different eras of warfare. Don Featherstone's 1962 *War Games* would be the most prominent example. The "rules" that Gygax aspired to publish were effectively addenda to these, preaching only to the converted, people already versed in the basic principles of Wells, who could parse slender pamphlets filled with dense charts describing how far miniatures could move in a turn, or how dice could resolve battles between certain types of historical combatants.

Getting people to spend real money for these sorts of rules was a very doubtful proposition. Serious hobbyists knew how to design their own conflict systems, and for some it was a point of pride that every little war was fought with its own customized ruleset. But the manufacturers and distributors of miniature figures had their own interest in the availability of rules for the toy soldiers they sold. Simple metal miniatures representing individual soldiers might sell for as little as 30 cents each in the early 1970s—a six-pack of soda cans might cost you 75 cents then—but large and ornate miniatures could command two or three dollars apiece. To stage a sprawling battle with miniatures could require dozens, or more likely hundreds of toy soldiers. Manufacturers of miniatures thus viewed rules promoting large-scale wars as something like a marketing expense: they would happily give rules away for free, or close to free, in the hopes that they would pull in bulk sales of cold metal. They also sponsored forums to encourage hobbyists to share rules: a miniature figure caster named Jack Scruby founded the first American magazine dedicated to miniature wargames, the 1957 *War Game Digest*, to let players disseminate conflict systems among themselves, thus expanding Wells's ideas in new directions. The *Digest* also conveniently provided a vehicle for Scruby to advertise the miniatures he himself cast for use in such battles. The typical designer of miniature wargame systems was transported with joy when any amateur magazine deigned to circulate a personal set of rules to a few hundred scattered subscribers, and when the designer realized a few dollars in return, that would be the exception rather than the rule.

Gary Gygax was among the first wave of hobbyists who bought an early copy of Avalon Hill's *Gettysburg*, but it took him until the mid-1960s to become active in the wargaming community, especially the more rarified circles of miniature wargame players. "Cardboard counters can never capture the spectacle that miniature figures display when arrayed on the battlefield," Gygax once explained back in the day, "neither can they impart the historic 'feel' that miniatures do." He participated heavily in wargaming's open and collaborative environment: if you were to single out any member of that tiny and far-flung community most likely to start their own wargaming company, it would surely be him. He founded local clubs and joined national ones; with his aptitudes and enthusiasm, he quickly vaulted to their leadership. As it was a community largely made up of teenagers and college students, he loomed as a thirtysomething de facto patriarch among them.

Gygax's ambitions in one club, the International Federation of Wargaming (IFW), involved him in planning a small gaming convention in Pennsylvania in 1967. It was an audacious idea, one heavily promoted by the hobby press of the day: one article called it the "first successful attempt at uniting game fanatics from different states." While the gathering did successfully

promote the hobby, it lost money for the IFW, almost dealing a death-blow to the club. Nevertheless, after changes in leadership, the IFW scheduled two follow-up events the next year: first a New York convention in June, and second, a Midwest convention that might attract Chicago-area IFW members, which Gygax volunteered to host in his home town of Lake Geneva.

A ninety-minute drive north from Chicago, Lake Geneva was once known as the "Newport of the West," as the shores of its namesake Geneva Lake are dotted with mansions built by wealthy Chicago families who would summer there. There were nineteenth-century estates like the Loramoor, later home to Franciscan friars, and imposing turn-of-the-century edifices like Stone Manor. Gygax's mother Almina was a daughter of the respectable Burdick family; her father had been the local district attorney around the turn of the century. She married Gygax's father, Ernest Gygax, when she was thirty and he was fifty-three. They lived in Chicago for some years, but Almina always brought the young Gary along for summer visits back to her father's house on Dodge Street in Lake Geneva. When Gygax was around eight, his parents moved back to Lake Geneva, and the young man made friends there: he could be found in 1947 at the tenth birthday party of Mary Jo Powell, along with his friend Donald Kaye. He enrolled in Lake Geneva high school, but never graduated—at the age of seventeen, three months after his father's death in January 1956, Gygax walked into a Marine recruiting station in Milwaukee and shipped off to Camp Pendleton. But the military life did not suit him, and soon he was learning the insurance trade in Chicago. In 1958 he wed Mary Jo Powell. Like his parents before him, they resided in Chicago at first—but by 1966, they were renting the white corner house at 330 Center Street in Lake Geneva with their four children. Lake Geneva had a way of drawing its people back.

In the 1970s, Lake Geneva society was hardly built around lavish mansions: most year-round residents struggled to find local work in the rural Wisconsin economy, and Gygax's own standard of living was more typical of the current community. Following in his father's footsteps, Gygax commuted via rail to a job in Chicago. His modest home on Center Street stood just one block from the Horticultural Hall, a holdover from the town's Roaring Twenties opulence, which hosted weddings and similar gatherings within its vaulted, timber-frame banquet room; its ivy-covered walls extended into an arcade enclosing an outdoor courtyard—they styled it the Loggia—where more tables could be set up if weather permitted. It was the sort of place where the Lake Geneva Garden Club, still administered by the Wrigley family, held an annual summer flower show, which Gygax had to avoid as he scheduled a gathering of wargamers to invade its sanctum.

Despite its grand name, the IFW only had about fifty members in 1968, about half of whom showed up for Gygax's Lake Geneva Wargames Convention, but the event managed to draw another seventy-five attendees, some of whom went on to join the IFW. A regional newspaper from nearby Beloit described the conventioneers as "a group of well-mannered, well-dressed intellects," but this belies the fact that most were lanky teenagers who could scarcely contain boisterous outbursts. The article gave special notice to Gygax as the convention host—surely the first time any of his gaming activities warranted the attention of mainstream media. The convention's success established that Gygax had the wherewithal to run a profitable event: directly before it, Gygax had told Don Greenwood of *Panzerfaust* magazine—one of the small-press amateur "fanzines" chronicling the subculture—that of the monthly gatherings of wargamers he had previously held at his house, the largest to date had drawn only eight people. Now that Lake Geneva had proven itself as a venue, there were plans for a sequel the following summer, and potentially even an annual tradition.

The Geneva Convention drew the attention of gamers from around the country to Gygax and his quaint hometown, but a hundred-person convention could only generate so much revenue: it yielded around $50 for the IFW's coffers. Its real value was in the sense of community it instilled in both gamers and game companies. Avalon Hill supported and promoted the event, dedicating a cover of its magazine, the *Avalon Hill General*, to photographs documenting it; SPI's *Strategy & Tactics* ran a two-page feature about it. By organizing the event, Gygax raised his own profile considerably, and with it more deeply embedded himself into the wargaming hobby. Through his convention, his voluminous correspondence, and his tireless production of fanzine articles, Gygax endeared himself to the humblest hobbyists as well as the haughtiest of wargame companies.

Everyone who plays tabletop games as avidly as Gygax eventually tries their hand at game design. Many, like Gygax, start by developing variants tweaking the rules of existing board games. Even *Monopoly* is subject to "house rules," and as homebrew systems grow more elaborate, they can evolve into completely separate games. A small interest group calling itself the War Game Inventors Guild, which counted Gygax as a member, promoted the publication of such variants and small-press titles. For example, guild member Dane Lyons designed an ancient wargame about Alexander the Great called *Arbela*, which Gygax later punched up—he had a knack for improving other peoples' designs. *Arbela* was more than just "rules," it was a "game" in that it sold with a hundred counters, a black-and-white photocopied map in sections to be colored and assembled (board not included), along with a rulebook. To help raise money for the IFW, Gygax advertised *Arbela* for mail-order sales in wargaming zines in 1968, promoting this venture as "Gystaff Enterprises," Gygax's first half-serious effort to step into hobby gaming as a business. The *Arbela* package sold for $3, which helped add $17 of profit to the IFW's coffers by the end of 1968—not a meaningless sum, given the club's paltry finances.

The sales generated by Gygax's hobby activities amounted to just pocket money—he was in it for the love. In a contemporary autobiographical aside about his fascination with games, he quipped, "There has been no real opportunity for me to think of subjects not allied to wargaming—in my free

The Lake Geneva Wargames Convention (GenCon) in 1968. Above: Gary Gygax addresses the crowd from the podium. Photo courtesy of Paul Cote. Opposite: Gen-Con attendees, including Mike Carr, then age sixteen, on the right.

time, that is." Not that he lacked for other pursuits: "Certain things like my family, religion (JW, you know), work and sex—not necessarily in order of appearance—always find a place sometime during the day." For Gygax, all this wargaming was a passion, but not a vocation. Gygax was a conservative Midwesterner, then sporting a neat mustache and sideburns; only rarely did a photograph capture him without a cigarette in hand. He was a family man with a career as an underwriter at the Fireman's Fund Insurance Companies in Chicago, a veteran of more than eight years in that firm, where he now made perhaps a $1,000 a month. He took his faith as a Jehovah's Witness seriously enough that he frowned on Christmas as a pagan holdover, and

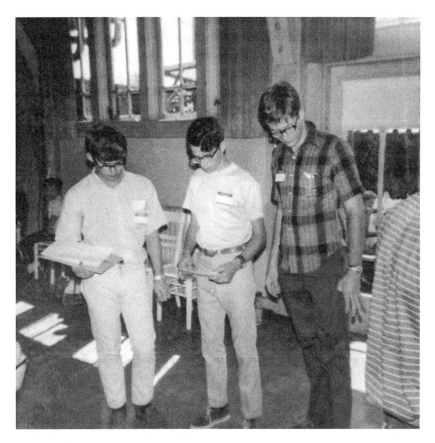

(continued)

every Sunday at nine in the morning the Gygaxes hosted a study group for Jehovah's Witnesses at their home. His formal education was just a patchwork. Having never quite finished high school, he took some night classes at a college level, and learned his trade from the Mutual Insurance Institute, but he read widely and never missed a chance to cite a source. He had a full life, so full that his passion for wargaming was bound to become a source of friction.

In the aftermath of the Lake Geneva Wargames Convention, Gygax had to step away from the hobby a bit. This was perhaps the result of an intervention. He had told *Panzerfaust* just before the event that he was dedicating something like three hours each day to wargaming, between writing articles, designing rules, and maintaining a wide swath of play-by-mail games. For the monthly gatherings he hosted, he lured players from nearby towns with a lavish miniature wargame accessory: a sand table with sculptable terrain, suitable for creating spectacular battlefields, which dominated his basement. His family could only be so patient with his obsession. In November, the day before Richard Nixon became president-elect of the United States, Gygax wrote to the founder of the IFW to explain why he needed to scale back his participation: "What got to me was that I was taking time from my family to wargame and doing it all too often. Now, I don't spend more than 2 hours/ week in 'gaming at home (that is my evenings and weekends are devoted to the wife and children, not that I go out to wargame)."

But gaming had a way of creeping back into Gygax's life. By March he would report to *Panzerfaust*, "When I was forced to give up all my [play-by-mail] and become inactive in the clubs I belong to because of lack of time I envisaged that there would be little or no time for writing—be it correspondence or articles. It now develops that there are about 2 hours every workday that I may utilize for this purpose." This was nominally time he found during the lengthy commute by rail to Chicago, or during the odd lunch hour. Though he affirms that "the only disappointing aspect is that it is impossible to work on game design here at the office," the word "here" betrays where he found the time to write this letter—and indeed in 1969 he typed and duplicated game rules at the Fireman's Fund office, just as he had with *Arbela* the year before. He would not take such time away from his family to indulge his passion for gaming, but it still had to be borrowed from somewhere, a choice that would soon have its consequences.

Gygax and Arneson

Devout game fans from around the country again converged on Lake Geneva for the weekend of August 23, 1969, a warm and dry respite in a rainy Midwestern summer. Some met up with Gygax himself in Chicago that Friday, and joined him on the four o'clock train to his home town after he ducked out of Fireman's Fund early. There they found Gygax's house totally overrun already, a contingent of New York fans having splayed Avalon Hill board games on every available surface. Downstairs in the basement, a dedicated few played Second World War miniatures on Gygax's sand table. Gygax's wife Mary served as a hostess and charmed the teeming guests. Early in the evening, an advance team marched from the Gygax home to the Horticultural Hall, where not long before, the Garden Club had hosted a speaker from the FBI. Now, industrious young gamers rearranged the furniture in preparation for the opening of the Hall the next morning. Some, having no other place to go, ended up spending the night there, borrowing sleeping bags to slumber within the grassy enclosure of the Loggia beneath the stars. Hotel rooms were scarce, and only a lucky few would find an unoccupied mattress on the floor of the Gygax home where they could collapse for a brief repose.

The 1969 convention, an ambitious two-day gathering, grew to around 150 attendees, thanks in part to advance notices in venues like the *Chicago Daily News*—which liberally quoted Gygax, "a Chicago insurance executive." Gygax was late for his opening address Saturday morning at nine thirty, no doubt delayed by the throngs camping at his house just around the corner. As afternoon temperatures rose to the eighties, conditions inside the bustling great hall went from sweaty to sweltering, but most conventioneers were too engrossed in their hobby to mind.

Gamers made their pilgrimage to Lake Geneva not just to play, but also to sell games, fanzines, and miniatures. One attendee's inventory of the various goods for sale in 1969 concluded with a mention of "the 1:1200 model sailing ships done by David Arneson of St. Paul, Minnesota." Arneson, a newcomer to the convention and a student at the University of Minnesota at the time, attended with a large contingent of his school's wargaming club, with whom he participated heavily in Napoleonic miniature simulations. In contrast to the gregarious Gygax, whom he met for the first time that weekend in Lake Geneva, the stockily built Arneson was more guarded and introverted; he showed up to the convention with a buzz cut, thick-rimmed glasses, and a Midwestern mustache.

Lake Geneva was a provincial town, but Arneson came from the metropolitan Twin Cities, where his club attracted dozens of members who had, since the mid-1960s, transitioned from a focus on miniature collecting to gaming. Large wargaming clubs tended to be fractious and prone to schisms; Arneson was a veteran of such political struggles in the course of organizing multiplayer wargames and editing his group's newsletter, the *Corner of the Table*. It also meant that Arneson had bonded with a coalition of loyal friends who were practiced in defeating political rivals as well as wargame opponents; it might be said that cutthroat coalition-building games like *Diplomacy* set the tone for their interpersonal disputes. It was a studious and inventive group that explored all aspects of the hobby, collaborating tightly on board and miniature wargame ideas. They came to Lake Geneva in part to recruit for their club: as tiny and fragmented as the gaming community was, their best chance of meeting new gamers from Minnesota was to find them at a convention in Wisconsin.

In the aftermath of this second annual convention—which people now began to call GenCon for short—you could see Gygax's picture once again on the cover of the *Avalon Hill General*. He had become a minor celebrity in this most modest of hobbies, someone whose name could elevate any project. Right after returning to the Twin Cities, Arneson reported to *Corner of the Table* that "I am in the process of working up a set of Napoleonic naval wargame rules in co-operation with Gary Gygax," rules to accompany the sailing ship miniatures Arneson had sold at the convention. Arneson even ordered a copy of *Arbela* from Gystaff Enterprises—but by the time he did, he found Gygax unresponsive.

In the wake of another successful GenCon, Gygax once again flirted with a "retirement" from gaming: he still had trouble balancing his hobby with his family, his work, and his religion. After an acrimonious flame war over his Christian faith in game fanzines in the spring, we should not be surprised that he cited piety as a justification for stepping back from wargaming. In a September 1969 letter, he explained, "I've resigned from IFW and quit most 'gaming in order to devote more time to the Christian ministry." Whatever sparked this move, news of it spread quickly as Gygax delegated some of his fanzine editorships to others. But just like the year before, he could not successfully sever himself from his beloved hobby. By the New Year he was back in the IFW and taking bold steps to drive his involvement to its deepest level yet.

In early 1970 Gygax's neighborhood club, then a group of no more than seven, adopted its grand title, the Lake Geneva Tactical Studies Association. Rather than meeting monthly, this group now convened every Saturday in Gygax's basement, where usually four or five members would turn up to play miniature wargames on Gygax's storied sand table. They included Gygax's childhood friend Don Kaye, as well as a handful of younger local gamers and a few others who commuted to Lake Geneva from nearby Illinois. Since Gygax had become increasingly interested in miniature wargames simulating the medieval period, he soon founded a second group called the Castle & Crusade Society as a subset of the IFW. The Castle & Crusade Society remained quite tiny for a national club, boasting dozens of members at its peak. Its meager dues largely went to publishing and mailing its crude fanzine, the *Domesday Book*, which shared rules for wargames featuring swordsmen and archers, jousting, and castle sieges. Arneson had also experimented with the medieval setting, so he was among the first to join; he sent the *Domesday Book* numerous contributions on historical subjects. The tireless Gygax edited and published the zine, and his "LGTSA Medieval Miniature Rules," a collaboration with Rockford, Illinois, gamer Jeff Perren, would be the most influential contribution to it.

During this period, Gygax and Arneson opened a longstanding correspondence that would grow to cover a wide range of topics in the wargaming field. Gygax arranged for his Lake Geneva club to participate in an ongoing Napoleonic simulation campaign refereed by Arneson, which kept them in close communication as Gygax relayed the orders of his group to the Twin Cities. Gygax and Arneson made good on their promise to work on naval miniature wargame rules for the early nineteenth century, a project that took the name *Don't Give Up the Ship*. Gygax favored collaborating on rules above tackling projects by himself: he worked best reacting against the ideas of others. Arneson, for his part, produced piecemeal chunks of miniature wargame rules all the time and distributed them in the pages of his *Corner of the Table*, though he dedicated little time to organizing them into a coherent system. There is no reason to suppose that Gygax and Arneson embarked on this first collaboration with any grander ambition than just circulating a few ideas through fanzines.

The path toward a company called Tactical Studies Rules began when Gary Gygax left the employ of Fireman's Fund Companies late in October 1970. No doubt in his struggle to balance his job with his hobby, the job suffered: we find much of his correspondence to fellow wargamers that year delivered in Fireman's Fund envelopes, and for personal stationery, Gygax sometimes used a company letterhead with the word "fire" blotted out, as well as the final "d" in "fund," which left only "Man's Fun Companies." He seems to have typed the first five issues of his Castle & Crusade Society's *Domesday Book* on a company typewriter, and no doubt duplicated it with the company copier—now Gygax had to hand over editorship to another member of the club. Probably he had long tested the patience of Fireman's Fund. Earlier in the year he had written, "I can't stand this job much longer, and I plan to switch as soon as I can get another," but leaving the job without a new one on the horizon was not his idea.

In the aftermath of this dispiriting dismissal, we can readily imagine a heroic Gygax who would resolve to stake everything on the impossible dream of designing games for a living. But the real Gygax did not have the luxury to be so romantic. He was a family man, providing for his wife, their four children—and a fifth imminently to arrive in November 1970. At the end of the year, he reported in a personal letter that "I lost my job in late October, and have yet to find another," and as a result he was "squeaking by on unemployment comp." This left him "very busy job hunting, scraping up odd cash here and there and the like." He had grave difficulties finding a suitable situation in his hometown. "I hope to be able to find some sort of work around Lake Geneva," he wrote wistfully in another letter, but that posed some challenges. "Lake Geneva is a small resort town of about 6,000 population," and although "it is a very pretty little place too," it was not a hotbed of employment opportunities. "Before the recent interest in winter sports it was pretty dead in the cold months. . . . The Playboy Club Hotel nearby has enlivened it a bit." If you had the money to enjoy the town's amenities, it was a charming place to visit—but it was a tough place to make a living after a mid-career setback.

It would take nearly ten nail-biting months for Gygax to find steady work, but faced with a stint of unwanted idleness, he took advantage of the opportunity to indulge his sweet tooth for gaming: "During this temporary (forced) vacation I am working on a couple of board games for semi-commercial sale and trying to get some work in on miniatures rules," he wrote. We must not lose a nuance in that phrasing: Gygax's "board games" like *Arbela* were "for semi-commercial sale," while the "miniatures rules" were different, not something that people normally expected to pay for. Nonetheless, Gygax's "temporary (forced) vacation" from gainful employ had created fresh possibilities for his game designs in progress. At last, he had the opportunity to immerse himself into his hobby with the abandon he had always craved, and thanks to his incessant networking, he had the necessary connections in the game community to test whether his work could be marketable.

Gygax's first publisher in the industry would be Don Lowry, a former air force officer whose passion for games had become a vocation. Lowry owned a mail-order hobby business called Lowrys Hobbies out of Evansville, Indiana. It was a far more ambitious undertaking than Gystaff Enterprises: Lowry had built a business on a scale to support himself and his small family. Since wargamers were spread thin across the country, and gaming at the time was such an obscure hobby, many potential game buyers lived nowhere near shops that sold wargames, and would instead send away for games from shops like Lowry's. He had risen to prominence in the IFW through his illustrations and articles for its magazine, the *International Wargamer*; as the IFW grew its membership from a few dozen into the hundreds, Lowry became the first to start placing paid advertisements in the magazine for his wares. He resold replica firearms along with miniatures representing troops and vehicles from World War II, as well as board games published by Avalon Hill at 15 percent off retail.

In a summer 1970 advertisement, alongside a selection of tank miniatures selling at around 35 to 45 cents each, we can also find Lowry pushing a rule book called *Fast Rules* by Michael Reese and Leon Tucker that detailed how to fight wargames with those figures. That modest twenty-four-page pamphlet, self-published by Tucker, sold for just 75 cents—so why not tack that on to an order for a few dozen miniature tanks? And it so happened that Tucker and Reese were both among the handful of members of the Lake Geneva Tactical Studies Association, and they were already working together with Gygax on a more detailed treatment of the same wargaming period, a ruleset to be called *Tractics*.

Lowry had announced his intention to enter the game and rule publishing business in the spring of 1970. Lowry and Gygax were already acquainted through the IFW as well as Lowry's visits to GenCon: at the third GenCon that summer, Lowry and his wife went out to dinner on Sunday night with Gygax and a few other veteran gamers, enjoying a conversation that carried on until midnight. They had plenty to discuss. As Gygax collaborated on rules with Tucker and Reese, whose work Lowry already carried, it was only natural that he would ally with Lowry to publish his planned "semi-commercial" games. Gygax alerted Arneson to the imminent release of several titles in a March 1971 letter: "Lowry says that he'll soon be publishing the following items that I did: *Alexander the Great* (rework of *Arbela*—much better, I think), *Chainmail* (the medieval et al. rules), *Dunkirk* (France, 1940), and *Little Big Horn*." Jointly, these games and rules titles formed the planned initial releases of Lowry's new imprint, Guidon Games.

Three of those Guidon Games titles were board wargames, boldly positioning Lowry to compete with the likes of Avalon Hill. Gygax had previously distributed a prototype of his *Little Big Horn* game to the War Game Inventors Guild, and *Dunkirk* was a perennial work-in-progress of his. The case of *Alexander* was a bit trickier, since it was a revision of the game Gygax had originally sold via Gystaff Enterprises as *Arbela*, credited solely to Dane Lyons. But when Gygax developed or expanded the work of another designer, there was some threshold he could cross where he felt that he had transformed the idea enough to warrant adding his own name as a co-designer, and sometimes even another threshold after which he dropped the name of the original author entirely. His "rework" *Alexander the Great* contained no mention of *Arbela* or its original author, but it would not look much like that earlier title: Lowry promised to ship it in a large box with a bright cover, packed with die-cut counters, sturdy maps, and a long, detailed rulebook featuring material Gygax had added after taking over responsibility for *Arbela* from Lyons. Lyons had dropped out of wargaming—it was a hobby some people retired from successfully—so he likely did not even know that Gygax had adapted his original idea into this new form. Wargamers largely treated game rules as a sort of intellectual commons, one without any agreed practices for assigning credits other than what seemed right at the time.

The sole Guidon release that was not a board wargame, but simply miniatures "rules," was *Chainmail*, a fifty-page pamphlet Gygax adapted from his earlier work with Jeff Perren in the Castle & Crusade Society on the "LGTSA Medieval Miniatures Rules." By printing *Chainmail*, Lowry entered a largely uncontested market: companies like Avalon Hill did not publish miniatures rules, and apart from one-off efforts like *Fast Rules*, almost no one else in America did. A very few miniatures manufacturers distributed rules to complement their figures: Bruce "Duke" Seifried, whose Custom Cast firm sold miniatures under the brand name Der Kriegspielers, also published a small series of Napoleonic miniature rules leading with *Frappé!* As Lowry's mail order business resold Custom Cast figures in 1970, he also offered the *Frappé!* rules in his advertisements. Surely Lowry saw an opportunity to capture more of this small market by printing similar rules himself. But Lowry was not a miniatures gamer, just a board gamer in the Avalon Hill tradition, so effectively he delegated decision-making for the "Wargaming in Miniatures" branch of Guidon Games to Gygax.

In his March letter to Arneson, Gygax further explained that *Chainmail* would contain "revised Medieval rules" building on those he had published through the *Domesday Book*—though he adds the tantalizing promise that "wizards, dragons, and all that good stuff are included" as well. Here, Lowry and Gygax again pushed gaming into virgin territory: Avalon Hill and SPI exclusively published historical combat simulations; no one sold rules for fantasy wargames at the time. Gygax had been interested in Tolkien-themed games since at least 1968. An aspiring fantasy novelist, he had published a few articles on the taxonomy of different-colored dragons in 1969 that informed how *Chainmail* represented them. His fantasy rules borrowed from earlier ideas on Tolkien circulated by a New England gamer named Leonard Patt. As he had similarly done when revising Lyons's *Arbela*, Gygax refined and expanded Patt's existing rules to a point where he deemed them his own invention, at least when it came to assigning bylines.

Chainmail marked a controversial step, because wargamers in general considered their hobby to be a serious adult pastime, not to be sullied with the childish trappings of fairy tales. Don Greenwood in his *Panzerfaust* review of *Chainmail* recommended discarding the fantasy elements: "Interesting though they may be to some, rules about dragons, wizards, ogres, etc. must appear somewhat foolish to the majority of wargamers." But these rules effectively opened a new market: an untested one, which made it hard to predict how big or small it might be.

Lowry stirred up much fanfare about the debut of Guidon Games, but we need to put that into perspective: his publishing interests were simply a modest diversification of his mail-order hobby shop. *Chainmail* was a digest-sized rulebook made from folded typewritten paper, with a monochrome illustration by Lowry on its cover, so the $2 charge for the product was a substantial markup over the cost of materials. In a summer 1971 interview with Greenwood in *Panzerfaust*, Lowry emphasized how little he had to do with honing the rules and games: "the Lake Geneva Tactical Studies Association play-tested various prototypes all along the way." Gygax could rely on its membership—his own eldest son Ernie, Don Kaye, Mike Reese, Leon Tucker, and local teenage brothers Rob and Terry Kuntz—to do much of the quality-control work. The same would be true for the forthcoming LGTSA title *Tractics*, the flagship of Guidon's miniatures line: a three-volume boxed set, supplemented with reference sheets, selling at a princely $7.50. Famously, *Tractics* called for the use of a twenty-sided die, at the time an exotic commodity, and yet another accessory that Lowry could resell through his hobby business.

Lowry named Gygax the Rules Editor for Guidon Games, but this was not a job that paid a wage as such—that would require the venture to make money. While Lowry insisted to Greenwood, "I expect to make a profit," he also downplayed the likelihood of doing so. He was forced to make "a small run of each game now due to limited capital. The profit on these will be used to produce more." For the initial boxed board game titles, which he planned to sell for $7 or $8, Lowry also had to compensate Gygax: "On this first run, after Gary gets his cut (he has a profit-sharing deal rather than royalties), we'll probably make two or three dollars a game." But, as Lowry hastily explained, even "this isn't 'profit,' actually," as much of the proceeds would go to Lowry and his wife in compensation for their many efforts getting things off the ground. With such thin margins, wholesaling would be a distant prospect. "We'll have to get costs down some in order to start wholesaling the games (let alone selling to wholesalers). Retailers usually pay 60% of retail for such things. That's a good sized bite out of the apple right there." Miniature wargame rules pamphlets like the $2 *Chainmail* would surely yield much less for Lowry, just pennies.

It was a much simpler thing to produce "rules" than it was to produce "games," Lowry would discover. The *Chainmail* rules pamphlet shipped from Guidon Games in the spring of 1971, but the board games faced endless delays. "Sales of *Alex* & *Dunkirk* are pretty slow due to Lowry having so many problems in producing the games," Gygax fumed in a July 22 letter. "It's been one thing after another. Graphics, mis-centered counters, etc. have all conspired to throw the release date further and further off." Gygax could point to one bright spot: "*Chainmail* is doing quite well, as almost everyone wants to play the fantasy game—wonder of wonders!" It turned out that its "Fantasy Supplement" had connected with a group of interested gamers who wargaming publishers had previously neglected—fans of Tolkien, of Robert E. Howard, and the other authors whose epic fantasy battles *Chainmail* could enable gamers to recreate.

No small part of the success of *Chainmail* can be traced to Gygax's direct advocacy, especially socializing the game in person—he had plenty of time on his hands and made a favorable impression, now sporting an avuncular beard he had grown the year before. A wargamer who encountered Gygax at a small convention at a Chicago high school in 1971 remarked, "I was and still am very impressed with Gary Gygax." He was approachable and eager to tutor gamers, to the point where "total randoms, like me, would just walk up to him and he'd make you feel terrific," and he would spend "almost the entire day helping guys design games and then judging a game of fantasy miniatures." People who learned *Chainmail* from Gygax got it immediately: "Imagine the fight between the Balrog and Gandalf occurring before your very eyes."

But even as *Chainmail* was doing "quite well," it could not have meant more than a few dollars in returns for Gygax. There was no prospect that the work Gygax did for Guidon Games could support him and his family, and unemployment checks and food stamps would only go so far. He could rely to some extent on the good graces of the Burdick family; his cousin had a decent plot of land a few miles west of town where the Gygax family "had to have a garden for survival," as his wife Mary would put it in a later interview, musing, "I never did that before."

For the sake of his family, Gygax needed steady work. As late as July 1971, Gygax could only report that "employment in this area is low, but I have put in applications at a bank, factory, and shoe store, and I believe one will come thru fairly soon—a month or two at worst." By August, it became clear that the third of those possibilities would pan out, as Gygax had then begun "training as a shoe repairman." When the local cobbler Fred Sesselman passed away and his apprentice son made plans to leave town for schooling, a rare entry-level vacancy became available. A month later, Gygax had to admit that "as I am so busy trying to learn the shoe repair business, supporting a family of seven in the nonce, that I have no time" for frivolities like wargaming. Once the bulky cobbling apparatus—a nearly $3,000 acquisition subsidized by his mother—moved into his basement, displacing the wargame sand table that had long enticed gamers to his home, Gygax's typical concluding refrain in letters became, "I have to get back to shoe repairing." His "Corner House Shoe Repair" was not a very lucrative business, perhaps bringing in a hundred dollars a week or so, but it was better than unemployment.

Gygax did manage to scrounge up a bit of time to work on continuing wargaming projects as his "temporary (forced) vacation" came to its welcome end. Gygax and Arneson had a phone call on September 8 to discuss their various joint ventures, including the Castle & Crusade Society and their continuing work on *Don't Give Up the Ship*. Over the summer of 1971, they had serialized a draft of those naval rules in the IFW's *International Wargamer*—a fanzine that, as of April, Lowry himself printed. Gygax and Arneson had also demonstrated the rules at GenCon in the summer, where by this point 275 gamers congregated in Lake Geneva over the weekend, and Arneson's Twin Cities club took charge of an elaborate demonstration of Napoleonic rules on land and sea.

Guidon Games was eager to print *Don't Give Up the Ship*: in a September letter, Gygax promised Arneson, "I'll do a preface also, and Lowry will load it with illustrations, so it should turn out to be a beautiful job." Taking a casual stab at how they might divide the proceeds, he ventured: "I assume that a 50/50 split is fair." The discussion of royalties could be so informal because payments were unlikely to amount to enough for anyone to fuss over. Gygax would later project that "royalties should run 20%, or from 40–50¢ per copy (retail—24–30¢ wholesale)," and most sales would surely be in the wholesale category. If they managed to sell out an entire print run of one thousand copies—by no means a sure thing—each author could hope to see one or two hundred dollars in total royalties. To put it in a broader perspective, the sum Lowry paid Gygax for all game work and proceeds in 1971 amounted to about $375.

A few hundred dollars was the upper bound anyone could imagine making from wargame "rules." By the end of 1971, Guidon Games managed to publish the three-volume boxed set of *Tractics* rules. Even for a deluxe set in its form factor, Gygax estimated that "they would bring in something like $20/month for the author(s)." Referring to the *Don't Give Up the Ship* royalties he soberly admitted, "We won't get rich, but every little bit helps, and it is fun to be published." The honor of working on a set of rules that might become popular in the gaming community was the lion's share of the compensation. It would take a miracle for a venture like this to end up providing someone with a livelihood—let alone a fortune.

With his newfound responsibilities in the shoe business, Gygax did not have as much time to dedicate to *Don't Give Up the Ship* as he had hoped. Arneson, though an enthusiastic and creative gamer, was a notoriously poor typist with a loose command of grammar and spelling. Arneson thus enlisted another Twin Cities gamer named Mike Carr to assist in editing and expanding the manuscript. One of the attendees of the first GenCon, Carr had self-published a World War I aerial combat game called *Fight in the Skies* back in 1968, and he had a talent for editing games. By the second week of December, it was clear that Mike Carr was doing enough work toward *Don't Give Up the Ship* that Gygax proposed, "I do think that Mike should get a piece of the action—particularly if you fish him into preparing a final copy."

Eventually they decided to divide the meager *Don't Give Up the Ship* royalties into thirds. The difference between a half and a third of the royalties for a set of wargaming rules like this was not enough money for even someone in Gygax's distressed circumstances to fret over. *Don't Give Up the Ship* might sell a few hundred copies if they were lucky, yielding royalties as little as one quarter per copy, then split three ways: it had no prospect of contributing meaningfully to anyone's finances.

Although Gygax felt the stakes were low enough for him to casually part with royalties, he approached the rules themselves like his reputation was on the line. Carr helped organize the draft rules for submission to Guidon Games, but Gygax afterwards altered them as he saw fit. Hearing from Arneson that Carr objected to some of those patches, Gygax replied imperiously, "Too bad if Carr doesn't like my changes. As a co-author, and as the Editor of the entire Guidon series, I'll blasted well use my own discretion in making such." If the honor of publishing good game rules was the primary reward of the work, then being satisfied with their state trumped all other concerns. Since Arneson had done the bulk of the work on the rules themselves, he received the first credit on the cover: it listed "Arneson, Gygax & Carr," though the inside gave the more formal credits as "Dave Arneson and Gary Gygax with Mike Carr."

Lowry included *Don't Give Up the Ship* in his April 1972 catalog, on sale for the same $2 as *Chainmail*. True to the interests of any hobby shop owner, he simultaneously began selling a set of four 1:1200 scale metal sailing ship miniatures which ranged from inch-and-a-half-long frigates to ships of the line more than twice that size, priced between $1.35 and $1.50. Thus the rules cost only slightly more than one of the miniatures: they would be a negligible expense for anyone assembling a fleet for battle. Lowry's miniature ships, incidentally, were of Arneson's manufacture, the same sold at GenCon back in 1969; since then, Arneson had been toying with working professionally as a figure caster. Gygax had acquired a few model ships from Arneson the year before by trading inventory of Guidon Games, including multiple copies of *Chainmail*, and then recommended to Lowry that he resell Arneson's vessels along with the *Don't Give Up the Ship* rules. For his part, Arneson used the *Chainmail* rules in his local activities surrounding the Castle & Crusade Society's "Great Kingdom," an imaginary world in which Gygax assigned members various territories; Arneson's was a barony in an area originally called the "Northern Marches."

But many changes were coming in the summer of 1972 for the wargaming community. First, Gygax went into another low-energy period in March, once again swearing off his hobby. He wrote to Arneson, "I must tell you I'm quitting all wargaming . . . no time for family if I don't, and they're most important." Then Tom Shaw of Avalon Hill, having long admired Don Greenwood's *Panzerfaust*, recruited Greenwood to edit the *Avalon Hill General* magazine and to assist with new game acquisitions. This induced Greenwood to sell *Panzerfaust* to Lowry, who was already acting as its printer. Thus Lowry now had a lot on his plate, especially given that he planned to relocate his family, and business, to Maine that summer. Publication of the *International Wargamer* lagged, which is one of several reasons that the IFW then began to falter. GenCon very nearly failed to happen in 1972, as Gygax was out of the picture and the dwindling IFW offered the convention little support—it took place on the other side of Geneva Lake, in a venue that was hard to find and harder to navigate. But the approach of GenCon seemed to revitalize Gygax: he made an appearance Sunday to play in Arneson's Napoleonic "Battle of the Nile," and shortly thereafter returned to helping Don Lowry plan future Guidon Games titles. The convention however effectively dealt a death blow to the IFW, smothering it under a $750 debt that it had no prospect of honoring.

After the release of *Don't Give Up the Ship*, Arneson found himself with a heap of leftover rules from the naval components of his Napoleonic simulation campaign, which Gygax invited him to let Guidon Games publish. Arneson thus began preparing two separate sequels: *Ships of the Line* and *Naval Orders of Battle*. Gygax saw drafts of both in the spring, although at the time he had little energy to address them: "I've felt more like reading and drinking beer of late, as the shoe repair business has been keeping me very busy, and what with work around the house, and entertaining the wife and jumping jacks commonly called my progeny, I need a little rest and relaxation." But he got around to it eventually, and a surviving copy of *Ships of the Line* contains a preface written by Gygax on September 15, 1972, in his capacity as Rules Editor for Guidon Games. When they had played together at GenCon in August, Gygax was again impressed with Arneson's talent for casting miniature ships; he then learned that Arneson had also started work toward casting fantasy figures suitable for use with *Chainmail*, which Lowry had just republished in a second, expanded edition. Although *Chainmail* had only created the market for fantasy figures the year before, Lowry and Gygax were both eager to make fantasy figures available, so Gygax encouraged Arneson's efforts in that area as well.

Before Lowry could get more work out of Arneson, however, he had to disburse the modest royalties accumulating for *Don't Give Up the Ship*. Lowry did pay Gygax a bit less than $450 dollars for all royalties and services over the course of 1972, but his co-authors went uncompensated. Throughout the final months of 1972, Gygax repeatedly sent vague promises to Arneson like, "Hope Lowry will send you your full monies soon! You'll be pleased with sales, as *DGUTS* is doing pretty well." Or he would take an action item like "will write to Lowry Sunday and get after him about your royalties."

When a check finally did arrive in November, Arneson reported that his bank refused to cash it, and that Mike Carr had the same experience. Gygax spoke to Lowry and could only relay, "The explanation of why the checks bounced is unbelievable—all MasterCharge's fault. He is (or has) made it up." So Arneson's first real interaction with Gygax in business was one where payment for work was not forthcoming, and it fell on Gygax, who had arranged for the publication of *Don't Give Up the Ship*, to try to explain it away—a precedent that surely informed the way Arneson perceived Gygax going forward.

Fed up, Arneson snapped in a December 1972 letter, "I still have not heard from Lowry and until I do I have no desire to either send him any of the new items or have any dealings with him." Arneson continued, "Until then, I'm not going to do a damn thing. Sorry but that's the way I feel, after all I have never received a single penny from DGUTS since it was published and that's hardly calculated to instill confidence." This required more hand-holding from Gygax: he insisted that Lowry's shop was "the brightest hope for the free-lance designer and writer, but there are handicaps. If Lowry can manage to get it together there (mainly manage to get enough capital in liquid form) we will all prosper accordingly." But he had to acknowledge that "until he can really afford to do it right—and advertise plenty—we'll have to settle for the small change."

Gygax had to mollify Arneson, as Guidon Games needed a pipeline of titles ready for publication, and the Twin Cities boasted a larger and more dynamic wargaming scene than Lake Geneva. Earlier in 1972, Lowry had published a new boxed edition of Mike Carr's board game *Fight in the Skies*, and within the ranks of Arneson's local club, then called Midwest Military Simulation Association, there were numerous other works in progress. Dave Wesely, whose referee-driven playstyle had heavily influenced Arneson, hoped to find a professional venue for his self-published Napoleonic land rules *Strategos N*. So, Arneson offered a potential revision and expansion of Wesely's rules to Gygax for Guidon's consideration. Lowry carried Napoleonic figures in his store and desperately wanted more rules, leaving Gygax to explore several leads—closer to Lake Geneva, for instance, he worked with Rick Crane on a set of rules to be called *Tricolor*. But Wesely's rules were a strong candidate. Anyone reading Arneson's *Corner of the Table* fanzine would see several other prospective projects circulating within, including a science-fiction campaign run by John Snider and Arneson's own Blackmoor fantasy campaign, which was set in the Castle & Crusade Society's "Great Kingdom."

This is not the place to lay out the intricate web of influences and innovations leading up to *Dungeons & Dragons*, which would require a larger treatment than there is room for here. At a high level, Gygax and Arneson got into business together on *D&D* as a natural extension of their previous activities working with Guidon Games and participating in the Castle & Crusade Society. At the end of 1972, Gygax had begun making plans for a third edition of *Chainmail* to be published by Lowry. Throughout the year, Gygax had read Arneson's reports on Blackmoor in personal correspondence and also in the pages of *Corner of the Table* and the *Domesday Book*, including allusions to sending squads of fantasy heroes to explore dungeons. Intrigued, Gygax asked Arneson in a December postcard to send over any *Chainmail* modifications for potential inclusion in the third edition, offering to "give you credit + free set of rules." Arneson demurred, insisting that his alterations to *Chainmail* for Blackmoor were "fairly minor" and that "the big change was laying out the dungeon for exploration and the like." Arneson had also integrated into his campaign the Avalon Hill game *Outdoor Survival* to cover adventures above ground. But he mainly stressed the importance of the referee, especially a "sadistic referee," to the experience of play—that was a role Arneson furnished himself, around the table in the Twin Cities. He sent Gygax some charts and notes from the campaign at the start of 1973.

When Arneson planned a visit to Lake Geneva in February, he offered to bring in tow Twin Cities gamer Dave Megarry. Late in 1972, Gygax heard from Arneson about a project of Megarry's, a dungeon fantasy board game with links to Blackmoor and *Chainmail*, which Guidon Games might want to evaluate for purchase. Megarry had already co-authored a known "semi-commercial" title called *Guerilla War* and had begun shopping his new fantasy idea to major games publishers like Parker Brothers. But that company received some three thousand board game solicitations per year at the time, and virtually never accepted outside submissions.

So, Gygax was eager to assess Megarry's board game as a prospective acquisition for Guidon Games. During the visit, Arneson ran Gygax, Megarry, and some of the LGTSA members through a Blackmoor adventure. Gygax found that experience, and Megarry's dungeon board game, tremendously inspiring. He first dispatched Megarry to Don Lowry to demonstrate his game, then called the *Dungeons of Pasha Cada*. By the first week of April, Gygax proposed to Arneson that the two of them collaborate on developing his dungeon adventure concept into a commercial product for Guidon Games. Gygax had already begun running adventures himself with the Lake Geneva crowd, centering on a town called Greyhawk that he added to the "Great Kingdom" map.

Gygax requested copies of any game system Arneson had drafted to date, but he preemptively seized the initiative when it came to authoring the rules: "I'll whip out a booklet (Gygax and Arneson, I trust) for your approval, so groups can play their own games." Putting his own name first reversed the order their names had appeared on *Don't Give Up the Ship*, and implied that Gygax expected to do the lion's share of the dungeon game design—Arneson had after all sworn to do no more work for Guidon Games until Lowry started paying royalties. When it came to this project, Gygax approached compensation with the same casual "I assume that a 50/50 split is fair" attitude he had adopted for the *Don't Give Up the Ship* rules, floating in a postcard to Arneson, "Trust you'd like to split royalties on a 'Blackmoor' rules booklet with me." He made this offer on April 15—long before it would be clear how much writing either Gygax or Arneson would contribute to the finished product—based solely on some vague expectation that the two would work together, no doubt modeled after their prior experience with *Don't Give Up the Ship*. There was no reason at the time to think their collaboration would result in anything but another slim rule booklet published by Guidon Games that might, if successful, yield a few hundred dollars of total royalties for the authors.

Over the next several weeks, Gygax continually expanded the rules until he had a hundred-page first draft to send to Arneson—with a title page that read "*Dungeons & Dragons*." The game required a referee to prepare a half dozen or more levels of a dungeon on paper, populating this underworld with monsters and treasure. Players then select from one of three classes of adventurers—fighting men, magic-users, and clerics—and send these characters into the referee's dungeon, where they explore, defeat adversaries, and collect rewards. Successful characters gain experience points and advance in level, rendering them more powerful, and thus enabling them to explore deeper and more dangerous areas of the dungeon. Money could be spent in towns, and with sufficient resources, characters could build their own castles and hire private armies. Polyhedral dice were rolled to resolve combat and decide various random circumstances of the game world. Around half of the game text enumerated the various monsters, magical items, and spells found in the game. Unabashedly, it was merely a rules framework, a fragmentary set of ideas and tools that relied heavily on its players to flesh out how the game would work.

During the sprint to develop *Dungeons & Dragons* in the spring of 1973, there can be no doubt Gygax intended to publish the rules through Guidon Games. Most tellingly, the preface of the first draft of the *D&D* rules is signed by Gygax in his capacity as Rules Editor for Guidon Games. "I have been offered the number two spot in the firm," Gygax had explained to Arneson, "taking care of the things I do now pretty much, save that I'd be there to work with the fellows and be able to keep on top of items like bouncing checks immediately—unlike 'you know who.'" Guidon Games sold around 2,500 units for the 1972–1973 fiscal year, yielding revenue of maybe $5,000, a modest number even for the standards of the industry. But as late as May, Gygax sincerely hoped that Lowry would provide him a steady job and a new home. Gygax had started planning to relocate to the coast of Maine, and even wrote to Arneson, "If we get going, would you be interested in moving out to Belfast? Think this over now, for who knows what will happen in the not too distant future."

Arneson's situation in life might have made that move look attractive. He had graduated from the University of Minnesota in 1971 at the age of twenty-three with a degree in history; two years later, he lived with his parents in his childhood home, ensconced in a comfortable, leafy St. Paul neighborhood. He held odd jobs like house painting, or working as a ticket-taker at the Minnesota State Fair, making little more than pocket money—but still more than he made designing rules for Guidon Games or selling miniature sailing ships. In 1973, he took steps toward founding a travel agency he hoped to call "Adventures Unlimited," which would organize trips abroad. But other than designing some brochures, and enlisting Dave Megarry to assist with some of the legal forms, the idea stagnated.

Arneson had no need to decide on a move to Maine; the cover letter that Gygax attached to the *D&D* first draft when he mailed it to Arneson that summer updated the story. It concluded with an aside about Lowry marked "Utmost Confidence," in which Gygax whispered, "Don is overextended and plans to pull in his horns. The stupid move to Maine is just catching up with him, and he says he's hurting. Production will be slowed." Tentatively, Gygax ventured, "I'll be hanging on here yet until we see how he does in six months to a year."

As it happened, May 1973 would be the last month that Lowry would send Gygax any compensation for his work, or even an accounting of what he was owed. This was an embarrassment for Gygax, who not only saw Arneson and Carr go unpaid, but who had furthermore borrowed money from his mother in exchange for a share of the royalties in his games, which Lowry was to pay back to her directly. Guidon Games as an imprint more or less ceased to exist at this time, beyond the back catalog of copies held by Lowry.

This abrupt turn of events imperiled any plan to publish *Dungeons & Dragons*: six months or a year might be too long to wait for Lowry to right his ship. This of course meant that Guidon Games was in no position to publish Dave Megarry's *Dungeons of Pasha Cada* project either. "Lowry, as far as I can personally see, fools around and isn't a driver," Gygax complained to Megarry in a letter early in August. And when it came to the dungeon board game, "Lowry wouldn't do it right, I fear." So, who would?

Gary   Dave

The $300 Idea

"Some of us here are getting a bit of loot together in order to produce our own wargame rules and eventually games," Gygax hinted to Megarry in that letter. He had seen enough to decide that Lowry was adding little value: "I've done one hell of a lot of spade work for him. . . . I might as well do it for myself, and Lowry will still market our stuff anyway." His pipeline of titles slated for publication at Guidon Games could simply be rerouted elsewhere. Gygax believed he and his allies in the Lake Geneva Tactical Studies Association were equal to the task of publishing those rules themselves—including *Dungeons & Dragons*.

There were known strategies for launching a rule-publishing venture in the industry. You founded something that could provide a steady income in the space, like a hobby shop as Don Lowry did, or a miniature figure casting business as Duke Seifried had, and later added miniature wargame rules publishing to the portfolio. Gygax had no hope of raising the seed capital required for either of those enterprises, but perhaps there was another, more modest strategy: to build a self-sustaining business around selling rules alone, that might someday diversify into the board game space. There was at least a chance he could scrape together enough "loot" to enter just the modest miniature wargame rule business vacated by Guidon Games in the marketplace, and if it succeeded, he could use the profits to produce board games as well—including Megarry's.

A rules firm based in Lake Geneva could trade on the reputation Gygax had built publishing semi-commercial games and rules, both in fanzines and through the Guidon Games imprint. And Gygax had one asset that was absolutely integral to his strategy: GenCon. Following the collapse of the IFW, the Lake Geneva Tactical Studies Association effectively took over the stewardship of the convention in 1973. Lowry reported in *Panzerfaust* that the show brought over four hundred gamers to the Horticultural Hall for that summer weekend, but it attracted more than just individual consumers: miniature figure casters brought their wares to sell, hobby store owners paid for exhibit booths, and distributors decided what to carry by watching the crowds. GenCon was furthermore a place to test and demonstrate game titles in development. Megarry came with a copy of the *Dungeons of Pasha Cada* to show to some of the other LGTSA members, and Arneson that summer had the opportunity to introduce Gygax to additional members of his Twin Cities club. Gygax was particularly struck by a game he saw for the first time there, the draft rules for John Snider's "Stellar VII" science-fiction campaign. Don Greenwood, wearing his new Avalon Hill hat, made the pilgrimage himself that year, as the company put some sponsorship money into the convention. He participated in board wargame tournaments and praised the event in the pages of the *Avalon Hill General* as "an outstanding success." But one must suppose Greenwood was taken aback to see how focused on miniatures the convention had become since he last attended in 1969, when Avalon Hill's products commanded more of the local mindshare.

By the first week of September 1973, Gygax notified Arneson, "We're getting ready to roll." That month, the partnership got its initial capitalization, $1,000 supplied by Don Kaye, and Tactical Studies Rules was born. Kaye was not wealthy, but he had made a sufficient living for his family as a foreman at the Lake Geneva Metal Spinning Company owned by his uncle. Despite his own periodic bouts of unemployment, Kaye was willing to risk a considerable sum on Gygax's plan. Their roles in the partnership were starkly delineated: Kaye would handle the money and Gygax would handle the rules.

Using the industry connections he had cultivated, Gygax approached wholesaler buyers for TSR's debut offering: a single-volume set of wargame rules for the English Civil War, *Cavaliers and Roundheads*. It was crucial to introduce TSR to distributors through something familiar, a work in the traditional historical gaming genre with proven authors. *Cavaliers and Roundheads* had largely been designed by Jeff Perren—in a foreword Gygax calls his own contribution to it "trifling"—but it sold with "Perren & Gygax" on the cover, to trade on the name recognition that team had achieved with *Chainmail*. Its look and feel cloned the design of Guidon Games publications, a single digest-sized booklet with offset printing that TSR planned to sell for $3— Lowry had raised the prices of his booklets to $2.50 already. The TSR logo on the cover of *Cavaliers and Roundheads* showed an intertwined "G" and "K" for the last initials of the two founding partners.

Cavaliers and Roundheads did attract some promising pre-orders: Gygax could boast in a letter to Arneson that the distributor Jim Oden "is taking an initial 100, and good old Jack Scruby will take an initial dozen of anything we do!" Oden ran a Dallas-based toy soldier producer that cast American versions of the famous Hinchliffe firm designs from Britain, and his firm Heritage would go on to become one of TSR's best early customers—Heritage would be fatefully entangled with TSR well into the 1980s. As for "good old Jack Scruby," the father of miniature wargaming in America, Gygax had already been planning with him a line of fantasy miniatures for *Chainmail* that would readily carry over to *Dungeons & Dragons*.

But Gygax had no intention of stopping after publishing just *Cavaliers and Roundheads* and *D&D*: he ambitiously wrangled an ever-shifting schedule of projected releases that went well beyond what had been planned for Guidon Games. At the time, he hoped TSR could squeeze in both *Cavaliers and Roundheads* and Arneson's *Naval Orders of Battle* before the New Year. He slated both *D&D* and a Western gunfight simulation called *Boot Hill* for 1974, and more tentatively proposed publishing that same year his own ancient-era rules, followed by Napoleonics, and then John Snider's space game, which might occupy three volumes Snider had outlined as staggered releases. The lengthier Arneson project *Ships of the Line* slipped back in the schedule to 1975, along with other planned titles, such as a set of modern tank rules.

How realistic were these ambitions, and these dates? Gygax knew well that everything depended on the debut product line's reception. The initial releases were investments: if they made money, that money could be used to print future titles. He explained to Arneson, "Depending on how well sales go, we will increase or cut back production. Six releases/year could be possible, as could only one or two new booklets be possible due to money. Let's hope for the best." The example of Don Lowry and Guidon Games showed how difficult this path could be: in the last issue of *Panzerfaust* for 1973, Lowry had to disclose that he had laid off the two staffers he relocated to Maine, a fate that Gygax only narrowly avoided. Even with three business ventures in play—*Panzerfaust*, Lowrys Hobbies, and Guidon Games—"the whole triad just hasn't been making enough to support us all," Lowry conceded as he scaled back his efforts to the point where only he and his wife performed all the functions of the businesses.

By the last days of December 1973, during the crunch time for proofing and finalizing the *Dungeons & Dragons* booklets, the project ran over budget, and it became clear that Arneson's *Naval Orders of Battle* would have to wait. Gygax returned it and *Ships of the Line* to Arneson by mail, requesting extensive revisions. If the fixes could be turned around in two months, then, "I don't promise it, but there is a chance we'll use one or both next." By this point Gygax also expressed no small frustration with Arneson's contributions to *D&D* work. Even at the beginning of their collaboration, he had responded to one of Arneson's rule proposals with, "I thought you'd do a better job of meshing it with our (LGTSA) rules as plagiarized from your rules as drawn from *Chainmail*." Many times Gygax had requested revisions to material Arneson had submitted, and ultimately had to rewrite them himself at the eleventh hour because they did not conform to Gygax's *D&D* system. He struck a tone in those letters that Arneson would be justified in resenting: "We do want a set of rules that has internal harmony now, don't we?" Gygax demanded testily. "It isn't nice to design totally different rules for aspects of the same game, is it? No!" In the final stages of publication, Gygax had it his way, just as he had overruled Mike Carr on *Don't Give Up the Ship*.

When 1974 began, TSR had gone only halfway to becoming a company. The partnership of Tactical Studies Rules then consisted solely of Gygax and Kaye, and neither drew any sort of salary for their work, nor could they dare hope for profits. There is no better indication of how modest everyone's expectations were for *D&D* than the language in the game's royalty agreement, dated January 4, 1974. Gygax and Arneson would split a 20 percent royalty on "the selling price of the set or single booklet or any attendant part of the set other than art work," virtually the same agreement they had struck with Guidon Games. In exchange for that, "the co-authors shall assign to the publisher the copyright, the right to publish, sell, and distribute the set of game rules to be entitled *Dungeons & Dragons* as booklets, and any other similar rights." In the entirely plausible eventuality that the game met total indifference upon its release, the agreement permitted the authors to repurchase its rights from TSR if it went out of print at "a fair price based upon market demand at such time, but in no event exceeding three hundred dollars ($300.00)." What TSR thought they had in *D&D* was, at best, a $300 idea.

The process of printing *D&D* took several weeks to complete, as the lengthy rules were divided into three digest-sized volumes that had to be

AGREEMENT

By the signing of this contract, the several parties concerned,
E. Gary Gygax for TACTICAL STUDIES RULES, publisher, and
David (Dave) Arneson and E. Gary Gygax, co-authors, do
agree to the following:

That the co-authors shall assign to the publisher the copyright,
the right to publish, sell, and distribute the set of game
rules to be entitled Dungeons and Dragons as booklets, and
any other similar rights, in consideration of payment to the
co-authors by the publisher of a royalty of twenty percent
(20%) of the selling price of the set or single booklet or
any attendant part of the set other than art work (whether
the sale is retail, wholesale, or by job-lot) on each and
every item sold; this to be payable on a quarterly basis beginning 1 May 1974 with respect to David Arneson and on a
monthly basis beginning 1 March 1974 with respect to E. Gary
Gygax.

That, however, the co-authors shall have the option of purchasing
the copyright from the publisher at such time as the publisher no longer maintains the title Dungeons and Dragons as
an in-print title, and to do so as a fair price based upon
market demand at such time, but in no event exceeding three
hundred dollars ($300.00), is also understood and agreed.

This Agreement shall not be considered a valid contract until
signed by both the publisher and the co-authors and shall
take effect as of the date indicated below:

SIGNED: _____ (Publisher)

SIGNED: _____ (Co-Author)

SIGNED: _____ (Co-Author)

DATE: Jan. 4   1974.

Tactical Studies Rules copyright assignment and royalty agreement for *Dungeons &
Dragons*, executed on January 4, 1974.

proofed, printed, and bound separately. Gygax had dropped off the necessary material for the first volume, *Men & Magic*, at the local Graphic Printing
Company just before the end of 1973; the materials that came back were
stored in Don Kaye's garage, at 542 Sage Street in Lake Geneva, a distance of
about three blocks from Gygax's house. At that time, TSR also ordered the
first shipment of the woodgrain boxes that would house the booklets, and
had the printers begin producing the labels they would affix to those boxes
before sale. The second volume, *Monsters & Treasure*, would not go to the
printers until mid-January, largely because they awaited straggling pieces of
artwork. By February 7, the components had all come together, including
the third booklet, *Underworld & Wilderness Adventures*, and Gygax dropped
Arneson a quick postcard to say, "Printer has *D&D* nearly done, so your
copy should be in the mail by next week."

D&D had vastly exceeded its planned budget, a potential calamity for so
modest a partnership. Gygax estimated that "this is going to cost us closer
to three than two thousand, I believe, when boxes, separate charts, box
labels and advertising flyers are run (the art is costing about $100 too!)."
They managed to keep the art budget low by fielding out the illustrations
to teenagers who drew a bit, like Greg Bell, who was part of Jeff Perren's
circle in Rockford, and Keenan Powell, Mary Gygax's half-sister. At the last
minute, Arneson provided four of the monster portraits for *D&D* himself,
which earned him an illustrator credit. Despite these cost-cutting measures,
Gygax and Kaye had to admit a third partner, a more recent addition to the
Lake Geneva Tactical Studies Association: Brian Blume, a twenty-three-year-
old machinist from nearby Wauconda, Wisconsin, who worked in the shop
of his successful father, Melvin Blume. Blume would describe his job as
"watching a lathe go round and round," but he brought home a handsome
annual salary of around $20,000, which let him buy into an equal partner-
ship with Gygax and Kaye with a $2,000 investment. Recently divorced,
Blume found in wargaming a much-needed diversion, and joining Tactical Studies Rules was simply a way of extending his engagement with the
hobby. Once Blume joined, Gygax would describe the triumvirate partnership as follows: "Don Kaye is our wise and noble president, Brian Blume the
watchful vice president, and I am the oppressed and hard-working editor."

As the entire treasury of the partnership had gone to the printers, TSR
had no chance of producing anything further until sales of its existing
titles replenished their coffers. That economic reality would constrain TSR

Original *Dungeons & Dragons* (1974) boxed set of three booklets, with dice.

throughout 1974: to print one thousand copies of a new digest-sized rules booklet, a slender volume of thirty-two pages, at the Graphic Printing Company required a baseline outlay of around $750. *Dungeons & Dragons* cost $3 per copy to produce, and it shipped with a cover price of $10 per set, but most sets did not sell at full price: instead, TSR sold *D&D* largely through distributors, at wholesale rates of only 60 percent of the cover price—and job lots for less than half. TSR thus expected a return of three dollars or less on each sale, which royalties and other overhead costs would easily eat up.

And that was assuming anyone would buy it. *Dungeons & Dragons* was a tough sell in the wargaming community of the time: it lacked the board familiar from board wargames, and relied only indirectly on miniatures, instead using paper-and-pencil dungeon maps that had little direct precedent. It furthermore incorporated unusual polyhedral dice into many aspects of play, which were not included in the box and effectively raised the price of the product. With rulebooks that not only struggled to explain unfamiliar system concepts but also brimmed with fantastic elements some historical gamers rejected as childish—never mind a burdensome requirement for a neutral referee to invest hours into preparatory work on dungeon design—*D&D* seemed destined for total obscurity. It certainly did not sell well out of the gate. Royalties up to end of March 1974, which reflected the sale of eighty-one copies, amounted to only $106.40, so Gygax and Arneson each received a bit more than fifty dollars for that quarter.

It is perhaps clearer in this light why the original contract valued *Dungeons & Dragons* as a $300 idea. Optimistically assuming for the $3,000 investment on the first printing an "eventual return of about $6,000, less shipping, taxes, advertising, and royalties" for *D&D*, Gygax could only ruefully predict that "TSR will be lucky to break even on the first 'thou.'" He ventured that printing "the next 1,000 will be a whale of a lot cheaper—about one-half" the cost, as they already had the necessarily galleys at the printers, so any realistic potential for profit hinged on the response warranting a second printing of *D&D*. If the whole thing ultimately returned no more than $300 in profit to TSR, that would represent a 10 percent return on the initial investment of $3,000, and it was probably thinking along these lines that set the game's contractual valuation.

Don Lowry had learned the hard way that the usual trajectory of sales for miniature rulebooks was heavily front-loaded, with a long tail. *Cavaliers and Roundheads*, the first TSR rulebook, followed this path: while at the beginning of the year Gygax eagerly reported that the game had sold over 250 copies since its release the previous October, by June 1974 he would have to admit that its sales had "really slowed." TSR would finish 1974 with four hundred out of the original print run of one thousand still in its inventory. *D&D*, a pricier and less traditional title, did not enjoy even an initial flash of popularity. Its returns for the second quarter of 1974 would remain flat: TSR would owe Gygax and Arneson just shy of $60 each for royalties on tepid sales of a little over a hundred copies between April and June, or around $20 a month—the income Gygax had predicted a three-volume Guidon set might furnish for its authors. Anyone looking soberly at these

Handwritten tabulation of *Dungeons & Dragons* sales for the first quarter of 1974, broken down by job lot, wholesale, and retail rates, with royalty payment sum for Dave Arneson.

figures in the spring of 1974 would have been justified in concluding that both *D&D* and TSR had failed as ventures.

And Gygax desperately needed money. In March, he had learned that his landlord intended to sell the house at 330 Center Street where Gygax, his wife, and five children lived in cramped quarters. He had an option to buy the house which would expire June 1, but he struggled to borrow enough money for a down payment; even when his mother fronted some cash for him, no bank would approve a mortgage for the perennially under-employed Gygax. He even briefly considered relocating his clan to the Twin

Cities, inquiring with Arneson about rent and jobs in the area. Ultimately, Gygax only managed to forestall his housing crisis by striking a deal to help a neighbor buy his "wee hovel," as he called it, in exchange for another year's lease at $125 a month.

TSR was still only a hobby at this point, and the royalties for *D&D* would not cover Gygax's rent, let alone support his family. The shoe repair business was irregular, so Gygax took what work he could, but he had very limited prospects. Many locals in Lake Geneva worked factory jobs in nearby towns, which might pay two or three dollars an hour: a few members of the LGTSA commuted to collect an hourly wage from Sta-Rite in nearby Delavan. Book-ish but uncredentialed, Gygax's only choice was often manual labor to which he was ill-suited. He had to apologize to Dave Arneson and Dave Wesely after a May 1974 visit when he was too exhausted from a new job to receive them properly: "I was all black and blue (thighs and stomach), and my hands were so cut up and bruised that they'd hardly work right. If they'd have been paying more than $2.90—like about twice that—I might have stayed on, or if there was any foreseeable hope of getting off shearing 14 gauge steel." He phoned in his resignation from that gig shortly thereafter.

Something had to be done. Anxious for the capital to produce further titles, Gygax and Kaye explored admitting a fourth TSR partner. But given sales to date, who would consider it a sound investment? Gygax knew well of his original partner, "Don isn't about to come up with any more loot." His frustration was palpable in his correspondence at the time. "Gad! It is most difficult to make a firm run properly without plenty of capital!!!"

With new investment not an option, Gygax turned warily back to Don Lowry for a quicker path to grow the TSR product line, despite their ongoing dispute over royalties. In March, Gygax proposed that TSR acquire the rights to *Chainmail, Don't Give Up the Ship*, and *Tractics* for the sum of $400, and furthermore acquire any unsold stock of those titles. Again, that all three Guidon titles would have such a low buy-back value is a good indication of why *D&D* seemed at most a $300 idea. Lowry, beleaguered by creditors and teetering on the verge of bankruptcy, had little choice but to accept. Gygax still defended Lowry, but only for his intentions: in May, he would write that "Don's a nice guy—a piss-poor business manager, but a nice chap."

TSR also tried to accelerate production at the time by offering "vanity press" services, where rules authors could front production costs as a loan that would be repaid with interest as copies sold. If it took two years to sell a thousand-copy print run, the repayment would amount to 10 percent interest on the loan annually. Brian Blume, who still had some cash reserves to spread around, became the first to exercise this path by loaning TSR $1,000 to print his forthcoming World War II tank rules *Panzer Warfare*, though as Gygax intimated, he made the investment "simply to help TSR along," as it would take some time for those rules to see print. Gygax hinted that TSR might similarly pick up a more ambitious project like Mike Carr's board game *Fight in the Skies*, another former Guidon Games title, "if Mike will finance the production."

Navigating around the firm's poverty, Gygax carefully sustained a holding pattern of forthcoming titles, enlisting Arneson's assistance in keeping the designers in the Twin Cities eager but patient. Back in 1973, Lowry had advertised the Napoleonic rules called *Tricolor* as a forthcoming title. Now, Gygax redirected it from the Guidon pipeline to TSR, to be the first product to follow *D&D*. Comparing the sales of TSR's two prior releases, a traditional wargaming title no doubt looked like a safer bet than another fantasy offering. The Napoleonic era remained the most popular genre among miniature wargamers, so perhaps its release would save TSR from destitution. Arneson for his part now also hoped to produce an additional board game for TSR about the Crusades, as well as a set of American Civil War naval rules tentatively titled *Damn the Torpedoes*. Whatever other projects TSR had in play, it was clear that Gygax still harbored the bravest ambitions for *D&D*, despite its disappointing reception. He envisioned three supplements to come: the first would be his *Greyhawk*, followed by a second supplement by Arneson, and then a third potentially from a new author.

Diversifying TSR's product line was essential to effective outreach through advertising, an expense that TSR could scarcely afford. "It costs about $40 to set up the copy, and the ads will run about $125," Gygax had lamented to Arneson, citing figures that TSR could not spend lightly. "It doesn't pay to advertise without as large a selection of materials as possible. With, for example, a dozen sets of rules and a couple of games any ad has a far better chance of interesting more people, thus paying for itself and even making a bit of loot." Gygax agonized for want of enough products to fill both sides of the printed flyers he sent out with company correspondence. So, instead of paying for advertising in wargaming trade and fan magazines, Gygax wrote articles—thinly veiled advertisements in prose form—to promote TSR products, and repeatedly begged Arneson to do the same, to no avail.

When it came to Dave Megarry's *Dungeons of Pasha Cada*, Gygax managed that holding pattern personally, in part because Megarry was now living in Boston. As Megarry's project was a proper "game" with a board and pieces, not just rules, Gygax spent much of 1974 contrasting the treatment the game would likely receive from Avalon Hill against, in some hypothetical future, that of a TSR with the resources on hand to publish games. Gygax could speak from experience about designing for Avalon Hill: his own *Alexander the Great* jumped from Guidon Games to Avalon Hill in March, and so he could lambast the "ridiculous (I mean miserly!!!) royalty percentage" that Avalon Hill condescended to pay him. What Gygax did hope to derive from working with Avalon Hill was legitimacy, and a stronger relationship with Don Greenwood, who could provide something TSR currently lacked: a means to publish "games" rather than "rules." Megarry officially appointed Gygax his agent to sell the game, which Gygax quickly retitled *Dungeon!* But Avalon Hill expressed little immediate interest in picking it up—Greenwood had, after all, deemed the fantasy elements in *Chainmail* "foolish" back in 1971.

Gygax and his partners exerted only so much control over their product schedule: they had to react to market opportunities. This was vividly illustrated in June 1974, when Gygax had some "ultra-confidential" news to share with Arneson: "At GenCon there will be a new release by a figure manufacturer and by TSR." For that rush project, Gygax desperately needed maps of Barsoom, the fantastic reimagining of the planet Mars, which Edgar Rice Burroughs had drawn to accompany his famous John Carter books— and luckily Arneson owned a volume that reproduced them. *D&D* already included a few encounter tables with monsters from Barsoom—an area of the "Great Kingdom" campaign world had contained such creatures—but a miniature manufacturer would want dedicated rules for a major release of figures. This request came in to TSR from Heritage Models; their line of Barsoom figures would premier at GenCon in 1974. This tie-in promised to draw much-needed sales and further diversify the TSR product line. Nothing could convey TSR's impecunity so well as Gygax's explanation that he had to beg Arneson to photocopy the Barsoom maps as "we will eventually pick the book up, but it'll take some time to raise $12."

So TSR pivoted, abruptly, to a title not in Gygax's holding pattern: *Warriors of Mars*. Gygax and Blume both hurriedly developed rules throughout June, borrowing shamelessly from *D&D*. Fortunately, work on *Tricolor* had concluded by this point: the first copies were due back from the printers

June 21. This freed up the schedule for the Barsoom rules, which would be Blume's first design credit. It does not appear that TSR established any particular relationship with the Burroughs estate for the production of this book, but Heritage's English counterpart Hinchliffe had secured permission to manufacture their figures, and no one really paid much attention to miniature rules booklets because no one had ever made enough money on them to fret over. They were one step up from packaging.

One cannot overstate the dependence of TSR on Heritage as a distributor in 1974. As a result of the unforeseen urgency to produce *Warriors of Mars*, everything else at TSR slipped—even royalties for *D&D*. In August, Gygax had to apologize to Arneson for the delay, explaining that Heritage president Jim "Oden wanted TSR to do those ERB rules," and as Heritage "is about 40% of our business, we really had no choice. Anyway, that meant we had to sandwich in another set of rules, and the budget is really at the strained point." Gygax insisted that the money was on hand, and that Kaye would pay it out soon—but this must have recalled to Arneson the evasiveness of Lowry about royalties.

The fact that Heritage demanded *Warriors of Mars* in time for GenCon reaffirmed the immense strategic value of the convention—which in turn highlighted the question of who exactly controlled the convention, now that the IFW, its original sponsor, was defunct. Nominally, the LGTSA had run the convention in 1973, and Gygax faced an internal challenge within the LGTSA in 1974 from "jealous orcs," as he put it, within the ranks of the club. Although TSR took its name and its personnel from the LGTSA, club members who held no stake in the partnership felt the interests of TSR had superseded club ambitions, like renting a meeting space where they could play games. GenCon itself began to be shaped by TSR's priorities, rather than the consensus of the LGTSA.

After a tense confrontation with Gygax and Kaye, Tom Champany resigned as the chairman of the LGTSA, amid some dark mutterings about Gygax being a "tin god." Gygax knew that Arneson had been through similar political difficulties in his own club, so he asked him in a letter, "Why is it, do you suppose, that those who work hard and are creative become objects of envy and dislike (hate) from certain associates?" But then he added a dash after the question and wrote his own answer: "Just because I hold Tom and many of the others in rather obvious contempt." As personable as he was, Gygax spoiled a bit too eagerly for these sorts of fights, and he took satisfaction in punching down—like a victorious wargamer given to trash-talking. That attitude would not serve his public image well in the long term.

GenCon returned to the Horticultural Hall and expanded to three days in 1974—but the six hundred or so attendees crammed into its walls might have felt that the scope of the convention was narrowing. Some products by Avalon Hill were on sale there, but only thanks to the presence of hobby shops. Most of the exhibit booths at GenCon now focused on miniatures, and nearly everyone had some sort of fantasy offering to show. Duke Seifried was on hand to sell his Der Kriegspielers miniatures. He displayed prototypes of fantasy figures yet to be released, accompanied by a dazzling sales pitch for anyone who came within earshot. Right next to Seifried was the Heritage Models booth, where they sold the new Martian figures to accompany *Warriors of Mars*; "theirs was the best exhibit," according to the *Great Plains Game Players Newsletter* fanzine. TSR sold their own rules and also Jack Scruby's fantasy miniatures, as the two companies had struck a partnership that TSR hoped would induce Scruby to distribute more copies of *D&D*. The Twin Cities hobby shop La Belle Alliance, who to Gygax's delight had bought twenty copies of *D&D* back in May, was on hand: they took an informal poll of attending gamers to ask which was the better medium, board games or miniatures games, and found 47.8 percent chose miniatures over 30.4 percent who favored board games, the remaining fifth being undecided.

But the real story of GenCon in 1974 was not the many miniatures vendors. "This year's convention was centered mainly around the new set of Gygax and Arneson rules *Dungeons & Dragons*," as one fan reported. "On Saturday at least a dozen games were in progress and as soon as one ended another was started." It was "the hit of the convention with gamemasters having games going in all parts of the Hall."

Arneson very nearly missed GenCon in 1974, as it overlapped with the start of the Minnesota State Fair, where he was once again scheduled to work a ticket booth. Although Arneson pleaded for GenCon to be rescheduled in the future, Gygax could only reply that the "GenCon date is dictated by the Garden Club (Mrs. Wrigley et. al.)." Arneson did show Gygax a draft of a post-apocalyptic game designed by John Snider's brother Richard, tentatively called "Mutant," which Gygax added to TSR's product queue within a week. Arneson relished the opportunity to socialize with the many miniature figure firms in attendance that summer, including Miniature Figurines of New York. As they had a full slate of fantasy figures on display, MiniFigs reached an agreement with Arneson to produce a painting guide for their miniatures. Arneson was eager to work with them because he hoped to interest a major manufacturer in producing figures from his molds, though he would vacillate between a rotating cast of potential partners in this endeavor.

At the end of summer 1974, Arneson remained somewhat discontented with the state of *D&D*. Gygax constantly nagged him to write fanzine articles promoting the title, but in his correspondence, Arneson tended to focus more on historical wargaming in the Twin Cities, especially naval wargaming. Sometimes in his 1974 letters he would call the publisher of *D&D* "Test Series Rules" instead of Tactical Studies Rules, confusing TSR with one of SPI's lines of games. Arneson had groused about the published *D&D* design in his correspondence, and even went so far as to ask one of his correspondents to forward some of his concerns for publication in the *Great Plains Game Players Newsletter*. In that letter, Arneson suggested there was "a certain amount of communication breakdown" between himself and Gygax in the design of the game, reviewing a few places where Gygax had overruled his wishes. The editor of the *Great Plains* zine would hold off on publishing this letter for half a year, but the passive-aggressive way that Arneson aired his grievances publicly, in a venue where Gygax was actively socializing rules ideas for *D&D*, gives a sense of how dysfunctional his collaboration with Gygax had become.

An uptick in *D&D* sales became perceptible in late summer and into the fall; as of August, TSR was bringing in around $100 per week, about the same amount as Gygax's shoe repair business. *D&D* sales for the third quarter more than doubled, to around 275 copies, which would yield royalties just shy of $140 each for Gygax and Arneson. While it is difficult to trace this growth to any single cause, no doubt GenCon in 1974 had a considerable impact—not because TSR sold that many copies of the game there, but because it gave gamers the opportunity to learn how to play directly from Gygax, Arneson, and members of their immediate circles.

It has been remarked that the original *D&D* rules offer little by way of a practical introduction to the game: they explain how to generate characters, how to design dungeons, how to roll for random encounters, and how to determine the plunder won in battle, but there is little text that explains the objective, or even the moment-to-moment operation, of the game. A few hours of play around the table with an experienced referee would immediately clarify the many tacit assumptions behind the rules, and GenCon provided just such an opportunity to learn the game from its most outgoing ambassador. Gamers always remarked on Gygax's easy manner: one fan who arrived at the convention in 1974 reported on how "Gary Gygax recognized me immediately and we went out at night for pizza and beer at the local pub—what a ball." So gamers from around the country who convened in Lake Geneva that August returned home with the *D&D* rulebooks in hand, ready to indoctrinate their local gaming groups and spread the game from there. Zine articles detailing local campaigns began to pop up, sparking further interest.

By September, Gygax could report to Megarry that Avalon Hill "is now willing to look at *Dungeon!*—probably due to the growing popularity of the *D&D* game they'd give it a fair look." But to keep Megarry in the holding pattern, Gygax also shared in that same letter that TSR had engaged a Chicago advertising firm, where his friend Dave Dimery worked, to develop a prospectus for TSR to publish his game. That was enough to keep Megarry patient. But before the end of the year, Gygax would have to admit "we are still working on funding for *Dungeon!*," and could say nothing more confident than "we will see what develops there."

The interest of Avalon Hill in *Dungeon!* came as this foremost of wargame companies prepared to unveil a new front in its strategy. Avalon Hill announced in the fall their intention to host a convention of their own, in Baltimore, in the summer of 1975. They called it Origins, as Baltimore was the birthplace of the wargaming movement created by Avalon Hill's Charles S. Roberts. Don Greenwood circulated a note inviting influential gamers "to partake in the activities of wargaming's newest and (we hope) best wargaming convention." As a venue, Greenwood promised Avalon Hill had "almost unlimited access to Johns Hopkins University," and they fully expected a turnout of "over 500+ gamers plus whatever public response we can generate from local newspaper, radio, and TV exposure." Naturally they would promote this through the *Avalon Hill General*—which was in 1974 uncharacteristically quiet about GenCon. But as a concession to the influential Gygax, Avalon Hill did promise that their event would include "fantasy trips through *Dungeons & Dragons*." Greenwood surely did not see *D&D* as a competing product, at least not yet—a survey in the last issue of the *General* for 1974 tested the water for interest in fantasy gaming—but he aimed squarely at GenCon with a competing convention. Gygax immediately resented the challenge to his greatest asset, and it would become a grudge he just could not shake off.

Even a slight increase in demand placed stress on the supply chain of *D&D*, which reached only a smattering of retail stores through its distribution network. The few gamers who went looking for it had trouble finding copies. Gygax and Arneson both struggled to secure major distributors other than Heritage to carry the TSR product line, appealing to Jack Scruby and the wargame impresario Lou Zocchi. Beyond questions of availability, the price point made it difficult to translate interest into sales, as wargamers were accustomed to buying complete board games from Avalon Hill for less than $10—and there was nothing in the *D&D* box but paper, rules without any other components. Widespread photocopying of the booklets ensued; many felt morally justified in pirating rules sold at such an outrageous markup.

Although rules could be photocopied, the exotic polyhedral dice the game required could not—and the wholesalers who bought rulebooks from TSR did not immediately stock their dice, apart from Zocchi. At a time when every penny mattered, dice sales provided crucial revenue for the young TSR partnership, and there were weeks in 1974 when dice brought in half of the company's take. By the end of November, TSR was ordering sets of the five polyhedral dice in lots of two hundred each. "Although we don't make much on them, it does give us a few pennies, gets people used to ordering from TSR by mail, and we get a mailing list too!" Gygax would cheerfully write. They jealously guarded their supplier, Creative Publications in Palo Alto, California, to prevent customers from going directly to the source.

One inevitable consequence of mounting interest in *D&D* was the appearance of imitators. M. A. R. Barker, a Minnesota university professor, was an early adopter of *D&D* who quickly applied its principles to his homebrew fictional world of Tekumél, a setting he had been developing in amateur fiction since the 1950s. By August 1974, Barker had a mature manuscript for a game called *Empire of the Petal Throne*, and had licensed the game for publication to a local imprint called World at War, a small wargaming firm with a handful of digest-sized titles slated for print. Much like TSR, World at War modeled itself after Guidon Games; it was run by Bill Hoyt, a longstanding member of Arneson's Twin Cities wargaming club.

Arneson forwarded Gygax a draft copy of *Petal Throne* in November as a potential acquisition for TSR. But since the game was so obviously derivative of *D&D*, Gygax reacted with outrage rather than eagerness. He showed some points of similarity to an attorney: "Our lawyer said that in his opinion a suit could be instituted without much difficulty if the work was published in the form it is now in." Though Barker had received contrary legal advice, Hoyt quickly acknowledged that some sort of royalty or at least credit to *D&D* must be due. Gygax took umbrage at the whole situation: "What I really regretted was the lack of courtesy shown by Barker in the first place, for he never sent a copy of his adaptation to TSR. Barker kept mentioning the 'good of the hobby,' evidentially not realizing it is a business which TSR runs, business with several thousands in personal funds of the partners which are invested to show a profit." Gygax could moreover see that the problem might recur: "If we allow copyright infringement now, who knows where it will end." Arneson for his part was content to leave this to Gygax, writing back: "I do not wish to touch the Barker deal with a ten foot pole since I will have to live with it on this end." But nevertheless, Arneson insisted: "I felt, and still do, that Barker had something TSR could use." Once communications had opened with Barker and Hoyt, Gygax explored various ways to resolve this quandary with the pair of them over the next several months.

The investment that the partners had made in TSR had turned out to be something worth protecting, not just money down the drain. Direct mail-order sales had grown by the end of the year to over $100 per week, dice included, and wholesale brought in perhaps the same amount. At the end of November, Gygax would reaffirm that "Heritage is still our best customer. Jim just ordered 50 *D&D* and 150 *WoM*," that is, *Warriors of Mars*. Reviewing the fate of their first four releases, Gygax grumbled that "*C&R* and *Tricolor* are not moving very fast, but they are steady sellers." On the upside, "*WoM* is going pretty well, but *D&D* continues to be the top seller." Perhaps TSR's fantasy offerings would turn out, in the long term, to be more viable than traditional wargame rules. Rather than dropping off, fourth-quarter royalties for *D&D* nearly doubled again, to $428.90 on sales of around 420 copies. A total in excess of 900 had sold as the year wound to close, and given that a number had been given away as promotions—or found to be defective—TSR's stock on hand had nearly depleted. In the second week of December, TSR approved a second printing of *D&D*, and with it, a long-awaited opportunity for a profit.

With its financial situation improving, TSR had sufficient capital on hand to squeeze in one more title before the end of 1974. Although Gygax

projected that the printer's bill for John Snider's *Star Probe* could run up to
$1,400—it was more just than a pamphlet, as it included a folding map and
a few counters, enclosed in a zip-lock package that would sell all together
for $6—he felt confident in their ability to pay early the following month.
The target release date for the game was December 20, but shifting schedules led them to print the book with a copyright year of 1975. Now TSR
sported two science-fiction titles to supplement their fantasy and traditional wargame offerings.

All of this augured well for TSR achieving the impossible: building a business around "rules," one which might soon support a handful of employees.
Admittedly, Gygax's share of the fourth-quarter royalties would not cover
his rent for those three months, but it shined the dimmest ray of hope. Even
back in middle of the year, Gygax had already begun to hint to Arneson
that TSR might be able afford him a position in the future. "Once we get big
enough," Gygax speculated, "you are the logical addition to the firm, and
I think we'll reach the point where we'll be able to offer something at least
nominally reasonable in not too long." Then he backpedaled: "Too many
unknowns to say more now." But could he resist saying more now? "How'd
you like to live in this area?" Slyly, he planted the thought, and then directed
Arneson into a holding pattern. "Keep that all to yourself, and forget it for a
while. It may all be a pipe dream at this stage, but I have high hopes."

Arneson to date had only intermittent stints of temporary employment
and vague ambitions of starting his travel agency, or maybe casting figures
himself to make a living. But his manner sometimes got in the way of business opportunities. Although he had agreed to produce a guide to fantasy
figure painting for MiniFigs earlier in the summer, the draft he delivered to
Steve Carpenter contained a critique of the design of the figures as well as
instructions for decorating them. When Gygax politely inquired after the
piece, Arneson replied, in a letter written on the last day of 1974, "Note
from Carpenter indicated he was looking it over and B.S. about a Mini-Figs
painting guide should not review or editorialize." Arneson did not seem to
grasp why a figure caster would hesitate to publish a painting guide critical of its own figures. His letter to Gygax continued: "Said he would get
back to me (Polite dust off???). I can always peddle it elsewhere (Hopefully)." This painting guide would indeed become a project that needed a
new home: perhaps TSR, and perhaps TSR would become Arneson's home
as well. But burned by the previous fiasco with Lowry, as tiny as the missing

returns might have been, Arneson never seemed secure when he had only one potential publisher in mind for a given project. And the viability of TSR was far from certain.

Only when we understand the humble roots of Tactical Studies Rules, and the unpromising initial reception of *Dungeons & Dragons*, can we appreciate how far Gary Gygax would rise in the decade that followed, and what that ascent would mean to him. His climb from near destitution and odd jobs to millions of dollars and appearances in venues like *60 Minutes* is practically miraculous, given what a small splash the game made in the tiny pool that was the wargaming community of 1974. TSR had pulled in around $12,000 in gross sales that calendar year: given that on average they sold *D&D* at only slightly above half the cover price, we might attribute half of their take to that one title. Those sums had not yet made TSR a profitable venture that could furnish anyone with a livelihood—but TSR's journey from a club to a company was on the cusp of completion. The burden of taking TSR to that next level would fall squarely on Gygax's shoulders, for a very unwelcome reason.

II Adventurers in Business

1975: Sage Street, Goodbye

It happened on the last day of January 1975. "Had a very nasty blow Friday," Gygax would write to an early *D&D* adopter a few days afterwards. "My old-time buddy and partner, Don Kaye had a fatal heart attack in the morning—died within about an hour of the occurrence." Kaye was rushed from his home to Lakeland Hospital in nearby Elkhorn, but he did not survive. Terrifyingly, he was only thirty-six years old, just a month older than Gygax himself. All that Kaye would ever know of TSR, *D&D*, and the fate of his own investment and energy, is what had transpired up to that fatal moment.

It was an event that could easily have ended this hobby business, and with it, the short career of *D&D*. But many great adventures start with a shock, a calamity that upends a person's life, forcing them to take a path they would never have chosen otherwise. Gary Gygax's adventure in business would begin when tragedy required that he take a different role in Tactical Studies Rules than he had originally planned, and one for which he had little by way of qualifications. He had no intention of letting TSR falter—if anything, the resulting changes to the partnership would hasten a transformation, forcing the final step in progressing from a club to a company.

Bereft of its president, TSR found the partnership cast into serious doubt, as Kaye's one-third share came into the hands of his widow Donna, who had weightier matters on her mind than the fate of a fledging game-rule business. Gygax affirmed that "Mrs. Kaye is very capable, however, and she wishes to continue the firm as is," adding that "she enjoyed working closely to Don."

Partnerships have no requirement for public financial transparency, but an internal analysis of the total assets of TSR compiled February 1, 1975, gives a good sense of where it stood around its first birthday. Gygax has scrawled in capital letters "Confidential: Destroy After Reading" at the top of the page, a directive that was ignored, fortunately for posterity. It suggests that Kaye's garage now housed around $12,000 worth of product, including 750 copies of *D&D* remaining from its second printing, and about half of the initial print runs of *Tricolor* and *Warriors of Mars*. At the bottom of the page, the partnership generously adds to its assets a few subjective intangibles, monetizing the projected growth potential and good will of TSR's principals. By this point they had, at least, figured out that *D&D* was something more than what its original contract had promised: just a $300 idea.

The immediate survival of the firm depended on meeting the aggressive schedule of releases planned before Kaye's passing. Any delays might lead to an irrecoverable debt to the printers, who could only be paid after sales. Gygax summarized the deliverables in mid-February as follows: "*Chainmail* this week, *Panzer Warfare* in about 3 weeks, *Greyhawk* in about 5 weeks, *Tractics* in about 5 weeks." As TSR's flagship *D&D* rules recommended purchasing *Chainmail*, an update of those rules under the TSR imprint seemed like a sure thing—especially elevated to a $5 price point from the former $3. Provided the forthcoming titles sold, Gygax promised Arneson, then "we'll get the whole of the *DGUTS* trilogy"—that is, the update of Guidon Games's *Don't Give Up the Ship*, followed by Arneson's long-awaited *Ships of the Line* and *Naval Orders of Battle*—"out right after GenCon" in August.

From his base in St. Paul, Arneson thus had the daunting task of editing down the vast texts he had generated for those two titles, but that labor would have to compete with his other responsibilities to a company that did not yet employ him or anyone else. He had to help his fellow Twin Cities authors prepare their titles for TSR: he advised Richard Snider on making his "Mutant" game compatible with *D&D*, for example. Gygax also expressed continuing interest in the work that Dave Wesely had done toward American Civil War era rules, which Arneson had to oversee personally. Arneson had reported that at the end of January he was "hard at work" on both his Crusades board game and the next *D&D* supplement, *Blackmoor*. "Keep plugging there, Dave," Gygax would write, "for we'll eventually get to everything you do. TSR isn't about to fail or pull a Lowry on you."

Although it took some time to sink in, the passing of Don Kaye no doubt prompted much somber reflection on what kind of firm the principals of TSR wanted to run. For a venture like this to succeed, it had to be a labor of love for everyone involved—but Kaye's widow was no gamer, and in light of TSR's increasing momentum, Gygax and Blume could rely for only so long on her willingness to perform effectively unpaid work. Gygax himself

CONFIDENTIAL: DESTROY AFTER READING

AN ESTIMATE OF THE FINANCIAL STATUS OF TACTICAL STUDIES RULES

- Initial Capitalization   September 1973
- First Release   October 1973
- Second Capitalization   January 1974
- Estimated Period of Full-Scale Operation 2/74 -- 2/75

Assets: (Figures rounded down)

400	CAVALIERS & ROUNDHEADS	$ .660*
750	DUNGEONS & DRAGONS	3,750*
600	TRICOLOR	1,500*
500	WARRIORS OF MARS	1,250*
900	STAR PROBE	2,700*
1,000	CHAINMAIL	2,500*

*based on 50% of cover price
TOTAL ALL BOOKLET STOCK $ 11,360

1,000 boxes	100
200 sets dice	300**
Miscellaneous equipment, fixtures, etc.	340
900 copies The Strategic Review	300**

**assumes postal expense excluded as
figure is already reduced~~~~
TOTAL ACTUAL ASSETS $ 12,400

Liabilities:

Production loan @ approx. 10% interest $- 1,100

   TOTAL LIABILITIES $- 1,100

NET ASSETS	$11,300
Subjective Valuation of Growth Potential	11,300
Subjective Valuation of "Good Will"	4,400
TOTAL VALUATION OF TACTICAL STUDIES RULES (300 units)	$27,000
(Value of a single unit as of 1 February 1975	($ 90)

An Estimate of the Financial Status of Tactical Studies Rules, February 1, 1975, detailing physical assets, liabilities including a production loan to Brian Blume, and subjective valuation factors, used to price the "units of value" held by the three partners.

was squeezing what TSR work he could into Wednesdays, when his shoe repair store was closed. This made TSR a thing that existed mostly on paper, shunted into spare time, still more a hobby than a company—like a play-by-mail game, it lived in correspondence. They needed a plan for a TSR no longer tied to the Kaye family, and no longer dependent on volunteer labor: TSR needed a local habitation, and perhaps a new name. To get there, Gygax and Blume would need financial resources well beyond their current means.

Both Gygax and Blume felt that, given their mission as a company, they had to be wary about accepting just anyone's investment. In a note to Megarry early in March, Gygax made vows that would have lasting implications: "We will never allow TSR to become a company which is run by any outside group. That is, we may take others in as partners eventually, but we will never seek any non-wargamer capitalization." Although he recognized this would slow the growth of the company, he wanted TSR to remain a company that made products by gamers for gamers. The first step was connecting more with their customers. So, they launched a quarterly newsletter, called the *Strategic Review*, which served to promote their games and solicit feedback from customers. In the second issue of the *Strategic Review*, Brian Blume in his own words affirmed that "TSR is not around solely to make money. The members of TSR are long time gamers who have found that there is a good deal of satisfaction in creating and/or publishing a good set of game rules or an enjoyable game."

The growing prosperity of TSR made Gygax more adamant than ever that Arneson prepare to join the firm: "Further to what I said it is absolutely necessary for you to let me/us know if you will be willing to remove to LG in a year or two," he wrote. "The deal we will offer will be the absorption of your casting business (and your abilities) into TSR for a cut of the company." Arneson now had grand ambitions around making his own wargaming figurines; he had shortly before begun talking to MiniFigs about carrying his line of Napoleonic miniatures. He therefore retorted to Gygax that his casting business might be the one doing the absorbing. Gygax was quick to nip that in the bud. "Even if MiniFigs carries your ships you won't be in a position to buy TSR," he replied testily. "Heritage does about $1,000/month with us these days, and we have other distributors who are doing altogether an equal amount. All hobby shop and other wholesale orders amount to about half as much, and retail sales are coming pretty close to that too."

Arneson's skepticism probably had roots in how he saw his relationship with Gygax, especially in how their collaboration on *D&D* had gone.

Although they had known each other for five years, working on games together, and playing them in person when their travel schedules permitted, they remained more colleagues than friends. Arneson continued to criticize *D&D* in his correspondence with other figures in the industry. In describing TSR's flagship game to Tony Bath, one of the venerable sages of British wargaming, Arneson flatly confessed: "I am certainly not in the most desirable position of saying *D&D* is a perfect set of rules, they are far from it." From the reports he had heard from early adopters, he believed, "In fact they are very susceptible to being wrecked by a poor referee due to the poor layout and explanations." If there was one thing Arneson could not abide it was a poor referee. He did manage to offer faint praise: "Still, I feel that they are not all that bad." Arneson harbored a contrarian streak, an anti-authoritarianism, which negatively disposed him to the sort of editorial prerogatives Gygax exercised: Arneson did not have the extroverted temperament of a leader, but he hated being a follower. As Arneson quipped in an autobiographical aside, "I am always ready, willing and able to tell someone else what they should do but am somewhat averse to the reverse policy." He was also a bit hesitant to leave home; it took him until 1975 to get a driver's license, and with it the latitude to travel freely.

Undeterred by Arneson's reluctance, Gygax pushed hard to win him over. Brian Blume, as Gygax would reveal in a March letter, "is thoroughly sick of his job" at his father's tool-and-die shop, "and he is anxious to liquidate most of his assets elsewhere in order to get a hobby shop in LG going." A brick and mortar retail store operated by TSR partners would fundamentally change the prospects of the business, providing the sort of stability that Lowry had derived from his mail-order shop. That too Gygax imagined would happen "within the year—18 months at the outside." Yet Gygax had to concede, "No question that you wouldn't be exactly living on Easy Street with TSR at first, but, Dave, we have so much potential that you would be sorry if you passed the opportunity by." Gygax knew well that caution was warranted when considering this sort of opportunity: "I still shudder about how I almost accepted an offer from Lowry, and I am very anxious to see that no other person can be put in such a position due to any actions on my part."

TSR had no stronger ally in these early days than Heritage Models, and its president Jim Oden. While he was no fan of fantasy, Oden had big plans for future partnerships with TSR: he was cultivating a deeper relationship with the Edgar Rice Burroughs estate, one that would grant TSR exclusive rights to publish any associated rules. In the short term, however, his negotiations required the withdrawal of the existing TSR *Warriors of Mars* booklet from the market once the initial print run sold out.

TSR's close relationship with Heritage provided another opportunity to accelerate the firm's growth in March. As Heritage owned a printing press, switching from the Graphic Printing Company to Oden's firm would "save us about $300 on a typical run of 1000, so we will be able to use him for a number of booklets and increase production accordingly," Gygax explained to Arneson. "I believe that we will be able to provide Jim with from 100 to 250 initial copies of whatever we do through him at 40% face price, so that our actual cash outlay for any run will be very low indeed!" Heritage was willing to accept inventory from TSR in exchange for the cost of printing, which would free up TSR to deploy its scarce liquidity elsewhere.

The promise of a significant cost reduction meant that TSR could break into board games sooner than planned. Hurriedly, Gygax instructed Arneson to spread the word to his local compatriots: "Tell Carr that this will mean that we should be able to get at *FitS* very soon. I wish to do it first, then *Dungeon!*" Gygax also wanted to slate two new Twin Cities titles for imminent release. The first was *War of Wizards*, a fantasy board game that M. A. R. Barker had already self-published—TSR would gladly help distribute any lingering inventory before printing an edition with their own logo. The second would be Barker's *Empire of the Petal Throne*, the first imitator of *D&D*. It had become clear that Bill Hoyt's World at War could not afford to produce it, and so Hoyt on April 21 signed an agreement with TSR transferring his option on the title to TSR in exchange for a 5 percent royalty as a finder's fee—above and beyond the 10 percent royalty Barker would receive. In light of these and other Minnesota-born projects, like the planned sequels to John Snider's *Star Probe* and "Mutant," the other Snider brother's game, Gygax predicted "that TSR will absolutely dominate the entire fantasy/science fiction market."

Buoyed by the news from Heritage, Gygax's optimism was redoubled by the steady rise in sales of *D&D*. Its royalties for the first quarter of 1975 came in at $598.10, amounting to around $100 per month for each of the authors. Still not a sum that would entirely pay Gygax's rent, nor sustain Gygax's family of seven—and the five cats they kept, along with a slender dog named Harald—but it delivered every four weeks an amount roughly equal to the royalties *D&D* had earned for the first half of 1974. Moreover, effective April 1, Gygax and Arneson executed a new royalty agreement for *D&D* superseding their original 1974 contract with TSR. This revision granted them a joint 10 percent royalty on "the cover price of the game rules or game on each and every copy sold," instead of their former 20 percent royalty on the sale price, an amount which was often less than half the cover price. As such, it was a slightly more advantageous agreement for the authors. The new contract also now reverted the rights to the authors automatically if the game went out of print without requiring any fee— now *D&D* was surely worth more than $300.

Those same royalty terms would govern the April contracts that TSR signed for *War of Wizards* and the first *D&D* supplement, *Greyhawk*, each offering its authors a 10 percent royalty on the price of the product. The exact wording of the agreements, "the cover price of the game rules or game on each and every copy sold," sounded unambiguous at the time: *D&D* sold in only one form, a "woodgrain" cardboard box with a $10 price printed on the sticker affixed to its cover. Even though the *Greyhawk* supplement was an extension to *D&D*, an addition to the same basic idea, it was a separate product, covered by a separate royalty agreement executed by Gygax and Rob Kuntz, for which Arneson received no money. But in a few short years, the question of exactly what qualified as "the game rules or the game" in these April 1975 agreements would become the object of violently differing interpretations—with a fortune potentially hanging in the balance.

Greyhawk added rules for new classes of *D&D* characters—the paladin and the thief—as well as more monsters, spells, and magic items. Its positive reception demonstrated that sales of *D&D* would not be confined to the original base set: in a letter to Arneson in April, Gygax boasted that since there was "much demand for *D&D* supplements," he "would like to get ol' *Blackmoor* soon." As Arneson had promised he was "hard at work" on it back in January, the continuing nonappearance of a *Blackmoor* supplement became something of a point of contention—especially as Arneson maintained that his labors toward it delayed progress on his other obligations. Even as late as August 1975, Arneson would write to the subscribers of his *Corner of the Table*, "I have been occupied writing a supplement to the *Dungeons & Dragons* fantasy rules, which will be called *Blackmoor*. This has occupied the bulk of my free time for the last three months and caused a suspension of the Napoleonic Campaign during that period." Yet that further three months did not result in a finished manuscript arriving at TSR.

To take effect as of 1 April 1975, item 4. below notwithstanding.

THIS AGREEMENT is made between the the Author(s) specified
hereafter and Tactical Studies Rules, 542 Sage Street, Lake
Geneva, WI 53147, hereafter called TSR.

Author(s): __Gary Gygax, 330 Center St., Lk., Geneva, WI__

__Dave Arneson, 1496 Hartford Ave, St. Paul, MN__

_____

_____

_____

_____

1. The Author(s) hereby agree to assign to TSR the copyright, the right to publish, sell, and distribute, the set
of game rules or game entitled _DUNGEONS & DRAGONS_,
in any form TSR deems suitable for commercial sales, as well
as any other similar rights.

2. TSR hereby agrees to pay the Author(s) a royalty of TEN
PERCENT (10 %)of the cover price of the game rules or game
on each and every copy sold; this royalty to be payable on a
quarterly basis reported within 30 days after the end of each
quarter, with quarters ending 31 March, 30 June, 30 September
and 31 December of each year.

3. TSR also hereby agrees that the ownership of the copyright mentioned above shall revert to the Author(s) not more
than 90 days after the set of game rules or game is no longer
maintained in-print.

4. This Agreement shall not be considered a valid contract
until all parties concerned have signed and dated the contract, but upon so signing the contract shall take effect on
a retroactive basis from the date of publication of the set
of game rules or game.

TACTICAL STUDIES RULES

E. Gary Gygax   _7 April 1975_
E. Gary Gygax, Editor

Gary Gygax   _7 April 1975_
Gary Gygax

Dave Arneson
Dave Arneson

_____

April 1, 1975 Tactical Studies Rules revised copyright assignment and royalty agreement for *Dungeons & Dragons* executed by Gary Gygax and Dave Arneson. Its terms
would govern royalty payments into the 1980s.

To motivate people like Arneson to work faster, TSR needed a capacity to award equity or similar incentives. Shortly after Kaye passed away, the partnership had amended its agreement to allow for adding new stakeholders through a system of "units of value," which behaved in a manner similar to shares in a corporation. Each of the original three equal partners acquired 100 of these units of value under the revised agreement, with units worth $90 each. An allowance for new units of value permitted the partnership to admit Dave Arneson by granting him 5 units on May 1 along with an option to buy up to 50 more. A grant of effectively $450 worth may seem like a pittance, but recall that the royalties Arneson received for *D&D* for all of 1974 totaled just $465.92. His work for TSR no longer entirely uncompensated, Arneson now owned a tangible, if minor, stake in the business.

As the company grew, it began to attract the attention of the hobby game media. It is no small irony that the first interviewer who approached TSR for its story was Don Lowry, who profiled the company in May. He billed the piece as "*Panzerfaust* interviews TSR (in the person of Gary Gygax)." Gygax no doubt relished the opportunity to inform Lowry that TSR not only published game rules with far greater success than the now-dormant Guidon Games, but that it imminently planned to open a hobby shop as well to sell games, rules, and miniatures by mail order, in the model of the floundering Lowrys Hobbies. "Sound familiar?" Gygax had to ask, never one to resist twisting the knife. In recent months, Gygax had decided on a less complementary opinion of Lowry than he evinced the year before; in a March letter to Megarry, after Megarry expressed some sympathy for Lowry's situation, Gygax snapped, "Apologies to Don Lowry my ass!" before calling him a "two-faced shaft-master." A bit earlier to Arneson, he could only say, "Lowry was once a nice guy, but he was such a piss-poor businessman that desperation must have made him a trifle on the crooked side."

When Lowry asked if TSR would consider adding any other partners, Gygax remained open to the idea: "Possibly. We have one young artist in mind currently," whose identity he then did not reveal. Perhaps he meant Greg Bell, who the company had hoped to hire, but there is another possibility. One upshot of the production process of *Petal Throne* was that it brought to Gygax's attention a fantasy artist native to the Twin Cities. "Dave Sutherland's a really excellent artist," Gygax gushed in a letter to Hoyt at the time. "I've asked that he do more (Barker is well pleased with his work)." Getting someone of Sutherland's caliber on board would significantly elevate the quality of TSR's products.

Although Gygax painted TSR as something like a bustling workplace, he clarified for Lowry that "we all have to squeeze TSR work in our 'spare time,' and that means most of the work is done in our individual homes." The Kaye residence at 542 Sage Street still provided TSR's nominal place of business: "There we maintain our supplies, records, and so forth. We have a weekly meeting in order to co-ordinate all of our efforts for the next week's work." But for this part-time operation, "the principals of TSR take nothing from the company. Every cent that is taken in goes back into the company in one form or another." At the time, Gygax affirmed that TSR was prepared to let this situation prevail indefinitely: "All of us are quite willing to continue without any salary or profits distribution from the company for as long as necessary to ensure that the firm succeeds." But it turns out it would only be necessary for another month.

Second-quarter 1975 sales of *D&D* amounted to 661 copies; it had sold more than 1,000 copies in just the past four months. As stock of *D&D* was again nearing depletion, TSR took Jim Oden up on his offer to have Heritage Models print the game. Around the middle of June, Heritage returned 2,000 copies for the third printing; in partial payment for the run, Heritage printed and retained an additional 250 copies, which they then sold themselves. With the promise of the revenue this restock would yield, TSR could take its final steps toward becoming a real company.

In a hasty note dated June 2, just weeks after his interview with Lowry, Gygax scrawled to Arneson, "Am working full time for TSR now." In practice, this amounted to a salary of $80 per week, which would yield about $4,000 per annum. Gygax gave up shoe repair and odd jobs, and Blume gave notice at Wisconsin Tool and Stamping. A few weeks later, Blume would relocate to Lake Geneva, taking an apartment on Country Club Drive on the outskirts of the downtown area. At first, he drew no salary, adhering to the principle that the partnership should reinvest as much of its profits as possible into its product line. Blume's immediate goal was to start up the hobby shop, to be a division of TSR known as TSR Hobbies.

With the undivided attention of its two principals, TSR now began to ease its way into the competitive arena of the hobby games business. It was not a business where the stakes were particularly high, but sometimes, when the stakes are lowest the competition can be the most vicious. In most wargames, turns are divided up into phases: and for the adventurers in business of the 1970s and 1980s, the combat phase was the summer convention season. It was the time when the business was no longer just on paper, like a play-by-mail game: it was when companies showed up in person to joust with competitors and vie for customer dollars. For the initial sortie, the principles of TSR would go on a journey. It was not unusual for Gygax to travel throughout the state for conventions, or even venture north into Minnesota or south in Illinois. But this trip would take them deep into enemy territory, all the way to Baltimore. Gygax, his son Ernie, Arneson, and Blume all piled into Blume's chartreuse Volkswagen Rabbit for quite a long drive.

Since 1968, the summer for wargamers had belonged to GenCon. Avalon Hill had initially championed GenCon as a venue where fans could play its board wargames, lavishing it with free promotion. But 1975 would be the first year that TSR the company—rather than the LGTSA club, which had hosted the convention since the IFW became defunct—formally sponsored GenCon. So, alienated by the increasing emphasis of GenCon on titles other than its own, this year Avalon Hill created its own venue: Origins. The first Origins convention, run in its hometown of Baltimore, would come at the end of July, about a month prior to GenCon. As a gesture to the enthusiastic early adopters of *D&D*, Avalon Hill had graciously invited TSR to organize a small *D&D* event in the midst of its board wargame tournaments. The previous year's GenCon had given TSR the opportunity to indoctrinate Midwestern players into *D&D*, and to move a few boxes at the same time; this year would afford Gygax the chance to take his show on the road and compete against traditional wargames on the East Coast.

In contrast to the quaint Horticultural Hall in Lake Geneva, the Origins convention was staged on the Johns Hopkins University campus. While attendees at GenCon slept wherever they could, Origins could put up gamers in the dorms. Not that this was necessarily an improvement: a high schooler from New York in attendance deemed the Origins accommodations a "hell hole, which has no air conditioning, precious few lights, a badly-cleaned bathroom down the corridor, no running water, hard beds, no blankets. It's about 90 degrees in the dorm, and 80 outside."

Origins served several purposes for Avalon Hill. In addition to promoting its own products through tournaments and giveaways, it helped them honor what they considered important in the wargaming industry. As befits a convention called Origins, it celebrated the genesis of the hobby by bestowing the Charles S. Roberts Awards, the first of which went to Avalon Hill founder Charles S. Roberts himself—or, as the *General* called him, "the man who started it all"—who made a rare appearance at the convention and assisted in passing out the rest of the "Charleys." But the awards gave no consideration to anything that fell outside of the board wargaming market targeted by Avalon Hill and SPI, such as the rules printed in Lake Geneva. The *General* tried to put a more inclusive spin on the event, saying that Origins "proved that all of wargaming could get together behind a common cause to promote their hobby," but it very decidedly excluded products that did not fit the Avalon Hill mold.

Walking the halls of Origins, Avalon Hill executive Tom Shaw proudly shared word of his company's prosperity with the press. He told the *Washington Post* that in the past year his company had sold around 300,000 games, grossing $1.8 million in revenue, and that they expected unit sales to rise to 350,000 in 1975. These numbers represented the pinnacle of the hobby games industry—consider TSR moved less than 3,000 games in 1974. Just behind Avalon Hill, at around $1.6 million in net sales, was SPI, whose success rested almost entirely on the circulation of their magazine *Strategy & Tactics*.

Strategy & Tactics circulated to the hobby gaming community an annual survey of industry revenue that showed the overall scope and growth of gaming—which also served to enshrine the pecking order of game companies. If we look at the entire industry as a game, then Howard Barasch of SPI was the unofficial scorekeeper who counted everyone's points in the upkeep phase of each turn. Most companies happily participated in his survey, but not Avalon Hill: SPI usually had to estimate Avalon Hill sales from the company's overall reported earnings. SPI took advantage of this opportunity by classifying much of Avalon Hill's revenue as non-wargaming—putting them down to about $1.2 million for 1975—in order to paint themselves as the larger wargame publisher. SPI also added nearly $100,000 to their 1975 figure through "lifetime subscription" offers they extended to the readership—the sort of promotion that raises quick cash for magazine publishers but inevitably saddles them with an onerous obligation going forward. But perhaps the real purpose of SPI's scorekeeping was to make sure the entire industry knew there were only two firms that mattered: their rankings for 1974 had shown Avalon Hill and SPI as the two "super powers" and relegated all other firms to a "third world" with a combined revenue of around $100,000. The total retail sales market for wargames in 1975, SPI estimated, stood at five or six million dollars. In SPI's rankings, TSR would languish in the anonymity of the "Other" category at the bottom of the third world.

The patrician loftiness of superpowers did not intrigue some journalists at Origins so much as the enthusiasm surrounding that bizarre upstart from the third world, Tactical Studies Rules. A reporter from the *Washington Star* studying the curious crowds at Origins heard talk of *D&D* on many of their lips, and would observe that "Gygax is a kind of heroic figure in the world of gamesmanship, being the co-creator of a hit game. This is the pinnacle of gamesmanship. Gamers followed him around, asking him the most incredible questions about strategy and getting him to autograph their *Greyhawk* rulebooks."

Unmistakably, TSR came to Origins in July to challenge the orthodoxy of hobby gaming. In addition to its third printing of *D&D*, freshly acquired from the printing press of Heritage, TSR brought to the convention two new boxed sets: Dave Megarry's *Dungeon!* and M. A. R. Barker's *Empire of the Petal Throne*. Both were produced at a new printer TSR had engaged, Patch Press in nearby Beloit, Wisconsin. *Dungeon!* came together at the last minute in July, and represented TSR's first effort at a new board game that would compete more directly with Avalon Hill. Gygax planned an initial *Dungeon!* run of three thousand copies selling for $12.50. Production of *Petal Throne* also went down to the wire, in no small part because Barker demanded a custom royalty agreement that gave him a percentage of TSR's royalties for any miniature figures based on the creature designs in his game, a unique provision among TSR's contracts. In the nick of time, Patch Press made two thousand copies of its colorful box, lengthy rulebook, and two large maps; due to its lavish production, *Petal Throne* would sell for a punishing $25, by far the most expensive offering in the space.

TSR could only staff a modest booth at Origins, and they brought perhaps two hundred units of inventory total to sell, including thirty each of *Dungeon!* and *Empire of the Petal Throne*. Reports from the convention suggest that *Petal Throne*, even at its stunning price point, sold out by Saturday. They were delighted to part with all of their copies of *Petal Throne*, *Dungeon!*, *D&D*, and the *Greyhawk* supplement—though they did return to Lake Geneva with a handful of copies of *Star Probe* and *Chainmail*. Arneson, who pitched in with the rest of the TSR contingent at the booth, mused that Origins was very pointedly a board wargaming convention: "no figure manufacturers were present and their colorful wares were missed sorely judging by the inquiries at our booth." Avalon Hill no doubt wished to strike a strong contrast to the miniature wargame presence at GenCon.

TSR helped to make Origins a destination event for *D&D* fans by planning two events for that weekend in Baltimore: a seminar on *D&D* conducted personally by Gygax; and a tournament that promised to pit eight teams of fifteen players each against a formidable adventure. The tournament took place in the infamous *Tomb of Horrors* dungeon, a maze of arbitrary death-traps designed to whittle down parties to hardy survivors. In photographs of Gygax running the tournament, one of the Origins organizers, Neil Topolnicki, could be seen at his right hand, helping to oversee the event.

With its considerable marketing budget and facilities, to say nothing of its vast fan base, Avalon Hill easily attracted 1,500 attendees to Origins, a number that vastly exceeded the size of any prior GenCon—though like GenCon, it did not make much money. Avalon Hill praised the valiant members of a local club who furnished many volunteers, singling out organizer Topolnicki for special acclaim. Given the threat that Origins posed to his beloved GenCon, it is unsurprising that Gygax soon began courting Topolnicki for a position at TSR.

The summer conventions of 1975 also surfaced the first evidence of competition against TSR. While Gygax's intervention secured *Petal Thone* as a title for TSR rather than a competitor, he could not hope to do the same for the many challengers attracted by the modest success of *D&D*. Fans of the game wanted to make it their own: as one would write in to *Alarums & Excursions*, a fanzine founded in June 1975, "*D&D* is too important to leave to Gary Gygax." The *D&D* rules welcomed players to introduce any alterations or additions to play that would help make the game enjoyable. Some made changes so fundamental that they had, in their own opinion at least, invented a new game—we might be forcibly reminded of how Gygax could take a title like Dane Lyons's *Arbela* and modify it to the point where it became his own *Alexander the Great*. By the summer of 1975, others were doing the same with *D&D*. Barker's *Petal Throne* would hit the market nearly simultaneously with Ken St. Andre's self-published *Tunnels & Trolls*, a derivative simplification of *D&D* that sold for just $2 at a science-fiction convention early in July. While St. Andre had hastily assembled his *Tunnels & Trolls* at a university print shop in Phoenix, it soon attracted the attention of an Arizona publisher named Rick Loomis, who ran Flying Buffalo, a company well-known in wargaming circles for its computer moderated play-by-mail titles. Loomis soon distributed and published *Tunnels & Trolls*, becoming an industry face for competition against *D&D*.

As a cluster of games emerged based on similar system principles—*D&D*, *Petal Throne*, *Tunnels & Trolls*, and a few others—commentators tried to isolate what these games had in common and apply a label to them. Although the cover of *D&D* had claimed it was a wargame, that term never fit particularly well. Reviewers for SPI began using the term "role-playing" around this time to describe the series of games inspired by *D&D*, a product label TSR would start to embrace in 1976. The energy of the community became a source of inspiration as well as competition for TSR; for example, West Coast players began to popularize the phrase "dungeon master" in 1975, and before the end of the year TSR would adopt this felicitous construction, even putting it in their own books.

Fortunately for Gygax, the major hobby game companies showed no immediate interest in producing imitations of *D&D*. Avalon Hill shied away from the fantasy and science-fiction arena—for now—but others thought the allure of *D&D* was in its departure from historical wargaming genres, rather than any unique role-playing elements. Avalon Hill's more agile rival SPI released a science-fiction board game, *Starforce: Alpha Centauri*, and a fantasy wargame, *Sorcerer*, in 1974 and 1975, respectively. Upstart imprints, almost too many to enumerate, pushed out cruder bagged wargames that tapped into the science-fiction and fantasy craze. Fact and Fantasy Games, without any apparent relationship with the Tolkien estate, put out its *Siege of Minas Tirith* and *Battle of Helm's Deep* for *Lord of the Rings* fans, and Larry Smith self-published a *Battle of the Five Armies* for fans of *The Hobbit*. As TSR aspired to distribute the games of others as well as to publish its own, these Tolkien-based wargames soon ended up in its mail order catalog—all three were advertised on the back of *Strategic Review* no. 3, which shipped around August, just in time for GenCon.

A reporter from the *St. Louis Post-Dispatch* would attend GenCon in 1975, writing that "the big trend in wargaming today is toward sheer fantasy, a mixture of the medieval and the mythical." And "the high priest of the fantasy movement is Gary Gygax, a bearded wargaming veteran from Lake Geneva." Although he mentions that Gygax was the "co-originator of *Dungeons & Dragons*," the name of the other originator seems to have escaped the reporter's attention, as it did with many others. The article proclaimed that "the game has been an enormous success," which enabled Gygax and Brian Blume to go on TSR's payroll. Not to be outdone by the "Charley" awards at Origins, TSR collected votes for its Strategists Club Awards to be given at GenCon; the honors included the "Best New Game of 1974," which unsurprisingly went to *D&D*, and the "Outstanding Designer" prize would be shared by Gygax and Arneson.

Ultimately, the summer conventions offered competing visions of which games were important, and victory in this contest would go to the venue that drew the biggest crowd. Gygax would not hear of the newcomer Origins outselling GenCon, which he represented as "the National Wargame Convention," so he initially claimed that GenCon had an attendance of 1,600—the actual "turnstile" number was probably around 1,000, counting both paid attendees and curious onlookers. This blatant exaggeration set off a minor flame war in the industry press, which only ended when Gygax eventually conceded that "Origins had a larger attendance than GenCon."

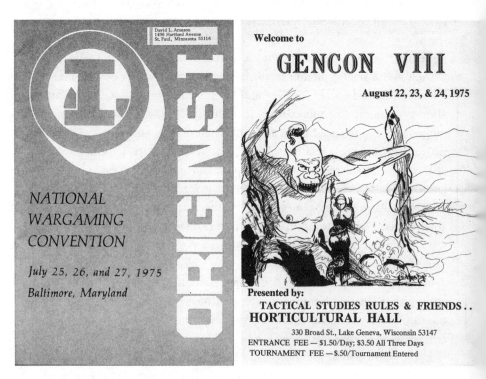

Program covers for the Origins and GenCon conventions in 1975.

Gygax's appetite for indulging in this sort of propaganda to attack TSR's rivals would become one of the defining characteristics of his tenure, and from the summer of 1975 forward, it would increasingly manifest in the company's internal and external communications. This proxy war between Avalon Hill and TSR over conventions would only escalate as the years went on and the stakes grew higher.

To support Brian Blume's planned retail games store, TSR Hobbies had formally incorporated on July 19. Back in March, Gygax had planned that Blume personally would foot the lion's share of the bill for founding the new hobby store from his savings, with TSR holding a minority stake in the business, in the expectation that TSR would buy Blume out when it could afford to. So, the plan was always to fold the two entities together eventually. But it would transpire that the transaction would go the other way around: TSR Hobbies would absorb the original partnership, as a way of buying out the stake of the Kaye family.

When they allocated the initial shares of TSR Hobbies stock on August 1, it was clear they intended it to be a joint venture of Gygax and Blume, not solely Blume's business. The stock agreement awarded Gygax 150 shares and Blume 100. It set the value of these shares at $100—being a private company, TSR's shares traded on no open market, so the shareholder agreement stipulates an algorithm that would guide future shareholder votes to determine the company's book value, taking into account corporate assets, profits, and "goodwill" worth up to five times the average net income of the company over the past five fiscal years. The shareholder agreement lists Gygax as the president of TSR Hobbies, and Blume as its secretary. Gygax held almost two-thirds of the shares in the company—TSR Hobbies belonged to him, at least for the moment.

Because this corporate transition had been triggered by the unexpected death of Don Kaye back in January, the language of that August shareholder agreement was fixedly, if not morbidly, preoccupied with the possibility that a shareholder might die. Since death was not the only eventuality that could sever someone from a partnership, this language also covered shareholders who wished to divest themselves from the company without shuffling off this mortal coil. The shareholder agreement effectively gave TSR Hobbies the right to purchase any shares belonging to a deceased or departing shareholder: if and only if the company refused, the stock then must be offered to the remaining shareholders on a pro rata basis. This pro rata clause effectively meant that the remaining shareholders were only entitled to purchase an amount of these shares proportionate to their holdings in the company: so hypothetically, if Gygax owned 60 shares and Blume held 40, then if 10 shares became available, pro rata Gygax would be eligible to purchase 6 and Blume 4. Such mechanisms prevent the dilution of the holdings of majority shareholders, ensuring that shareholders could maintain the same overall percentage of control of the company, provided they were willing to buy the offered stock. But if none of the existing shareholders are willing to buy the earmarked shares, the shareholder agreement then permits them to be sold to a third party. These provisions put some teeth behind Gygax's promise to protect the company from outsider control.

For its first few weeks of existence, TSR Hobbies effectively owned no assets. How much of a war chest would it need to absorb the original partnership and pay for a retail store? Per the original division of the partnership into "units of value," each of the three equal partners held 100 units of value ostensibly worth $90 each. As such, something a bit less than $30,000 would have been required to buy out all three partners and the miscellaneous additional units which had been awarded to parties like Arneson for their service to the partnership. But since two of those three partners were buying themselves out, really these figures just put a price tag on the Kaye family portion of TSR, enabling Gygax and Blume to take over the company for themselves.

To raise the necessary capital, TSR Hobbies accepted a substantial investment from the Blume family in September. This came in two portions: first, the purchase of 200 shares by Melvin Blume, Brian's father and president of the Wisconsin Tool and Stamping Company, at a cost of $100 each; and second, the purchase by Brian Blume of a further 140 shares at the same price. While the latter may seem like an investment perhaps beyond his means, we should probably understand that $14,000 dollars as Blume buying out his own 100 units of value in the partnership, thus canceling out $9,000 of the cost, leaving a $5,000 investment in the future of the company. Effectively, the Blumes injected $25,000 into TSR, enough to buy out the partnership and to supply sufficient liquidity to take on new projects. This was the sort of seed money needed to secure facilities and stock up a hobby shop. Gygax as well reinvested some of the money he realized from the buyout of the partnership into TSR Hobbies, purchasing 30 shares of stock at $100 each on October 8—he really needed to keep the rest of the cash.

It might seem that accepting Melvin Blume as a shareholder violated the promise Gygax had earlier made to Megarry about accepting non-wargamer investment. But Melvin had stepped away from day-to-day responsibilities at his firm and spent most of his time golfing in Washington State; he would be a silent partner whose interests would be handled by his son Brian. While the Blume family investment immediately rendered Gygax a minority shareholder in TSR Hobbies, he would nonetheless serve as president of TSR in the post-partnership era. Gygax was more than a decade older than Blume, and he knew the hobby game industry better than nearly anyone—there was no question who should run the firm. As the pair made up the entirety of TSR's board of directors, any key steering decisions would be made jointly by both.

TSR Hobbies purchased the assets of the original partnership on September 26, 1975. The purchase price reflected the "units of value" of the partnership, which included assets like the 923 copies of *D&D* remaining from the 2,000 that Heritage had printed in June. So, TSR said goodbye to the partnership's Sage Street headquarters, moving TSR's stock into Gygax's basement, where only recently the cobbling machine had loomed, until the company could acquire its own building. The transfer included all rights to the rules and games, so the original royalty agreements of the partnership remained in place at TSR Hobbies—including, most significantly, the revised 10 percent royalty agreement that Gygax and Arneson had executed for *D&D* in April. Those were the terms that would fall under legal scrutiny in the years to come.

The transition occurred right at the end of the third quarter of 1975, which marked a new high in *D&D* sales: 1,371 copies in all, if we include the copies Heritage retained to cover printing costs. This more than doubled the previous quarter's figure. So, Gygax and Arneson split $1,371 worth of royalties under the 10 percent cover-price rate set by the April agreement. At long last, Gygax's half could cover his rent and then some—at least before taxes. This sharp increase reflected heavy engagement following the summer conventions, spread by converts who returned from those events to their homes, schools, and game clubs.

With a newfound ability to make payroll, TSR Hobbies brought on its first two hires who were not partners effective October 1: LGTSA member Terry Kuntz, and a GenCon attendee and recent Southern Illinois University graduate, Tim Kask, who took over responsibility for editing the company's periodicals. For the moment that meant the *Strategic Review*, so

Kask had time for editorial work on forthcoming *D&D* supplements as well. TSR was a start-up, so "Tim will also do some design work, shipping, floor sweeping, etc., just as the rest of us must do," Gygax affirmed.

Immediately after TSR Hobbies acquired the assets of the original partnership, Gygax began the delicate process of bringing Arneson on board. His responsibilities, as Gygax put it publicly in the *Strategic Review*, would be to "produce material like a grist mill (Crack! Snap! Work faster there, Dave!)." That sentiment linked to the admission on the same page that "*Blackmoor* is late," but did not exactly suggest the sort of arrangement that Arneson would enter into willingly.

Gygax had spent years now twisting Arneson's arm about joining the company, and back in August, Arneson was already forecasting "within the next three months I will, in all probability, be moving my place of residence to Lake Geneva, Wisconsin," to work for TSR. But now that the long-promised day had arrived, Arneson had some justification to be wary of TSR: he knew that Gygax had recently cut the royalties paid for *Petal Throne*, and that Dave Wesely furiously contested the terms of TSR's proposed royalty agreements for his Revolutionary War rules in development, now called *Valley Forge*. So, Arneson insisted on an employment contract with TSR. Gygax felt this was a mere formality, and entrusted drafting it to his Uncle Hugh, who got it in the mail to Arneson on October 10. The duties listed in the contract stipulated that Arneson would work for TSR "as a creative artist to create manuscripts and game components involved in the production of games and game rules for the Employer," though "the precise service of the Employee may be extended or curtailed from time to time at the discretion of the Employer." The contract as written covered an initial span of six months, with an optional extension of the same length, at a salary of $125 per week. In lieu of royalties for his design work, the contract further awarded Arneson 30 shares of TSR stock—then valued in total at $3,000—in exchange for all rights to six of his works in progress: *Blackmoor*, *Ships of the Line*, and *Naval Orders of Battle*, and then three newer projects, *Crusader*, *Narvik*, and *PT Boat*. It furthermore stipulated that "during the term of his employment all game and game rules and design efforts produced by him become the sole and exclusive property of the Employer." Separately, TSR offered Arneson an option to purchase 5 more shares of stock at $50 each, and an additional 5 at twice that.

On October 14, Arneson returned the contract unsigned and accompanied by numerous objections: most fundamentally, that "the contract would deprive me from seeking any work within a broad spectrum of areas extending from history to model making." Arneson wanted the freedom to assist others with designs, contribute to periodicals, and continue work with figure casters like Custom Cast. Regarding works in progress, Arneson protested that "our verbal discussions involved only the turning over of the *Blackmoor* manuscript to TSR," rather than the five additional games, and that "the contract would deprive me of all rights to original work completed, but unsold, prior to the date of my employment" as well as work "submitted to, but rejected by, TSR Inc. after the date of my employment." Moreover, he found the compensation meager—it amounted to about $2.60 an hour, when federal minimum wage in 1976 would be $2.30—and saw no provisions for pay raises, bonuses, or profit sharing. Arneson also rejected some fairly standard language that would allow TSR the right to terminate him for "gross insubordination" or "failure to perform his duties," stating that both those provisions are "far too general to offer protection against misuse by the Employer." As such, Arneson concludes, "I cannot consider the possibility of signing the contract you issued October 10."

The response to Arneson came not from Gygax, but from Blume, in his capacity as the Chairman of the Board of TSR Hobbies, Inc. "We were very surprised, and disappointed, that you did not find the contract satisfactory," the response read. Blume was quick to reject one of Arneson's principal demands: "There is no question of going any higher on the benefits or salary—you'd be making more than either Gary or I do." Blume elsewhere claimed he collected less than $6,000 from royalties and wages in 1975, and the amount they offered Arneson amounted to a bit more than that. "It was also disappointing to see how little trust you displayed in us with regard to the wording of your contract—your idea in the first place." Blume contrasted Arneson's cynicism with the faith evinced by another recent hire: "Tim Kask moved all the way from Carbondale, Illinois, to work with us. Although he's a graduate in communications, he is not receiving more than a token salary and the chance to get in on the ground floor of this operation, and he has no contract of any sort." Nowhere in Blume's letter did he suggest that TSR would be open to further discussions about employing Arneson.

But Blume did add, "We hope that you will continue to submit your design efforts to us for publication," mentioning perennial works-in-progress such as *Ships of the Line* and *Naval Orders of Battle*. His remarks became quite cutting, though, when it came to another of these efforts: "There is a great problem with *Blackmoor*." Blume generously relayed, "Gary has explained to me that the reason the manuscript was in such horrible condition was that he had you running around taking care of other people instead of allowing you to do your own work." As Blume intimates, it was only "because of this highly extenuating circumstance we can justify the 100 or so man-hours put into it so far to make it a usable design." If Arneson would not join TSR, Blume suggested the company's willingness to pay him a royalty for *Blackmoor* rather than stock: "Your name will appear on the cover as sole author, naturally, although inside we will give proper credit to those who contributed ideas and aided in the total rewrite." The tragicomic saga surrounding the publication of the *Blackmoor* supplement is too complex to detail here, but Tim Kask, who was tasked to edit it into cohesion, was clearly stunned by the whole process, even venting his frustrations publicly in the pages of the *Strategic Review*. Decades later, he still seems traumatized by it.

So much for Brian Blume—or as he signed company memos, B^2—as the bad cop. On October 20, Arneson telephoned Gygax, and over the course of their conversation, as Gygax would summarize, "much of the mutual misunderstanding has been removed." At a high level, Gygax promised Arneson that when it came to compensation, "there will be increases for all of us if possible." While accepting stock instead of royalties might seem like a fixed payout, he proposed, "our plan is to give you bonuses if sales of assigned titles exceeds stock appreciation, or if the titles simply generate a large profit immediately." They agreed to meet in person to hammer out the details. Arneson would not relocate until TSR had secured a workplace in Lake Geneva; TSR had settled on a little gray house at 723 Williams Street, but the mortgage had not yet closed.

Still, as late as November 10, Arneson expressed lingering concerns about exactly what it meant to assign rights for a title like *Blackmoor* to TSR in exchange for stock options. What counted as *Blackmoor* in that agreement? "I want it very clearly understood," Arneson wrote, "that material that was sent in with the manuscripts but was not used in the final draft, is not included in the deal. I feel that this is only fair since you will be getting the best parts of the ms. for the booklets." In the same letter, Arneson also griped about his inability to afford the stock options TSR had offered. Graciously, Gygax was willing to let the second batch of 5 shares go at a lower price—but totally unwilling to part with the unused fragments of *Blackmoor*. "We ask that we have permission to retain all portions of *Blackmoor* unused for eventual use in some manner." Gygax also gently reminded Arneson that many portions of *Blackmoor* had been written by others, and that effectively Arneson was getting those to use in his booklet as part of the deal.

"Deal?" Gygax asked. And a deal was struck. As such, the agreement that Arneson signed for *Blackmoor* on November 18 awarded him a royalty of 0 percent. In lieu of money, he received the 30 shares that made him, as Gygax pointed, "now the fourth largest stockholder in TSR," as it went from "Brian, Me, Melvin Blume, you." Gygax at the time had 334 shares, Blume 420, and Blume's father 200—all stockholders other than those four then owned just 1 share each.

Arneson was not the only prospective employee that Gygax courted at the time. Dave Megarry as well felt the full force of Gygax's entreaties at the end of 1975. Just two days before the New Year, Gygax sent Megarry the stock agreement and the forms necessary to purchase 3 shares, with an optional allowance to purchase more. But he warned, "I would not recommend that you buy a large amount of stock unless you do plan to eventually work for TSR." At the time, Megarry preferred to remain in Boston, but Gygax left the door open: "While I cannot state flatly you will have a job whenever you wish, we will certainly be willing to notify you at such a time as we do have a position—and you can write to us when you are again thinking of it too!" Megarry would not manage to hold out for long, especially once Arneson came to Lake Geneva.

The public appetite for *D&D* could not wait for staffing, or housing, or anything. By November, TSR's *D&D* inventory required replenishment. International sales had begun to ramp up, especially as a UK firm called Games Workshop had begun reselling *D&D* there. The rate of sales made a reprint of merely another thousand or two wholly inadequate. Therefore, TSR contracted for a fourth printing of 5,000 copies from Patch Press, after positive experiences with the printing of the *Dungeon!* and *Petal Throne* boxed sets. Patch Press moved away from the woodgrain box adorned with stickers of the first three printings, using instead a white box on which the art was directly printed. Having settled on Patch, TSR would continue to use them for the remainder of the lifetime of the original *D&D* game. TSR took this opportunity to alter the box cover art, substituting Greg Bell's rearing rider for a dungeon scene of a wizard facing off against monstrous adversaries by Dave Sutherland, who was rapidly becoming TSR's go-to artist. Before the end of the year, Sutherland would be supplying *D&D* art to the *Strategic Review*, and would also be drafted to provide some incidental art for the *Blackmoor* supplement.

Meanwhile, TSR focused on transforming 723 Williams Street into a suitable workplace. "The shop is going slowly," Gygax reported to Arneson in November. "Needs: new roof, new heating plant, new wiring, some plumbing repairs, painting (after plaster repair), carpeting, stock and miscellaneous fixtures and furnishings." And even after all of the hand-holding Gygax had done to coax Arneson into joining the company, Arneson still seemed to feel underappreciated. When the gregarious Gygax came up to the Twin Cities for some meetings, Arneson expressed some resentment about not being the center of his attention. "I hate to be pouty about it," he wrote to Gygax, "but your most recent visits saw a great deal more information exchanged with others than myself, which has also occurred on my other visits. I really do become rather irked by such things." Sensitivity about points like this augured that his tenure at TSR might not be a smooth one.

As the year wound to a close, *D&D* had now sold in excess of four thousand copies, with more than three-quarters of those trading in the past twelve months. All told, across its various product lines, TSR brought in perhaps $60,000 for 1975. Accounting remained somewhat opaque, but now that TSR Hobbies was incorporated, there would be a proper fiscal year tally forthcoming for 1976, which would be closely monitored by the industry mavens who charted the total scope of the hobby. The vast majority of TSR's revenue paid for printing costs, royalties, advertising, facilities, and so on. But the remaining amount was sufficient to pay a handful of people slightly above minimum wage to work the business full time. Under Gygax's leadership, TSR had made it through a year that could easily have seen the end of the enterprise, and with it the demise of *D&D*. It had never been the plan that Gygax would serve TSR as anything but an editor and designer, in a partnership that was more of a club than a company, but he had shown a capacity to do much more.

TSR Turn Results for 1975

Revenue: $60,000 (Barasch ranking "Other")
Employees: 5
Stock Valuation: $100
GenCon attendance vs. Origins: 1,000 vs. 1,500

Avalon Hill revenue: $1.8M

1976: Stab

When the TSR partnership was reborn as TSR Hobbies the company, the project of making *Dungeons & Dragons* transformed from a hobby into a career—and not just for Blume and Gygax, but for the growing party of adventurers they recruited for their business. As TSR became a workplace where employees reported every day to jostle against one another, its own corporate culture began to develop. Being a game company, run by gamers, that culture was playful, but a certain amount of competition—and then factionalism—would soon follow.

The ten-room corner house at 723 Williams Street was about four blocks from Gygax's home. If we picture Lake Geneva as a town built around the proverbial intersection of Main Street and Broad Street, where Main Street runs parallel to the shore, then "Williams is actually Broad St., but when it takes a jog at the railroad tracks they change its name to Williams," as Gygax explained. Gygax and Blume closed on the house in January at a cost of $27,500, secured with a fifteen-year mortgage. TSR Hobbies itself did not actually own the property at 723 Williams Street—instead, Gygax and Blume formed a separate partnership that purchased the property, and TSR paid rent to their partnership. This had tax benefits, but also profited the partners some small amount.

Everyone who worked in the building had a nominal job, but had to pitch in wherever the need arose. In a personal letter dated February 2, Arneson explained his situation at the beginning of his employment at TSR: "My work here in Lake Geneva is going quite well and keeps me very busy from 8:30 to 6:00 every day of the week. In addition to my job as Director of Research I am also in charge of the Shipping Department and overall management of the operations of the Hobby store we have set up."

The little gray house at 723 Williams Street in Lake Geneva, TSR's first property and original home of the Dungeon Hobby Shop, as drawn by Dave Sutherland, *Strategic Preview* no. 4.

The company was a start-up, so every employee had to be a jack-of-all-trades—even the director of research needed to work the mail room.

TSR Hobbies was not solely a mail-order business: 723 Williams Street would serve double duty as the company's headquarters and its retail outlet. "It has been remodeled to house our offices on the second floor," as Gygax described it, and "the first is given over to 'The Dungeon' hobby shop—as well as accounting, design, and receiving, and the basement serves as a mini-warehouse for small quantities of products we produce and sell." Terry Kuntz, who had done much of the heavy lifting to get the first floor into shape, would man the retail till at the Dungeon, balancing his time with design work toward his "Robin Hood" game.

Between frantic editing jobs, Tim Kask had his hands full managing TSR's in-house magazine. From its humble origins just one year earlier, the *Strategic Review* had developed a credible circulation of around 1,500. Those volumes paced sales of *D&D*, and justified the first reorganization of the young company. The board of TSR Hobbies, Inc.—which is to say Gygax and

Blume—met on February 22 to "create a new division of the corporation for the purpose of publishing one or more professional journals" which "would begin by transforming the current house publication, the *Strategic Review*, into a publication of non-house nature which would survey the entire industry impartially." The mention that the board reached a "unanimous" decision is typical of the time: since the board had only two members, both of whom needed to agree to any major decision, every successful vote was unanimous. Hints of the coming transformation to the *Strategic Review* had appeared since the fourth issue, which contains a cryptic space-filler box proclaiming "the Dragon is coming!" It would however be something of a challenge for this new magazine, *Dragon*, to establish enough independence from TSR to earn a reputation for impartiality.

For his part, Gygax still brooded over the summer conventions. By waging a war of words against Avalon Hill over the respective attendance of Origins and GenCon, he revealed how he saw his own position and that of TSR in the industry. In a letter from mid-February, which would run in the final *Strategic Review*, Gygax portrayed himself as a pioneering outsider who had been unexpectedly vindicated, defying the predictions of "the hobby's 'big guns.'" As he related, "I have touted miniature wargaming when most of the hobby in the U.S. thought that wargaming meant boardgaming. I have talked about fantasy gaming and been referred to as all sorts of an idiot, up a creek, and so on." But in spite of all that naysaying, "TSR had developed and produced a whole new aspect of gaming," a success that "has astounded many of the more stodgy minds of the industry and hobby—as well as prompting the release of large numbers of rules and games of fantastic nature by competitors."

The emergence the year before of imitators like *Tunnels & Trolls*, as well as the first forays into fantasy wargaming by larger publishers, made Gygax intensely protective of TSR's precarious success. Wary of any effort to ride on their humble coattails, TSR retained a local law firm, Allan & Lenon, and began sending cease-and-desist letters to any commercial venture, no matter how modest, that invoked the name of *D&D*, as *Tunnels & Trolls* did in its advertising. One surviving communication from the firm attests: "The game *Dungeons & Dragons* and the title of that game are copyrights of TSR, Inc., a Wisconsin corporation, and were filed in January of 1974. Therefore any continued use by you would be a breach of this copyright and would subject you to further legal proceedings." Anyone familiar with the distinction between copyright and trademark might find that statement dubious;

moreover, TSR was a bit tardy in filing either trademark applications or copyright registrations for their works. Luckily for TSR, the targets of these cease-and-desist letters had no appetite for a legal struggle and met them with grumbling acquiescence.

The challenges sallying forth from 723 Williams Street became more strident as the growing company had more at stake. The April *Strategic Review* announced that Dave Megarry had already joined TSR staff, and that Mike Carr would follow imminently. A TSR Hobbies board meeting on April 14 officially raised the number of corporate officers to four. Gygax remained the president, and Blume in addition to secretary was named the "first vice president." But since he had some management experience—in the restaurant business—Mike Carr was named "second vice president" reporting to Blume. Dave Megarry became treasurer and quickly took charge of TSR's books. The board set the salary for both of these new officers at $10,000; it also raised the salaries of Gygax and Blume from the $11,000 figure set just months earlier to $13,000. But the minutes of the meeting talk about officers taking "voluntary cuts in salary, as last year, if deemed necessary to increase the cash flow of the corporation," and Gygax himself would draw less than $9,000 in wages from TSR in 1976.

These salaries paced the steady increase of the business. In the first quarter of 1976, TSR Hobbies sold 1,462 copies of *D&D*. Arneson's half of these first-quarter *D&D* royalties amounted to $731.10, a nice supplement to his modest paychecks as he settled into his new home. He even received from TSR a further $59.84 as one-third of the 5 percent royalty on 359 sales of their edition of *Don't Give Up the Ship*, likely the first cashable check he received for his work on that game.

It likely was as well for Mike Carr, who as vice president would take charge of all of TSR's production, so Arneson now reported to Carr. Dave Sutherland as well agreed to join the company around this time, though he would be an intermittent presence before the summer. The arrival of familiar faces from Minnesota surely comforted Arneson, but it took him some time to settle in to his new environs—as he would say his move "from the Arctic of Minnesota to the sub-arctic of Wisconsin"—and he made frequent trips back to the Twin Cities for months to come. His 1967 Volkswagen, affectionately nicknamed "Rudolph," made these sojourns possible. Some of those trips resulted from his association with the Way International, a Bible study group. Arneson had completed the organization's introductory course, the "Power for Abundant Living" seminar, last December in the Twin Cities. He maintained a lively correspondence on the subject and also drove to nearby Racine for "fellowshipping" with other Way members a few times per week.

Arneson's primary responsibility as director of research was working with external freelancers and partner game companies. In March, Arneson was assigned to develop a proposal from Patrick Wilson of Oklahoma, whose club approached TSR to publish a set of World War II naval rules that would eventually appear under the name *Cordite and Steel*; Wilson was able to front a production loan of $1,000, one half the expected outlay for the booklet. At the same time, everyone had to wear several hats, and Arneson also corresponded with companies whose games TSR might sell at the Dungeon Hobby Shop. He reached out to Marc Miller of Game Designers' Workshop, for example, to inquire after titles in their line, Arneson being a fan of their game *En Garde* in particular. And then of course there were unglamorous tasks like helping out with shipping. But Arneson had to balance these day-job responsibilities with his obligation to deliver on his designs in progress, creating a tension that would increase over his tenure in Lake Geneva.

Our best window into the first employees of TSR, and its corporate culture at the time, comes from a periodical the company issued in the middle of the year called the *Strategic Preview*—not to be confused with the *Strategic Review*. Subtitled "TSR Jobbies," the *Preview* began just as TSR transitioned into running *Dragon* and *Little Wars* magazines. In the pages of the *Strategic Preview* we see the talents of Dave Sutherland as a cartoonist on full display. Every issue contained an episode of his comic "David Megarry, David Megarry," a workplace parody of a contemporary television show called *Mary Hartman, Mary Hartman*, itself a satire of soap operas.

In the debut issue of *Strategic Preview*, Sutherland introduced "the 'characters' who made up TSR and would be featured in the continuing saga of 'David Megarry, David Megarry.'" The first is Gygax, who is portrayed as a fountain of dark hair with a nose and glasses, who wields a cat-o-nine-tails to motivate the workers and perpetually has one finger poised above a "panic button." Many caricatures derive from game design projects: thanks to his work on *Boot Hill*, Brian Blume is depicted as a cowboy with six shooters at his sides with his face obscured by a ten-gallon hat nearly larger than his entire body; Mike Carr is dressed as an aviator and surrounded by miniature

biplanes from *Fight in the Skies*; and Terry Kuntz is done up as Robin Hood.
Tim Kask wears an oversized newsboy cap and incessantly puffs smoke of
some undetermined substance from a long pipe. Dave Arneson is rotund
and mustachioed, wearing a visor and a collegiate "Blackmoor U." shirt.
Dave Megarry is himself always poring over TSR's ledger, his nose red and
his head surrounded by cartoon bubbles that betray drunkenness; Sutherland introduces him as "the lead character in this continuing story, living
his soap-opera existence every day at TSR—a man who might go far except
for his drinking problem." A humorous exaggeration, though Megarry has
been known to enjoy his scotch after hours.

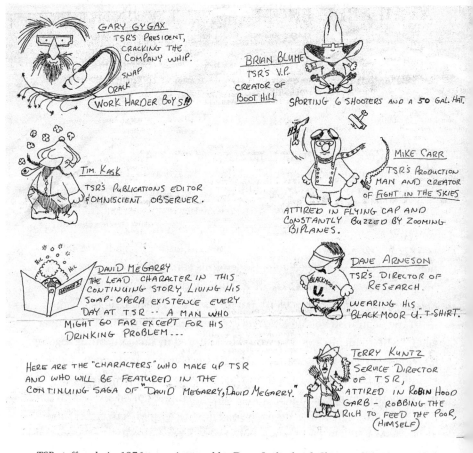

TSR staff early in 1976, as caricatured by Dave Sutherland. Shown: Gary Gygax, Tim
Kask, David Megarry, Brian Blume, Mike Carr, Dave Arneson, Terry Kuntz, from *Strategic Preview* no. 3.

These seven employees, plus Sutherland, formed the core team who went to work every day at 723 Williams Street in the spring of 1976. To understand their interpersonal dynamic, it is crucial to remember that Gygax, at age thirty-seven, was by far the oldest: the rest were all in their twenties. Arneson and Kask would be the next oldest, but apart from Gygax, who already had five children, Kask was the only staffer working for TSR who was then married—Blume was divorced. Thus it is unsurprising that Gygax led the company with a sort of paternalism that some might have seen as authoritarianism.

As four of these employees were transplants from the Twin Cities, they unsurprisingly banded together into something of a coalition. Arneson found a second-floor apartment at 830 Wisconsin Street, just around the corner from the Horticultural Hall, which he would share with his friend and co-worker Megarry. Carr and Sutherland similarly roomed together about four blocks further down the same road. In the evening, Carr, Megarry, and Arneson could often be found together at the Korner Bar on the first floor of the Hotel Clair at the intersection of Main and Broad Streets, which had a ten-lane bowling alley in its basement.

Sutherland's "David Megarry, David Megarry" narratives parodied office life at TSR in ways that spoke to the travails the small business endured. In one episode from June, Kask emerges to tell Megarry that the third D&D supplement *Eldritch Wizardry* is finally complete, a cause for celebration—but then Carr interrupts to inform the pair that the United Parcel Service has just gone on strike. Unable to ship the product, Kask and Megarry both collapse in despair. A strip in the second issue gives a glimpse into office politics, one that foreshadowed a coming schism within TSR. "Where's Arneson?" Megarry demands, as he browses through his ledger next to an overflowing outbox. In the next panel, the outbox now nearly reaches the ceiling, and Megarry exclaims, "Hey!!! What's wrong with shipping!!!!?" Only in the final panel do we see Arneson lying on the floor in the mail room, helplessly entangled in packing tape, prompting Megarry to conclude, "I think we'd better get him back to game design!!" This early reference to TSR squandering Arneson on clerical tasks in the shipping department, when his talents might have been better used in the design department, surely reflects a perception that Sutherland and other TSR staffers from the Twin Cities shared.

As new staff joined TSR during the summer, Sutherland added their characters to the dramatis personae of "David Megarry, David Megarry."

Dave Arneson is all tangled up in shipping, in an episode of Dave Sutherland's comic series, "David Megarry, David Megarry," from *Strategic Preview* no. 4.

Ernie Gygax is portrayed as a barbarian, slumped over drunk next to emptied cans of Tree Frog Beer imported from the *Fabulous Furry Freak Brothers*. Twenty-year-old Rob Kuntz, labeled "Restocker of the Dungeon," is shown as a cavorting child in a robe and wizard hat clutching a toy beholder by one of its eye stalks. Both of those youngsters had pitched in around the partnership the year before as well, but now they formally came on staff: Kuntz would work the mail room and replenish the Dungeon's shelves while pursuing game design projects on the side. Neil Topolnicki, the Baltimore gamer who did much work for Avalon Hill in founding the Origins convention, had come on board in April; he is portrayed arms akimbo in smart Napoleonic attire atop a stack of wargaming books. Finally, a character identified only as "Shlump da Orc," who has a feather and inkwell in place of a typewriter, stands in for Sutherland himself, and would become something of a mascot for TSR's art department as it grew.

With so many gamers packed into a workplace, a lot of gaming occurred as well. Gygax hinted that in April he was "readying a small fantasy campaign" to play around the office. Rather than building this around his city of Greyhawk, Gygax invented the new village called Hommlet; it was menaced by servants of the nearby Lost Temple of Elemental Evil, which lay in ruins along the shores of Nyr Dyv. As part of setting up Hommlet, Gygax assigned players responsibility for some of the town residents and establishments: Dave Arneson, for example, specified the trader who lived in the far northwest of the town, the first house on the road when traveling from nearby Verbóbonc.

It was not all play and no work at 723 Williams Street. One of Arneson's most urgent projects was to drive Dave Wesely's Revolutionary War–era miniatures rules to completion in time for the two hundredth anniversary of American Independence in July 1976. Wesely had, per TSR's "vanity press" agreements, fronted part of the cash for publishing the book, which gave it priority in the printing schedule. As that project wrapped up, Arneson drove almost biweekly to the Twin Cities, ostensibly to work with people there— but also for social occasions, like the weekend of June 5 (for his high school reunion), and then June 19 (for Mike Mornard's wedding), and then of course for the long Fourth of July weekend. Over this time, however, it is unclear how much work Arneson did in his capacity as director of research engaged "as a creative artist to create manuscripts and game components," as his contract had stipulated. Of the six projects he signed over to TSR when he joined, one was already complete at the time—*Blackmoor*—and the remainder seemed to stagnate. It is striking that of the others, four were naval warfare games, and the last a medieval wargame building on *Chainmail*; none were fantasy titles or related to *D&D*. For the first issue of *Little Wars*, Arneson pitched in an article about the historical accuracy of World War II naval gaming scenarios, but his byline otherwise remained absent from TSR's periodicals.

During his painful negotiations prior to joining TSR, Arneson had fretted about signing over the rights to his designs in exchange for stock, rather than royalties. If he still harbored reservations about it, he may have been comforted to see that Gygax himself did precisely that in the middle of the year, in some cases even exchanging existing royalty agreements for one-time grants of shares. In July, Gygax signed new contracts for *Classic Warfare* and *Little Big Horn*, and revised agreements for existing titles written jointly with Blume like *Boot Hill* and *Warriors of Mars*, all yielding to him a royalty of zero. Although Gygax, Arneson, and Carr had just executed a royalty agreement for the TSR edition of *Don't Give Up the Ship* the previous October, as of July 1 they all signed a new version of the contract that bequeathed them zero royalties as well, in exchange for stock. Over the course of the year, Arneson would accumulate 30 more shares, bringing his total position to 60.

Through these little boosts, the stock holdings of Gygax and Blume steadily increased; Blume made sure he always had a little more, but their stakes were comparable. The most fateful change in TSR's corporate governance that summer was made on July 30, when the pair granted themselves twin options to buy 700 shares of TSR stock at $100 each. An option agreement of this form encourages executives to increase shareholder value, as it locks in a cost for stock that can later be "exercised" at that strike price even if the book value of shares grows much higher: say, if four years later, TSR stock rose to a book value of $1,000, Gary and Brian could exercise those shares at only $100 and make a $900 profit on each. Options thus create a considerable incentive to increase book value for the executives holding them. For either to exercise his massive option in 1976 was far beyond their means: it would take a check for $70,000. Nor would either stand to gain much from it at the time; as of November, the annual shareholder meeting would set a new book value for TSR stock at $110, so the option would not yield a large enough profit to warrant taking out a loan for such an investment. But if either Blume or Gygax did exercise his option, it would immediately grant controlling interest in TSR Hobbies—though if both exercised, neither would own more than 50 percent of the stock. There was no hurry to explore this path, as the cost was prohibitive and the option would not expire until 1986. But in just a handful of years, TSR stock would indeed be much more valuable, and control of the company would amount to control over a modest business empire. These twin option grants bided their time in TSR's files like ticking bombs—both would ultimately go off in 1985, with dramatic consequences for the company.

The worth of TSR's shares depended largely on one title: *Dungeons & Dragons*. In the spring of 1976, TSR had two new *D&D* projects in the works; both were incremental additions to the game. Jim Ward and Rob Kuntz had already completed work on *Gods, Demi-gods & Heroes* before Arneson came on staff; it was slated for a release before GenCon. The other title was *Eldritch Wizardry*, which came out promptly on May 1. Although Gygax and Blume were listed as the authors, the ideas within adapted a number of proposals from the community. Dennis Sustare was credited as "the Great Druid" for contributing the druid character class, and Steve Marsh, who had previously done aquatic monsters for the *Blackmoor* supplement, got a credit for of his work on mental powers, which dovetailed with Gygax's own ideas to form the psionic abilities given in *Eldritch Wizardry*. The book was rounded out with an anthology of powerful magic items; like the other supplements, it was thus something of a grab bag, contributing to various parts of the *D&D* system. As that system grew disparate and unwieldy, the overall architecture of *D&D* had increasingly scattered across a diverse set of slender booklets and magazine articles. The need for a reorganization of the material into a package suitable for newcomers grew as TSR attracted more customers from outside the wargaming community.

TSR could now afford to advertise in magazines targeting the science-fiction fan community, for example: we can find full-page notices for *D&D* in venues like the May issue of *Fantastic Stories* magazine. With these boosts, *D&D*'s audience expanded well beyond its wargame heritage. Jerry Pournelle, in an article he wrote that summer, remarked on how games had taken over the science-fiction conventions of the time, including "a thing called *Dungeons & Dragons*, which seems to be a form of collective psychoses complete with audio-visual hallucinations."

Summer brought with it the "combat phase" of the game industry calendar, and this time, TSR had reinforcements to deploy. Almost the whole crew, in their cartoon form, can be seen on the cover of *Strategic Preview* no. 5 heading to Baltimore for the second Origins convention in July. Only Dave Megarry remained behind to mind to the fort at 723 Williams: TSR sent nine people on the twelve-hour drive to Origins II, though they could only cram eight into their van, along with all of their product. Neil Topolnicki drove his own car separately, as he needed to arrive early to assist with setting up the convention, honoring an earlier commitment to Avalon Hill.

Despite Gygax's ongoing feud with Origins over which was the "national" wargame convention, he still relished the opportunity to connect with East Coast fans. He again ran a *D&D* tournament at the second Origins in 1976, this time the famous science-fiction mash-up *Expedition to the Barrier Peaks*. Attendance of the *D&D* tournament doubled to 240 participants—it was the largest event at the entire convention, a development that was no doubt disconcerting to Avalon Hill. Separately, Gygax conducted a seminar explaining the game to newcomers by introducing them to the first level of the Greyhawk dungeon.

Maybe there was something to non-historical gaming after all. Avalon Hill that summer acknowledged this growing market with the release of their own board wargame adaptation of Robert Heinlein's novel *Starship Troopers*. This led Tim Kask to write in the second issue of *Dragon*: "Even the 'big two' of gaming, Avalon Hill and SPI, have come around to the view that fantasy gaming is here to stay. This change in attitude is evidenced by the fact that both of them have produced fantasy games," as in his estimation "fantasy gaming encompasses fantasy, swords and sorcery, and science fiction." TSR had its own plans to license literary works, but in the interim, it acquired the rights to Larry Smith's Tolkien-based board game *Battle of the Five Armies*, to be printed under TSR's imprint as of July 1. Smith, it would turn out, had no license in place with the Tolkien estate, but no one noticed—at least not right away.

The crowd at the second Origins was reported as a teeming throng of 2,500 persons. Wary of tying the event too tightly to one company, Avalon Hill and SPI agreed that in 1977, Origins III would relocate from Baltimore to New York City to allow SPI a chance to host it. For some time to come, Origins would be an itinerant convention, with a steering committee that would hear bids for future venues. Everyone seemed to agree that the fourth Origins should be in the Midwest in 1978, and that it would be desirable for the fifth to be on the West Coast in 1979. In a letter written August 18, Avalon Hill's Don Greenwood predicted that "Gygax and TSR will probably be admitted to the steering committee as the successful sponsors of Origins IV." Since TSR had already announced its plans for a California "Gen-Con West" in September 1976, Greenwood could only anticipate gloomily, "They will have little difficulty in ensuring that the site for Origins V is what is now being termed GenCon West." But for Gygax, the question would be whether to embrace Origins or try to smother it—GenCon was too dear to him to suffer Origins' attempts to overshadow it.

Four weeks after Origins, the ninth GenCon had nothing like its competitors' numbers. In the aftermath of the event, *Dragon* reported, "Paid attendance was in the vicinity of 1,300, with crowds of over 1,000 on both Friday and Saturday." The biggest coup of GenCon was the presence of Fritz Leiber to promote his new licensed TSR board game *Lankhmar* on the first day of the convention. Leiber addressed a lively crowd in the main room of the American Legion Hall, just around the corner from 723 Williams Street, which had space enough for one hundred folding chairs and a podium—and there was standing room only. Gygax introduced Leiber with a confession that "he has created some excellent Swords and Sorcery, which I admit to lifting a few ideas from when we did D&D." But the two of them had first met in person only the day before; Leiber would describe Gygax in an article for the *San Francisco Examiner* a few weeks later as "a mustached man of youthful middle years reminiscent of Buffalo Bill." In answer to the question on everyone's mind, Leiber had to confess to the GenCon crowd that he had not yet played *D&D*, and he had only just had the opportunity to review the rulebook.

Leiber hung around to pose for photographs at the convention, where he rubbed elbows with M. A. R. Barker and the principals of Games Workshop,

Ian Livingstone and Steve Jackson, whose British business had grown to the point where a pilgrimage to Lake Geneva was a practical necessity. Gygax was eager to play host for Games Workshop, as their relationship grew in importance with the expansion of the market for *D&D* overseas. But TSR had reached a point where it needed to choose between its industry allies for the sake of revenue.

The day after GenCon ended, TSR executed a licensing agreement with Miniature Figurines of New York, the American branch of the British firm popularly known as MiniFigs. Under this contract, MiniFigs gained a three-year exclusive right to produce miniature figures co-branded with the *Dungeons & Dragons* game in return for a 2.5 percent royalty, effective retroactively from June 1. While the officially branded MiniFigs *D&D* figures would not appear until the following year, the ramifications of the deal quickly became apparent: it precipitated an immediate schism between TSR and the many other companies who produced fantasy miniatures for the *D&D* audience, most significantly, Heritage Models. Heritage at the time marketed its line of "Fantasy Fantastics" miniatures, and advertisements for these figures appeared in the pages of *Dragon* next to those for Duke Seifried's "Fantastiques" line and for MiniFigs. Now TSR stood to gain from the sale of one of the brands more than the others, and questions about bias in advertisement acceptance and placement would soon follow. When *Dragon* bumped a Heritage ad entirely—ostensibly because space was oversold—the matter went to the courts in Texas. Almost overnight, Heritage went from one of TSR's most dedicated supporters to a bitter rival.

Relationships with partners became more enticing as the success of *D&D* brought new entrants into the market who did not hope to compete with TSR, at least not openly. The Judges Guild unveiled their first product at this GenCon, a sprawling urban adventure setting they called the *City State of the Invincible Overlord*. The founders of the Judges Guild, who had visited TSR earlier in the summer, proclaimed "personal thanks to Dave Megarry, Tim Kask, Dave Arneson, Rob Kuntz and the TSR legions for the encouragement and +1 blessing given the founding of the Judges Guild." The absence of Gygax's name from that list is striking. When they produced their *Guide to the City State* after GenCon, it appeared with a notice on its cover that it was endorsed by Dave Arneson, "famous fantasy game author." As they worked toward a revision to appear early the following year, the Judges Guild shared in their newsletter that Dave Arneson not only endorsed it, but he was "writing a complimentary commentary in the introductory notes."

One might well ask why Arneson had extended a personal endorsement to the Judges Guild rather than securing some sort of arrangement with TSR. By the summer, Arneson had already become a bit distant from his employer. He was away from Lake Geneva quite a bit, traveling coast-to-coast after TSR extended the 1976 summer convention season into September by holding its satellite GenCon West in San Jose, California. But during this itinerant time, he increasingly soured on TSR, and the fracturing of a coalition grew imminent.

It had become clear that "director of research" may not have been the best title for Arneson's responsibilities. He did continue developing Twin Cities projects, like the games of the Snider brothers, but new TSR products did not make it into his hands—especially not *D&D* ones. When John Eric Holmes, a neurologist at the University of Southern California, wrote to Gygax volunteering to reorganize the *Dungeons & Dragons* rules, Gygax seemed happy to delegate the task to him; Holmes had independently come to believe that the rules, scattered and ambiguous as they were, simply provided little useful instruction to new players, and he had a vision for paring down the system into a digestible introduction. Then in October, Gygax received a letter from a student at Iowa State University named Merle Rasmussen pitching the idea of a game "somewhat similar to the intriguing fantasy booklets of yours in the *Dungeons & Dragons* series and *Boot Hill*," though Rasmussen's game would focus on "the world of espionage." Gygax, Blume, and Carr greenlit the project—which would eventually be titled *Top Secret*—but TSR's research director was not involved.

One day in the autumn of 1976, Dave Arneson listlessly committed to a piece of scrap paper a few rhetorical questions about his situation in life. He cycled through TSR's works in progress, many on subjects he considered his bailiwick but none being works he was assigned to develop—everything from wargaming projects to the "*D&D* rewrite." He then scribbled down four points that characterized his tenure at the company:

1) No original work has been published,
2) Unlikely that any will be,
3) No original work has been allowed during term of employment,
4) Unlikely any will be.

Why indeed did TSR publish none of Arneson's original work, and exclude him from development projects he would have relished? In other correspondence from the era, Arneson would describe his past months at TSR as being mostly "concerned with shipping (4 months) and then editing others' rules," and he maintained that "there was no prospect of any of my work being published by TSR." But it is no simple matter to explain why.

Arneson would accuse Gygax and Blume of reserving for themselves the choicest work at TSR, or at best redirecting it to freelancers, in order to avoid paying royalties to employees. But TSR's heavy use of freelancers in 1976 surely had more to do with the fact that they collected production loans from the authors of outside submissions to finance publishing their works. Moreover, Arneson's original works *Ships of the Line* and *Naval Orders of Battle* had by that point existed as drafts for more than four years, and the rights for both had the year before been signed over by Arneson to TSR in exchange for a stock grant. Gygax repeatedly asked for urgent revisions to them both, and Arneson repeatedly avowed his faith in their imminent publication to his friends, even as late as October 1976, but they simply never materialized. As of the summer of 1975, TSR had announced both as forthcoming titles in the third *Strategic Review*, which suggests that the company did indeed plan to release those products eventually. If Gygax were cynically deceiving Arneson, just stringing him along with no intention of publishing either game, why then would TSR have paid upfront for those titles with a stock grant, rather than offering a royalty agreement which would cost them nothing if the rules never went to the printers?

Arneson's melancholy was no doubt exacerbated by the fact that he never really took to the sleepy lakeside community that TSR called home. "The night life around Lake Geneva is zero so that aside from going out drinking (which makes me sick after the first couple), [there's] playing pinball," Arneson lamented in a letter to John Snider, who was then stationed in Germany. In another personal letter of the time, he complained that his "forlorn love life took an apparently fatal dive" when he moved to Lake Geneva, as he was unlikely to meet any women there, and visiting the local Playboy Resort—Arneson was a "keyholder"—was a dispiriting substitute. Clearly homesick, he held out hope for returning to Minnesota. In October, he hinted in a letter to Snider's brother Richard that "there is a chance that TSR will open a branch office in the Cities as early as January of next year." He became fixated on the idea that he and the other members of the Twin

Cities coalition would be back home by the spring, where more of their old gaming group could enter the TSR fold.

By the middle of September, Arneson maintained an intermittent presence at 723 Williams Street at best. Most afternoons after lunch, he retired to his apartment on Wisconsin Street and worked from there. While he secured the permission of his supervisor, Mike Carr, his absences were conspicuous in a company with just a dozen employees. Writing to John Snider, Arneson listed some of the projects he was working on at the time: while it included *Ships of the Line*, he also mentioned "a set of role playing rules for medieval Japan" as well as one "for 18th century pirates." He explained it was "all quite hush hush, cannot even tell you their final names, but it keeps me busy." For some of these projects, it is unclear to what degree Arneson disclosed his activities to TSR. When October sales came in low, and management started exploring cost-cutting measures—Gygax even circulated a memo demanding that employees use less heat in the office, as winter loomed in Wisconsin—things did not bode well for Arneson.

Matters came to a head at the November 3 annual shareholder meeting of TSR Hobbies, held the day after Jimmy Carter was elected president. Unlike the previous year, the meeting was not simply a perfunctory interval of time Gygax and Blume passed in a room by themselves—now Carr, Sutherland, Arneson, Megarry, Kask, and Terry Kuntz filed off their posts at work that Wednesday afternoon to vote their stock holdings. Even Rob Kuntz, who owned no equity at the time, was permitted to attend "by special permission and unanimous consent of the shareholders." After Megarry had delivered the treasurer's report on the situation of the company, and Gygax had dutifully expostulated on future areas of expansion, something of a confrontation ensued.

A motion was raised to expand the TSR Hobbies board of directors from two persons to four in order to aid in long-term strategy. Although the minutes do not record the originator of the motion, the 289 votes cast supporting it represented the entire Twin Cities coalition: Arneson's stock, the holdings of Megarry and Carr, and Sutherland's 5 shares thrown in as well. As Gygax and the Blume family collectively held more than 1,500 of the 1,807 shares outstanding, they could easily defeat such a measure—which they promptly did. Arneson may have mistakenly believed that Blume would support him, but if so, this is what in a *Diplomacy* game would be known as a stab.

Heated words were then exchanged. Arneson made some oblique reference to who had done what for the company besides merely investing money in it, as he felt his own support for TSR in 1974 and 1975, efforts largely uncompensated at the time, entitled him to a say over company direction. Gygax countered that any obligation that TSR had to the Minnesota group—and Arneson felt this was directed squarely at himself—had been amply repaid with the wages of employment. Ominously, Gygax intimated that any employee was replaceable, as money could always buy talent. He furthermore made it perfectly clear that when the company's interests were at stake, his family's welfare was threatened, and that he would treat such challenges accordingly.

Arneson reported that Megarry resigned the day after the shareholder meeting, "citing illegal company activity, failure to honor the company's commitments to him in *Dungeon*," and he noted that Megarry "did not feel he could undertake legal action while in the company's employ." At the board of directors meeting that day, when the board approved its slate of officers and salaries for the following year, Megarry was no longer listed as treasurer—that role was now held by Blume, in addition to his positions as first vice-president and secretary. Blume would only occupy the treasurer position as a caretaker for a week or so before bringing in a replacement: his younger brother Kevin. Though Kevin had taken some business classes, he had majored in biology in college, and earlier in 1976 had been employed as a Medical Service Specialist by the Air Force, working in hospitals in Washington and abroad in Thailand. While it cannot be said that Kevin was a gamer, he was family.

Gygax made an effort to reach out to Arneson the day of the board meeting in a private conversation, among other things reassuring him that his opinions did matter, and that Gygax's remarks about the Minnesota coalition were not a personal attack on Arneson. But the pair quickly ran out of pleasantries. Arneson reminded Gygax of his promise, articulated in a letter the past October during contract negotiations surrounding the *Blackmoor* rights, that "our plan is to give you bonuses if sales of assigned titles exceeds stock appreciation." As roughly 6,000 copies of *Blackmoor* had sold at this point for $5 each, did Gygax feel that just 30 shares of stock, then valued at $110 each, was adequate recompense for all the titles Arneson had signed over to TSR? Gygax responded that he did, especially given how little of *Blackmoor* Arneson had actually written; Arneson recalled in a letter to a friend that Gygax had shot back "that TSR would never have paid me more than 5% royalty for the poor work manuscript submitted." To this, Arneson retorted that TSR stock was unfairly overvalued, and the actual worth of 30 shares was less than even that reduced royalty. The exchange only heightened tensions and propelled TSR ever deeper into a schism.

That same day, November 4, Gygax also sent a memo to the company outlining "our official policy regarding the following areas of professional activity," which covered consulting, game design analysis, and research. It forbade employees from working with outside firms on such matters without going through proper company channels: TSR offered "consultation services" that "range from $25 upwards per hour" and very decidedly stated that "we do not give free consultation." This language no doubt targeted persistent suspicions that Arneson was moonlighting for other firms during his long solitary afternoons at home—perhaps Duke Seifried's Custom Cast, perhaps the Judges Guild, or others.

This memo, or least the sentiment behind it, induced Rob Kuntz to tender his resignation from TSR, according to Arneson. Though Kuntz cited health and personal issues, he surely had other reasons: his responsibilities at the company were poorly defined, and like Arneson, he seemingly flitted between the mail room and design meetings, charged with accountability for too broad a set of tasks. Gygax accused Kuntz of quitting the company solely so he could still do external freelance design work; certainly Kuntz did not sever himself completely from TSR, as he continued to contribute to *Dragon* as well as write for other companies. His departure most likely signaled solidarity with the Twin Cities coalition and defiance toward Gygax; Kuntz would amply express the latter in his ongoing correspondence with Arneson.

Arneson did not take the memo well either. A copy survives in which he has crossed out Gygax's title, "President," and replaced it with "Dictator." The memo was originally addressed to "Gentle folk," and this Arneson has corrected to "Slaves." Other references to the whole company as a decision-making body are blotted out in exchange for "Gygax."

This subversive unrest reacted to an atmosphere of professionalism dawning at TSR, one which sometimes veered into martinetism. Four days after the board meeting, Gygax announced the imminent release of a new employee handbook, as well as the implementation of a time clock for hourly employees. The section in the handbook on "Attendance" contains a very pointed section on absences, stating that "employees are required to be on duty during their work hours and must not leave the Company premises except on approved Company business without permission of their immediate supervisor." The end of the handbook also details a list of disciplinary infractions and their associated punishments; its section on "minor offenses" begins with "habitual absence," then goes to "habitually reporting late," and "habitual failure to be in attendance on company premises." No doubt Arneson's predilection for working from home in the afternoon inspired such restrictions. Workers guilty of transgressing these rules would accrue points—a system worthy of a game company—which could trigger reprimands and in sufficient quantities harsher punishments. Under the most heinous "intolerable offenses" is listed "leaving the premises during working hours without notification," which warranted enough points for an automatic termination of employment.

The time clock became an immediate source of morale problems. The handbook commanded that "you must use the time clock if you are an hourly employee," not just at the beginning and end of a working day, but additionally punching out and in again around a lunch break. Salaried officers were exempt from using time cards, but Arneson's compensation was now structured at an hourly rate of $2.75 for six eight-hour days a week. To Arneson's fury, Tim Kask was excused from punching in even though he was not yet a salaried officer; of the remaining employees, only Arneson, Terry Kuntz, and Neil Topolnicki became thralls of the clock.

The day that Gygax announced the handbook, November 8, he sent Arneson a "Written Statement of Ownership of Games et al. Produced during Employment by TSR." It aimed to revise Arneson's employment agreement, levying stricter controls over outside work. Where Arneson's original contract had stated merely that "during the term of his employment all game and game rules and design efforts produced by him become the sole and exclusive property of the Employer," the new language targeted some gray areas around freelancing on the side. It required that "each and every game, set of game rules or game related concept and/or any portion thereof, which I originate, create, develop, prepare, edit, write, playtest, and/or cause to or aid to be published, during the term of my employment by TSR Hobbies, Inc., is the sole and exclusive property of TSR Hobbies, Inc." This agreement would go into effect retroactively from the beginning of the year, and would moreover still apply after Arneson left TSR.

TSR had not singled out Arneson for special punishment: all employees were immediately required to sign a version of the agreement. Gygax clarified that they were making a generous exception by allowing Arneson some time to consult legal counsel before executing it. But this generosity had a time limit. Gygax's letter concluded with an ultimatum: "As signing the statement is a condition of employment, failure to so sign will be considered as a resignation of employment effective on the deadline for signature, 15 November 1976."

Arneson received this notice on a Monday, and his signature would be required the Monday following. Over the intervening weekend, he took the five-hour drive up to the Twin Cities in the company of Brian Blume and Mike Carr. Comparing notes with Carr, Arneson learned that only the two of them, plus Gygax and Blume, had to sign this onerous version of the agreement, as hourly workers outside the creative side of the business would retain the rights to work done on personal time.

Arneson's Uncle George—uncles then being the preferred source of legal counsel for both Gygax and Arneson—urged him to sign nothing, characterizing Gygax's ultimatum as unmistakable "coercion." Arneson insisted that they formulate a counterproposal, which the pair of them developed over the course of the weekend; effectively, it would let Arneson retain ownership of all design ideas he developed at TSR, while granting TSR only a right of first refusal to publish his work. On the long drive back on Monday, he learned that Carr had decided to sign TSR's agreement, but only after appending to it a list of games he had invented before joining, to mark them as exempt from the company's ownership. Arneson also had plenty of time during the trip to discuss the situation with Blume, who hinted that TSR might be willing to look at his counterproposal. The three of them did not make it back to Lake Geneva until late on November 15, however, so it transpired that Arneson was out of the office on the day the ultimatum came due.

Arneson returned to the office at 723 Williams Street on Tuesday, November 16, at around nine thirty in the morning. When he arrived at work and picked up his weekly check, he immediately noticed that $40 had been deducted from his usual wage. Inquiries about his reduced pay revealed that he had been docked for taking his trip home to the Twin Cities, on the grounds that it was unauthorized and done on company time. Incredulous, Arneson pointed out that he had actually accompanied his immediate supervisor, Carr, as well as Blume himself, on this journey— surely the company must have been aware.

Angered by this reprimand, Arneson typed up a formal letter to Gygax in the office that morning. He wrote, "Unless the management of TSR is willing to negotiate the terms of the agreement, I must assume that TSR has terminated my employment, as I cannot, in good conscience, sign the agreement as it now stands." He added his resolute insistence that Carr "had approved my leave as a paid absence."

After dropping off the letter to Gygax, who read it in silence, Arneson packed up some of his reference materials, departing the office a little after one o'clock. According to Arneson, by the time he left, 723 Williams Street had emptied for lunch. Gygax would describe a very different scene: After Arneson learned he would receive no wages for the days he was absent on his trip, "he turned livid, but he said absolutely nothing. He spent approximately one-half hour packing various belongings into a container, and then he left." Gygax found this unusual because, "When Mr. Arneson left the offices of the corporation to work at home he always obtained his supervisor's permission to do so first. On the occasion in question he not only failed to do so, but from his obvious state of rage, and the slamming of drawers, books, etc., none of his fellow employees cared to ask what he intended. Mr. Arneson then literally slammed out of the office, possessions in hand."

Livid or not, Arneson made his way from the office on Williams Street to a lakeside diner, a town institution called Popeye's Galley and Grog, to take his lunch. Arneson loved all things naval, and it was a restaurant with harpoons decking its walls and boats suspended from the ceiling. Then, as he would later relate the events of the day, he drove Dave Sutherland's car to Delavan to get it repaired, because Sutherland was ill. When he returned to his apartment on Wisconsin Street in Lake Geneva, at about four o'clock, Neil Topolnicki informed him that a letter from Gygax awaited him at the office.

In his letter, Gygax rejected Arneson's view of the new employment agreement. "Those employees of TSR who are doing creative work are doing so strictly for the benefit of TSR with regards to their designs," Gygax explained. "As you do not wish to sign the statement, we cannot have you continue as research director. Hence forward, you are transferred to shipping. Your hourly rate will be $2.30 per hour, with a basic forty hour week." Cruelly, Gygax construed this demotion as an act of mercy. "Please note that we are transferring you despite the fact that you committed an intolerable offense by leaving the premises today without the courtesy to notify anyone." Gygax refused to budge on whether Arneson's trip to Minnesota was authorized: "Mr. Carr informs me that he did not, in fact, state that you would be paid for the two days you were absent, but the matter depended on the amount of vacation time still remaining due you." Still, Gygax agreed to retroactively authorize those as vacation days—but he would not do so for Arneson's current absence on Tuesday, November 16. In punishment for that truancy, Gygax wrote, "we must suspend your employment for ten days without pay."

After receiving Gygax's letter, Arneson furiously wrote to his father, to his friends, to everyone. He composed a few draft responses to TSR that he never sent, some curt and dismissive, others stretching for pages, telling the story from his side, complaining that he never had an opportunity to defend himself. The letter he actually sent on November 20 was much shorter, just four sentences, stating that he resigned effective November 16, and that his mail should be forwarded to his parents' house in St. Paul.

At first, Arneson was understandably disconsolate. "I have no future plans," he wrote in a mass mailing to the Snider brothers and to Steve Rocheford, "as I am basically unemployable . . . I will certainly try and continue writing but it is unlikely I will find a publisher anywhere." It was clear that he now saw Gygax as a villain, painting him as "Gary Gygax, hereafter referred to as EGG," a nickname that recalls the Egg of Coot, the adversary in his Blackmoor setting. Arneson mused that he could only aspire to a position as a parking lot attendant or a security guard. At his darkest depths, he could only add: "Hopefully they will still pay my *D&D* royalties so I can live."

That hope would become the basis for some of the most explosive episodes in the history of *Dungeons & Dragons*. From the outside, the prospects of TSR and *D&D* looked quite modest at the time. When Howard Barasch at SPI posted his statistics ranking the hobby games industry sales for the 1976 fiscal year, he put TSR in fourth place, with a revenue of $121,900 on total unit sales of 22,436. This was less than $40,000 behind the third-place contender, GDW, though of course they both were well behind the two "super power" wargaming companies who boasted over a million in sales each. Barasch noted however that TSR sales only cover the period from October 1, 1975—the time that TSR Hobbies incorporated—up to April 30, 1976, a little more than half a year. With the addition of two summers of revenue, the race for third place in the ranking would have been closer. As TSR tabulated its first fiscal year ending with that October 1 date, they represented the total for their 1976 year as closer to $300,000, on the strength of strong recent sales.

Then, over the final quarter of 1976, those sales began to undergo a dramatic transformation. October had been a slow month, with the number of fifth-print white boxes of *D&D* that sold amounting to a tepid 466 copies, regressing to levels last seen a year earlier. But then November sales climbed to 866 copies. In December, with holiday shoppers on the prowl, sales for that single month leapt to 1,125, a sum comparable to the total for all of 1974. As Arneson received 50 cents per copy, were he to realize this amount every month, *D&D* royalties alone would very nearly equal his former TSR salary. It turned out these figures indeed reflected a sustained trend in sales, which would average comfortably above a thousand copies per month over the next year—though Arneson would be none the wiser until he saw his next quarterly payment.

Still, after a week of reflection in the safety of his parents' home, Arneson emerged from this dark night of the soul determined to jump back into game design. He wrote to John Snider, "I will be starting a company here in Minnesota to publish and market rule books." Arneson knew he needed staff, and he had four people already in mind: "an editor (Mike Carr), artist (Dave Sutherlands), research editor (me), and an accountant (Dave Megarry)." Two of them, of course, remained employees of TSR at the time, but how long would that last, under Gygax's tyrannical rule? In order to prevent anyone else from suffering his fate, Arneson swore that in his company, "authors would retain the copyrights to their work and the company would only hold a short-term licensing agreement that would be renewed in each subsequent run of the booklet." He even knew what to call it: "the name of the company will be Adventures Unlimited, the name for the proposed travel agency some years back." He had a handful of unfinished titles he could migrate to a new firm—though it was unclear what claim TSR might lay to them, or what Arneson took with him of *Dungeons & Dragons*.

TSR Turn Results for 1976

Revenue: $300,000 (Barasch ranking 4), profit $19,000
Employees: 10
Stock Valuation: $110
GenCon attendance vs. Origins: 1,500 vs. 2,200

Duration of Arneson's stay in Lake Geneva:
around 11 months

1977: The Great War

The breaking of the Twin Cities coalition left Gygax and Blume effectively unchallenged within TSR Hobbies—but that did not assure them of control over *Dungeons & Dragons*. As 1977 began, the entire hobby wargames industry began to pivot toward the role-playing space, searching for any vulnerability in TSR's armor. And from within that industry, Arneson would stake his own claim on the future of *D&D*.

The most obvious weakness of *D&D* in the beginning of 1977 was the sprawling and disorganized state of the rules, spread across an accretion of rulebooks, supplements, and magazine articles. Shortly after leaving TSR, Arneson announced his own stopgap solution: he would publish a one-volume index to the disparate *D&D* bibliography, an encyclopedic reference where you could look up the location of any *D&D* rule. TSR was not about to publish it, but Arneson wasted no time in following the example of Dave Megarry by offering his services to Duke Seifried at Custom Cast. By a fortuitous chance, Custom Cast had just merged with Heritage; Megarry thus found himself relocating not to Ohio, but to Texas, to work for Jim Oden. Also feeling betrayed by TSR, Oden this year had decided to compete openly in the role-playing game space: he finally succeeded in licensing John Carter from the Burroughs estate, and furthermore secured the rights to Star Trek from Paramount, aiming to release role-playing titles for both properties. Bringing Arneson on staff to oversee those and other projects would be a publicity coup and a dramatic rebuke to TSR.

A frank note from Mike Carr a few days into January made it clear how TSR felt about Arneson's index project: "TSR asks that you not go ahead with your plans to commercially publish the *Dungeons & Dragons* index." Carr had to remind his old friend that "the name and copyright are held by TSR," and thus no product branded as *Dungeons & Dragons* could be sold without TSR's permission. TSR hurriedly registered a number of its works with the US Copyright Office in January, which went some ways toward making that assertion less of a paper tiger than it had been a year before. Arneson returned a genial reply promising that both he and a lawyer would check the manuscript to "avoid any TSR copyright infringements real or claimed." He could not resist an aside, driving a little wedge between Carr and TSR: "I also think that in the future 'TSR' should write their own letters and not put you up to it."

But the index would be only the start of Arneson's plan to fix what he felt TSR had broken. He had articulated to his friend John Snider a grander plan to work toward "a line of role-playing game booklets," beginning with a "basic booklet" that would contain "information that would otherwise have to appear in each and every role-playing book, no matter what the period or mythos, taking up valuable space that would be better used to enhance the period or mythos covered by the book." With those foundational rules in place, then "each mythos or period would begin with a first, very simple volume, meant to capture their imagination, not use a referee extensively, and get them hooked." Additional volumes and supplements that delved into the details of particular settings and genres, matters like social advancement and military actions, would then follow. He would pursue this design under the umbrella of his Adventures Unlimited, in a partnership, as yet to be ratified, with Heritage.

At the beginning of the year it seemed unlikely that Arneson would lure away Carr for his new venture, and Dave Sutherland did not immediately respond to any of Arneson's entreaties to contribute to the index project. Carr did equip Arneson with a warm letter of recommendation, one that touted Arneson's many innovations in the gaming field, qualified only with the generally accepted admission that "Dave's weakness seems to be putting these ideas in final, polished form," a disadvantage "easily overcome when he can work with a competent editor."

Another person still in the orbit of TSR who remained sympathetic to Arneson was Rob Kuntz. Although Kuntz had resigned in November, he remained in Lake Geneva and did work for TSR while retaining the freedom to freelance. He spread to Arneson the sort of gossip that could only intensify the schism. "Have you been bad mouthing TSR or something," Kuntz teased, because "word has gotten back to Gary that you have and he has been calling people like Oden and putting in a bad word in for you."

Arneson would later remark that in his quest for employment, he had to "overcome a lot of bad P.R. from TSR about not being productive." Kuntz portrayed himself as flagrantly courting Gary's displeasure: he told Arneson how he had submitted an article about *D&D* to a rival company's newsletter, Fantasy Games Unlimited's *Wargaming*, with the defiant gloss, "Bet you Gary gets really steamed! I don't care much anyway." Kuntz had his own game designs in progress, and pointedly kept Arneson abreast of titles that Adventures Unlimited might consider for future publication.

Kuntz also related to Arneson the everyday indignities that TSR heaped on his brother Terry, most recently an internal memo encouraging employees dissatisfied with their work situation to resign. "Same old crap," Rob sighed. In fact, both Terry Kuntz and Neil Topolnicki would leave the company early in 1977. Within a few months, staff would shrink briefly to just nine persons—whittled down like an adventuring party in a trap-filled dungeon—and at this juncture, TSR began to look like a family business: Gygax's wife and son were on payroll, as were three members of the Blume family. Few would read into the name "Jo Powell Agency," the advertising agency created to manage placements in *Dragon*, the maiden name of Gygax's wife—Mary Jo Powell—but she was effectively the agency's sole employee, and booking advertisements for TSR periodicals quickly took precedence over her secretarial work she initially had been doing. Incidentally, Victoria Miller, who in a couple years would marry Brian Blume, soon took up those clerical responsibilities. But off TSR's books, the Jo Powell Agency funneled the commissions for periodical advertising into a three-way partnership split between Gygax, his wife, and Brian Blume. It would gross nearly $30,000 before the end of 1977, providing both families a bit more income.

Apart from immediate family, a few key individuals drove the work at TSR. Tim Kask began the year as a general editor, though he increasingly focused on managing *Dragon* as its subscriber base grew. Sutherland was then the only staff artist. Carr not only ran all production, but he also edited games and was responsible for the Dungeon Hobby Shop at 723 Williams. With such a skeleton crew, TSR set a light publishing schedule for the year, focusing on a few large releases for *D&D* planned for the summer and fall, rather than the wide spread of "vanity press" wargaming products it had offered the year before.

This reduction in staffing at the start of 1977 did not bode well for the company's health. It might have been a sign that TSR was about to go under. Afterward, for the Twin Cities gamers, there might be some hassle recovering the rights to games from the wreckage of the company, but there was every reason to think they could salvage games in development limbo, like the further installments in John Snider's stellar empires series. Those titles could then be redirected to greener pastures—say, to Heritage in Dallas.

After holding a few preliminary phone calls, Arneson wrote to Jim Oden and Duke Seifried in the third week of January to share a proposed employment contract with Heritage. Not that he intended to relocate to Texas: Arneson planned to rent his own place in St. Paul on Galtier Avenue, starting on the first of February, so he hoped to secure $600 a month as a retainer from Heritage, with an additional $15.00 per hour for any editing or playtesting he did on Heritage's projects. The contract itself drew heavily on his recent counterproposal to TSR: it largely offered Heritage a right of first refusal, but no ownership of Arneson's designs. "It may seem," Arneson preemptively countered, "that I am indeed asking for the sky and the moon with sugar on it but I feel that my proposal does form a basis for negotiation and that when I make the company its first $100,000 (next year at least!) I can justify every penny."

Arneson knew well that Heritage would be reluctant to take legal responsibility for his *D&D* index, but he needed Heritage's printing press to mint it. So, he brought the project under his Adventures Unlimited imprint, predicting that "as publisher and author TSR will have to nail me first." He expected to complete it imminently: "The local trolls start proofing it next weekend," he wrote. He enlisted Mike Mornard to help him debug the indexing work, which Arneson admitted was "about as exciting as doing a telephone book and just as tedious."

The employment agreement that Arneson proposed to Oden and Seifried covered numerous planned projects. In addition to working for Heritage to produce role-playing booklets for their newly licensed properties, he offered to "work up a *D&D* supplement and then turn to the *D&D* rewrite." He assured Oden that the "index and supplement should sell 4–500 a month easy," about half of monthly sales of *D&D* at the time. But a supplement could only be an interim measure: the brass ring was the rewrite, the promise of creating a novel and superior game that would replace *D&D* itself.

To provide assistance on the rewrite, Arneson enlisted Richard Snider. Snider currently resided in Mankato, Minnesota, where he was working toward a college degree, but in between that and fretting over TSR's silence

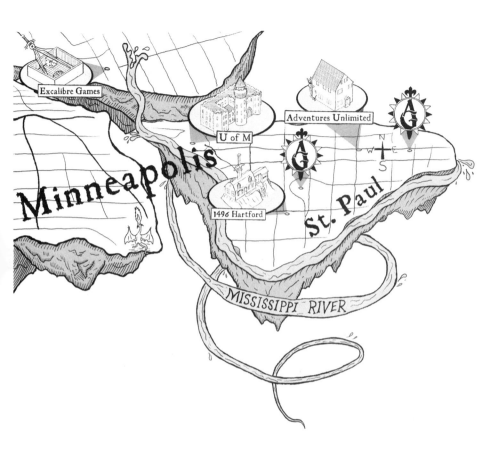

about his "Mutant" draft, he had some time to help Arneson implement his fundamental reworking of role-playing games. As originally envisioned, the project was divided into two segments: a "role-playing" booklet that furnished generic, foundational rules, and then an application of those core rules to a "fantasy" period aimed at superseding the setting of *D&D*. Arneson proposed Snider would work on some aspects of the fantasy setting, especially related to monsters and magic, while Arneson would tackle the rest.

But Arneson had some other chores to complete first—he offloaded some of the work on the index project to Snider as well. Securing Dave Sutherland's help as a freelance illustrator for the index proved difficult, but Arneson won him over in the end. Sutherland sketched a cover design for it, as well as a few smaller pieces for the interior, though Arneson promised to keep Sutherland's contribution a secret to protect his position at TSR. One of the interior illustrations Sutherland drew for the index, a stout dragon, Arneson promoted to the logo for Adventures Unlimited, widely reprinting it on letterheads and business cards. No doubt Arneson found it easier to persuade Sutherland in the face of his continuing mistreatment at TSR. Sutherland explained in a letter to Arneson that he had announced his intention to leave, but "Gary 'pulled' me into the office and asked me to stay. He offered a 25¢ hourly raise now and an average of a 20¢ hourly raise every three months." While Sutherland agreed to those terms after discussing the situation with his fiancée, the actual increase to his wages turned out to be just 20¢. Gary was, Sutherland sighed, "up to his old words and promises blowing in the wind trick. But hell! I expected as much."

Arneson wasted no time mounting his first challenge to TSR. On March 23, he sent a draft of the *Dungeonmaster's Index* to Heritage for an initial print run of one thousand copies, with the understanding that Dave Megarry would take responsibility for editing the final product, and that—following TSR's example—"Heritage will take in payment of the printing bill such booklets as are required to satisfy this printing bill." Apart from fifty copies that Arneson would distribute personally in Minnesota, he granted Heritage exclusive distribution rights to the *Index* and allowed them to purchase copies to resell at 60 percent off the cover price. Heritage intended to retail the *Index* for $3.50, though privately Arneson fretted to Megarry over whether the sum was too great. As the text went to the printers, it said nothing about who published it—it did not even contain a mention of Adventures Unlimited. It was however "Dedicated to the Four Musketeers, may they soon ride again!" The closest the text comes to acknowledging any "musketeers" of the Twin Cities coalition by name is crediting Dave Sutherland for his art as "S."

Although he continued to negotiate an employment agreement with Heritage, Arneson ferociously defended his status as a free agent, evading any constrictive corporate shackles. The draft contracts they bounced around in 1977 carefully preserved Arneson's latitude to publish work rejected by Heritage elsewhere. Arneson was negotiating not just for himself, but also for his friends in the Twin Cities: he wanted John Snider to do Heritage's Star Trek project, and invited his friend Greg Svenson to tackle the John Carter role-playing game. "By the end of the year there should be 5–7 games on the market," Arneson forecasted to John Snider, reiterating the figure he had earlier given to Oden of "bringing in $100,000 in revenue." If that kind of money came in, he might even be able to lure Carr and Sutherland away from TSR.

"The best part is that I am my own man in this case!" Arneson gushed. Success, for Arneson, meant that no one was telling him what to do: he could get games into print without having to commit to any single employer who would then hold leverage over him. Snider, for his part, had executed a February contract with TSR for future installments of his stellar empire game series that made him hesitant to wade into the Heritage Star Trek project, as his TSR agreement included a "restrictive covenant" clause that barred him from working on competing titles. While he signaled his willingness to help Arneson with the Star Trek property, as Snider remained overseas in Germany in the military, there were plenty of reasons why work towards the Star Trek game progressed quite languidly.

Eschewing direct employment meant that Arneson had to struggle for financial security. He mentioned in his correspondence with Heritage that, in addition to *D&D* royalties from TSR, he also hoped to collect some unemployment payments. People who quit their jobs cannot receive unemployment, and after his initial request for benefits was rejected, Arneson testified in St. Paul on March 24 that the ultimatum he received from TSR to sign a new employment agreement was tantamount to a termination. The state was inclined to support his claim, but when contacted about it, TSR appealed the decision, arguing that Arneson had left willingly, as Gygax had merely demoted him to the shipping department and suspended him for ten days without pay for his absenteeism. This became a first point of legal contention between them; Gygax, Blume, Carr, and Arneson would then tell their sides of that confusing story to the courts, a dispute that would drag on into next year.

Arneson would open another, more consequential legal question at the beginning of April by sending TSR a letter—its text carefully drafted by Dave Megarry—that questioned whether he was receiving appropriate *Dungeons & Dragons* royalties. The letter restates the terms of the April 1975 royalty agreement for *D&D* and speculates that "TSR Hobbies, Inc. may well have failed to fulfill this obligation" in four specific areas. The first related to Heritage: as Heritage had received 250 copies of *D&D* as partial payment for producing the third printing of the game in 1975, Arneson maintained that those copies constituted a "sale" under the royalty agreement, and he was understandably curious if that meant he was owed any money for them. Second, Arneson questioned whether royalties were properly paid for a promotion at the end of 1975 that sold odd copies of the first and second booklets in the original *D&D* set. Then in the third case, Arneson demanded an accounting of the agreement with Games Workshop to sell *D&D* in Britain, and what royalties might be due from such sales. Finally, he obliquely noted that "I have received information that the rules known as *Dungeons & Dragons* are to be rewritten in a new format by person(s) other than the original authors," and he requested details on that turn of events. Arneson expected a response by the end of April.

A reply would come April 26, from Brian Blume's pen, rather than Gygax's. It reported succinctly that "to the best of my knowledge, any and all royalties due the authors of the game entitled *Dungeons & Dragons* have been paid." Briefly, to Arneson's third point, he elaborated that copies then sold by Games Workshop in England were all imported from America and that they were accounted no differently than domestic sales. "I hope that this sets your mind at ease," he concluded.

One thing that Blume did not address was Arneson's allegation that *D&D* would be revised, or at least revisited, by "person(s) other than the original authors." Arneson knew well that work toward a "Beginner's Set" was already underway before he left TSR; surviving drafts of Holmes's "*Dungeons & Dragons* for Beginners" from early 1977 listed the authors as Gary Gygax and Eric Holmes, with no mention of Arneson. TSR had little interest in elaborating on their strategy, which involved not just the efforts of Holmes to condense and clarify what been released before, but a broader initiative to rethink the game from the ground up—what would become the *Advanced Dungeons & Dragons* game.

In parallel, Arneson began to marshal other forces to militate against TSR. Beyond plotting for a *D&D* rewrite with Heritage, he also planned to publish a reversion to the original principles of the game, this time with the Judges Guild. By mid-April he had entered negotiations with that firm to edit and publish notes from his original Blackmoor campaign, including maps of his dungeons and the overworld area. Arneson did not strike this deal behind Heritage's back. He won Jim Oden's consent to it, in part by downplaying the project: "the Blackmoor dungeon," Arneson hastened to explain to Oden, "will probably remain a novelty item at best and not sell on the same level as the *Index*." But Arneson foresaw another, more strategic outcome in allowing the Judges Guild to take on the project: "I also think that should Judges Guild come out with Blackmoor Dungeon, TSR will then cut off Judges Guild and open up yet another front in the great War." Whether or not that outcome was realistic, Arneson was willing to exploit his relationship with the Judges Guild to provoke TSR into further isolating itself from the rest of the industry in this "great War."

Oden amiably agreed, "Blackmoor by Judges Guild is fine with us." The Judges Guild hoped to sell copies through Heritage, so the consent of a powerful distributor was very welcome. Arneson agreed on a deal with them, a base 10 percent royalty on the expected $9 cover price, over the phone at the end of the month. The product, which would be called the *First Fantasy Campaign*, was put together quickly so that it would be available for the summer conventions that year. The Judges Guild positioned itself as a firm willing to do the heavy lifting: "I think we could do a good job for you, with a minimum amount of work on your part." Arneson sent the Judges Guild a grab bag of notes: beyond the current Blackmoor dungeon map, there were some fragments of troop assignments and settings from his original Blackmoor campaign, an article he had published through the *Domesday Book* in 1972, chunks of system he had sent to Gygax in 1973 for inclusion in *D&D*, some revisions he drafted after the publication of *D&D*, an unpublished "Infamous Characters" article he had signed over to TSR, even some bits of system by Richard Snider for good measure. To make all this cohere, Arneson furnished connecting text to explain some of the more abstruse components. But for the most part it remained, as the foreword of the book would call it, the "unpolished gem" of Arneson's original fantasy setting.

Now Arneson would come to the summer conventions of 1977 ready for battle with two new *D&D* products: his *Dungeonmaster's Index* and his original campaign notes in the *First Fantasy Campaign*. Unmistakably, Arneson intended to pursue TSR aggressively on whichever fronts he could. He had already informed the company of his intent to sell 7 shares of stock, with the express purpose of transferring three of those shares to Heritage, which would grant Heritage the right to inspect TSR's books. The "great War" had begun.

The first battleground of the war that Arneson foretold would be Staten Island, New York, at the Origins convention the weekend of July 22. After Avalon Hill had hosted Origins for its first two years at Johns Hopkins, SPI ran this year's event at Wagner College, with responsibility largely falling to Howard Barasch. Registration snafus led to long lines, rivaling those for the film *Star Wars*, which had entered wide release about a week before.

Gygax and Arneson had begun maneuvering forces for this battle the year before. TSR had previously planned to have Arneson and Rob Kuntz represent the company at the Origins convention, but in January, Gygax wrote to SPI to rather pointedly disinvite Arneson from TSR's seminar. This prompted Arneson to schedule his own talk, where he could speak to his plans for the industry. Moreover, as Gygax declined to furnish a *D&D* tournament or even attend the convention on account of the feud over the respective attendance of Origins and GenCon, Arneson would design and oversee the *D&D* tournament at Origins instead.

By this point, TSR had received ample intelligence of Arneson's forthcoming releases, and surely knew that the cover of the *First Fantasy Campaign* would advertise the contents as "the history and details of the original fantasy roleplaying game." As Gygax would not be present at Origins to tell his side of the story, he instead wrote a preemptive rebuttal to Arneson in the June issue of *Dragon*. The piece was called "Origins of the Game" and it opens with the observation that questions about the invention of *D&D* often came up at convention seminars, which had prompted him to set the record straight, in writing, for posterity. Gygax must have been frustrated with Arneson at the time: with the emotional confrontation at the board meeting last November; with his flight into the employ of a competitor, one whom TSR was already legally battling; with his persistent accusations that TSR was cheating him on royalties; and with his new efforts to publish *D&D* material outside the company. By taking this matter to the readership of *Dragon*, he would not settle the question of the game's origin, but instead throw down a gauntlet that would inevitably be picked up.

Gygax's editorial explained the evolution of the Castle & Crusade Society, *Chainmail*, and the Blackmoor campaign up to the point that *D&D* was published. When it came to the drafting of *D&D* itself, the account did not differ much from retrospective remarks Gygax had made prior to Arneson's acrimonious departure from TSR: he wrote that he received "18 or so handwritten pages of rules and notes" from Arneson before he embarked on "a brand new manuscript" of around "100 typewritten pages." But the tone in which Gygax described Arneson's contribution was now decidedly less generous. The editorial maintained that "*Dungeons & Dragons* differed considerably from Dave's 'Blackmoor' campaign," though it was short on details to back that assertion, except in so far as he says that Arneson "complained bitterly that the game wasn't right." Thus, Gygax considered that the first true games of *D&D*, as opposed to Arneson's "variant *Chainmail*," were played in Lake Geneva. Most damningly, he summarized Arneson's contribution to the game as only nominally that of an equal: "Although *D&D* was not Dave's game system by any form or measure, he was given co-billing as an author for his valuable idea kernels."

Characterizing Arneson's contribution as merely "kernels" drew a stark battle line that would quickly escalate the "great War" into a conflict over two mutually exclusive alternative histories: that the essence of the game came from Gygax, or that it came from Arneson. A furious Arneson wrote a June 10 letter to *Dragon* stating that "the facts as to the origins of *D&D* put forth" in the last issue by Gygax were "at variance with and in contradiction to previous public statements and articles published by TSR. As the co-author of *D&D* I insist on being allowed to present a rebuttal to Mr. Gygax's editorial in the next issue of *Dragon*."

Kask responded with a postcard about ten days later, allowing that Arneson was "more than welcome to submit a manuscript," but giving fair warning that "I conducted my own verification, unbeknownst to Gary, and had all the cardinal points of the piece independently verified before I elected to run it." To that, Arneson could only reply in a follow-up, "I am at a loss to understand how valid it was as you failed to contact myself or apparently any other member of the Minnesota group to ask about the Blackmoor Campaign. If you had, you would have discovered the true origins of *D&D* in greater detail."

Under separate cover, about a week before Origins, Arneson sent Kask his rebuttal, titled "The Roots of *D&D*," which he produced with some light edits by his *consigliere* Dave Megarry. Arneson felt strongly enough about it that he sent it by certified mail. Unsurprisingly, *Dragon* declined to publish it, despite Arneson's persistent threats that he would see it published elsewhere if *Dragon* refused to air it. Arneson would soon have the opportunity at Origins to rub elbows with the principals of many other companies competing with TSR in the marketplace, a crowd who he could now consider kindred spirits, and he could surely find someone there willing to print it.

Since Gygax's editorial was on Arneson's mind as he came to Origins, it is best to consider his seminar remarks and his "Roots of *D&D*" piece jointly. Arneson's "Roots" positioned the role-playing practices in Dave Wesely's "Braunstein" tradition as the true catalyst in the invention of *D&D*, downplaying the influence of any particular wargaming systems—most pointedly *Chainmail*. He maintained that he lighted on medieval fantasy purely from his interest in the films and books of the genre. Although in Blackmoor, "actual combat used the *Chainmail* system," Arneson explained, his group developed substantial additions and modifications which "have been used locally ever since, far removed from any 'variant' of *Chainmail*." This sentiment is perhaps at odds with Arneson's 1972 letter to Gygax, in which he had written that his changes to *Chainmail* were "fairly minor." No longer was Arneson willing, as he was just months earlier in the *First Fantasy Campaign*, to volunteer various other ways that his Blackmoor campaign drew on *Chainmail*. His newfound reticence surely reacted against Gygax's characterization of Blackmoor as "variant *Chainmail*." In the "Roots" piece Arneson argued that systems like *Chainmail*, tied to particular genres, could never be essential to the invention of role-playing games, as the practice of role-playing was not tied to any given genre. Effectively, Arneson described an activity isolated within the Twin Cities: his piece does not merely imply that Gygax made no contribution to the invention of *D&D*, it does not even deign to mention Gygax or TSR.

Leaving the overarching conclusions aside, "Roots" directly challenged Gygax's account on very few points of historical fact. Instead, it simply told a different segment of a compatible story, so that each piece filled in gaps in the other: Arneson made no mention of the Castle & Crusade Society; Gygax made no mention of Braunstein, of which he may well have been effectively ignorant. Crucially, Arneson did not contradict any of Gygax's account of how the text of *D&D* came together—he did not contest Gygax's assertions about who wrote the published rulebooks of the game. Over time, Arneson would increasingly argue that the basic idea behind the game mattered more than its codification into a text.

Arneson's messaging at the summer conventions would reinforce those themes, and he found an attentive audience ready to absorb it. His panel at Origins on "the state of fantasy gaming today" got off to a rocky start: none of the other panelists turned up. Arneson had to invite an audience member to fill in with an impromptu lecture on dungeon design. But Arneson still had ample opportunity to discuss his feud with TSR; one attendee recorded that Arneson described himself as "excommunicated from TSR by the all-powerful who reside there." Arneson teased his plan to bring out "his original rules (which TSR edited to death) through Judges Guild sometime soon." By casting TSR's role in the development of the game as a merely clerical one, of "editing to death" his original rules, Arneson upped the stakes a bit, implying that Gygax had not taken the initiative to write up the *D&D* rules himself.

The war between Arneson and Gygax at Origins was not just a war of words: each also released products there. The *Dungeonmaster's Index* debuted at the dealer tables on Staten Island that weekend. Another attendee of the seminar noted how Arneson described the *Dungeonmaster's Index* as "a trial balloon," since "if they don't successfully sue him for that, they won't get him for anything reasonable." Arneson sought to test how much control he could have over *D&D* without working directly with TSR. One can easily read that into Arneson's foreword to the *Index*, which hints that it will "pave the way for greatly expanded subsequent efforts."

But on the other side of the war, Staten Island also saw the latest from TSR, the long-promised *Basic Set* revised by Eric Holmes. Both offerings, in their own way, attempted to remedy the disorganization of *D&D*. Contrary to Arneson's fears, the *Basic Set* still credited him as a co-author with Gary Gygax—Holmes is listed only as an editor of the booklet. This too would have lasting implications as the "great War" escalated.

In place of Gygax, Tim Kask walked the halls of Wagner College at Origins. Kask was perhaps not the most diplomatic emissary that TSR could have dispatched to the event: he was already known to the fan community as someone who disparaged commercial efforts competing with *D&D*, and who reserved especial contempt for the amateur press. "You thought you hated Kask before," wrote one fanzine author who attended TSR's seminar. "Well, wait 'til you read this." Kask intimated that TSR would sue imitators of *D&D* out of the market, and deemed competing titles like *Tunnels & Trolls* to be "trash." He addressed the crowd in terms recorded as: "If you see a fantasy game, you will know that it is either *D&D*, or something that we are allowing to exist." Another quoted him as threatening, "We will go after anyone who uses anything we invented—any monsters we invented, the level system, anything." The prevailing sentiment seemed to be, "Overall, it appears as if Tim Kask and TSR are on a witchhunt."

If anything, TSR's seminar at the 1977 Origins hardened their opposition and cemented alliances on the other side of the "great War." Nowhere was that solidarity more evident than at Scott Bizar's seminar. The head of Fantasy Games Unlimited, Bizar put Dave Arneson on stage alongside Dennis Sustare, author of the FGU role-playing game *Bunnies & Burrows* released the year before, with the authors of FGU's latest offering *Chivalry & Sorcery*, Ed Simbalist and Wilf Backhaus. Those last two had tried to fix the problems with *D&D* by reinventing it from the ground up, just as Arneson hoped to; the longer Arneson waited to unveil his "*D&D* rewrite," the more such competition he would face. Ever eager to play the field, Arneson had already begun working with Bizar, and would in fact start publishing articles through FGU's magazine *Wargaming*, following the lead of Rob Kuntz. That was where Arneson would eventually publish his "Roots" piece rejected by *Dragon*, though it would take some time to appear in print.

The audience at Origins witnessed the battle lines of the "great War" being drawn. In the pages of *Alarums & Excursions*, one observant fan wrote, "Politically, the rapidly widening schism between Gygax and Arneson factions of 'traditional' *D&D* came into the open at Origins. The *Dungeons & Dragons* tournament there was run by Arneson et al., completely independent of TSR, and prizes were supposed to be furnished by Heritage Models." The fan community could see both sides of the issue: "Arneson may feel that if there is to be any single name associated with FRP gaming, it should be not Gygax but Arneson. In this he would have some justification; after all, Blackmoor was the first reasonable approximation to a modern D&D campaign. But Gary Gygax is the man who pushed D&D into the marketplace, and for that he deserves all our thanks." The combatants themselves surely lacked the perspective to see matters so impartially.

The success TSR had enjoyed remained a precarious one, under constant threat. On Friday night at Origins, a group of about fifty industry and community members gathered to discuss the future of the convention. Whereas the first three annual conventions had been effectively run by Avalon Hill and SPI on the East Coast, they had opened the fourth iteration of Origins to bids from companies and clubs around the nation. The five largest companies in the industry were eligible to vote on these bids, that is, Avalon Hill, SPI, Heritage, MiniFigs, and TSR: two board wargame companies, two miniatures firms, and one oddity. Don Greenwood had been certain that TSR would bid for GenCon to host Origins, but by this point, Gygax would rather have abolished Origins than embraced it. Only two serious contenders lobbied to run the convention in 1978: Game Designers' Workshop, who proposed to hold the convention at Illinois State University in Normal, and Metro Detroit Gamers, who offered convention facilities in Ann Arbor. In either case, this would shift Origins from the East Coast to the Midwest, putting it in direct competition with GenCon next summer. Although a potential conflict with GenCon was raised in the room, when the final vote was taken, the bid from the experienced conventioneers in Michigan prevailed. It is no surprise that TSR took this as a direct assault on their business, and Gygax's hatred of Origins only increased.

It seemed like nothing TSR could do would fail to draw competition. When they finally released John Snider's *Star Empires* a bit after Origins, fortuitously in the wake of the release of *Star Wars*, they now had to contend with GDW's *Traveller* role-playing game. Snider was purportedly furious about how his game was handled—it was "pretty well butchered by TSR," he would write to Arneson—and because *Star Empires* lacked rules for personal characters and adventures, *Traveller* captured early market share with ease.

Arneson counseled Snider to "raise as big a fuss as you dare about it," eager to drive new wedges between his friends and TSR. TSR further provoked the Twin Cities coalition when Jake Jaquet announced a forthcoming game to be called *Gamma World*. As a college friend of Tim Kask's, Jaquet had sometimes filled in as a freelance editor—in the March *Dragon*, Kask called him "my voluntary associate (meaning unpaid)," though that issue also began crediting him as "associate fantasy editor." Jaquet had been given a parcel of rules circulating at TSR under the name "Mutant" in order to determine what it would take to turn them into a workable design—that would be Richard Snider's game. Although Jaquet reported that the original manuscript was unsalvageable, he felt that with fresh direction, the core idea could be developed into a worthy product, namely *Gamma World*— which meant that "Mutant" would have no future at TSR. But at the time, Arneson had more pressing matters to fight: he found time before GenCon to fire off another stern letter to TSR about royalties, which was met with another perfunctory response from Brian Blume.

This year GenCon relocated to the largest available space in town: the Lake Geneva Playboy Resort. This would be the only year the convention— an event notorious for juxtaposing the youthful geek culture of the gaming community with the staff of a Playboy property—would occupy the venue. But GenCon did not entirely forsake the Horticultural Hall in 1977: Dave Arneson was scheduled to run a large *Don't Give Up the Ship* event there starting Saturday morning, competing directly with the official *D&D* tournament at the Playboy Club. Arneson had joked in his correspondence with John Snider that he worried about meeting with an "accident" in Lake Geneva, and in fact he did not attend, pleading last-minute car trouble.

Although Arneson personally did not make it to GenCon, his work was on sale there, most prominently at the booth of the Judges Guild. While the cover of the *First Fantasy Campaign* promised to reveal "the history and details of the original fantasy roleplaying game," it pointedly did not name any game in particular, and included the disclaimer, "fantasy game system not included." Nowhere within does the text invoke that dreaded designation *D&D*, nor is Gygax mentioned in the text by name—but the section about the "Egg of Coot," the adversary in Arneson's Blackmoor setting, has passages that echo his experiences working with Gygax at TSR. Arneson had for the past months referred to Gygax as "EGG" in his correspondence, and the text about the Egg stresses its supreme egotism and authoritarianism. "All close servants of the Egg undergo rigorous mental conditioning that is aimed at crushing all their mental initiative. This is then replaced by the overwhelming desire to serve the Egg and do exactly what it wished." This was the purest evil to Arneson. Arneson also portrays the Egg as someone who "is known to hold an unshakeable grudge against anything that has ever in any way caused it difficulty," which leads the Egg to "direct its efforts exclusively towards the demise of this force." While the character of the Egg of Coot had its roots in earlier rivalries in Arneson's Twin Cities wargaming club, it seemed to apply equally well to his current nemesis.

Arneson had predicted that the publication of the *First Fantasy Campaign* would induce TSR to sever its relationship with the Judges Guild. What happen instead at the close of the convention season, around the beginning of September, was that TSR placed the Judges Guild under a new and more onerous licensing agreement, to apply for the next three years. In addition to paying TSR a 2.5 percent royalty on any *D&D* related products, the Judges Guild was required to submit any such products to TSR for review. "Each individual article shall require individual approval by TSR regarding the quality, style and content of the article." Perhaps most visibly, the sets of the *City State of the Invincible Overlord* that Judges Guild then released, which had an endorsement from Dave Arneson on the cover, now shipped with a sticker to cover up that statement with a revised testimonial that the product was "created and approved for use with *Dungeons & Dragons*." Yet the person with the distasteful job of applying those the stickers did not always efface Arneson's endorsement very fastidiously.

Symbolic efforts to pave over Dave Arneson only intensified a perception in the court of public opinion that TSR was obscuring his contribution to the invention of *D&D*. Edward Simbalist, author of the 1977 game *Chivalry & Sorcery*, purchased a copy of the *First Fantasy Campaign* at GenCon, and it inspired him to write some encouraging words to Arneson in private correspondence. "It is clear to me who lit the way for the rest of us to follow," Simbalist attested to honor Arneson. Then, without naming Gygax, he continued, "and those who would usurp you from your rightful place in the world of fantasy wargaming will get short shrift from me."

For the small publishers of competing role-playing game products, Arneson became a martyr, a symbol of the victimization of an entire industry by TSR's tyranny and greed. Everyone was outraged by the cease-and-desist orders TSR had circulated the year before, and the public schism with Arneson was a potential weakness in TSR's armor. Fans could read reports, like one in the *Wild Hunt* fanzine, that "Arneson is reputed to have left TSR for Heritage Models in Texas, and is rumored not to have left his fraction of the rights to *D&D* behind." While that was not strictly accurate, the community rejoiced at the prospect of a *D&D* not under TSR's control.

But by the end of the summer, Arneson's relationship with Heritage had already begun to sour. They continued to bounce around unsigned contract language. So, in the interim, Arneson assumed some provisional position in games publishing at the firm. Arneson complained to John Snider in August, "Generally, they do not know what they are doing, they have failed to take my advice, and do not consult me about games other than those I present to them." The things he had promised to deliver to them, including the Star Trek and John Carter games, had fallen behind schedule as Arneson struggled to delegate them to reliable designers. Although Arneson had promised Jim Oden a title called *Source of the Nile*, developed by his friends Dave Wesely and Ross Maker, that too would fail to appear under the Heritage imprint, as Avalon Hill made a better offer. Arneson did manage to secure a few projects for Heritage's GameTime Games board game imprint, but after Heritage acquired a company called Battleline Games, and assigned its management to vet such internal submissions, Arneson found it difficult to get new work accepted.

As for Richard Snider and his work toward Arneson's *D&D* rewrite, things were not progressing there as smoothly as everyone had hoped either. The two sent draft material back and forth throughout the year. Snider would later write that they proposed to divide the labor such that Arneson had responsibility for the "game mechanics, combat and most of the monster section" while Snider needed to do "some monsters and the magic," but as he puts it, "things didn't quite work out that way." Instead, he says, Arneson's contribution "came in the form of loose notes." Snider was thus left "to

put his material into shape" as well as to his do own work and edit together
the final product.

Although he skipped GenCon, Arneson would return to Lake Geneva that fall,
in November, for the annual shareholder meeting, which again summoned
a familiar crowd to the little gray house at 723 Williams Street. Arneson was
still a shareholder, but he had managed to pass on a few of his shares to his
allies: Heritage Models now held 3 shares, and Dave Wesely 1, which let him
attend in person as well. Megarry, remaining in Texas, chose not to attend,
so Arneson held his proxy: together with Megarry, he had 212 shares to vote.

Gygax opened the meeting with a bullish report on TSR's success: revenue
looked a bit shy of $550,000, with the firm reporting $38,912.74 in profit.
When SPI's industry rankings were published for the 1977 year, TSR easily
moved into third place in the industry. Its stock valuation was increased
to $120 per share, and there was even enough cash on hand to pay out a
dividend of $1.10 per share to shareholders. The treasurer's report delivered
by Kevin Blume suggested that TSR's growing business would benefit from
a professional audit, which was approved for the following year. He continued by giving a report on recent hires. As *Dragon* became more prominent,
someone needed to help out with its sister publication, *Little Wars*, and this
responsibility fell to Joe Orlowski. As the volume of art needed for both
Dragon and the many new *D&D* products in the pipeline had grown beyond
Dave Sutherland's capacity as the single paid artist, Tom Wham and Dave
Trampier had come on board to help out with these responsibilities. Now
the company began to develop structures to support their employees, such
as benefit plans and even a profit-sharing plan. With all of this growth,
there was talk of seeking new offices for the company. Tim Kask and Kevin
Blume would both be salaried employees for the next year.

When his moment came, Arneson proposed that the board of directors
be expanded. This time, rather than asking for there to be four seats, he
only asked for three. The 212 shares he could vote were the only support for
this motion, which Gygax, Carr, and others easily voted down. But Brian
Blume, who with his father's proxy could vote nearly 1,000 shares, chose
to abstain. This became a topic of debate at the one-hour board meeting
of Gygax and Blume that followed directly after the shareholder meeting
concluded; the board meeting minutes note obliquely that "the desirabil-
ity of having a third director on the board was discussed." Blume could

apparently foresee a time when it might make sense to have a third voice on the board—though surely he had no one from the Twin Cities in mind.

Arneson could not have expected his motion to succeed, and one might well wonder why he bothered to show up. But Arneson had another motive in visiting TSR that week. Accompanied by his legal counsel, Arneson returned to 723 Williams Street the day after the shareholder meeting to extract from Brian Blume an accounting of overseas sales of the original game, as well as royalties for the new *Basic Set*. Gygax did not join them.

Confronted with Arneson's skepticism in person, Blume jotted down on a piece of paper three categories of sales: those of the "old" original *D&D* set, the "new" *Basic Set*, and then British sales. For the quarter ending in September, he tabulated 3,519 sales of the original game, 2,927 of the *Basic Set*, and 741 through Games Workshop in the UK. But while the first category of "old" sales yielded to Arneson a royalty of $1,759.50, his allotted 5 percent, for the second category of "new" sales he would be paid only $731.75, just 2.5 percent of the cover price, even though the *Basic Set* sold for the same $10 as the "old" rules. Blume explained this discrepancy by pointing out that Arneson was being paid his full royalty for the *D&D* rulebook included in the *Basic Set*, which was valued at $5, or half the price of the boxed set—but no royalty for the other items that then shipped in the *Basic Set*: not the dice, the *Dungeon Geomorphs* nor the *Monster & Treasure Assortment*, which would have totaled $6.50 sold separately.

There was a certain logic in Blume's position: after all, the *Dungeon Geomorphs* had been on sale since the end of 1976, well before the publication of the *Basic Set*, and Arneson had not demanded a cut of their royalties then: What about packaging them in the *Basic Set* box suddenly entitled Arneson to a share of their proceeds? Arneson had done no more work on them or the *Monster & Treasure Assortment* accessory than he had on any number of other accessories marketed outside the *Basic Set*, like say the *Eldritch Wizardry* supplement. And as for the dice, even though *D&D* had always required their use, dice up to this point had been sold separately by TSR at a hefty markup, and Arneson had never received nor requested any share in those profits. Blume argued that the *Basic Set* was effectively a product bundle that sold the game rules along with some accessories at a slight discount, and that the royalties owed to Arneson were for the game rules, not the accessories.

Though dissatisfied with Blume's explanation, Arneson took the sales data back to the Twin Cities to study alongside the original contracts. A few weeks later, he had weightier matters on his mind: Arneson was briefly hospitalized, and soon diagnosed with diabetes. As he adjusted to a new diet and care regimen, he effectively was unable to travel for some months, and doubtless his work on the "*D&D* rewrite" suffered accordingly.

Overtaking *D&D* in the marketplace was becoming progressively more challenging. At Origins, the Holmes *Basic Set* had attracted only modest attention, selling perhaps 350 copies of the boxed set and a further 150 or so of the standalone rules booklets. But back on TSR's home turf at GenCon the following month, sales of the *Basic Set* edged out the best sales month ever for the original *D&D* game: the three little booklets sold 1,280 copies in August, but the *Basic Set* sold 6 more. Sales always dipped just after the summer conventions, but once print advertisements began to ramp up, sales of the *Basic Set* climbed: in November, the *Basic Set* sold 1,556 copies, about 400 more than the original game. Then in the month of December, sales of the *Basic Set* nearly doubled, reaching 2,767 copies, a figure vastly in excess of any prior *D&D* monthly sales. Something had changed—and it would appear that TSR had arrived as a force in the hobby gaming industry.

As a consequence, Arneson's income in 1977 came predominantly from *D&D* royalties paid by TSR, even though he no longer worked for the company. He received about $1,650 from the Judges Guild for his *First Fantasy Campaign* royalties, and perhaps $1,250 from Heritage, covering their sales of the *Dungeonmaster's Index* and his various work in editing and shepherding other games. But his *D&D* royalties for the year came in at $7,343.11.

The performance of the *Basic Set* would throw into sharp relief the disappointing reception of the *Dungeonmaster's Index*. In October, Heritage advanced Arneson $300 against future royalties, to avoid the bother of writing small checks for the long tail of sales that might trickle in. When Arneson later inquired after the title's performance for the final three months of the year, Oden would bluntly inform him that there were only returns and then nothing: "October, minus six, November, zero, and December, zero." Arneson had raised the possibly of printing more—but Oden replied that "for all purposes the *Dungeonmaster's Index* is out of print" and "I think you can see why we are not too anxious about reprinting."

Arneson would fume to Megarry that Heritage had not done enough to promote the *Index*: that a poor dealer discount rate had been offered, that they sent no flyers or advertisements, but instead just listed the product name and number in mailings. Around the end of the year, Arneson sent out 120 flyers of his own to dealers and managed to secure orders for 124 copies as a result, which he considered a vindication: with proper advertising they could at least put the booklet on some more shelves. But this modest response could not disguise the fact that TSR's *Basic Set*, especially considered together with the looming release of a bestiary called the *Monster Manual*, rendered the *Dungeonmaster's Index* obsolete—and any material those TSR releases did not cover would imminently be reorganized for the remaining *Advanced Dungeons & Dragons* books. So, the *Index* became a subject of largely historical curiosity almost immediately upon its release.

The *Monster Manual* was expected well before the year's end, but came to the public late. This was in part because of a last-minute bar raised by Tolkien Enterprises, a division of the Saul Zaentz licensing company, which controlled the nonliterary rights to the Tolkien estate's intellectual property. Famously, they sent a cease-and-desist letter to TSR late in 1977, coinciding both with the November 27 airing of the Rankin/Bass animated adaptation of *The Hobbit* on television and TSR's release of the *Battle of the Five Armies* game repackaged in a box which prominently declared its adaptation from *The Hobbit*—which had never been licensed. Once Zaentz's lawyers began inspecting TSR's offerings, they similarly objected to the use of "hobbit" in *D&D*, as well as Tolkien terms like "balrog" and "ent." Rather than hazard an escalating confrontation, TSR hastily extirpated the offending language from their products and settled the case, which was heard in a Milwaukee federal court in December. TSR admitted it had "misappropriated" the material, and in return, Tolkien Enterprises permitted them to sell their remaining 1,500 boxed copies of *Battle of the Five Armies*—provided they could do so before March 31, 1978. All copies unsold by that date had to be destroyed.

TSR's failure to license the Tolkien intellectual property exposed an obvious vulnerability to competitors, if not a glaring hypocrisy in a company that rashly unleashed lawyers on fans and imitators alike. SPI, the host of Origins in 1977, had secured a Tolkien license for their *War of the Ring* (1977) game—and closer to home, Heritage Models had licensed the rights for fantasy figures from Tolkien Enterprises, and would publish a Tolkien-branded painting guide. The attention of Zaentz's lawyers may have been drawn to TSR by any number of little birdies on the other side in the "great War."

In the year's final issue of *Dragon*, Gygax gave an update on TSR's plan to fix *D&D*. "'Basic' *D&D* was the first step, and the release of *Advanced Dungeons & Dragons, Monster Manual* is the next. I am personally developing the next two volumes," by which he meant the forthcoming *Players Handbook* and the volume then tentatively titled the *Referee's Guide*. But the focus of Gygax's year-end address was the position of *D&D* and TSR in the industry. "Not surprisingly, we take the view that the creators and publishers know best how to develop the creation." In Gygax's mind, however, the "creators" did not seem to include Arneson, nor indeed anyone not then working at TSR. Gygax effectively doubled down on the rhetoric Tim Kask had expressed at Origins. "Quite a few individuals and firms have sought to cash in on a good thing by producing material from, or for, *D&D* . . . For most of these efforts, TSR has only contempt."

"I cannot resist the analogy of a lion standing over its kill," Gygax explained by way of conclusion. "The vultures scream, and the jackals yap, when the lion drives them off without allowing them to steal bits of the meat." But it is clear here that the "kill" for Gygax was the release of a commercially successful product around *D&D* more so than the conception of a game, and this he credits to TSR alone. "TSR was the lion which brought down the prey, and we intend to have the benefits derived therefrom. If we share with anyone, it will be on our terms."

TSR Turn Results for 1977

Revenue: $545,000 (Barasch ranking 3), profit $39,000
Employees: 13
Stock Valuation: $120
GenCon attendance vs. Origins: 2,300 vs. 2,200

Hobbits in the *Monster Manual*: Supposedly 0
(Actually, a couple snuck in.)

1978: Stolen Glory

Half way through January 1978, Arneson's lawyers sent a letter to TSR posing the most consequential legal question of his royalty dispute: When we read the 1975 contract between Gygax, Arneson, and TSR, how should we understand what constitutes the "set of game rules or game entitled *Dungeons & Dragons*"? Does it only mean the product that TSR had published in 1974, those three copyrighted rulebooks that listed Gygax and Arneson as co-authors? Or does it mean something more expansive, which would encompass anything based on an essential "original idea" behind the game?

The point of dispute homed in on the linchpin clause of the 1975 contract, the one requiring that TSR pay *D&D*'s two co-authors "a royalty of ten percent (10%) of the cover price of game rules or game on each and every copy sold." How should we apply those words to products published after the original *D&D*? Arneson's legal team argued that the "cover price" applied to a product like the Holmes *Basic Set*, which they deemed a repackaging of the game rules: TSR is per the contract within its rights to distribute *D&D* "in any form TSR deems suitable for commercial sales," so maybe we should understand that to include not just the three original boxed booklets, but anything enclosed in a box with the rules.

Whichever form the packaging of the rules might take, it was the price on the product cover that determined Arneson's due compensation, according to this line of thinking. The sought remedy was to immediately send "a check in the amount sufficient to cover all unpaid royalties due Mr. Arneson as calculated on the $9.95 cover price on the new *Dungeons & Dragons* game." A failure to comply within two weeks would compel his lawyers to "take whatever action may be necessary to protect Mr. Arneson's royalty rights, and his interest in the copyright." Appearing below a law firm's letterhead, these words explicitly threatened to take the matter to the courts, in order to secure disputed royalties which at the time amounted to $731.75—though once the uptick in sales at the end of 1977 had registered, that sum would steadily climb.

The fundamental question underlying this legal dispute would redouble with the unveiling of the *Advanced Dungeons & Dragons* game. The *Monster Manual* set a new bar for production quality: this large, hardcover volume with a full-color cover by Sutherland looked nothing like any product of the gaming community to date. Its $10 price tag valued it the same as the entire original *D&D* boxed game. Virtually no one saw the *Monster Manual* before the New Year, so we can safely say *Advanced Dungeons & Dragons* debuted to the public in early 1978. Perhaps no one was less happy to see it than Dave Arneson.

When Arneson had a chance to review a copy of the *Monster Manual* in February, he dispatched a letter to his lawyers fuming that the book "gives no credit to any of the authors who contributed to any of the *D&D* works or supplements. It is all given to Gary." Arneson could only mutter as an aside, "My God, he seems to be out to get everyone." Gygax did make a point, in the preface, to boast that "all new monsters are strictly of this author's creation—just as all those which appeared in *The Strategic Review* were." But he then went on to give various credits for the monsters that were not new: to Steve Marsh for the aquatic monsters extracted from *Blackmoor*, to Terry Kuntz "who was never thanked for his prototypical beholder," to the artist Erol Otus, to his son Ernie, and "to the whole crew at TSR," a credit which could charitably be read to encompass employees past and present. The acknowledgement was broad enough that *Dragon* at the beginning of 1978 could plausibly attest that "author Gary Gygax, in his prefatory remarks, spreads the credit around." Yet in his own copy of the *Monster Manual*, Arneson wrote in three more names that he felt belonged there: his own, and those of Jim Ward and Rob Kuntz.

More materially, Arneson felt the credits in the *Monster Manual* "would seem to indicate that no one will get any royalties but Gary/TSR." Yet there was "no way of checking that," so he suggested: "Maybe you can just ask and get back their answer in writing." But for "answer" Arneson initially wrote the word "lie," which he then lightly struck through and replaced with "answer."

This is not to suggest that Arneson endorsed the *Monster Manual* as a worthy endeavor. In a letter to Dave Megarry in March, he jeered, "What a bunch of clods, wasting money and effort like that on *MM*. Hardbound Whoopee!" Yet in other moments, Arneson expressed frustration and regret at his inability to participate in the game's ongoing development. In a February 12 letter to Games Workshop, he confessed, "I would have greatly liked to have worked on the new D&D and the *Monster Manual*, but my present relations with TSR prevented that, not that they even asked me to do so." To try to rectify that situation, after praising the diverse industry coverage in Games Workshop's new magazine *White Dwarf*, Arneson proposed that he submit a series of articles called "the Unwritten Dungeons & Dragons" in order "to explain some of the areas inadequately covered in the original D&D as well as the new reprint version." Given the degree to which Games Workshop then depended on TSR's beneficence, this could hardly have seemed a risk worth taking to them, and no such articles appeared.

Arneson's fixation on the fate of *D&D* at the time perhaps reflects the difficulties he was experiencing with Heritage and his plans for a *D&D* rewrite. At the beginning of the year, Arneson had written to Jim Oden, reporting that his "fancy Chicago lawyers" had some further suggestions for the employment agreement with Heritage, which had been mired in negotiations for a year. As an example of what he was seeking, he held up the monthly stipend he received as an advance on royalties from the Judges Guild, but Oden saw Arneson's ongoing freelance work for the Judges Guild as a conflict: "I would not really care to see more booklets promoting D&D come out, nor would I think designing new games for other companies would be allowed under our contract," Oden wrote. Arneson remained loathe to tie himself to any single firm, and constantly explored new freelance opportunities in the industry. He even reached out to Avalon Hill, only to be rebuffed by a curt note from Tom Shaw to the effect that "apparently there is some misunderstanding between you and Heritage Models" as "our current sources state that you are tied up with an employment contract with Heritage Models. Therefore, we would not be free to work with you until such time as you are free of this agreement."

For his part, Oden expressed increasing impatience about Arneson's deliverables, the ones promised to yield Heritage $100,000 by this year. "What's the deal now on the new fantasy game?" he asked. To add a little motivation, Oden shared that Heritage had "obtained the rights to publish the new fantasy rules from England, *Bifrost*, and are wondering how much emphasis to put on it." If Arneson dragged his feet, Heritage would simply move on to republishing the back catalog of an outside firm. This provoked a hasty reply from Arneson, in which he signed the Heritage contract with no further dawdling and insisted that any proposed work for Judges Guild gave no cause for concern. "All the stuff I was planning on sending them, subject to your approval, was done some time ago (before I even worked for TSR!)." Indeed, he planned to send the Judges Guild the notes for scenarios from Blackmoor which had roots in the campaign prior to the publication of *D&D*.

When he was done conceding and reconciling, Arneson then leveled with Oden: "You should realize Jim that nothing is ever really going to wipe out D&D." Their best hope was simply that TSR would sabotage itself with its misguided revisions. "We (meaning me and Heritage) are fortunate that TSR decided on their rewrite. It is so expensive and yet so poorly done (i.e. none of the many errors in the original rules have been corrected!) that they are suffering as a consequence." Having perhaps not yet seen figures from the last three months, Arneson seemed to be under the impression that sales of the *Basic Set* were actually declining, and demand for the original set increasing: "People know a rip off when it hits them." While he might not be able to "wipe out" *Dungeons & Dragons*, Arneson promised that his rewrite, now under the working title *Adventures in Fantasy*, "will simply be the very best set of fantasy rules on the market today." Everything from "the very best" on was in all capital letters.

The fight over royalties, the most material of the battles between Gygax and Arneson, would be fought by lawyers, in their own arcane cant. TSR's outside legal counsel John Beard replied to Arneson's challenge on April 11. After reviewing the terms of the April 1975 royalty agreement that Gygax and Arneson executed with TSR for the original *D&D* game, Beard largely reiterated Blume's talking points on the *Basic* rules by stating that "it is TSR's position that the proper royalty base is the current market or cover price ($5.00) for the separately printed game booklet or game rules entitled '*Dungeons & Dragons*.'" Beard then insisted: "The fact that TSR has chosen to market the *Dungeons & Dragons* game rules and the separately developed playing aids as a 'basic set' (currently priced at $9.95) does not entitle Dave Arneson or, for that matter, Gary Gygax, the President of TSR, to a 5% royalty on the entire market price of the 'basic set.' That is because at least $4.95 of the $9.95 price for the basic set is attributable to the separately developed playing aids," including the *Dungeon Geomorphs* and *Monster & Treasure Assortments*, which—as Beard helpfully pointed out—did not exist at the time the April 1975 royalty agreement was signed.

The argument hinged on the essential question of what the "set of game rules or game" meant in the April 1975 *D&D* royalty agreement. Beard asserted TSR's position that those terms "are synonymous to describe only the printed game booklet." To support this point, he posed a hypothetical case: "If TSR were to choose to market together in the same box the *Dungeons & Dragons* game rules ($5.00) with gold and silver miniatures having a separate market price ($1,000.00) as a 'basic set' of *Dungeons & Dragons*, at a total price of $1,005.00, surely you would agree that Dave Arneson is not entitled to a royalty payment of 5% times the entire $1,005.00 price." Beard argued that the same applied to the current situation, that "both Dave Arneson and Gary Gygax are only entitled to 5% of the market price ($5.00) attributable to the *Dungeons & Dragons* game rules, which they co-authored." Beard glossed over the question of who might have authored the additional material included with the *Basic Set*—and whether that might in fact be Gygax, who would then receive a separate royalty for those titles—but the position of TSR is clear: "TSR has faithfully paid Dave Arneson a 5% royalty on the market price (currently $5.00) for each copy of the *Dungeons & Dragons* game rules sold." Beard hinted that it would not be in Arneson's own best interests to force TSR to abandon a *Basic Set* and only publish rulebooks separately from playing aids, as selling those together bolstered sales and thus Arneson's payout.

Arneson, unsurprisingly, did not find TSR's argument persuasive. He compared defining the "game or game rules" as simply the rulebook within the box to doing the same for an Avalon Hill board wargame, neglecting its board and pieces, where it would be "not complete, one without the other." But his primary rejoinder was that since he developed fundamental components, the "original idea" of *D&D*, he should be entitled to compensation for any work based on that core idea. So, although the *Dungeon Geomorphs* and *Monster & Treasure Assortment* did not exist in 1975, he countered, "without *D&D* they would not exist today or have any commercial value without *D&D*." In his frustration, Arneson lamented, "No longer is *D&D* an idea or a concept upon which so much is being done." He was aware that he had not been involved in writing the Holmes *Basic Set*, but he found that irrelevant: "By reducing my part of things to a simple job of writing they destroy the idea that it was the 'concept' of the 'game' that I developed and upon which all this stands today."

But royalty contracts involving copyright assignments are usually understood to cover creative products resulting from "a simple job of writing," and not to extend to things like "an idea or a concept." When in 1975 Arneson signed a contract with TSR for "the set of game rules or game entitled *Black-moor*," he clearly believed that it applied only to the written content submitted for the printed booklet—certainly it did not apply to the idea or concept of Blackmoor itself, which Arneson felt free to detail in his *First Fantasy Campaign* in 1977. But Arneson seemed to interpret the original *D&D* contract very differently. If indeed Arneson, by virtue of his role in creating *D&D*, was entitled to compensation for any and all playing aids built on top of the game, then one must wonder why he had not yet demanded royalties for *Greyhawk* or *Eldritch Wizardry*, or from other firms who produced similar *D&D* accessories, like the Judges Guild.

Concerns about the *Basic Set* were only the first battle in this "great War"—in his correspondence with his lawyers, Arneson also fretted that TSR had not addressed "the *Monster Manual* royalties." Arneson knew well that the *Monster Manual* was more detailed than the description of monsters in the original *D&D*, and that he had not personally participated in that process of expansion. "They will," Arneson anticipated, "bring up the point that I have done no additional work for them, while others have done so." Addressing that possibility, Arneson could only reply with a wounded snarl, "They never even hinted that they wanted to see my stuff after I left nor considered (reacted to) any overtures I made after I left." Given how unpleasant his parting was for everyone concerned, TSR's unresponsiveness could hardly have been a surprise.

Extending Arneson's line of argument about the additional *Basic Set* contents to *Advanced Dungeons & Dragons* had potentially dire implications for the industry. Back in 1971, when Gygax adapted and expanded Dane Lyons's *Arbela* rules, he reached a point where he believed he had developed a new game, which he titled *Alexander the Great*. Gygax evidently felt he passed a similar threshold in the development of *AD&D*, where he had altered and elaborated the original rules until the result was a distinct game, with a slightly different name. But he was certainly not the first to cross that line.

In the introduction to *Tunnels & Trolls*, Ken St. Andre wrote of his own such modifications: "So it is no longer *Dungeons & Dragons*—it is now *Tunnels & Trolls*. Our thanks go to Gary Gygax and Dave Arneson who created the original *D&D*, but this is basically a completely different game, bearing about the same relationship to *D&D* as *Careers* does to *Monopoly* or Chevrolet does to Ford." This last analogy perhaps does not serve St. Andre well, as stripped of the logos, many drivers might have trouble differentiating a Chevrolet from a Ford: they basically work the same way and do the same thing. As the originator of foundational concepts behind *D&D*, was Arneson then entitled to a share of the royalties for *Tunnels & Trolls*, or say *Chivalry & Sorcery*? And then why would TSR have not sued for the same already? The answer was that TSR knew they would lose: copyright law does not protect adaptations of "original ideas," but instead copying substantially from particular written works.

Regarding the *Monster Manual*, Arneson fumed that "Robert Kuntz and I are evidently not getting anything when over half the contents originated with the two of us (and almost a third from me alone)." Even if many of the monsters originated with Arneson, the question of how much Arneson contributed to the original *D&D* had little bearing on his access to royalties: Gygax started taking that question off the table back in 1973, when he offered, "I'll whip out a booklet (Gygax and Arneson, I trust)" and then "trust you'd like to split royalties." Once he tendered that proposal, and then agreed to the 1975 contract, Gygax largely mooted the legal question of who contributed what to the game. Provided that the contract was valid, and that it applied to these later works like the *Monster Manual*, Arneson was entitled to his half of the royalties no matter how much or little he personally contributed to the game's development.

In May, when Arneson assembled a curriculum vitae enumerating his "Books in Print," he listed the *Monster Manual* under his "planned 1978" titles. And Arneson certainly planned to clarify to TSR that he was in fact a co-author of it, per a letter he would send to them in June. "This item," Arneson posited, "clearly consists of material from *Dungeons & Dragons*," a fact that is "stated within the work itself." So while he politely entertained the possibility that "there has been a bookkeeping error and the check was not sent," he quickly homed in on another alternative, "that TSR is in violation of my *Dungeons & Dragons* contract."

If TSR could not explain the situation, Arneson threatened, "I will be forced to expand my present legal activities now being undertaken on my behalf, to include the matter of royalty money for the *Dungeons & Dragons Monster Manual*." The reply from TSR's Milwaukee attorneys returned to the essential question: What did the "game or game rules" in the 1975 contact really mean? "Simply put," Beard responded, "it is TSR's position that the April 1, 1975 agreement relates only to the specific game rules entitled *Dungeons & Dragons* which existed at the time of that agreement." By contrast, the *Monster Manual* is "an original work authored solely by Gary Gygax, and was separately copyrighted by TSR in 1977," and thus "there are no unpaid royalty payments due" to Arneson for it. Arneson would never accept that position, and the conflict intensified accordingly.

TSR staff increased only gradually through 1978, but as a newspaper article in March observed, the business had "16 young, imaginative employees packed into a small, two-story house at 723 Williams Street in Lake Geneva." Cramming their activities into that single-family home made for close quarters, and prevented any real expansion. As early as March, Arneson had already caught wind that TSR would "buy the downtown bowling alley and upper floors of the Korner Bar" where he and the Twin Cities coalition had been wont to hang out.

This referred to the property at 772 Main Street in Lake Geneva, which had for much of the century housed the Hotel Clair. Famously, the basement of the hotel was a bowling alley, though Lake Geneva residents of the day knew the place mainly for the first-floor Clair Lounge—the back of the GenCon programs for 1973 and 1974 advertised the lounge as a nearby destination "for your listening and dancing pleasure." TSR purchased the building from Genevieve Payne, the last surviving member of the Lazzaroni family; her father had bought the building in 1918, at which time it housed an ice cream parlor and boarding rooms in the upper floors. The acquisition of the Hotel Clair closed in June—though just as was the case with 723 Williams Street, it was not TSR that purchased the building, but instead a partnership consisting of Gygax and Blume, who would then lease the building to TSR. As the building cost $140,000, the down payment they placed on it easily exceeded the $27,500 mortgage they had taken out on 723 Williams just two years before.

When TSR took over the Hotel Clair, an iconic location in the heart of Lake Geneva, they began to change the face of the town. But they found the property in a state of dire disrepair. The dilapidation of the building was no secret: fifteen years before, in 1963, a partial ceiling collapse at the Tic-Toc Grill in the Hotel Clair had injured several diners and led to a series of expensive law suits against the Lazzaroni family. But TSR staffers weary of the cramped conditions at 723 Williams happily raided the front desk of the hotel and took room keys as souvenirs. The first floor was redone as a retail space, the future home of the Dungeon Hobby Shop, and the basement bowling alley would serve as a warehouse. The two upper floors became new office space for the staff of TSR—apart from Dragon Publications, which would remain headquartered at 723 Williams.

Dragon had moved beyond a circulation of 7,500 at the start of the year, and it would transition from a bimonthly to a monthly magazine in April. By this point, it had become a prominent venue for not just games but fantasy literature. February marked the publication of a teaser for Andre Norton's forthcoming novel *Quag Keep*, the first fantasy novel that adopted *D&D* as its setting. It featured real-world gamers who are transported into the world of Greyhawk, foreshadowing a rapidly approaching time when the broader

The entrance to the Dungeon Hobby Shop at 772 Main Street in Lake Geneva, circa 1982 (top left); the back of the building, still advertising the Hotel Clair (top right); and a room key from the defunct hotel (bottom). Top left and right courtesy of Merle and Jackie Rasmussen.

public at large would wonder how separate playing these games was from the fantasies that they depicted. By June, the book was out, just in time for the summer conventions.

Going in to the convention season, TSR was struggling in the court of public opinion despite its growing media platform: the community just found Arneson's talking points more compelling. The Chaosium's book *Authentic Thaumaturgy*, which had reached fans before the end of April, matter-of-factly refers to *Dungeons & Dragons* as a work "by Dave Arneson, edited by Gary Gygax." Gygax continued to assiduously promote his own contribution with his July editorial in *Dragon*. In it, he once again positioned himself as the font of fantasy gaming, given that "the 'Fantasy Supplement' to *Chainmail* (copyright 1971) would pioneer a whole new form of game." But if he hoped to convince the fan community, he quickly undermined himself by casting shade on game systems that are "currently in vogue amongst the fringe group which haunt the pages of 'Amateur Press Association' publications" like *Alarums & Excursions*, offhandedly asserting that "APAs are generally beneath contempt, for they typify the lowest form of vanity press." Seething, Gygax insinuated that "certain small publishers of amateur magazines or second-rate work have accused TSR of maintaining a proprietary interest in *Dungeons & Dragons* from a purely mercenary motivation," though he could only infer they did so to further their own ambitions in the market. In the interest of something like full disclosure, Gygax did spare a footnote for that admission: "I have been the target of some pretty vicious and petty attacks from some of the 'APAs.'" Nonetheless, he accused his attackers of "paranoia and persecution complexes," apparently without any self-consciousness. In some ways, Gygax was as embittered by his success as Arneson was by his exclusion.

At the traditional battleground of Origins, Gygax would return that summer in person to confront his many challengers. Debate about the respective attendance of the conventions returned to public view in the letter column of Don Lowry's magazine *Campaign*, the successor to the old *Panzerfaust*, early in 1978. As usual, Avalon Hill, in the person of Don Greenwood, feuded with Gygax over which should truly be considered the national gaming convention. Greenwood had been an eyewitness to the birth of TSR, at GenCon in 1973, and he maintained that "GenCon is what got TSR off and running," whereas he insisted that Origins was independent of Avalon Hill. Even Gygax could see the futility in this feuding as he admitted, "those that have communicated their desires to TSR have stated that the controversy about GenCon and Origins is silly." But Gygax could not let the matter rest, wading into the debate with stubborn scorn, because this year Origins posed its most direct challenge to GenCon yet: the previous three Origins had transpired on the East Coast, but now it would come to the Midwest, just weeks before GenCon, in a move likely to siphon attendees and lessen Gen-Con's impact. The bid last year from the Metro Detroit Gamers had secured a place for Origins in Ann Arbor, Michigan, centered around the sprawling Bursley Hall of the university there.

Despite his misgivings, Gygax would run the Origins *D&D* tournament— after all, the commute was relatively short, and it was better that TSR handle it than Arneson and the Twin Cities coalition. Famously, TSR ran a progressive three-part adventure that confronted parties with hill giants, frost giants, and fire giants. The story "is tied to that which will be run at Gen Con, so that those gamers who attend both conventions and play in the D&D tournies at each will be doubly pleased," Gygax promised *Campaign*. No doubt in retaliation for his apparent cameo appearance as the Egg in the *First Fantasy Campaign*, Gygax could not resist caricaturing his co-author in this adventure setting: the hill giant chief was named Nosnra— which spells "Arneson" in reverse, minus the "e"—and the background text describes him as "a grossly fat and thoroughly despicable creature, sly and vicious, loving ambush and backstabbing." This only slightly coded reference was probably overlooked by the tournament participants, but Gygax surely delighted in leading groups to slay that loathsome adversary. And this dig would not be solely for the benefit of the 275 convention attendees who competed in the tournament: at the conclusion of the event, TSR sold published copies of the adventure as "modules," with the first being the *Steading of the Hill Giant Chief*. *D&D* modules quickly became a lucrative side business for TSR, and they carried Gygax's insult to a far wider audience than the summer conventioneers.

The dispute between Arneson and TSR escalated at the awards ceremony held at the end of Origins, on Sunday afternoon. Traditionally, the organizers had bestowed the Charles S. Roberts Awards for excellence in board game design; this year, in a bid to reposition Origins as a convention covering the entire gaming scene, they instituted a new awards category, the H. G. Wells Awards, which recognized achievement in miniature wargaming. By their reckoning, *D&D* fell under the miniature category, and from the ballots tabulated at Origins, it received a number of accolades:

unsurprisingly, it took "All Time Best Role Playing Rules," and it tied for entry into the miniatures Hall of Fame. But it was more surprising to see a fantasy role-playing game awarded "Greatest Contribution to the Hobby, Game or Rules, 1967–1977."

Representatives of TSR happily collected plaques for these honors—but Dave Arneson beat TSR to the podium to claim the "All Time Best Role Playing Rules" plaque for himself. At the time, no one wanted to make a scene, but shortly after Origins, Arneson was asked to return the plaque to the Metro Detroit Gamers so that it could be given to TSR, who had lodged a complaint. As Arneson would explain, "I was informed that traditionally all awards were given to the company that published the winning game, or set of rules, and not the author, or designer."

Arneson flatly refused to return the award—instead, he demanded that he be given the plaques for the other two H. G. Wells Awards bestowed on *D&D*. He widely circulated a letter detailing his reasoning, comparing the situation to "Bantam Books receiving the awards for J. R. R. Tolkien's works or 20th Century Fox, *Star Wars*'s Oscars." He concluded with a plea on behalf of the individual, the freelance designer without any supporting employer: "If the state of this hobby has already reached a point where creativity is neither recognized nor appreciated then something should be done about it." In a brief postscript, Arneson could only grouse that, "if you want to receive the award for the game you designed, you are best advised to be there to run up (and I do mean run) and get it, for you will certainly be unlikely to get it any other way."

If Arneson hoped this controversy would advance his cause in the "great War," the response was surely disappointing. Within a few weeks, TSR had received a copy of the "All Time Best Role Playing Rules" plaque, furnished by the Origins committee, but Arneson did not receive duplicates of the other two awards that he had demanded. Whatever their disagreements with TSR, several of the large companies behind Origins simply could not support Arneson's position. Writing on behalf of Avalon Hill, Don Green-wood explained, "We do not agree with Mr. Arneson that in all cases the awards should go to the designer; as in the case of Avalon Hill games, the designer oftentimes has done a good deal less than 50% of the eventual game which the public sees." Indeed, as Avalon Hill "takes the responsibility of paying a full-time staff to correct design submissions submitted by others, we feel that the awards should rightly go to the publishers." The

Dungeons & Dragons product including the Holmes boxed *Basic Set* (1977), the *Players Handbook* (1978), and the module *Steading of the Hill Giant Chief* (1978), with dice.

situation prompted the steering committee for the awards to amend the official policy going forward: "In cases of doubt as to who designed what, the person/company stated by the game manufacturer will be used, for they should have an idea as to who did what." But in the future, they "hope this is not needed."

GenCon in 1978 would transpire in the aftermath of that drama. Having outgrown the capacity of Lake Geneva, even with the addition of the Playboy resort, TSR took a page from the Origins playbook and relocated its convention to a college campus: the University of Wisconsin at Parkside, in nearby Kenosha. But after all of Gygax's fierce positioning of GenCon as the foremost gaming convention in the country, GenCon XI was a crushing disappointment. In March, Gygax had told a reporter that "we're expecting between 4,000 and 6,000 people" to make it to Parkside, but actual attendance came in lower than the year before, at perhaps below 2,000 people—a figure little better than half the turnout for Origins a few weeks before.

There was no shortage of externalities to blame. Torrential rain on Thursday and Friday prompted Tim Kask to speculate, "we figure that we lost some 500 attendees to the weather alone." Less plausibly, Gygax suggested in *Dragon* "some nasty people in Lake Geneva actually misdirected people or told them that GenCon was cancelled this year!" But Kask knew the real culprit: "There is no way to estimate how much attendance damage GenCon XI suffered from the proximity in time and space to Origins 78. We feared that it would have an unpleasant effect, and our fears seem to have justified to some extent." As such, Gygax would be forced to swallow his pride and concede, "There is no question that MDG and Origins beat GenCon hands down in most categories in 1978." He joked that "crow is not unpalatable when properly parboiled and baked in a humble pie."

In hindsight, the release of the *Players Handbook*, the first substantial chunk of the *Advanced Dungeons & Dragons* system, overshadowed most other events of consequence at GenCon in 1978. In the preface to that volume, Gygax articulated how he saw his role in the industry. "Authoring these works means that, in a way, I have set myself up as the final arbiter of fantasy role playing in the minds of the majority of *D&D* adventurers." This did not strike Gygax as an undeserved position: "Well, so be it, I rationalized. Who better than the individual responsible for it all as creator of the 'Fantasy Supplement' in *Chainmail*, the progenitor of *D&D*; and as the first proponent of fantasy gaming and a principal in TSR, the company one thinks of when fantasy games are mentioned, the credit and blame rests ultimately here." Missing from this statement is any concession to the original co-author of *D&D*, though toward the end of the preface, he acknowledged some twenty or so people by name, with Arneson first among them—but only because the list was in alphabetical order. In the court of public opinion, this would not go over well: as one commentator in *Alarums & Excursions* held, "The manner in which persons other than Gygax get credit seems a little chintzy. They get a small mention in the introduction as a string of names."

But there was another development at GenCon that year, one that had little visible impact at the time but serious long-term implications. Nine-thirty Sunday night, at the Wisconsin Beer Garden, more than twenty games companies held an impromptu meeting to vent about TSR's mistreatment of exhibitors and dealers at Parkside: aside from the many issues about placement and location of booths, they were inadequately lit when the sun went down, which led some furious dealers to move lights around, causing widespread circuit failures. The general anti-TSR sentiment in the room led to the founding of a new trade group, initially called the Association of Game Manufacturers, soon to be known as GAMA. The group aimed to allow small publishers to band together to share some of the costs of developing the market and protect themselves from the whims of larger firms: originally, they intended to restrict the group to manufacturers with sales of less than $500,000 per year who marketed at least one game with a print run of one thousand or more copies. Each company would be granted one vote in association decisions regardless of their size. Rick Loomis from Flying Buffalo took the initiative to help organize the membership, and found Avalon Hill and SPI were both amenable to joining on equal footing with these smaller companies despite their size. This trade industry association would soon position itself as the authority behind the Origins convention, and a counterweight to GenCon and its administrators in Lake Geneva.

Licking its wounds after a disappointing GenCon, the "Game Wizards"—as TSR now called themselves—nonetheless had plenty to celebrate. Their relocation to the Hotel Clair began shortly after the convention, at the end of the summer. A notice printed at the back of *Dragon* announced the forthcoming change of address of the Dungeon Hobby Shop, advising shoppers to expect a "Grand Opening Week Celebration in the autumn." TSR remained small enough that this move incurred some significant post-GenCon delays to processing orders, for which Gygax issued an apology in a note to Don Lowry's *Campaign*. The wait would be worth it.

"Our new building is quite large," Gygax explained proudly, "and over the next year or so it will be remodeled to house all of TSR's operations. Initially, only shipping, processing, accounting, and the shop will move." A place of pride in the new building had been set aside for TSR's most recent acquisition: a Burroughs computer, which would occupy "a sacrosanct and pure room." Gygax promised that thanks to the new computer, and more spacious quarters, order fulfillment would improve by October. Next to the Hotel Clair itself, that computer was the most expensive thing TSR Hobbies had ever bought, at a cost of over $40,000 dollars on an extended lay-away plan.

When it came to TSR sales, "the 'Best Seller' list is topped by the *Advanced D&D Players Handbook*, closely followed by *D&D Basic Set*," Gygax reported. In the first three months after its release, the *Players Handbook* sold around ten thousand copies, and its numbers would only go up from there. Soon, TSR planned to publish the 1975 and 1976 Origins tournament dungeons in module form, as the *Tomb of Horrors* and the *Expedition to the Barrier Peaks*, respectively. On the horizon, *D&D* fans could look forward to the "long awaited *Advanced Dungeons & Dragons Dungeon Masters Guide*."

Mike Carr had already begun to scale up the development and production staff to meet the demand for new releases, bringing on Allen Hammack and Tim Jones to help whip games into shape—Carr had to edit the *Players Handbook* personally. But to meet the seemingly insatiable public appetite for *D&D* products, TSR also needed to shift some of the burden for game designs off of its overworked president. So, they posted a job opening in the twentieth issue of *Dragon* seeking "an individual to work directly with Gary Gygax on fantasy of all sorts—D&D and AD&D principally." The position required: fluency with *D&D*; the ability to write and design, and to vet and develop freelance submissions; and the public presence to represent the company at conventions and similar gatherings. Applicants had to complete a written test on the *D&D* system and submit a sample dungeon level; hiring would not begin until after the New Year. The test included open-ended queries like "What happens to paralyzed characters?" or "Give three reasons why magic-users can't wield swords in *AD&D*."

One person who took a predictable interest in measuring TSR's expansion and success was Dave Arneson. He had, in October, dispatched Dave Megarry to TSR to "exercise his right as a shareholder and as an agent of Mr. Arneson, a shareholder, and Professor Barker, an author with right of inspection, to examine the corporation's books and records of account, minutes and/or record of shareholders." Barker joined this action as he continued to seek better terms for licensing his *Petal Throne* projects outside the TSR umbrella. But primarily, Megarry was tasked to assess exactly how much money might be at stake in the formal lawsuit that everyone knew was coming. Arneson's lawyers helpfully reminded TSR that "Mr. Megarry is familiar with the

A brown paper bag passed along for signatures at TSR offices, circa early 1978, which features Ernie Gygax, Ken Reek, Tim Jones, Joe Orlowski, Tim Kask, "Shlump da Orc" (maybe Sutherland, maybe Dave Trampier?), Dave Sutherland, Mike Carr, Vicki Miller (later Blume), Kevin Blume, Mary Blume, and Gary Gygax. Notably absent: Brian Blume.

corporation's books, and thus, his inspection should not interfere with the operation of your business."

Anyone who scrutinized TSR's books that autumn would have found a very different company than the one that existed only two years before. Over the past year or so, Gygax and Blume had converted the bulk of their remaining royalty agreements into stock grants to maximize their stakes in the company. Consequently, this marked a time when the governance of the company was effectively fixed: Gary Gygax held 671 shares to Brian Blume's 775. While other minor shareholders would come and go over the next seven years, the holdings of the company's two main owners would remain steady at those levels.

Under a 1978 offer, many of the early employees now held 5 shares of stock, including Kevin Blume's wife Mary, who had been staff since around the start of the year. Even people like Ken Reek from shipping had their 5 shares. Gygax's son Ernie now held 15 shares, and Mary Gygax had amassed 35. Jointly, including the 200 shares held by family patriarch Melvin Blume, the Blume family holdings of 990 shares represented 48.6 percent, just shy of half the stock outstanding in the company. This preserved the board-level structure that treated Gygax and Blume as partners, where neither had formal control, and both of their consents would be required for any major venture, even though Gygax was nominally president and Blume the secretary. In a letter earlier in the year to Bill Hoyt, Gygax explained that on matters of contracts, "I cannot make a unilateral decision, for anything that TSR formally agrees to must be signed by both the President and the Secretary," and TSR contracts of this era do universally show signature blanks for both.

The first shareholder meeting to be held at the Hotel Clair, on the afternoon of November 8, welcomed a far more diverse attendance than the unhappy meeting at 723 Williams Street two years before. Arneson had no business with the shareholders this time, and no dramatic vote was proposed to expand the board of directors. The shareholders approved the acquisition of the new Burroughs computer, and reaffirmed Gygax and Blume as directors. A nearly unanimous vote—only Dave Wesely, wielding his single share, opposed it—held the value of TSR stock at $120, the same as the year before, despite the fact that revenue now neared $1 million.

Afterward, the two members of the board held their annual meeting, at which they approved salaries for the officers of the company. Gygax's yearly wages were set at $20,000; Blume's salary was fixed at $17,500. But "in view of the continuous nature of the service provided by the directors," the pair then approved for themselves separate annual compensation for their roles on the board, at $5,000 for Blume as chairman and $2,500 for Gygax as a director, which effectively gave them equivalent salaries. They derived compensation from other sources as well: the partnership of Gygax and Blume that leased TSR its two buildings received monthly payments of $2,113 from TSR, which delivered Gygax and Blume a net profit of a bit over $1,000 for the year. And then, there was the Jo Powell Agency, which went from grossing around $30,000 in 1977 to $50,000 in 1978, yielding a few thousand more dollars of net profits for the Gygax and Blume families.

But of course, Gygax stood to gain more from royalties than from salary or side perks: over $30,000 for 1978 alone. Gygax had signed a comprehensive agreement early in 1978 for future game design work, which would encompass all *Advanced D&D* book royalties. It awarded him a flat 2.5 percent royalty on "any and all items designed by the author from 1 January 1978 to the termination of his employ at TSR." The contract Blume originally typed up had only 2 percent—Blume was always bargaining to drive royalty rates down—but a hand-correction initialed by both of them shows that Gygax was able to convince his penny-pinching partner to bump the figure to 2.5 percent.

Aside from setting salaries for themselves and the remainder of the officers, then including Kevin Blume, Mike Carr, Tim Kask and Dave Sutherland, TSR's board in 1978 also reserved a $16,000 salary for an anticipated hire: Will Niebling, who they expected to join the following year as an assistant vice president of sales and marketing. They must have been thrilled to staff that position with a gamer: a long-time member of the Metro Detroit Gamers circles, a participant in the original Detroit "Ryth" *D&D* Campaign, and a veteran of many GenCons. Gygax trusted Niebling well.

Arneson saw no point in attending the shareholder meeting when his energies could be better spent prosecuting his "great War" in the court of public opinion. Arneson remained preoccupied with the H. G. Wells Awards scandal from Origins that summer, perhaps because it served as a ready metaphor for his entire situation. At around this time, he wrote a parable about "Blog the Cro-Magnon," whom he depicted as inventing the essential idea behind the wheel by rolling a heavy load across a fallen log. Following Blog's foundational discovery, a host of other Cro-Magnons made incremental improvements to the design; Gazork, for example, pared away some of the roots and branches from the log, and Zebelok found a better way to fix the cargo to the trunk. Ultimately, the work of several later innovators resulted in something we might recognize as the axle of a car. Arneson uses this parable to argue that "those who take another's idea may well shape and refine it to the point where it bears little resemblance to the original," but "without that idea we would still be walking around lugging stuff on our backs."

So too it was with *D&D*—Arneson could accept that what he built was just "a rough prototype" and that some other people, no one he would care to name, had afterward improved it. But all their "fancy packaging" and "promotion and advertising" were worthless unless they sold something people wanted. He mounted this entire argument to reach the conclusion that game designers should get awards rather than publishers who profit from games, because "too often the person whose ideas gave them that profit make little or nothing." The initial inventors of ideas deserve the glory, and presumably the money, because "without their spark, no matter how dim, there would be nothing."

Arneson had trouble finding a venue interested in publishing the story of Blog the Cro-Magnon, but he had no shortage of other public outlets to tell his side of the story. Howard Thompson of *Space Gamer* magazine reached out to Arneson after Origins and secured an interview with him in the fall, which begins with a somewhat cautious editorial note explaining that Arneson "had a major role in the creation of the classic *Dungeons & Dragons*." The interview questions were delivered by mail, and Arneson was at the time so preoccupied with the ongoing controversy over the H. G. Wells Awards that he simply wrote in a new section about it. Overall, Arneson in that interview expressed new levels of disconnection from the narrative about the history of the game advanced by Gygax.

Thompson attempted to engage Arneson on some of the historical particulars frequently mentioned by Gygax, such as their mutual participation in the Castle & Crusade Society—which warranted notice in the foreword to the 1974 *D&D* books. When asked point blank, Arneson was willing to concede that "the Society set up a mythical map where 'kingdoms' were assigned to the 'lords' of the Society and a society-wide campaign, using medievals was proposed, which never got anywhere." But he did not volunteer anything about how Blackmoor was indeed his personal spot on that map. Instead, when pressed with the question "How did you come to create that infamous first campaign, Blackmoor?" Arneson sidestepped that background, answering: "One Saturday after reading several S&S novels, eating popcorn, and watching horror/monster movies all day, I designed a maze-like dungeon and populated it with orcs and similar beasties." While the idea of dungeon adventures may have arisen just how Arneson described it, the question that Thompson actually asked involved the Castle & Crusade Society in several respects. Arneson also passed over the fact that the selection of "orcs and similar beasties," as he had freely put it in the *First Fantasy Campaign* the year before, "began with only the basic monsters in *Chainmail*." *Chainmail* received absolutely no mention in the interview.

Arneson also very much bemoaned the process through which *D&D* was created and the lamentable state of the published product. This led him to walk a very fine line between criticizing *D&D* and disowning it, one that his legal advisers might not have encouraged. In part, Arneson surely did this to promote his work for the Judges Guild; for example, he claimed in one breath, "I was not consulted on many aspects of the final work" on *D&D* and in the next promised that in the *First Fantasy Campaign* he had "tried to show where I would have liked *Dungeons & Dragons* to have gone." When Thompson drilled down on the question of how the collaboration had operated, and asked directly, "How was the final rules draft developed?" Arneson explained: "All editing on the final draft was done in Lake Geneva and I did not see it before it went to press. It was very much a case of me providing various ideas and concepts but not having any say as to how they were used." For the first time in a public venue, Arneson alluded to the looming lawsuit: "I am reluctant to say more due to the present legal situation."

This line of argument was something of a double-edged sword for Arneson. While he was eager to show that Gygax had delivered a poor product and acted in bad faith, Arneson portrayed himself as so removed from the process that he did not even get to review the work Gygax was doing. This was a far more expansive version of complaints Arneson had been making for years about the "errors" in *D&D*. But ultimately it did not bode well for Arneson's *D&D* royalty challenge if he "did not see it before it went to press" and he effectively contributed nothing more than "various ideas and concepts" with no say over whether or how they were used. These words would be read by TSR's legal team with no small interest.

When Thompson politely inquired about his current works in progress, Arneson name-dropped *Adventures in Fantasy*, though he was unsure if it would be published by Heritage or Fantasy Games Unlimited. His "agreement with Heritage is only a right of first refusal and nothing more," he ruefully explained. "Mostly they have refused."

Arneson did seem to collect incomplete projects over the years, things that simmered on a back burner in search of a publisher or some other impetus to complete them, like his idea for a fantasy figure painting guide. Arneson characterized himself as a freelancer, pointing out how he had any number of projects in the works across the industry: he suggested that his Japanese role-playing project formerly called "Bushido" would now be called *Samurai*, and that the Chaosium was in talks to publish it. This renaming was no doubt motivated by the publication of a 1978 role-playing game called *Bushido* by Tyr Games. Arneson also named the two dungeon projects for the Judges Guild that Jim Oden had viewed so unfavorably at the beginning of the year: "Island of the Wolf" and "City of the Gods." As Arneson had promised to Oden, these were not exactly fresh material, but instead campaign work Arneson had done for Blackmoor long ago. Yet getting them into print remained elusive.

Arneson's prospects to see his work accepted by Heritage did not improve when, at the end of the year, a few key managers left the company to start their own venture, Yaquinto. Rather than clearing the way for Arneson to accept a more senior role guiding the direction of development, this instead induced Jim Oden to lure Howard Barasch over from SPI to join Heritage; Barasch in turn quickly brought in his own person to manage Heritage's miniatures projects. These changes only further reduced the likelihood that Arneson would see Heritage publish *Adventures in Fantasy* or any of his other designs, despite the contract he had hastily signed at the beginning of the year.

The uncertain fate of *Adventures in Fantasy* made Arneson's claim on *D&D* more crucial to his professional future. By this point, the steady growth in *D&D* sales had begun to afford Arneson compensation well beyond what he would have received as a TSR employee. For the first half of 1978, Arneson received combined royalties on the original *D&D* game and the *Basic Set* amounting to $5,611.1. For the third quarter of 1978 alone, TSR gave him $5,759.14. In the fourth quarter that rose to $6,635.50, so in total, he received more than $18,000 in royalties from TSR for the year—a little more than half as much as the $30,000 Gygax received. While the story of Blog the Cro-Magnon warns that inventors often "make little or nothing," Arneson's share was, say, larger than Brian Blume's base salary at TSR. Augmented by over $2,000 from the Judges Guild, and perhaps $500 from miscellaneous work for Heritage, this afforded Arneson a good living by the standards of game designers of the day. But Arneson felt that his contribution to *Dungeons & Dragons* entitled him to far more, and he intended to get it.

TSR Turn Results for 1978

Revenue: $930K (Barasch ranking 3), profit $58,000
Employees: 19
Stock Valuation: $120
GenCon attendance vs. Origins: 2,000 vs. 3,400

Disputed H. G. Wells Awards: 3

III The Everfull Purse

1979: Treasure in the Steam Tunnels

The most famous move in the battle for *Dungeons & Dragons* would play out on February 7, 1979. That was when Arneson's legal team issued its summons to Gygax in the long-anticipated legal action brought by Arneson against TSR. It was a game changer, an escalation that seemed sure to dominate the story of *D&D* for the next year or more—it was unthinkable that anything would overshadow it. What could?

Arneson's complaint cast a wide net, naming not just TSR Hobbies as a defendant, but also Gygax himself, and even the defunct partnership of Tactical Studies Rules—surely because his contract for *D&D* was with that partnership. First, the complaint represented that Arneson was unjustly deprived of his contractual 5 percent royalty on the cover price of the *Basic Set*, the *Monster Manual*, and the *Players Handbook*. It reinforced that point by alleging that the publication of *Advanced D&D* as "solely authored by defendant Gygax" effectively has "stolen the rights of Plaintiff as the co-author of *Dungeons & Dragons* to receive royalties upon the said work and its derivations." Arneson thus demanded not only that he receive his 5 percent royalty on all of those works, but a minimum of $50,000 in "pecuniary damages resulting from the willful omission of Plaintiff's name as co-author" and "false representation of Defendant Gygax as the sole author" of those works. Add to this punitive damages in excess of $50,000 to reflect the harm to Arneson's "reputation in his profession." Finally, the complaint insisted that the court prevent TSR from any "further publication of *Dungeons & Dragons* or any work copied, derived or adapted therefrom without disclosing Plaintiff's co-authorship thereof upon the cover or box-top of such game or game rules."

At the time, the combined value of all the shares outstanding of TSR stock stood at around a quarter of a million dollars. Although TSR racked

STATE OF MINNESOTA

COUNTY OF HENNEPIN

DISTRICT COURT

FOURTH JUDICIAL DISTRICT

David L. Arneson,

      Plaintiff,

vs.

Gary Gygax, Tactical
Study Rules, a partnership
consisting of Gary Gygax and Brian
Blume, and T S R Hobbies, Inc.,
a corporation.

      Defendants.

COMPLAINT

Comes now the Plaintiff, David L. Arneson, and for his cause of action against the Defendants, states and alleges:

JURISDICTION

1.1   At all times herein material, Plaintiff has been and now is a resident of the State of Minnesota.

1.2   At all times herein material, Defendant Gary Gygax (hereinafter referred to as "Gygax") has been and now is a Wisconsin resident residing in Lake Geneva, Wisconsin.

1.3   Defendant Gygax was a partner in Defendant Tactical Study Rules, a partnership consisting of Gary Gygax and Brian Blume until on or about July 14, 1975, when said partnership incorporated itself as Defendant T S R Hobbies, Inc., a Wisconsin corporation, having its principal place of business in Lake Geneva, Wisconsin.

1.4   Plaintiff is informed and believes that Defendant T S R Hobbies, Inc. is the assignee of the rights of the said partnership and has assumed the obligations thereof.

1.5   Plaintiff is informed and believes that at all times material hereto, Defendant Tactical Study Rules, and Defendant

-1-

Cover page of Arneson's 1979 complaint against Gygax and TSR.

up almost a million dollars in gross sales for 1978, the company only made around $58,000 in profit, and had $30,000 or so in cash on hand. For the year 1978, Gygax was paid roughly $16,000 in wages by TSR, along with a further $30,000 in royalties, including all royalties for the *Advanced D&D* titles under the master agreement he signed with TSR at the beginning of 1978 which granted him a 2.5 percent royalty on his work—effectively, Arneson demanded double what Gygax received for those titles. Gygax's personal holdings of TSR stock would be worth around $80,000, and at this point TSR Hobbies had, since its founding in 1975, paid Gygax some $50,000 for all game royalties across all titles. The minimum $100,000 that Arneson demanded, above and beyond any royalties, well exceeded the amount anyone had made from *D&D* to date: if the court sided with him, Arneson likely would not only end up controlling TSR, but might even bankrupt Gygax. It was a rather dramatic escalation from the $750 Arneson had sought just one year before.

The legal process would be spearheaded by Michael Hirsch on Arneson's side and John Beard on TSR's side. Some preliminary maneuverings over whether the case should be heard in Minnesota or Wisconsin would take the first half of the year to resolve, but the news hit the hobby press almost immediately. The Chaosium's new magazine *Different Worlds* gossiped, with only a slight exaggeration, "Dave Arneson is suing TSR Hobbies, Inc., for $300,000 in back royalties for *Dungeons & Dragons Basic Set* and the *Monster Manual* for which TSR refuses to give him credit." Incidentally, that gossip column appeared under the name "Gigi D'Arn." Any resemblance to the initials of Gary Gygax, combined with a contraction of Dave Arneson's first initial with the leading syllable of his last name, was surely coincidental.

As the legal situation heated up, Gygax betrayed his insecurity with increasingly ill-advised and self-defeating outbursts in the press. To the February issue of *Dragon*, which would have been prepared as the lawsuit loomed, he contributed a new long-form piece called "*Dungeons & Dragons*: What It Is and Where It Is Going" that retold the history of *D&D* with a special emphasis on the vast conceptual gulf he claimed between the original game and his new *AD&D* system. Excerpts from the forthcoming *Dungeon Masters Guide* in the same issue hastily sketched the parts of the system yet to be published. In a separate article from the same issue, Gygax lashed out at a single-paragraph blurb in *Strategy & Tactics* that had described the *Players Handbook* as "a method to get you to buy what you already have," or a greatest-hits compilation: "Now you already have everything on the album, in one form or another, but you wouldn't be caught dead without the new item." For Gygax, this dig not only threatened his arguments that *AD&D* was more than just something "you already have," but also surely reopened old wounds from Gygax's long-standing struggle to promote fantasy gaming in the face of the indifference of SPI and Avalon Hill, along with echoes of the conflict over Origins and GenCon. Gygax chalked SPI's slant up to "personal or professional jealousy." Bafflingly, elsewhere in that same issue of *Dragon*, Gygax decided to pick on fanzine editors by singling out a sixteen-year-old Canadian who had cobbled together a project called *The Apprentice* at his high school print shop, which further stoked the outrage that was already growing in the fan press.

The animosity that Gygax recklessly sowed in the fan community had to create an opportunity for competing products: like the ones planned by Arneson. Gossip reported in the second issue of *Different Worlds* indicated "Dave Arneson apparently tore up his contract with Heritage to publish *Adventures in Fantasy*, Dave's new FRP game," and that Excalibre Games "will get first crack at *AiF*." The principals of that company were Twin Cities gamers Arneson had known since the 1960s; Dennis O'Leary of Excalibre had even distributed *D&D* for TSR there in 1975. The other principal was one Randy Hoffa, a rival of Arneson's from the days of old, whom Arneson had caricatured in the *First Fantasy Campaign* just two years ago as the villainous Ran of Ah-Foo. They agreed to take on the project because the printing was "privately financed" by Arneson and his friends in a manner reminiscent of the production loans TSR collected before publishing rules years earlier. But before Excalibre could publish *Adventures in Fantasy*, Arneson needed to finish it. The longer his projects dragged out, the more likely it became that similar games would beat them to the marketplace, as had happened with *Bushido*—which Arneson would offer to acquire for Adventures Unlimited that summer, unsuccessfully. As late as July, Arneson was still polishing *Adventures in Fantasy*, which with every passing month would face more competitors.

Arneson's lawsuit cast a pall over TSR, but its executives had the opportunity to enjoy some of their success in 1979. Brian Blume married Victoria Miller in May, and at his wedding reception signed a stock option agreement for their latest officer, Will Niebling, which granted him a ten-year option to purchase 500 shares of TSR stock at $125 each. While that would require a substantial outlay on Niebling's part, it would if exercised make him the third-largest shareholder, behind Gygax at 671 shares. The option demonstrated that Gygax and Blume were willing to trust Niebling with a substantial amount of control over the company: this would be the only offer of such magnitude they extended to any prospective executive. Such a lavish incentive was necessary to lure Niebling away from his steady work as a pharmacist, given that he would take a substantial pay cut to join TSR. With Niebling on board, they finally had someone to drive sales and marketing apart from the founders.

Early in the year, the Gygax family had started house hunting; their current residence on Chapin Road in Lake Geneva, which they bought in 1977, was no longer aligned with either their needs or their means. In February, they had made an offer to buy a fourteen-room stately manse with a columned porch, a pool, and twenty-three acres of land in the Fox Hollow subdivision of nearby Clinton, Wisconsin. By the time they closed the deal in July, the two eldest children of the Gygax family could live independently—both had jobs at TSR—so the Gygaxes had plenty of room in the 5,000-square-foot home. The previous owners had kept some farm animals on the property, which led the Gygaxes to take custody of a twenty-eight-year-old horse that came with the house. The family took a liking to equine husbandry, and over the next few years would steadily grow a herd of horses—which in turn required the acquisition of a separate horse ranch nearby. "Dragonlands" quickly became the nickname for this estate. Clinton was a half-hour drive from Lake Geneva, and Gygax did not drive, so a company car, designated TSR1, was reserved for the particular use of chauffeuring Gygax between his home, office, and various other appointments.

The preoccupation of the executive team with other matters, and the mounting popularity of *D&D*, meant that the creative work at TSR fell increasingly to the growing staff. A gamer named Lawrence Schick had spoken at length with Tim Kask at GenCon in 1978, and on the basis of their conversation submitted a number of articles to *Dragon*, including a series on well-known characters of fantasy literature and mythology that Schick had written with Tom Moldvay, a fellow Kent State student. Schick had seen the advertisement in *Dragon* that fall for a game design position at TSR, and like many hopefuls he applied for the position. In response to TSR's request for a sample dungeon design, Schick sent in his adventure, called *White Plume Mountain*, and was hired in the new year.

Schick was one of a small team of designers recruited early in 1979 to staff TSR's new design department. Jean Wells came onboard at around the same time, as Gygax put it, "to give the game material a feminine viewpoint—after all, at least 10% of the players are female!" By late February, she was already answering inquiries sent to TSR for rules clarifications, which increased in volume in the period after the *Players Handbook* was published but before the *Dungeon Masters Guide* filled in the gaps in the *Advanced* system. Before the end of the year, Wells's "Sage Advice" column in *Dragon* would make her clarifications a matter of public record rather than something she needed to repeat for individual letter writers. Gygax assigned Schick to work on "science fantasy and science fiction role playing adventure game material" as well as standard *D&D* fare; developing a TSR game worthy to compete with GDW's *Traveller* was a priority, and Schick had responsibility for delivering it. Schick and Wells would be joined on the design staff by Moldvay, as well as a Nebraska high school teacher named Dave "Zeb" Cook, shortly thereafter. While Gygax kept his hand on the till of the *Advanced* game, further development of *Basic D&D* became the remit of this organization.

Gygax may have delegated design responsibilities, but he could not leave Arneson's "great War" to any surrogate. When the fourth issue of Fantasy Games Unlimited's *Wargaming* finally saw print in the spring of 1979—after what *Different Worlds* would call "a long absence," far longer than a year, for a putative quarterly—it was only by historical accident that it fell after the filing of Arneson's lawsuit against TSR. But it carried "the Roots of *D&D*," Arneson's rebuttal to Gygax's June 1977 article in *Dragon*, the one that Tim Kask had declined to print, and which Arneson had threatened to take elsewhere. Now it had manifested abruptly after a two-year wait in a time capsule.

Arneson's belated sentiments there would quickly be followed by his feature in *Different Worlds* no. 3, this one a fresher piece. With two more years of conflict behind him, Arneson was less generous toward Gygax's *Chainmail* rules, saying only that he had used them "to handle combat at first." But his core message remained consistent: that "in the Twin Cities, role playing has always been popular." He enumerated a number of role-playing activities that preceded the publication of *D&D* and summarized that "applying a fantasy setting to RPG was merely another outgrowth of an already established tradition (albeit one without any real rules) in various non-fantasy settings." This notion that the rules mattered little became a common talking point for Arneson, a way of denigrating the process of actually writing the game, which Gygax had appointed to himself. The rules were an inessential development next to some ineffable role-playing concept that emerged from play; but the more Arneson stressed that argument, the more he implicitly acknowledged that his original contribution to *D&D* had not been to authoring its text.

No doubt interpreting the appearance of these two articles as a coordinated attack by Arneson, Gygax could not let them go unchallenged. So, he returned to the dispute in *Dragon*, which had a print run now nearing ten thousand, to reinforce his side of the story. Reading Arneson's "Roots," Gygax no doubt sensed how damaging Arneson found his characterization of Blackmoor as a "*Chainmail* variant"—so he turned up the volume on that a few notches. His new article showed how Blackmoor's single greatest system innovation, the dungeon adventure concept, could be argued to have roots in *Chainmail*. "Following *Chainmail's* advice to use paper and pencil for underground activity such as mining during campaign game sieges, taking a page out of the works of Howard and Burroughs *et al*, he brought the focus of fantasy miniatures play to the dungeon setting." He even discussed the other key innovation, Arneson's experience system, in terms that emphasized the potential influence of *Chainmail*: since in *Chainmail*, a Hero fights as four men, and a Superhero as eight, Gygax stated that "Dave decided he would allow progression of expertise for his players, success in games meaning that the hero would gain the ability of five, rather than but four men, eventually gaining the exalted status of superhero."

But Gygax's true occasion for his renewed polemic was to reiterate, in tireless keeping with his previous statements, that "*Advanced Dungeons & Dragons* is a different game" than the original *D&D*. He explicitly argued, in words quite salient to the legal dispute, that "there is no [more] similarity (perhaps even less) between *D&D* and *AD&D* than there is between *D&D* and its various imitators produced by competing publishers." Whether it was indeed a different game would be central to the outcome of Arneson's lawsuit.

A ruling from the United States District Court in July affirmed that Arneson's suit would proceed in Minnesota. The decision hinged on how much business TSR and Gygax did in the state, a condition for determining jurisdiction under Minnesota's "long arm" statute. As Gygax had personally traveled to Minnesota, secured contracts there for works TSR would publish, encouraged others in the state to market the game, and so on, this simply was not an argument he was going to win. It was a blow to TSR to have to fight this case in another state, but not one that augured either way how the judicial system would weigh the merits of the complaint.

As the lawsuit began in earnest, *D&D* had achieved a level of recognition that eluded most titles in the wargaming hobby. A widely syndicated July 1979 *Los Angeles Times* article about *D&D* showed how deeply the "burgeoning subculture" around the game had taken root in that city. It quotes Gary Gygax estimating that a quarter of a million Americans played *D&D*, and that sales of the *Basic Set* alone now hovered around five or six thousand copies a month. *Games Magazine* ran a feature article that summer on *D&D* by Jon Freeman, author of the forthcoming *Winner's Guide to Board Games*, which included a final chapter about *D&D* and the role-playing game industry it had inspired—although it would not come out until October, its text was surely written before the middle of 1979. *D&D* is "appallingly addictive," Freeman summarized, and as a conclusion for a book surveying all tabletop aspects of gaming, he attested it is "far and away my favorite game." Indeed, he suggested it is something more than just a game: "*D&D* may be one of the most exciting discoveries of your life."

While it still lived just outside the mainstream, TSR began to connect with a realm of business beyond the confines of the traditional wargame hobby. Wary of the Game Manufacturers Association spearheaded by Rick Loomis and its focus on Origins, Gygax steered TSR toward an alternative industry association. Largely due to the success of *D&D*, the Hobby Industry of America (HIA) created a Hobby Gaming and Military Miniatures division, and immediately appointed Gygax its president pro tem. Gygax hoped to use this industry group to drive for higher standards in packaging and design, and he even expressed some willingness to give GenCon over to the direction of the HIA—no doubt reflecting his concern about the future of the conference after its poor showing against Origins the summer before. Where GAMA focused inward on consolidating the hobby, Gygax gazed outward at the broader market for toys and crafts, and sought a place there for TSR.

Going into the summer, Gygax saw quite a bit of upside for his company. "The corporation employs some 20–25 persons now," he told the magazine *White Dwarf*, "and by this time next year that figure will certainly have grown to 30—possible as many as 40, for we expect to grow considerably." As Gygax wrote in a personal letter to Steve Marsh on August 8, "TSR is really doing well now, and I am pretty well off too. We'll be moving upwards to become the largest hobby game publisher in the next couple of years, barring anything unforeseen happening."

It transpired that something unforeseen was about to happen. And so the midpoint of 1979 provides a good opportunity to review the success of *D&D* in relation to the rest of the industry. Howard Barasch continued to provide his annual survey of the earnings of the industry—as well as juicy gossip—in *Strategy & Tactics* after he moved from SPI to Heritage. His 1979 figures show a hobby gaming industry still dominated by Avalon Hill and SPI: Avalon Hill brought in around $3.7 million, and SPI $2.4 million. TSR by his reckoning had made $900,000, though due to differences in fiscal calendars, that reflects the company's 1978 total. Almost all other companies Barasch tallied made less than half a million dollars. Overall, Barasch reckons that the hobby games industry drew in $9.2 million, and shipped nearly two million units of product in the past year.

TSR's revenue came almost entirely from role-playing games at this point: apart from *Chainmail*, its wargame booklets rarely registered sales above double digits in a given month, sums that could boast no improvement on Don Lowry's Guidon Games business of the early 1970s. A boxed TSR role-playing game like *Gamma World* or *Boot Hill* would reliably sell a thousand copies per month in 1979, about equal to a competing title like *Chivalry & Sorcery*, and double the sales of *Traveller* or *Runequest*. Sales that strong would have unleashed jubilation at TSR just a few years earlier—but the revenue resulting from these titles would amount to little more than a rounding error in tabulating the surging sales of *D&D*.

The original *D&D* boxed set had, since its release more than five years before, sold just below 60,000 copies. Its first supplement, *Greyhawk*, could claim 50,000 sales by this point, and the other three supplements more than half that. The reigning unit sales champion was the boxed *Basic Set*, which had, since its mid-1977 release two years before, already moved over 70,000 units, and a further 12,000 copies of the standalone *Basic* rulebook. But combined, the *Advanced* game books had already eclipsed that: the *Players Handbook* had been out for roughly one year by the summer of 1979 and had already sold almost exactly 50,000 copies. Then add to that 47,000 for *Monster Manual* sales, and consider the imminent release of a third volume, the *Dungeon Masters Guide*, which boasted an initial run of 44,000 books that had been pre-ordered before the first of August. Accessories had also become popular: each of the six modules released during the 1978 summer convention season sold in the vicinity of 10,000 copies over the year that followed, at $4.50 to $6 apiece, which added a tidy sum to the *AD&D* total. And although the *Tomb of Horrors* and *In Search of the Unknown* modules entered the market a half year later than that first round of six, their sales only lagged a couple thousand copies behind by mid-1979. All told, very nearly a half million units of *D&D* product had traded to date.

As impressive as the growth of *D&D* had been, it is important to tally these sums now because of the incredible transformation that *D&D* sales were about to undergo as the summer of 1979 drew to a close. Take just the flag-ship *Basic Set* as a representative example: in its two-year lifetime, up to the end of the second quarter of 1979, it had sold 73,358 copies. But in just the third quarter of 1979 it would add to that 33,715 more sales, nearly 12,000 a month, a 45 percent increase to its overall total. In the fourth quarter alone, it sold a further 93,796 copies, a sum that comes close to equaling all previous sales of the product. And then the next quarter, TSR would move a stunning 139,857 copies of *Basic Set*, which was now on a trajectory to reach nearly a half million sales in just one year. Without exaggeration, the summer of 1979 marked an inflection point that would change not just the role-playing games hobby, but the entire games industry. So, what happened?

This turning point came soon after GenCon. In the hopes of attracting a more mainstream audience, TSR advertised GenCon in radio spots using the voice of the newly created character "Morley the Wizard." This was a summer when the fifth Origins had reached a new attendance record of 4,100 at Widener College in Chester, Pennsylvania, with modest sup-port from a TSR now desperate to keep GenCon alive. TSR planned this year's GenCon around the triumphant release of the *Dungeon Masters Guide*. Inevitably, there were logistical problems coordinating the release of 44,000 copies of a new title: the bindery that TSR engaged for the book informed the company on August 10 that it would deliver only half of the promised print run due to other obligations. But TSR managed to get as many cop-ies as they could to distributors, while keeping enough on hand to satisfy the audience at GenCon, including a dozen copies each day that had been autographed by Gygax and cover artist Dave Sutherland.

At GenCon as well came some new modules. *White Plume Mountain* pol-ished up the dungeon Lawrence Schick had submitted to TSR as a job appli-cation. The release of Gygax's *Village of Hommlet*, which revisited the office campaign run at TSR in 1976, afforded him another opportunity to vent about the legal situation. In the original Hommlet campaign, Arneson had controlled the trader to the northwest of the town, so in the published *Village of Hommlet* that trader, numbered on the map as building 13, is named "Rannos Davi." It must be said that "Rannos" is a more subtle scrambling of "Arneson" without the "e" than "Nosnra" from the *Steading of the Hill Giant Chief* the year before. Rannos, a tenth-level thief, is described as "slow, fat, clumsy, and placid." But Gygax does not reserve his mockery for Arneson alone: Rannos is accompanied by "a tall and thin individual, with sharp features and protruding eyes" by the name of Gremag: a distortion of "Megarry." Although the pair pose as townsfolk, they are both chaotic servants of the Temple of Elemental Evil. Players who trade with Rannos and Gremag will find themselves cheated in business because these two thieves overvalue their own wares and underpay for anything offered to them.

One GenCon attendee spotted a familiar face in the crowd: "Arneson was handing out a thick pad of playtestable FRP rules to be published sometime next year, possibly in time for next GenCon." Braving the scorn of his former employer and legal opponent, Arneson did show up for GenCon to circulate a playtest edition of *Adventures in Fantasy*, but apart from distributing it at the summer conventions, it went out only to a limited audience of mail-order customers. It was an oversize photocopy, crudely edited and typeset, with maps and illustrations drawn by Arneson. At the end of the convention, Arneson would hurriedly ship off to the West Coast for Pacificon—the successor to the GenCon West event TSR had run in 1976 and 1977—where he ran the Blackmoor dungeon for delighted participants.

After the thrashing GenCon took in competition with Origins the year before, TSR had high hopes for the 1979 attendance figures: people presumably knew how to find Parkside now, and the *Dungeon Masters Guide* promised to be a powerful lure. Disappointingly, all this brought in just 2,135 paid attendees, barely more than half the draw of Origins. Based on an informal tally of unregistered attendees, TSR would gamely circulate that the total number present was above 3,000.

Things had settled down a few weeks after the convention, and a TSR employee named Rose Estes was in the middle of writing up a piece about GenCon for a hobby magazine when she received a call from the *Dayton Journal-Herald*. Estes was a spokesperson for TSR at the time, and was accustomed to trying to explain the game to baffled reporters. After hearing complaints from the reporter that game was totally sold out in Dayton, she was then asked to comment on the situation with the missing boy.

"What boy?" she replied.

GenCon had ended on August 19. The Michigan State University paper, the *State News*, ran a headline the following Saturday, about an "MSU student reported missing for two days from Case Hall," one of the university dormitories. It accompanied this article with a picture of a young man, just sixteen years old, captioned with the name Dallas Egbert. It explained that Egbert was from Dayton, Ohio, that he was an Honors College student at Lyman Briggs College, and that the last time anyone could be sure he had been seen at the dorm was August 15—the day before GenCon started.

Egbert was attending a summer semester because an illness had forced him to drop some of his spring classes: officially, he was still considered a freshman. The *State News* suggests that a friend of Egbert's indicated that Egbert had been "known to leave campus before for destinations unknown." She added, "Fall term he took off and told me he was going. He was gone for two weeks." A university official observed that this was "not a unique situation. He's 16 and brilliant. We're concerned due to his age." His roommate reported that Egbert was ordinarily one to play his stereo to the point that it "pounds the wall down but I haven't heard that lately." Apparently, he had no driver's license, and regularly took buses to get around.

Someone missing for a couple days is not news, but after another week passed, on Sunday, September 2, the story had spread to local papers and become a police matter. In the Lansing, Michigan, *State Journal*, a front-page article that day wondered, in its title, "Did Missing Student Leave Clue?" That paper reported that Egbert's room was uncharacteristically orderly, stripped of its bedsheets and a customary ream of posters, and that in their place "perched on an otherwise cleared desktop was a neatly printed note two lines long, telling what Egbert wished done with his body 'should' it be found." In what could be generously called an understatement, police investigators conceded he might be suicidal.

Searching for leads, the police took a tarot deck they found in the room to a fortune teller to inquire if some sort of message could be found in the ordering of the cards. But the deck was not the most enigmatic object left in his dorm—that would be a corkboard leaning up against a wall, with thirty-six plastic and metal tacks embedded into it, which investigators scrutinized for hidden meaning. In that same September 2 article, Egbert's mother, who reported that she had played games with her son in the past, proposed that it might be some sort of message, perhaps a map. "This year," the *State Journal* related, Egbert had "told her about a new game he had learned, called *Dungeons & Dragons*." Rather matter-of-factly, the newspaper attested that "the tacks on Egbert's board resemble a dungeon used in the game," and that Egbert's friends did not remember seeing the board there before he disappeared.

According to Estes, the campus police at the time were unaware that *D&D* was a commercial product: they found no rule books in Egbert's room, and assumed it was a game that had been invented by students at the university. Since they could find no students willing to come forward and explain the game, they spoke to the press about it as a "bizarre and secret cult," which naturally created some interest in the game, and in the curious bulletin board "map" that they had associated with it.

A cluster of blue and white tacks formed a rectangular block in the lower-right corner of the board, something that might be the shape of a room or building. A single yellow tack by itself occupied the upper-left corner. The remainder of the tacks seemed randomly positioned. But police determined, upon comparing the board to a campus map, that "some of the locations of the tacks matched the locations of manhole covers leading into the university's steam tunnels." Extrapolating from that hypothesis, the cluster in the lower-right corner might depict a power plant.

But these guesses at the meaning behind the board were admittedly conjecture. By September 5, a UPI story was reporting that police "called in computer and logic specialists plus those familiar with an elaborate board game popular among college students in an effort to decode the board." That game was "a highly complex game involving fantasy and role playing." Bill Wardwell of the MSU police had been trying to find people who played the game with Egbert, without success. "I'd hate to say it's a secretive game, but you get into it only by invitation," Wardwell told the media. The authorities had now caught wind of a Wisconsin *D&D* convention that took place around the time Egbert vanished: GenCon. They reached out to TSR Hobbies, sending photographs of Egbert and the mysterious thumbtack board, which were apparently lost in the mail and had to be resent.

Asked if the police were grasping at straws by inquiring with TSR, Wardwell conceded, "A little bit." But no straw would go ungrasped when, the next day, the megaphone of the media landed in the hands of William Dear, a private investigator hired by Egbert's desperate parents. Dear launched a series of expensive and flamboyant measures, like flyovers of campus in his private plane, to gauge how well the bulletin board corresponded to an aerial view of the campus. His daily rate was $500 to $700, plus expenses. There was talk of shipping in specially trained tracker dogs from Texas. Naturally, Dear needed to search the steam tunnels personally, although police had already done so a week before: nearly fifteen miles of tunnels, in which the temperature was 115 degrees, requiring an eight-hour search. Dear would take nothing for granted: the note found in Egbert's room describing how he wanted his remains to be treated was, according to Dear, a suspected forgery, a case where "we think someone was trying to mimic his writing." Press reports began to suggest that Egbert's parents, who had offered a reward for information leading to their son, were convinced their son had been abducted, and that the physical evidence on the scene in his dorm room was intentional misdirection.

But it was the "highly complex game" that Dear most sensationalized for the press. Dear demonstrated his understanding of the game when he suggested, from the configuration of the bulletin board, that "the number of different pins indicates the beginning of the game," and that players familiar with the game might try to implement "Egbert's pattern" in order to divine his intentions.

On September 7, the story broke nationally through the Associated Press and the Knight Ridder system, but it was less a story about a missing college student than it was a rash amplification of Dear's most lurid speculation about *D&D*. "Game Might Have Turned into Deathtrap," the *Appleton Post-Crescent* headline supposed. "Fantasy Game Death Feared," read the *Des Moines Tribune*. "Game May Have Killed Computer Whiz," according to the *Wausau Daily Herald*. Or, "Fantasy Game May Have Claimed Missing Genius," as the *Los Angeles Times* would have it. Nightly news reports on television were little better. Dear's quotes in these articles go beyond just grasping at straws; his understanding of *D&D* is summed up by preposterous allegations like, "Someone is put in the dungeon, and it's up to them to get out." The only subject Dear spoke to more confidently than *D&D* was Egbert's almost certain death at its hands: "If he's where he's supposed to be," that is in the steam tunnels, "then he's dead." Or, "it is our opinion that the boy is dead," as he was widely quoted as saying.

Rose Estes at TSR ended up fielding the September 7 press calls in Lake Geneva, most of them frantic demands to explain *D&D* within minutes of meeting their deadlines—which, as anyone who has played the game knows, is no mean feat. She patiently attempted to communicate basic facts about the game, like that there were now an estimated 300,000 players nationwide. That number was not about to shrink when articles running over the next week would feature the box cover of the *Basic Set*, sometimes obligingly held up by William Dear himself. The Associated Press quoted Estes denying any live-action component in the game, insisting that "in all of the variations— and there are a great many—we know of none that are actually physical." Apart from anonymous and unsubstantiated rumor, there was no indication of any real-world, real-space game of *D&D* taking place at MSU. The *New York Times* deemed the "bizarre intellectual game called *Dungeons & Dragons*"— illustrated with a snapshot of William Dear heroically exploring the steam tunnels that had already been searched a week before—a tabletop experience "for the players to find a way out of an imaginary labyrinth to collect great treasures." Speculation grew so intense, Estes recalled: "The only way to stop a national broadcasting system from going on evening television and labeling the game a sado/masochistic torture cult was to call campus police and insist that irreparable harm would be done to their university if they didn't call the reporter and stop them."

This all must have lit up the switchboards in East Lansing. A higher-ranking officer took over public relations for the investigation as of September 8: Captain Ferman Badgley would dismiss all of the game theories as "merely speculation," and more candidly relate, "we don't have any clues we can hang our hat on." Indeed, Badgley feared that the intense press coverage could be keeping Egbert in hiding.

By September 9, the futility of continuing tunnel searches had become evident—even Dear would inform the captivated national media that "we're satisfied that he's not in there"—but that did not let *D&D* off the hook. Now headlines like the *Fort Lauderdale News's* "Missing Genius Reportedly Seen at Game-Playing Cult's Convention" dragged GenCon into this mess. A day later, the game was still the "No. 1 Clue in Genius Search" according to the *Tampa Tribune*, in an article that began by listing a summary of clues available, including "a suicide note, a cult game convention in Wisconsin and his ties with the gay community." Badgley, with his typical circumspection, explained what police interviews with GenCon attendees had revealed: "Nobody has positively identified him, but a couple of people may have seen him up there."

Then by September 11, the excruciating frustration of Egbert's parents turned to suspicion of the college and its responsibility for oversight of their son. But the press continued on. "Did Dragons, Dungeons Swallow Dallas Egbert?" asked a headline in the *Press and Sun-Bulletin* of Binghamton, New York, on September 12. Badgley decided to end daily press briefings as there had been no new developments in the case. Will Niebling at TSR could report that the police had some information in the mail, and that "we will take a look at it and see if we can deduce anything." The gaming hobby was still small enough that TSR staff members recognized Egbert when they finally saw the pictures, though no one could quite place whether they'd seen him at a past GenCon or perhaps at a WinterCon in Michigan. Egbert had not registered for the 1979 GenCon—though with nearly a thousand unregistered persons counted in attendance, official records could not tell the whole story.

And then suddenly, on September 14, newspapers reported that Egbert had been reunited with his family after he contacted Dear, who arranged a private plane to transport him from Louisiana to Texas. He had not died in any steam tunnel, and had not been playing *D&D*.

Dear was not about to admit any error on his own part: he now shifted to represent himself as the guardian of a secret that Egbert did not want divulged, and as such, Dear refused to clarify whether *D&D* had been a factor in Egbert's disappearance. He would at least freely volunteer that *Dungeons & Dragons* proved meaningless in the search for Egbert. This let some of the more reckless press outlets off the hook: in follow-up articles they could say it was unknown if and how *D&D* had factored into Egbert's situation, rather than admit that prior reporting was all nonsense. Egbert's parents had nothing further to say publicly about the matter, for the moment. The media, however, was in no hurry to exonerate *D&D*, and there was plenty of coverage in the form of "details surrounding the discovery and condition of the 16-year-old computer science student with a taste for the offbeat remain uncertain." The full story would have to wait for the following summer, when it returned for a sad conclusion.

One thing that last UPI bulletin said was that *D&D* "has a cult-like following at many colleges." That word, "cult," and the connotations it carried now became attached to *D&D*—it had been less than a year since almost one thousand people died in Jonestown under the influence of a cult, and the Manson family's crimes remained fresh in American memory. A few *D&D* fans took it upon themselves to try to correct these misapprehensions in the popular press, but these sorts of rebuttals would do little to sway a new court of public opinion that was convening around the game.

These events, which loom large in hindsight, played out on the national stage over the course of only about a week, between September 7 and 14. Game-industry periodicals like *Dragon* were at best monthlies—*Different Worlds* was bimonthly—so by the time they could weigh in, it was all over. Tim Kask wrote an editorial in *Dragon* lamenting how the "detective hired by the parents has made some incorrect statements regarding the game that have only fueled the controversy." But he had to balance that against the fact that *Dungeons & Dragons* was "getting the publicity that we used to just dream about, back when we were freezing in Gary's basement in the beginning." In its October issue, *Different Worlds* ran two clippings from September 9 and September 14, with the speculative headline, "Fantasy Cult Angle Probed in Search for Computer Whiz," pitted against the breaking news, "College Fantasy Game Victim Recovered Alive." Although the latter article qualified its text with Dear's refusal to divulge the cause of Egbert's disappearance, the headlines would always remember Egbert as that fantasy game's "victim."

Egbert's adventure in the steam tunnels was no more real than a game of *D&D*—but there was real treasure at the end of it. In the wake of the Egbert incident, media coverage of *D&D* pivoted from its former frenzied speculation to the story of the game and its unexpected success. An article at the end of September summed up the situation nicely, that *D&D* "was a relatively obscure pastime until the August disappearance of a 16-year-old computer wiz from Michigan State University catapulted the game into national prominence." It cites anecdotal evidence from various hobby stores, including "Something to Do in Louisville, Kentucky," which reported that the game was becoming a bestseller, and a statement from ABC Hobbycraft in Evansville, Indiana, that *D&D* "tops the fantasy games that now account for 20 percent of the store's business." An October 3 article in the *New York Times* reported a similar situation in Washington at a game store called Your Move. "I can't keep the *D&D* reference books in stock," exclaimed the store's manager. "Every other phone call is about the *D&D* books." In a way, the Egbert situation was a magical event for TSR, something that transmuted supposition into gold.

For TSR, the most material consequence of the "steam tunnel" incident was a new business partnership, which, as Gygax hinted to Steve Marsh, promised "important gains in distribution, advertising, promotion, sales, products, cash, etc." This was the distribution agreement TSR secured with Random House. Millie Marmur, a vice president at Random House, had two teenage sons who played the game, and once it became the subject of a national conversation, she forged a deal with TSR that would become a boon to both companies. With this agreement, effective January 1, 1980, TSR products would no longer be relegated to the shelves of hobby shops, but could now expect to appear in key retailers like K-Mart, Waldenbooks, and other mainstream brick-and-mortar stores of the time.

But the national media would never consider the story of the game complete without a human-interest subject, and Gary Gygax found himself the focus of as much interest as the game itself, with his unforgettable name and his compelling rags-to-riches story. This started during the Egbert affair itself: "I did about a dozen interviews," Gygax recalled, "and was on two Milwaukee TV stations who filmed games in progress here in my living room." But even that did not prepare him for what would be in store over the coming months.

It was one thing to host a Milwaukee affiliate, but another matter to be invited to appear on a network television talk show. If there was any moment when Gygax could be said to have arrived as a national celebrity, it was November 8, on the late-night show *Tomorrow* with Tom Snyder on NBC. Apparently, right before the show, Snyder loosened Gygax up by asking him directly, "Isn't it true that this is really a stupid game?" Gygax replied earnestly, "No, the game is really very good."

Snyder was very clear on one point: he singled out Gygax as "the inventor of *Dungeons & Dragons*," concluding "you've had a fantastic success." Arneson recorded an audio tape of the show as he sat in front of his television watching. When Gary enumerates the character classes available in the game, at the point when he mentions that there is a thief class, you can hear Arneson mutter, "That's you."

Different Worlds snarked at Gygax, "Predictably, he didn't mention Dave Arneson." Most of the media followed his lead. An *Us Weekly* magazine feature in the October 30 issue, titled "The Mind Behind *Dungeons & Dragons*, the New Campus Craze," showed images of Gygax running the game with the caption, "Gary Gygax, who invented and designed the *Dungeons & Dragons* game, strikes an eerie pose in front of five players."

Even within the narrow confines of the gaming industry, the notoriety of *D&D* led the trade press to gravitate toward Gygax rather than Arneson.

Rudy Kraft of *Gryphon* magazine interviewed Gygax directly after the steam tunnel press, where Gygax could now report that the *Basic Set* had sold twelve thousand copies in the last month. Asked to speculate about what that would mean for TSR's bottom-line revenue over the next year, Gygax could only say, "It's getting pretty hard to guess, 4 to 6 million. It's so hard to tell at this point because of the recent publicity *Dungeons & Dragons* has received and also because we are successful and growing and establishing new means of penetrating the market." Although Gygax had reportedly contributed 1,500 hours of work to the *Dungeon Masters Guide*, the way he explained things to Kraft, those days were over: the administration of the business had taken the place of further creative work on his part.

Kraft did reach out to Arneson as well, but with one condition: "I would also like to interview you for the magazine but I would like to hold off on conducting the interview until after you and TSR have settled the lawsuit." Kraft did not hesitate for fear of a reprisal from TSR, but instead because he knew well that "most of the generally interesting questions people would like to have asked of you are ones you would not currently answer."

Gygax could not resist noting in his interview with Kraft that "the bigger you get the more profitable it becomes to litigate against you." Then he added, "I don't believe anybody has ever accused us of swiping ideas from them but it could happen." Somewhere in Minnesota, Arneson no doubt howled at that. But the sudden uptick in *D&D* sales necessarily raised the stakes in the lawsuit—to exactly where, it was not yet clear: perhaps to a place where $100,000 would not threaten to bankrupt TSR or Gygax; perhaps also to a place where the 5 percent royalty Arneson demanded would amount to a fortune. But for now, the uncertainty only made the lawsuit pose an even greater threat to TSR's future.

Since Arneson's lawsuit had demanded everything from TSR, it is perhaps unsurprising that TSR's legal team responded that Arneson was entitled to nothing. TSR's strategy was not just to parrot Gygax's line that *D&D* and *AD&D* were fundamentally different games but furthermore to insist that Arneson's contribution to the original game had been so small that he had not actually deserved any of the royalties he had already received. TSR argued that Arneson had only been designated a collaborator on the game in the 1975 contract through a "mutual mistake," as neither Gygax nor Arneson understood copyright law well enough then to ascertain whether Arneson had generated anything copyrightable that he could assign to TSR.

As recently as his article in *Dragon* in June, Gygax credited Arneson with some of the core ideas in *D&D*—dungeon adventures and the experience system, for example—so it might seem utterly preposterous for TSR to now argue that Arneson's contribution was *de minimus*, as they say in legal circles. They were not arguing that Arneson had never furnished those "valuable idea kernels," but rather that "valuable idea kernels" were by their nature not copyrightable, and thus could not be the legitimate subject of a copyright assignment like the 1975 contract.

Legal precedent had long held that game rules were not copyrightable: the words in a rulebook are copyrightable, and the image on a game board is, but the uncopyrightability of basic concepts surrounding how games work had long allowed imitators to ride on the coattails of innovative games, provided they explained the basic concepts in their own words and with their own illustrations. If basic ideas like dungeon adventures and the experience system were copyrightable, TSR would have long since shut down *Tunnels & Trolls* and similar imitators who borrowed those concepts from *D&D* and simply paraphrased them. While Arneson undoubtedly conceived many of the basic ideas, all game system concepts were effectively in the public domain in the eyes of the law; it was only a specific text like the *D&D* rulebooks that could be copyrighted, and thus could be covered by a copyright assignment like the one Gygax and Arneson had executed in 1975. The problem, TSR argued, was that neither Gygax nor Arneson understood this back in 1975, and thus by mutual mistake they entered into a contract that TSR now argued was invalid.

Ironically, when Arneson complained the year before that, "by reducing my part of things to a simple job of writing they destroy the idea that it was the 'concept' of the 'game' that I developed and upon which all this stands today," he was making precisely TSR's case: the "simple job of writing" is what results in something copyrightable, not the development of the concept behind a game.

Although it is tempting to try to understand Arneson's lawsuit as exploring essential questions about who contributed more than someone else, the legal arguments would depend on far more complex technical questions about how the "joint work" of collaborators is defined for copyright purposes. The legal precedents for joint work have a requirement of intent: meaning that ideas were developed with the specific intention to merge them with a collaborator. But the basic ideas of the experience point system and dungeon adventuring originated in the Blackmoor campaign before anyone had the idea that Gygax and Arneson would work together on *D&D*, so were they really part of a joint work? Had Arneson intended to merge those ideas into a new project with Gygax when he created them? If not, then arguably, Gygax simply adapted Arneson's uncopyrightable ideas the same way that St. Andre later would with *Tunnels & Trolls*. When Arneson himself characterized the situation as "me providing various ideas and concepts but not having any say as to how they were used" while Gygax was controlling the text, this made his legal situation quite doubtful, as counterintuitive as that might be to Blog the Cro-Magnon.

As the legal arguments played out, there was relatively little disagreement about who did what when during the development of *D&D*—the lawyers were fixated on these finer technical issues. But to the remainder of the industry, who breathlessly waited for the resolution of the suit, the expected verdict would deliver nothing less than the final say on who really created *D&D*.

Near the end of the year, a fan asked in *Alarums & Excursions*, "What happened to Dave Arneson?" The fan noted, "I realized I haven't heard anything about Arneson since *Blackmoor* and the *First Fantasy Campaign* were published." He blamed this on how "EGG has taken the spotlight" and cut Arneson out of the production of *Advanced D&D*. Most of the gaming community had no idea that *Adventures in Fantasy* had even entered a limited release. The task of finding an audience for it became immeasurably more difficult when the sudden fame of Gygax and *D&D* began to transform the industry.

Adventures in Fantasy was at least fortunate to have avoided publication by Heritage: the rising tide of *D&D* did not lift Jim Oden's boat. As *Space Gamer* reported in November, "Rumors had been circulating about Heritage's impending demise for several months." Oden—who had been TSR's first real ally, and then its first real enemy—sold his interest in the firm late in the year rather than face bankruptcy; Ray Stockman, who bought Oden's stake, elevated Duke Seifried to run the company. Or as the gossip column in *Different Worlds* had it, "One night Duke was complaining loudly at a restaurant about the state of the company and how he would do better if he ran it. The proverbial Texas millionaire overheard the conversation and offered on the spot to put up the money." With Heritage's cash crunch throughout 1979 and this reorganization, major projects stalled, and Excalibre would prove a readier publisher for Arneson's work.

Tectonic shifts in the industry made all sorts of projects falter. Before the end of the year, Gygax visited the United Kingdom—for the first time—to have an earnest conversation with the two partners who ran Games Workshop, Ian Livingstone and Steve Jackson. They had distributed *D&D* in Britain since 1975, and their success had paced the growth of TSR in the United States, allowing for their own conventions and providing a local market for their *White Dwarf* magazine. An article from July 29 in the *London Observer* suggested Games Workshop had sold 20,000 copies of *D&D* so far; under a recent agreement with TSR, they would now begin manufacturing the *Basic Set* under license. The game sold for £7.50 there, and the total business of Games Workshop was now over £400,000 per year. The question, naturally, was whether TSR should acquire them, or structure some kind of merger. But Gygax and Blume were unable to come to an agreement with Livingstone and Jackson, who ultimately decided to go their own path. The separation of TSR from Games Workshop left a planned collaboration between the two in limbo: the *Fiend Folio*, a sequel to the *Monster Manual*, which was meant to appear before 1980. As the relationship between Games Workshop and TSR shifted, the *Fiend Folio* project slipped into a realm of murky legal questions where it would remain mired for years.

TSR was in a position to consider such acquisitions because they simply had more money than they knew what to do with. Monthly sales for the *Basic Set* in November came in at around 50,000—remember that just two years prior, the *Basic Set* had sold only 1,500 copies that month. Thanks to his stake in the *Advanced* titles, Gygax's royalty payments for the calendar year 1979 rose to $75,983. With the further $27,570 in salary he drew from TSR, his income cracked the six-figure mark. And that leaves out the many smaller sources of income that came in for him, like the $1,250 he was now paid per quarter as a director of TSR, or the $12,000 or so that he split with Brian Blume for the lease on TSR's buildings. He and his wife Mary took in a further $16,000 from the Jo Powell Agency in 1979, which was just the commission on more than $120,000 in advertising buys for *Dragon* magazine. At the November TSR shareholder meeting, the book value of the stock was voted up to $250, double the previous year—a pretty dramatic jump after the prior annual bumps of just $5 or $10 at a time.

The benefits of this *D&D* windfall did not pass over Arneson. As the continuing beneficiary of royalties for the original game and the *Basic Set*, his take this year almost doubled, reaching $35,739.96. The year before, his royalties amounted to a bit more than half the amount Gygax had been paid; this year, thanks to the increasing prominence of the *Advanced* game, Arneson's royalties fell to a little less than half of Gygax's take. This amount of money still far exceeded the salary of any TSR employee—but was less than Arneson felt his contribution warranted. With the new valuation of TSR's stock, and the sudden bump in sales, the figures that Arneson's lawsuit had demanded at the beginning of the year no longer looked so stratospheric: perhaps, with continuing growth, they might even be sums the business could absorb without significant difficulty.

TSR Turn Results for 1979

Revenue: $2.2M (Barasch ranking 3), profit $160,000
Employees: 25
Stock Valuation: $250
GenCon attendance vs. Origins: 2,100 vs. 4,100

Persons Disappeared in Steam Tunnels: 0

Brian   Kevin

1980: The Spotlight

At the dawn of a new decade, everything was going to be different for *Dungeons & Dragons*. The "great War" between Gygax and Arneson was far from over, but it was now overshadowed by a battle fought on the national stage, where the game would be subject to challenges that were louder and less rational than disputes about credit and royalties. From this point forward, the American media played as large a role in defining *D&D* as did the game's creators.

A *People* magazine story about Gary Gygax from the second week of January relayed that "Ever since *D&D* was dreamed up, stores have been waging a losing crusade to keep it in stock." The article shipped with a full-page close up of Gygax's looming face, mugging gamely over a handful of fantasy miniatures, bearded, bespectacled, benevolent, but a bit manic as he twists his gaze down at these emblems of his unlikely success. Another picture attached to the same article showed Gygax and his wife under the covers in bed—a sort of John and Yoko moment—though in this case Gygax is reading from Andrew Lang's *Green Fairy Book* while Mary lovingly looks on.

The *People* article identified Gygax as "D&D's 41-year-old inventor," and it was rare for any notices to hint that someone other than Gygax had contributed to the creation of *D&D*. Even where a caveat identifies Gygax as the co-author of the rules, his counterpart routinely went unnamed. No doubt with each article that neglected Arneson the urgency of legal redress increased.

At the Hobby Industry of America's annual January show, everything had changed. What had begun the previous year as the Hobby Gaming & Military Miniatures division within the HIA had now taken on the simpler and more compelling name "Adventure Gaming." While it encompassed all manner of wargames and role-playing games, its flagship title, its exemplar, was necessarily *D&D*. Howard Barasch, who was in attendance, reported that, "Without a doubt *Dungeons & Dragons* was the most talked about product at the show." Barasch observed of *D&D* that "its success is helping draw attention to our entire hobby" and to one man in particular: "Gary Gygax is emerging as a top celebrity with his name, face, and product making it on national TV, *People*, *Us*, and *Parade* magazines plus a host of local shows and numerous articles." Barasch suspected that TSR had already surpassed SPI in total sales, and that "the way D&D and its support items are selling, TSR will probably become the largest company in the hobby." By the time Barasch would next tabulate industry sales, he would turn out to be right.

A report at the start of the year in *Space Gamer* predicted that "TSR Hobbies will emerge as the largest gaming firm if it can survive two hurdles." One was "the risk associated with moving to mass market outlets such a K-Mart," which could alienate the hobby market while triggering a spectacular but short-lived popular fad. The other hurdle was "a lawsuit by D&D co-copyright holder Dave Arneson. Loss of that case could have a major impact on the way TSR does business."

While his lawsuit slowly progressed, Arneson had the unenviable task of trying to gain a foothold in this market for his *Adventures in Fantasy*. Excalibre took out a full-page advertisement for it in the February issue of *Different Worlds*, which promised mail order copies of the autographed boxed first edition at the special price of $15. This offer was valid only while supplies last, and retailers were invited to schedule preorders to inform the size of an anticipated second printing. Having learned from his experiences at Heritage to do his own marketing, Arneson scheduled a promotional event at a small West Coast convention and sent out a mass-mailing to people who had bought the playtest copy from him the year before, offering them a $6 discount on the new Excalibre edition. That same flyer warned that the price would rise to $20 per copy after April 1. By the summer, when the first reviews of *Adventures in Fantasy* started to appear, the price had climbed to $25.

But early reviews showed just how hard the path ahead was for Arneson. *Space Gamer* suggested, "Had he and co-designer Richard Snider convinced Excalibre Games, Inc. to publish this game before 1979, it might have been a rival for D&D. Today, it is too little for too much money." Reaction among fans was less generous: In *Alarums & Excursions* the game was called "hopelessly unplayable" and "a real turkey." SPI's *Ares* magazine deemed, "The price is high, the graphics are terrible, the rules are worse, and many of the systems are overly complicated." While an executive at Excalibre sent an angry rejoinder to *Space Gamer*, calling its treatment a "hatchet job," in the 1980 survey of that magazine's readership, *Adventures in Fantasy* ranked second-to-last overall among role-playing games. Unfortunately, this was basically indicative of the coverage that the game received in the industry. The Chaosium did invite Arneson to contribute an *Adventures in Fantasy* section to a role-playing product based on the popular *Thieves' World* shared-world fantasy anthology, but it would only amount to a handful of pages. Otherwise, the game simply made little headway.

At the time, Arneson still intended to publish elements of his Blackmoor setting as unofficial *D&D* supplements through the Chaosium: for years they had anticipated the "Island of the Wolf" and "City of the Gods" scenarios Arneson had originally promised to Judges Guild. But *Different Worlds* reported in June that "Arneson is plugging away on two different Blackmoor campaign supplements, 'Egg of Coot' and 'Land of the Skandaharians.'" Arneson still hoped to deploy smaller firms as foot soldiers in his "great War" against TSR, but in that respect he was hopelessly overmatched: TSR, through its license agreements, wielded a disproportionate influence over much of the industry. The conceit that there was a stark distinction between the original *D&D* game and the new *Advanced* game was built into the very structure of their licenses: although MiniFigs held a figure license for the original game, TSR separately bid out a license for the *Advanced* game in the spring of 1980, awarding it to Grenadier. In addition to their license for the original *D&D* game, the Judges Guild had to sign a separate 5 percent licensing agreement the year before for the *Advanced* game, paying TSR first-quarter royalties for 1980 of $37,045.40, then $46,018.06 in the second. That deal would expire in another year, and they could ill afford any increase in that percentage fee—but nor was it clear they could survive without an agreement with TSR.

Some firms had sufficient standing to remain viable without TSR's beneficence. When TSR announced in the pages of Games Workshop's magazine *White Dwarf* that it had formed a UK subsidiary that would begin operating on March 30, the exclusive distribution agreement between TSR and Games Workshop had already come to a close. But if they were not to be allies, they would be competitors: the twentieth issue of *White Dwarf* featured an advertisement proclaiming in huge letters, in typefaces reminiscent of a certain film released that summer, that "the British Empire Strikes Back." There could be no doubt whom Games Workshop intended to strike back against: "After more than a decade of invasion by alien games, the Empire is at last prepared for the counter-attack," they explained. "We have watched, waited, and studied." Now they launched an initial slate of four boxed games, including a license of the popular *Doctor Who* television series, and had ambitions to enter the fantasy miniature gaming space shortly.

But at that point, would TSR rather ally with a hobby firm like Games Workshop, or the toy and electronics giant Mattel? Licensing with Mattel meant the development of a hand-held electronic *D&D* game, as Gygax explained: "The game will have a labyrinth-type display through which the player will maneuver his character." The Mattel agreement would encompass a number of future electronic games projects, and it was signed with an immediate advance of $25,000 and a 6.5 percent future royalty on net sales. A separate agreement also gave Mattel permission to develop *D&D* software cartridges for its video game console, Intellivision, under the same terms.

TSR could afford to play hardball with licensing as its game sales soared under its supercharged distribution agreement with Random House. When Random House received shipments from TSR, they paid an immediate advance of around a quarter of the expected retail sales. So, on March 6, after a flurry of February purchase orders, TSR received a payment from them of $79,000—and then, on March 12, another of $140,0000. The checks coming through this deal were simply staggering for the hobby industry of the time. Theirs was the sort of relationship where Will Niebling and Lawrence Schick would fly to Nassau, in the Bahamas, in the first week of May to brief TSR's distributor on forthcoming releases. Random House wanted to hear not just from a sales guy like Niebling, but also from Schick, the head of design, who could speak to creative direction. As a result of that meeting, Random House promised to distribute 25,000 copies of the 1981 *Dragon* calendar, and eagerly awaited the forthcoming *World of Greyhawk* campaign setting.

And then there were possibilities that could outshine even book sales. In June, the *Los Angeles Times* reported that a film based on *D&D* was in the works at Twentieth-Century Fox, gossiping about talks that had been in progress since at least February. A deal memo circulating in 1980 would grant Fox a two-year option from TSR for a film based on *D&D* for a down payment of $100,000 toward a purchase price of $250,000—though that number would go up if 1980 *D&D* sales were to exceed the 1979 figures. Gygax would develop a treatment for the project and receive an executive producer credit, as would Brian Blume, and they would have approval of the screenplay and key creative personnel. In compensation for their services, the producers would themselves split a six-figure sum and a generous cut of the net profits. Allowances would be made for potential sequels, and even a television series based on *D&D*. Gygax in particular became captivated by this project, but deals that large take time to work out, and negotiations dragged on throughout the year.

With Gygax dazzled by the spotlight of the national stage, work on fresh *D&D* product increasingly fell to TSR's small design department. Under Lawrence Schick as vice president, work was driven largely by Tom Moldvay, Jean Wells, and Zeb Cook. A department report from March 12 shows Moldvay and Wells revising the *Basic Set* and drafting the new *Expert Set*, which was due May 1. Originally, the plan had been to perform only minor revisions to the *Basic Set*, but once work started on *Expert*, they soon appreciated "the large changes needed in the design and the need for it to lock with the *Expert Set* also being written." The new plan was that *Basic* "will be designed for characters of low-level with powerful monsters and references to higher levels kept to a minimum, except where they can be explained adequately. More emphasis will be placed on how to play the game." As a crush of new players entered the *D&D* market, introductory explanations were more necessary than ever.

The efforts of the design team were spread thin, however. Cook and Schick were developing a new science-fiction role-playing game for TSR, something that could compete more directly with *Traveller;* the project, now called "Alien Worlds," was the subject of playtesting throughout the year. But the design department had a scope of responsibilities they simply did not have enough staff to discharge. "Apparently," a note at the end of the March report read, "higher executives are unaware of how soon we need a new design person. To this end we will be preparing a case showing how much time we lose just answering letters. It has started to become quite serious." It did not help that Jean Wells was sidelined around this time due to an incident involving the module *Palace of the Silver Princess*, which was notoriously pulped due to objectionable content. Apart from some sexually charged imagery, it also contained an Erol Otus drawing with numerous company in-jokes and perhaps caricatures of certain TSR executives. As of the April 15 design team meeting, Wells was "using her design skills to tackle our increasing letter load and doing typing and other work besides" under Cook's supervision.

As TSR staffed up, importing entire families to the sleepy town of Lake Geneva, it formed something of an isolated enclave where employees largely socialized among themselves: new hires might crash on another staffer's couch for a month or two, or even live out of the gray house at 723 Williams for a stint. If you brought family in tow, they too might find employment at TSR. When the design staff relocated Kevin Hendryx from Texas along with his wife Mary, she would soon work the retail counter in the Dungeon Hobby Shop, and this was not simple nepotism: they needed all the help they could get.

During the revision of the *Basic Set*, the design staff fretted, "There are problems in having to wait for Gary's decisions on seemingly fine points. Perhaps a clearer directive from higher up on the design concepts and how much leeway we have would help." It is hardly surprising that Gygax's time was hard to come by, given his national media prominence at that moment. TSR just could not manage to stay out of the spotlight: echoes of the Egbert affair continued to ripple through the national media. When TSR released Merle Rasmussen's new espionage role-playing game *Top Secret* early in 1980, they fell into another small publicity windfall. Apparently, some notes from Mike Carr's playtesting campaign had been left at a local Lake Geneva establishment, and because they ostensibly detailed a plot to assassinate an Israeli businessman named William Weatherbie, they ended up in the hands of law enforcement. A telltale logo on one of the pages led the FBI to the Hotel Clair, where they asked some polite questions before they were satisfied that the conspiracy was entirely fictitious. Carr quickly saw in this a marketing opportunity, and the press outreach for *Top Secret* incorporated the story of how the game was so realistic it had fooled the FBI.

But a new and less welcome front in TSR's battle to control its public image opened with news from Wasatch Middle School in Heber City, Utah, where an after-school *D&D* program founded at the beginning of the year had attracted around twenty high-performing students. At a March 27 meeting of the Heber school board, an attorney named Donald George, spokesman for a group of concerned parents, presented a detailed case for terminating the program. Some of his objection derived from the potential for sacrilege in the game, from the use of holy water to the practice of spells like Water Walk. But he mostly seemed to see it as a waste of time and resources. The Heber board ultimately voted against banning the game, and overwhelmingly, parents approved their children to participate when consulted—it turned out the group of concerned parents was just two couples.

Dissidents however raised the matter again at an April 10 school board meeting. School officials urged them to just let the program run its course, as students left to their own devices would turn to other interests soon enough; inevitably, the more *D&D* was perceived as a forbidden activity, the more kids would clamor to play it. Sales at a local game store reportedly doubled, and many students said they would now go on playing after the conclusion of the program. By the time the disgruntled parents tried to involve the state school board in the controversy, the exasperated superintendent announced that the program would be discontinued. He clarified that no scheduled activities had been canceled: "We finished out the cycle. . . . We did it on our own volition, without any outside pressure." But the syndicated news stories spread in the wake of this decision provided a more sensational and reductive account of the events in Heber City: that school officials had banned the game.

Moreover, reports on the Heber City controversy represented that *D&D* had been banned on religious grounds. One nondenominational Christian minister felt that the school board decision only scratched the surface of the real problem, that *D&D* "is very definitely antireligious," and indeed that "it comes from that old subversive source Satan." The new decade would bring with it a widespread "Satanic Panic" in American culture, one that painted various youth trends, including heavy metal music, as causes of anti-Christian behavior. Effectively, these critics argued the inverse of the previous narrative about Egbert: instead of claiming that this imaginary game could induce players to believe its fantasy was real, they believed that players mistakenly thought the fantasy of the game was imaginary, when it actually indoctrinated them into real-world witchcraft and demonology. In the eyes of these critics, Gygax and Arneson truly were wizards, who simply disguised their black magic as a game. The irony was that both of them strongly self-identified as Christians—Arneson even started working in the autumn with the Way International on a game for memorizing biblical verses.

The spotlight followed controversy, and the debt that TSR owed to alarmist press was beyond evaluation. An article published in *New West* in August 1980 quoted a *Model Retailer* columnist's advice to TSR: "They should raise a foundation to this Egbert kid. Except for the disappearance of that boy and the resulting national exposure, TSR could have remained a steadily growing hobbygame company instead of a skyrocketing one." Gygax, interviewed for the same piece, had to admit "it was immeasurably helpful to us in name recognition."

Those words were surely recorded before another, sadder echo of the previous year's publicity, as newspapers around the country reported the suicide of James Dallas Egbert on August 16. This led to a new spate of articles with sensational titles like "Youth Buried with His Secret," while William Dear despicably exploited the occasion to tease the press that he still held secrets about the past year's investigation that might, or might not, link Egbert's fate to *D&D*. "I've weighed it very heavily," Dear told reporters, but he could "see no use" in revealing what he knew. And so the press syndicates would affirm that "the mystery of his whereabouts for the month has never been cleared up."

But the *New York Times* discovered that after the young man's death, his anguished parents needed the truth to be told at last. Egbert's parents had withheld the details "at the urging of a flamboyant private detective who wanted them to sell movie rights to the story." The heart-wrenching truth was that Egbert had, in the summer of 1979, fled as far from his school as he could, to New Orleans, before drinking a mixture of root beer and cyanide in a hotel room. After he survived this suicide attempt, he worked at an oilfield in Louisiana until he was persuaded to call his mother—only then, when his mother connected him to Dear, had Egbert discovered the intense media attention around his disappearance.

While Egbert was still missing, Dear first approached his parents about the possibility of capitalizing on this remarkable story. He insisted that the sensational publicity he recklessly courted was, as the *Times* put it, "one of the best hopes of turning up witnesses and clues." When Egbert surfaced, Dear impressed upon him the potential value of the rights to the story, money that might be badly needed, especially as the showy and profligate search for Egbert had run up a tab reportedly nearing $40,000. For a time, Egbert and Dear were partners in this endeavor. Egbert's parents went along with the plan, even giving Dear power of attorney for the purposes of negotiating with Hollywood. But that permission was retracted with Egbert's passing, and instead, in the hopes of doing some good, his parents went public with the whole story. In time it would become clear that they did not manage to close all the avenues Dear might explore to profit from the story himself, however, and the popular imagination continued to contextualize Egbert's situation in a pattern of juvenile harm inflicted by *D&D*.

TSR could not afford to tolerate a recurring narrative in the press that *D&D* was harmful to children. An advertisement in the August *Dragon* solicited for

"Real-life Clerics" who could attest to "the game's helpful, positive influence on those who play it," and one obliging reverend shared his endorsement in the issue following. TSR also countered these reports by forming an education department with a mandate to leverage the TSR product line, including *D&D*, in classrooms. Spreading into the educational market was not merely an attempt to shed a pall of unwholesomeness, but was also an attempt at diversification, finding new markets—even if it was then unthinkable that the public's appetite for *D&D* was anywhere near saturation.

Branching out into areas like education is only one way that staffing swelled at TSR. By spring, the number of employees had grown to seventy-six, double the year before. Gygax's confidante Steve Marsh came on board temporarily to assist Zeb Cook with the *Expert Set*; the team report from May 15 explained that "Zeb has started on the section for players and Steve Marsh has taken over the monster section." Jim Ward, who had freelanced for TSR as early as 1975, finally quit his job as a schoolteacher and joined TSR on June 16, just as they were putting the finishing touches on his forthcoming *Deities & Demigods* book. Interestingly, Ward would join the sales department rather than design, so his addition did little to alleviate the mad rush there, which, in addition to rewriting the *Basic Set* and pruning the sprawling *Expert Set* rules, included preparing a large tournament for GenCon. Although the "Alien Worlds" project remained a priority, the design department report from June states bluntly that "no serious work" had been done on it in the last three months.

As of May, the company became large enough to need an internal newsletter, one called *Random Events*, which introduced new hires, advertised employee events and corporate initiatives, and furnished a healthy dose of TSR's corporate culture—at first, one decidedly from the perspective of staff, not management. One aspect of corporate culture that changed at the same time was the departure of Tim Kask from the helm of *Dragon*. A curt announcement in the May *Dragon* issue heralded the elevation of Kask's protégé Jake Jaquet to the editorship of the magazine, heading a team where he worked closely with Kim Mohan. Jaquet had great ambitions for TSR Periodicals, which they would rebrand Dragon Publishing: in May, he circulated an internal proposal to form an association for *D&D* and *AD&D* players focused on participating "in a nation-wide, multiple tournament contest for a national *AD&D* title." Naturally the platform of Dragon Publishing might keep the proposed association's membership abreast of events.

There was simply no question of cramming the expanding staff into the Hotel Clair and 723 Williams Street, so TSR leased a large facility a mile or two north at 281 Sheridan Springs Road. Sheridan Springs, incidentally, was named for the Civil War general Philip Sheridan, who visited the area in 1874 and praised the quality of the natural spring near that road—a century later, those waters bubbled into a Coca-Cola bottling plant. As the new TSR facility there had formerly been occupied by Leisure and Recreational Products, a company that customized vans, employees called it the LRP building. The previous occupants left behind enough material that the walls of TSR's front office were remodeled with automobile upholstering; the sales area, for example, was done in a light-brown vinyl with ornamental buttons. For the time being, the creative staff, including both artists and game designers, remained at the Hotel Clair. Commuting between the two, and especially parking at the LRP building, became a notorious bureaucratic hassle. It was only a taste of the growing pains expansion would bring.

There is no small irony that Origins found itself in need of a last-minute venue in 1980: the planned convention space, the University of Delaware, rescinded its permission, a move widely attributed to fears that some Egbert-like incident might befall the campus. So, the convention instead returned to Widener College in Chester, Pennsylvania, to the same lack of air conditioning—despite a promise to the contrary in the program—and with the exhibit hall cramming one hundred vendor booths into an even smaller space. "By comparison," *Random Events* would snark, "the Black Hole of Calcutta was a vast wasteland." Attendance was steady, with vague tallies indicating three or four thousand in all, but many reports spoke wistfully of the pinnacle Origins had reached in 1978 at Ann Arbor.

The irony of worrying over Origins attendees venturing into the steam tunnels, of course, was that Origins was supposed to be a bastion of level-headed wargaming—though that too was changing. On Saturday night, SPI head Jim Dunnigan made what one observer called an "impassioned plea to the historical gamers not to become overly paranoid about the growth of the science fiction/fantasy theme," no doubt because SPI was debuting its first fantasy-role-playing game, *Dragonquest*. The growing competition in the role-playing space was on full display at Origins. Someone asked Dave Arneson, whose booth offered autographed copies of *Adventures in Fantasy* for $25, to justify that steep price—only to be informed, as an attendee put it, that "autographed copies would be collectors' items in three or four years." Meanwhile, across the hall, *Dragonquest* traded briskly as a boxed set—like *Adventures in Fantasy*, containing 150 pages worth of rulebooks—for just $9.95. Even the boxed version of *Runequest* would come in at $19.95, and it contained the core rulebook, which then traded for $11.95 alone, in addition to six dice, a module, a book of monsters, and a tutorial on *Basic Role-Playing*. Pricing certainly kept *Adventures in Fantasy* in the margins.

Perhaps the most striking debut at Origins was the presence of Microcomputer Games, a new subsidiary of Avalon Hill selling commercial wargame software. Where TSR had been happy to field out a license to Mattel to adapt *D&D* for computers in exchange for royalties, Avalon Hill invested in a substantial move into the computer space. They were not the only wargame publisher branching out in this space: Dave Wesely's Discovery Games, no doubt funded by the Avalon Hill release of *Source of the Nile* the year before, spent 1980 developing a "Squadron Leader Series" of World War II aerial combat computer games, all running on the same engine. Under the rubric of 4-D Interactive Systems, a company founded by four Twin Cities coalition veterans whose names began with "D," Arneson worked on these Discovery Games titles as well. Ultimately, Avalon Hill's Microcomputer Games division would end up distributing some of the titles that Discovery Games produced.

At the conclusion of Origins, the Game Manufacturers Association took formal charge of the future of the convention, cementing the convention's position as the alternative to TSR and GenCon. The consortium of five key manufacturers at the helm of GAMA heard bids for 1981 and, having long intended to hold a West Coast Origins, awarded the convention to the organizers of Pacificon, who had run the former GenCon West convention in the Bay Area. Immediately thereafter, they scheduled the 1982 Origins for Baltimore, a return to its original venue.

TSR made a token showing at Origins, with a small delegation to manage tournaments for *Top Secret, Gamma World, Dungeon!*, and the *D&D* properties, largely overseen by Will Niebling in Gygax's absence. Gygax and Blume were in Los Angeles in July, with Mattel, exploring further directions for electronic *D&D* games, and no doubt with other parties continuing to discuss Hollywood opportunities. The Origins *D&D* tournament, a Zeb Cook design called *Dwellers of the Forbidden City*, was organized around just three sessions with four groups of six adventurers each: so around seventy-five people would play in total, less even than competed in the first Origins tournament in 1975. While TSR would not neglect Origins entirely, they had every reason to view it as an inhospitable venue, and redouble their own focus on GenCon.

GenCon in 1980 would be the first place most people would see the *World of Greyhawk*—its absence at Origins, where it had long been promised, was lamented by many attendees there. This would be the first campaign world setting that TSR brought to the market, though many of their prior modules were nominally situated in it. In the context of the ongoing legal dispute, the release of the *World of Greyhawk* showed the general populace of *D&D* fans for the first time a map, albeit a heavily revised and expanded one, of the Great Kingdom of the Castle & Crusade Society, and by implication how Blackmoor and Greyhawk were rooted in it. Blackmoor itself warrants only a brief paragraph deeming it a "little known territory" with an anonymous ruler and a ruined castle under which "extensive labyrinths are supposed to exist." TSR printed 50,000 of the folio to start—and thanks to their distribution deal with Random House, half of those copies were spoken for sight unseen.

But the main release for GenCon would be a *D&D* debut, the hardcover *Advanced* book *Deities & Demigods*. This expansion and update to the 1976 supplement *Gods, Demi-gods and Heroes* added a number of real-world pantheons, including entries for Babylonian and Native American religions, but also a warm salute to the fantasy fiction that inspired *D&D*. TSR had licensed the setting of Nehwon from Fritz Leiber for its *Lankhmar* game back in 1976, so that was a natural addition. Eric Holmes had generously supplied a version of Lovecraft's *Cthulhu* mythos to *Dragon* late in 1977, and those elements would be wrapped into *Deities & Demigods* along with a section based on Michael Moorcock's Elric series. By 1980, however, the Chaosium had secured a license to publish games based on Lovecraft's Cthulhu mythos from Arkham House—and, before publishing their 1977 board game *Elric*, they secured "all game rights to the stories of Elric of Melnibone," as their press release proudly announced back then. So, a hasty second print of *Deities & Demigods* would soon feature an acknowledgment reading: "Special thanks are also given to Chaosium, Inc. for permission to use the material found in the Cthulhu Mythos and the Melnibonean Mythos." But this intellectual property issue should not overshadow the reality that a company trying to overcome perceived Christian sacrilege might have thought twice before releasing a book about deities that characters could worship, especially one that includes quite a few adaptations of real-world faiths outside the Judeo-Christian tradition.

After years of trailing Origins in attendance, GenCon finally caught up. *Dragon* would put the final attendance figures at 4,300 for Origins and 4,500 for GenCon—but internal TSR documents suggest it was a tie, with GenCon also coming in at 4,300. No doubt the spike in attendance was driven partially by the massive *Advanced D&D* Open tournament, which encompassed more than eight hundred players in parties of nine overseen by more than forty dungeon masters, with seven rounds of play spanning all four days of the convention. The adventure, which pitted players against the slavers of the Pomarj—familiar to purchasers of the *World of Greyhawk*—would soon be published in a series of four modules, beginning with the *Slave Pits of the Undercity*.

Now GenCon attracted the sort of coverage mainstream industry trade magazines would usually reserve for the Hobby Industry of America conventions. *Playthings* gave GenCon six pages that summer, and it neatly explained how it measured up to its longstanding rival: "the two shows are highly competitive, but Origins emphasizes board war games and GenCon has become the world's capital for fantasy role-playing." Companies like Heritage knew to bring those offerings to GenCon: Duke Seifried was on hand to demonstrate their new role-playing game, *Knights and Magick*, which tried to return adventure gaming to its roots in miniatures. *Playthings* observed that one could readily perceive an industry schism on display at GenCon, between those companies who clung to the legacy of wargaming and those who embraced the new "adventure gaming" path blazed by *D&D*. Eric Dott, the president of Avalon Hill, indignantly told the magazine that "people can call it what they want, but when you're in a military conflict situation, it's still a war game."

Interest in *D&D* was hardly confined to industry reporters. Around GenCon, Tom Hoving of the television show *20/20* would visit Lake Geneva and tour the Hotel Clair offices with Gygax, surrounded by a full camera crew. A few pictures from the day appeared in *Random Events*, though the footage would not air until the following year. And then a reporter from *Forbes* came to visit the new TSR office after GenCon, where he found Brian Blume in a three-piece suit and Gygax wearing a t-shirt. "Is *Dungeons & Dragons* the Hula-Hoop of the Eighties?" the reporter asked. *Forbes* noted one factoid about the median age range of *D&D* purchasers, which over the past two years had dropped decidedly, from ages 18 through 22 down to ages 10 through 14. Demographic figures released by TSR showed that 46 percent of *D&D* sets in 1980 were purchased by or for children between the ages of 10 and 14, with another 26 percent for those between 15 and 17. There is a variety of data to similar effect available: over half of subscribers to *Dragon* in 1980 were under 18, for example, and the median age of subscribers had already dropped to 16. While the youth market was attractive to anyone in the toy and hobby business, it was a market that came with certain constraints and limitations that might be hard for TSR to navigate—especially as the Satanic Panic grew.

Now, close to the ten-year anniversary of the date when Gygax lost his job at the Fireman's Fund Insurance Company, a sort of corporate origin myth—maybe a character that Gygax played—started to solidify about how his termination had inspired a bout of self-reflection and ultimately a new career goal of inventing games. While it was true that Gygax used that "temporary (forced) vacation" from employment to work on amateur games for "semi-commercial" publication, no one in their right mind back then would have aspired to make a livelihood designing the sorts of miniatures rules Gygax then favored. Nonetheless, the November issue of *Playthings* had it that "Gygax quit his job as an insurance underwriter to write for various gaming publications," and *Forbes* delivered a similar line. The spotlight had begun to shape how Gygax saw his own character.

Gygax and Blume hinted to *Forbes* about greater ambitions; they were considering "some bank financing" to fund their plans, which would be unusual, as "up to now we've basically been pay-as-you go." To date, TSR had only taken on debt to purchase its Burroughs computer; even the mortgages of the two buildings in Lake Geneva had been done through the separate partnership controlled by Gygax and Blume. "It's a decisive moment at TSR," the *Forbes* article concluded. "Dark corridors stretch off in the distance in several directions. Brian Blume looks over at Gary Gygax almost as if he were rolling the dice in his hand. 'Nobody's ever had anything this hot . . . ,' he says, peering in vain down those corridors."

It was not easy to decide which businesses TSR needed to be in. Sometimes emergencies demanded action, like when supply chain problems resulting from the runaway success of the *Basic Set* forced TSR to ship boxes with a sheet of cardboard "randomizer chits" instead of dice. As they had been mass-importing those dice from Hong Kong, the most economical path forward was for TSR to begin manufacturing its own dice. In time for GenCon, Kevin Blume had arranged for in-house "Dragon Dice" that would be sold separately and packaged into future game products. Not that they could do this on the cheap: TSR had molds made, at a cost of around $100,000 each, and contracted out to a firm in Beloit to forge an initial run of a half million dice, in eighteen colors. Famously, although these dice were stamped with numbers on their faces, the numbers were difficult to read unless colored in with a crayon that would ship with them.

In his role of controller, and as *Random Events* put it "Chief Overseer," Kevin Blume had become indispensable to the company. Around September, a reorganization positioned Kevin Blume as TSR's treasurer, and explicitly as third in command to his brother Brian and Gary Gygax. At the time, Mike Carr was the company's general manager and remained "in charge of the people who create, produce and market TSR products," meaning all of sales, marketing, design, development, art, and production. Will Niebling thus reported to Carr at the time, as did Lawrence Schick. But now Carr worked under Kevin.

Following this reorg, the extent to which the Blume family had staffed certain areas of the company with relatives started to become conspicuous. Doug Blume, brother to Kevin and Brian, was elevated to vice president of personnel and training. And after Kevin became treasurer, Judi Witt, his wife's sister, took his former position. Among her direct reports was her own husband, Steve Witt, who was in charge of operations. *Random Events* would sometimes poke fun at the Blume family's growing ranks, as when it detailed how Brian's wife Vicki, who "used to work for Doug, her husband's brother" had moved in the organization: "now she works for Steve, her husband's other brother's wife's sister's husband," which is to say Kevin's wife Mary's sister Judi's husband Steve. And then in the autumn, Judi Witt's brother Jack Sloan came on board in product engineering, which covered purchasing from vendors, and before the end of the year he would be joined in that capacity by his—and Mary and Judi's—father Bob Sloan. The collective purview of the Blume family effectively gave them a lock on most questions of how TSR spent money.

If Gygax were concerned about Blume family nepotism, he was not in much of a position to complain. He had placed his son Ernie in charge of

Dungeon Hobby Shop, a position where he was being groomed to take over all consumer-facing aspects of the business. His wife Mary continued to run the Jo Powell Agency, placing advertisements for the increasingly successful *Dragon* magazine, which gave her personally around a 10 percent commission on buys that were now hundreds of thousand dollars a year. Gygax's daughter Elise was on payroll acting as his personal assistant. Even Heidi Gygax, who would be starting her junior year in high school in the fall, took a summer job at TSR. He also continued to rely on old friends: Dave Dimery, who had been best man at Gygax's wedding, had his own vice presidency in store. Dimery was an old advertising hand in Chicago, who quickly put together a campaign structured around Morley the Wizard as TSR's new mascot. The success of *D&D* was something Gygax understandably wanted to share with those closest to him.

By that autumn, the full impact of *D&D* sales on Gygax's personal finances became apparent. A tabulation of royalties paid to him for the nine months leading up to the end of September 1980 totaled $291,662.88. Royalties for the *Basic Set* alone contributed nearly $100,000 to that, and the three hardcover *Advanced* books piled on a further $140,000 or so. And September would show that sales had further room to grow: it was TSR's best sales month ever, bringing in revenue of $1.8 million, an amount approaching TSR's revenue for the entire 1979 fiscal year.

TSR had come a long way since its humble beginnings. In honor of the fifth anniversary of TSR Hobbies, counting from the dissolution of the original partnership, TSR held a "Founders Day" event early in October, featuring a cake depicting Gygax and Blume's faces: a picture on the back of *Random Events* shows Gary pretending to cut the cake with an axe.

But something about Gary Gygax started to change at the end of summer 1980. Surely these enormous royalty payments had life-altering implications, but whether they were the sole cause of the shift is difficult to say. Gygax complained in a letter to Steve Marsh that back on the final day of GenCon, "I was stricken with a strange illness which kept me in bed for about three weeks." Although he was briefly hospitalized and subjected to all manner of tests, "no diagnosis could be made." In Gygax's subsequent correspondence throughout the year, he complained of lacking energy, of being unable to work at a hundred percent. Toward the end of October, he wrote to Marsh that he was happy "to postpone full recovery for as long as possible," in part so he could enjoy a few wargames at the Dungeon Hobby Shop. But

CAPITALISM INACTION DEPT.

The secret RE ballpoint camera took these photos to give every-one an idea what happened at the TSR stockholders' meeting. The big news was that Gary almost chopped Brian in half for buying a car that costs as much as a house. In the end, Brian put down his knife, apologized, and promised to dress real funny (below) so Gary would laugh. The meeting ended with a big poker game to determine divi-dends and divisors. Guess who won.

Reconstruction of the back cover of *Random Events* 1 no. 7 (1980), showing events at the October 3 TSR "Founders Day" party at the Red Eye Restaurant, with photographs by Bill Frantz; the "Capitalism Inaction" text was a parody, playfully reinterpreting the images as depicting the November 3 shareholder meeting.

troublingly, he reported, "I do not have any particular creative urge at this time." It is unclear, though, how much occasion he could have to satisfy that urge, as "there is enough administrative work here at TSR to keep me pretty busy from day to day." Surely managing the growing prosperity of TSR drained Gygax of any energy he might then have dedicated to game design.

And then, not long after he wrote those words to Marsh, Gygax lost his mother to a heart attack, while she was visiting Dragonlands ranch. Gygax had been just seventeen years old when his father died. "I expected my mother to live on for many years. Well, what can one say?"

In this state—unwell, famous, bereaved, wealthy, and stymied creatively— Gygax came to the November TSR shareholder meeting, which fell on the day voters would go to the polls to elect Ronald Reagan as the next US president. TSR's business at this point was simply gangbusters. Ed Sollers, who would start November 5, was the one-hundredth employee. Revenue had effectively quadrupled over the previous year, with the company bringing in around $8.3 million. Accordingly, at the shareholder meeting, they set a new book value for TSR stock at $1,000. The Blume family stake in TSR was now worth around a million dollars. As a measure to protect that substantial holding, a shareholder vote that night brought about a change long in the works: after holding the titles of controller and treasurer, Kevin joined Brian and Gygax on TSR's board of directors.

But of course, there was one outstanding worry that TSR's newly constituted board had to resolve. "Who was the fat guy with the bald lawyer nobody would sit next to?" *Random Events* wondered pettily in its report on the shareholder meeting, the last where Dave Arneson would appear in person. The scorn he faced in that room was not lost on Arneson, either: as he wrote in a letter to Chaosium founder Greg Stafford at the time, "Ever sat for an hour with 38 people glowering at you?"

Arneson knew well that the strong sales reported at the shareholder meeting meant more royalties for him, enough that he could take over his own distribution and publishing. By this point, Excalibre had lost its appetite for publishing *Adventures in Fantasy*, sitting on a large amount of inventory that simply would not move. On November 12, they signed over all rights to Arneson's company Adventure Games—it was around this time that Arneson stopped using the name Adventures Unlimited, so the contract marking this transfer of rights has the old company name crossed out and the new one penciled in. The transaction would be covered by the hobby press; *Strategy & Tactics* ran a brief blurb to the effect that "Dave Arneson has been disappointed with the low sales and high price of his game, *Adventures in Fantasy*, produced by Excalibre Games. To remedy this, he has bought back the game and will publish it under his own company name, Adventure Games, for $20.00." Arneson planned to open a new office in St. Paul on November 15, and had already convinced Dave Megarry to come back home from Boston to work there. He also negotiated toward a new contract with Richard Snider for the rights to his still-unpublished "Mutant."

Arneson's willingness to spend cash probably reflected the optimism of his legal team about their prospects in his dispute with TSR. The fundamental uncopyrightability of game rules was one of the larger difficulties that Arneson's legal team needed to overcome if they followed his narrative that their client's main contribution to the "joint work" was some essential, uncopyrightable "original idea." Much of the resulting argument is quite technical, and dependent on the authoritative treatise *Nimmer on Copyright*, the standard guide to copyright law. A passage in *Nimmer* highlighted by Arneson's legal team does suggest that uncopyrightable ideas can qualify as a contribution to a joint work: "if authors A and B work in collaboration, but A's contribution is limited to plot ideas which standing alone would not be copyrightable, and B weaves the idea into a completed literary expression, it would seem that A and B are joint authors of the resulting work." But to be counted as "work in collaboration," the authors would have to intend to collaborate on it: it was not enough if Arneson had previously and independently invented "original ideas" like dungeon adventuring or experience points, and those ideas were only later observed by Gygax and woven into a completed work. No one disputed that Arneson had sent rules text to Gygax, who freely volunteered he had received eighteen or twenty such pages, but those basic ideas dated before Arneson had any intention of collaborating with Gygax on *D&D*.

Reviewing the historical record, Gygax and Arneson had shared a postal correspondence and a number of phone calls in 1973 during the development of *D&D* which showed an intent to collaborate—but linking that to concrete contributions that Arneson newly created for *D&D* was not straightforward. Arneson had playtested the rules, written comments on the draft, and sent along further contributions, but the letters showed Gygax rejecting or rewriting Arneson's submissions specifically because they were not written to be merged into "our (LGTSA) rules as plagiarized from your rules as drawn from *Chainmail*." The legal requirements to demonstrate collaboration are however quite lenient. *Nimmer* stipulates that the contributions made to a joint work do not need to be comparable in quantity or quality in order for the parties to be co-authors under copyright law. As long as they could prove that Arneson created literally any contribution with an intent to merge it into *D&D*, the case for joint authorship could be made. For example, case law precedent allowed "joint work" in cases where one party contributed the images and another the text for a given book, so Arneson's legal team held up his four illustrations of monsters as indisputable examples of copyrightable work created by Arneson intentionally for the *D&D* project that appeared in the published work unchanged. It is sobering to think that those images only barely made it into the published game, as Arneson sent them at the eleventh hour, and the decision to include them in the published booklets was decidedly arbitrary.

Gygax continued to maintain, as he told the press that summer, that "Dave Arneson didn't write a word of the first three booklets." Yet, ultimately, Arneson's legal team argued that "Arneson and Gygax knew exactly how much Arneson had contributed to the work when the royalties contracts were drawn up by TSR, the work published with Arneson named as a co-author, and the copyright notice submitted with Arneson designated as a co-author. There was no mutual mistake regarding Arneson's joint authorship and the entire argument is a sham." But surely nobody had given this matter much thought six years earlier, back when no one could have imagined this would be an idea worth more than $300. Or the year before that, when Gygax casually proposed to Arneson, "I'll whip out a booklet (Gygax and Arneson, I trust)" and then "trust you'd like to split royalties." When Gygax wrote those words, he had no way of knowing how much or little work Arneson would later do toward the development of the game—especially given that Gygax hoped to publish this through Guidon Games, and Arneson had refused to do further work for Guidon until he had been paid back royalties. Gygax's offer was simply an acknowledgement that he was building on ideas that Arneson had generated, with an expectation that Arneson would help down the road. The 1974 and 1975 contracts in no way measured some later percentage of contribution; they simply followed the initial "split" that Gygax had promised.

All this line of argument addressed only TSR's counterattack against Arneson. To make the case that the *Advanced* game was effectively the same game as the original *D&D* for the purposes of the 1975 contract, they needed a different set of evidence. Arneson's legal team went through the original *D&D* booklets and cut out the descriptions of various monsters, spells, magic items, and so on, along with parallel passages in the *Advanced D&D* books discussing those elements of the game, and then pasted these clippings side-by-side on pages that filled binder after binder that they submitted into evidence. So, on one side of the page, you would see the text for the owlbear that appears in the *AD&D Monster Manual*, and on the other, the very similar text from original *D&D*, to illustrate how directly the former derived from the latter.

But the case of the owlbear is a curious one, as its original text came from the *Greyhawk* supplement, authored by Gary Gygax and Rob Kuntz, for which Arneson received no credit or royalty. If Arneson had not demanded royalties for the *Greyhawk* supplement, which existed at the time the 1975 contract was executed, as a component of "the game or game rules" that made up original *D&D*, why did he think he was entitled to claim things like the owlbear as part of the original game now? The answer is that Arneson's legal team had another tool at their disposal: the Holmes *Basic Set*, which borrowed liberally from the *Greyhawk* monsters and spells, and for which Arneson received credit as a co-author and also royalties. So, the legal binders submitted into evidence contained numerous clippings from the *Basic* rulebook, including for the owlbear.

Early drafts of the "Beginner's Set" had only Holmes's and Gygax's names on them; we can merely speculate how the legal landscape might have changed if TSR had published the *Basic* rules with those credits. The decision back in 1977 to instead treat *Basic* as simply an edit of the original game, and thus as something notionally created jointly with Arneson, was a choice that undermined TSR's later strategy of representing the *Advanced* game as something entirely new and separate. How much more similar to the original game was *Basic* than *Advanced*? Both were rewrites, with rules changes, of the original game—but the first Arneson received royalties for, and the second he did not?

Arneson's legal team also engaged an expert witness to testify that *AD&D* effectively was the same game as original *D&D*: Jon Freeman, author of the *Winner's Guide to Board Games*, who was now gaining prominence as the designer of a popular early computer adaptation of *D&D* called *The Temple of Apshai*. Gygax could not have been happy to see Freeman appear as an expert witness for Arneson, as Gygax had accredited Freeman personally after reading his article on *D&D* in *Games* magazine the year before, gushing in a letter published in the January 1980 issue that "Jon Freeman absolutely knows and understands the game." Freeman's deposition effectively splits into two parts: the first intended to show the vast conceptual gulf between *Chainmail* and *D&D*; and the second demonstrating the lack of the same between original *D&D* and *Advanced D&D*. "There is nothing of any consequence in *D&D* that is not included in *AD&D*," Freeman posited. He named many monsters, spells, and magic items which are reused between the systems, and singled out the names of the games themselves as a key part of this connection: "if *AD&D* is not *D&D*, it can't call itself *AD&D*." After all, he said, "People are buying the *AD&D* books because they believe them to be *D&D*." In his assessment, the differences between the games were "trivial."

The minutiae of the legal questions that decide these matters are almost always unsatisfyingly disconnected from the questions of justice that we want settled. Regardless of what is technically copyrightable, and who wrote down the words on the page, Arneson clearly deserved substantial compensation for his contributions to the original game. And as the game's success grew, so did Arneson's take. Gygax pocketed eye-popping royalties for 1980—and Arneson's share of the royalties for the *Basic Set* and the original *D&D* game for that year amounted to $132,241.45 (in 2021 dollars, that would be around $425,000). To put that in perspective, Arneson received about $750 in 1980 royalties for *Adventures in Fantasy* from Excalibre. His share of the *D&D* proceeds was surely a larger amount of money than any game designer in the hobby made at the time other than Gygax himself; it was around a third of Gygax's royalty take. Was that adequate compensation for his "original idea"? Arneson could hardly pretend to "make little or nothing" from his spark of inspiration like one Blog the Cro-Magnon. But who could say what was fair, especially after so much enmity had built up? The legal instruments involved were not calibrated to determine whether that sum was too much or too little.

For TSR, the situation simply needed to be resolved. Arneson's legal team had managed to interpose itself into TSR's ongoing negotiations with Twentieth-Century Fox. A lawyer for the studio asked Arneson's counsel the somewhat leading question, "I would also appreciate your informal opinion as to which of the various parties involved has the rights in connection with *Dungeons & Dragons* as they pertain to motion pictures." It seemed that the continuing legal situation would cast a pall over any negotiations regarding the film rights.

Nor did it stop there. In the document discovery phase of the lawsuit, Arneson's legal team learned of TSR's licensing agreement with Mattel. They demanded copies of any electronic game designs, along with draft instruction booklets, to ascertain whether any potential "original idea" of Arneson's might have made its way into that product, which would debut in the coming year. Arneson's team also delved deep into the ongoing work on the *Basic* and *Expert Sets*, and had begun prying into new work on a new project then called the *Companion Rules* intended, in Gygax's own words, to be "a pickup of the three supplements to the original game— *Greyhawk*, *Blackmoor*, and *Eldritch Wizardry*—revised, expanded, edited, and improved." Did Arneson have interests there as well?

But beyond all these concerns was the sheer amount of money TSR was making, and the amount that they projected they would make in the future. If TSR had to settle with Arneson, would they rather negotiate a sum when they were a company making $8 million per year, or $16 million, or $32 million, or more? Their potential exposure could only grow if they waited. Something had to be done, and soon.

In the final weeks of 1980, Gygax had come to understand that a confluence of factors—including the business needs of TSR and his own struggles to activate his creativity—made it necessary for him to delegate not just work on the *Basic Set*, but the primary design of *D&D*. Gygax declared in a December letter to Steve Marsh that he had embarked on a quest to identify someone who could "co-write (or at worst, ghost write)" new *D&D* material. But Gygax embraced this path only reluctantly. "I would love to give up business for writing, but I cannot in good conscience do so for at least the next couple years."

A suitable understudy for Gygax had to be equal parts energetic and deferential. One TSR employee who fit the bill was Frank Mentzer, who had joined the production department earlier in the year. Currently, he was tasked with ramping up the proposed new membership group for *D&D*, the Role Playing Gamer's Association, or RPGA. For winning the Masters Tournament at GenCon that summer, Mentzer was recognized by a *Dragon* article proclaiming, "He's the Top Dungeon Master." He was moreover protective of Gygax personally, sending him a letter two days before Christmas reminding him, "We live in a turbulent time of great tensions. There are a lot of nuts out there, many of whom have a Cause." Pointing to an event that happened just two weeks before, he warned, "Observe the recent death

of harmless John Lennon. Also observe the religious zeal of many unin-
formed Christians against D&D." This was the downside of how brightly
the spotlight shone on Gygax personally. "Have you considered rent-a-cop
security for yourself, in public?" But the imminent threat at the time was
not from an assassin—it was looming in a Minnesota District Court.

TSR Turn Results for 1980

Revenue: $8.3M (Barasch ranking 1), profit $1M
Employees: 76
Stock Valuation: $1,000
GenCon attendance vs. Origins: 4,000 vs. 3,500

TSR Board Members: 3

1981: Identity Crisis

High atop a crenelated turret flanked by castle walls, there perched a wizard named Morley, who surveyed the teeming crowds below. It was part of what *Strategy & Tactics* would call "an elaborate B-grade movie set" with "a gateway guarded by a blood-shot eyed dragon (obviously a frequent guest at the TSR office parties)." The scene was the Hobby Industry of America trade show, at the end of January 1981, and TSR's medieval booth won an award for Will Niebling's animatronic showpiece. This was not TSR's first promotional stop of the year—Niebling and Gygax had manned the Mattel booth at the Consumer Electronics Show in Vegas to demonstrate the new electronic version of the game to distributors and retailers who hungrily anticipated its Christmas release. All would be on display shortly thereafter at the February Toy Fair in New York, part of a now ceaseless, expensive promotional roadshow. TSR had become a very different thing than it was just two years before.

At the beginning of 1981, no ceiling for sales of *Dungeons & Dragons* was in sight: the game was like a magic item that relentlessly generated gold. TSR's showy booths could now promote the repackaged *Dungeon!* board game by Dave Megarry, flanked by the *Basic* and *Expert Set* boxes—which were overdue the previous October, and just barely made it in time for the trade shows. It must have been of no small interest to Arneson's legal team that while the new version of the *Basic Set* booklet still listed Gygax and Arneson as authors, crediting Tom Moldvay as an editor, the *Expert Set* gave Zeb Cook and Steve Marsh as editors but mentions neither Gygax nor Arneson, nor what exactly that booklet was editing.

With every uptick in sales, the stakes in the Arneson lawsuit grew commensurately higher. The legal teams representing Arneson and TSR prepared for battle: Jon Freeman was deposed in San Francisco on January

15, and the case was slated to go to trial by April. The future of *D&D* was too bright to live in the shadow of a lawsuit. TSR simply had to settle with Arneson. The agreement, signed on March 6, forged a treaty in Arneson's "great War." As Arneson's press release at the time put it, "The terms of the settlement ensure authorship credits on the D&D game for Arneson as well as clarifying his rights to future D&D royalties. Arneson also received a financial settlement for his stock in TSR Hobbies, Inc."

While that press release represents the situation as a decisive victory, settlements tend to leave all aggrieved parties equally miserable: the terms were far more modest than Arneson's initial demands of TSR. In lieu of the six-figure cash damages requested in his complaint, TSR instead simply bought back the 56 shares Arneson owned: given their $1,000 valuation at the time, that did mean a significant windfall, but it also rid TSR of Arneson's unwelcome presence at shareholder meetings. In practice, the settlement more or less ignored the authorship credits Arneson had sought, as Gary Gygax's name would continue to appear alone on all of the core *Advanced D&D* books for the rest of the decade, and Arneson's name would not grace the box cover of future revisions of the *Basic Set*. Finally, Arneson's royalties on the *AD&D* game would not be the 5 percent he sought, but instead 2.5 percent—the same amount that Gygax himself received. While the agreement guaranteed for those royalties a minimum payment of $150,000 annually through 1984, the total royalties Arneson could gain from those titles was capped at $1.2 million. The likelihood that this agreement would make Arneson a millionaire surely made him overlook any concessions in his desired terms, but this last provision also virtually justified the entire settlement from TSR's perspective, as optimistically as they viewed their future sales prospects. For his other *D&D* titles, Arneson would receive a further guaranteed minimum of $20,000 per year for the duration of the copyrights.

Different Worlds gossiped admiringly about Arneson's settlement: "I bet that if you put five zeros after a number, you would be in the right order of dollar magnitude. That kind of money could capitalize quite a game company." Many apparently believed a court had decided in his favor, and the perception of a vindicating legal judgment cemented the growing consensus in the hobby that Arneson contributed the greater part to the invention of *D&D*. But Arneson himself, as part of the process of crafting the legal case, had recently been immersed in correspondence from 1972 and

1973, and now that his fortune was assured, he would deliver a more candid account of his own role in writing the game's text. On April 21, Arneson gave an interview to *Pegasus* magazine where he reported on the aftermath of demonstrating the Blackmoor dungeon to Gygax and the Lake Geneva group: "At the time, they had a lot more spare time than I did and they had a lot of ideas, so they came up with their own version of the rules. They sent theirs to us and we fooled around with them for a while. We exchanged letters for a while and just kind of slipped into it."

Arneson also used that April *Pegasus* interview to announce the future roadmap for Adventure Games, his lavishly financed successor to Adventures Unlimited. His immediate plans for the company included releasing a modern naval miniature wargame called *Harpoon* designed by Larry Bond, but he promised to follow that quickly with several titles long in the works: Richard Snider's "*Mutant* should be out for the conventions this summer." He also proposed to return to John Snider's "*Star Probe* and *Star Empires*," which Arneson said will "be presented in a series of about six booklets which will be released one at a time." Rounding out the Twin Cities coalition, he alluded to a new game design by Dave Megarry called *Pentantastar*. In reference to his own design work, he remained committed to the "Samurai" project for the Chaosium, observing that "two other people have beaten me to being published. But, time will tell which is best."

Arneson spoke with the greatest animation about continuing on with *Adventures in Fantasy*. Now that Adventure Games owned the title, he could cut the price and give it the marketing it deserved. But the independent review of *Adventures in Fantasy* that followed Arneson's interview in *Pegasus* was no more complimentary than the notices from the year before, even taking into account the reduced $20 price point. Arneson made much of how he could remedy price and production issues with a second edition, which he identified as another project in the works at Adventure Games. For the time being, he slapped an Adventure Games sticker on Excalibre boxes to obscure the former owner's logo.

The period around the settlement was not so triumphant at TSR: it was a tense and quiet time. *Random Events* went on an unannounced hiatus from February through April, upon its resumption reporting that the Dragon Publications staff were no longer able to produce the magazine themselves.

Gygax was also conspicuously absent from the pages of *Dragon*. His contributions had petered out a bit after GenCon the previous year, and his byline would be effectively absent until November 1981, when his regular column the "Sorceror's Scroll" returned with an admission that "not much magical ink has flowed from cockatrice quill to parchment for this column for a year now." It was in February when Gygax, perhaps taking Frank Mentzer's advice about the very real dangers of the spotlight, brought on staff Jim Johnson as "Administrative Aide to the President." Johnson served as Gygax's chauffeur and bodyguard.

Following the settlement, Gygax reported another bout of debilitating illness. In a letter to Steve Marsh, Gygax went into detail, saying "it is the same thing that struck me right after GenCon last year, this time it was more severe." Going back to April, he described a variety of ailments from an intestinal complaint to a pinched nerve in his lower back, and as a consequence he was "not up to working full-time at the office yet." Even at the end of the month he predicted, "I probably will not get back into full swing at the office for another month or so yet, for I do not care to risk another, possibly more serious, bout of illness again." As late as mid-May, the resumed *Random Events* noted that "Gary has been housebound of late this last week."

It was surely during this lull following the settlement that Gygax wrote a singular essay called "Who Am I?" It was a curiosity for any number of reasons, an almost confessional piece exploring what he wanted out of life. Like his many earlier retrospectives, it reviewed the founding of TSR and his tireless struggle to elevate it to its current situation, though surely Gygax now saw those events through the filter of the settlement. He began with his childhood, followed by the wargaming clubs and the first GenCon, continuing through the founding of the original Tactical Studies Rules partnership as something of a hobby, and the shocking death of Don Kaye. After that, he wrote, "In 1976 came an identity crisis. Was I a game player or was I a writer/designer?"

The modest initial success of *D&D* required that Gygax attend to so many TSR matters that actually playing games fell by the wayside. At first, Gygax found that "designing games was more fun than playing them." When the time came, as the business expanded and began to engage design staff, he thought perhaps he could enter more of an advisory position in which he could further indulge his passion for playing. But then in 1980, with the company pulling in over $8 million in sales, Gygax "once again faced an identity crisis. The demands of the corporation preclude being its chief executive officer and a designer/writer at the same time. Was I an executive, or did I wish to return to the creative end?"

Ultimately, Gygax resolved this dilemma by deciding to remain an executive. He felt a clear responsibility to his staff, now numbering more than one hundred people, to contribute in the capacity that was best for the company. "I hope I do not regret it in the time ahead," Gygax mused to himself, his inner conflict about renouncing game design on full display. This expanded on the sentiments Gygax expressed to Steve Marsh at the end of 1980, where he had admitted, "I would love to give up business for writing, but I cannot in good conscience do so far at least the next couple years."

By the end of the essay, Gygax seems to have convinced himself that he made the right decision. He approached business like an adventurer, exclaiming "business is a fun game, too!" He encouraged others to follow careers in adventure gaming, which at the worst would provide a paycheck, but advised that "if you approach the industry with gaming in mind, you will be ahead." He believed that "the logic and reasoning, planning and negotiation, learning and dedication which come from game playing can be of immeasurable help in business." His own example proved the point: a high school dropout and game expert had risen into the national spotlight, to the very cusp of being a household name.

Perhaps the greatest curiosity of all is that the piece appeared in the July issue of a competitor's magazine, *Space Gamer*. Why publish it there rather than in *Dragon*? Perhaps Gygax wanted to share these thoughts but also bury them a bit, safely out of the baleful gaze of *Dragon*, which had a circulation now nearing 50,000, up from just 15,000 the year before, and *Space Gamer* managed barely above a tenth of that. In its rapid growth spurt, *Dragon* surpassed the stagnant circulation of *Strategy & Tactics*—as that magazine conceded in its March 1981 issue—to become the dominant publication in hobby gaming, and it was still growing. People internally had begun to estimate when it might pass the 100,000 mark.

One name Gygax never mentioned in "Who Am I?" is Dave Arneson. That was consistent with TSR's corporate communications in the wake of the settlement. The May issue of *Toy & Hobby World*, a major retailer trade magazine, led with a "Corporate Profile" of TSR that focused almost exclusively on Gygax and his creative impetus. We learn from reading it that "in 1972, he took the big step and put aside his regular job to enter the speculative field of full-time game design." In keeping with the "heroic inventor" character he had adopted, the profile related how "creature comforts were few indeed for his family as Gary designed unsold games and sustained his household as a part-time cobbler." The ink on TSR's settlement with Arneson had barely dried, but there was no mention that *D&D* might have had a co-creator in the piece: it instead described how "Gygax began to apply his imagination to the creation of game systems that combined the best features of fantasy and gaming. He then introduced a new element to gaming—the play of a game 'character'—a personal touch that proved to be the key element in the birth of role-playing games." Similarly, in the June issue of *Playthings*, Gygax talked about the invention of games in terms like, "When I wrote the *Dungeons & Dragons* role-playing game, I wrote it for myself and for my friends, who had been playing war games and board games for years," with no mention that anyone else might have been involved.

The resolution of the legal situation thus would not end the rivalry between Gygax and Arneson. When TSR began promoting its new Role Playing Gamer's Association, it promised to offer a subscription service that kept players attached to the *AD&D* brand, something like the original business model of the Judges Guild—incidentally, the two-year license that the Judges Guild had signed with TSR to make *AD&D* products was due to expire imminently. Once the RPGA had been announced in the February *Dragon*, Arneson saw it as a blatant attempt to organize the community around the single pole of TSR, so he began working toward a competing organization: the International Fantasy Gaming Society (IFGS), which took its name from the recent science-fiction novel *Dream Park* by Larry Niven. To initially populate his IFGS, Arneson reached in June out to a regular "who's who" of game designers: Ken St. Andre, Ed Simbalist, Steve Perrin, Marc Miller, Steve Jackson, Mike Stackpole, and of course members of his own inner circle like Richard Snider, Dave Megarry, and M. A. R. Barker.

Arneson urged the IFGS not to rally around any single set of rules, which would repeat the "fallacy exemplified by another 'so-called' great designer who tried to be a 'god.'" Instead, Arneson stressed the position that rules were inessential to the game, that all great innovators in role playing had started without rules. This idea was not met with much enthusiasm from the likes of St. Andre or Perrin, who published rules and struggled to advance them in the marketplace. Still stung by his experience at Origins in 1978, Arneson stressed that the group should establish an award for the best role-playing game of the year, but on the strict condition that "this award would be given to the author/designers, not to the companies." Arneson's "great War" against Gygax and TSR had given way to a tenuous peace—a Cold War perhaps—but the battle for control of *D&D* and the industry it created would continue unabated.

TSR was beginning to have an identity crisis of its own. By May, staff had increased to 110, driven by an influx of young staffers bouncing off—or sometimes through—the walls of the deteriorating Hotel Clair. Many were college-age artists or designers; some were still teenagers. Gygax personally would not drive the creative process of the company—he had apparently "knocked off quite a few new monsters" for a planned sequel to the *Monster Manual* prior to his bouts of illness, as well as some work toward his long-promised *Temple of Elemental Evil*, but these were not forthcoming anytime soon. TSR was now dependent on a stream of modules and games developed by its boisterous design staff.

Hijinks inevitably ensued. The third floor of the Hotel Clair had a false ceiling, as it had originally been a cavernous ballroom, so there was the time when Erol Otus tried to crawl his way to the space above Zeb Cook's office with the aim of making spooky noises. The ceiling was so thin that Otus prematurely fell through right above the desk of Tom Moldvay, who was naturally startled to find half of a person suddenly dangling and flailing above him. Once, when a manager was late to unlock the doors at the Hotel Clair, Steve Winter simply scaled the fire escape, entered through one of the rickety windows at the art department, and then let everyone in. Or there was the time when Skip Williams saw a few unfamiliar people loading goods from the basement of the Hotel Clair into a car early in the morning; it did not strike him as an unusual situation at first, and only after striking up a conversation with them did he realize they were in fact burglars.

With Gygax scarce around the office, it would be Kevin Blume, wielding the title of chief operating officer, who would steer the company to adopt a more professional identity through the imposition of unfamiliar discipline. Harkening back to the 1976 employee handbook, staffers who failed to use the time-clock properly would be given demerit points for a "major offense." Blume's primary concession to softening the tone of his internal communication was by festooning his memos with clip art from the *Peanuts* comic strip. Under his direction, significant staff turnover began to change the face of TSR.

In the art department, Dave Sutherland was promoted to vice president of graphics and design, with Jim Roslof under him to manage the art team directly. TSR now had a mandate to recruit a staff capable of producing the caliber of art that adorned fantasy paperback covers, which would lead them to seek out talent like Larry Elmore. What followed was a changing of the guard: the prolific artist Otus departed in 1981 with a scholarship from TSR to help support his continuing education at Berkeley. Others, however, would leave under less amicable circumstances.

TSR's new policies soon alienated many of the founding members of its design department. Since 1978, TSR had offered staff an effective royalty on products developed in-house; most recently through a "creative bonuses" program. By 1981, Lawrence Schick, whose understaffed design team had perennial difficulties making deadlines the year before, had stepped back from his vice presidency to refocus his efforts on the "Alien Worlds" project he spearheaded along with Zeb Cook: as early as the February, the game's official title *Star Frontiers* had begun to leak. But when a decision was made to end the creative bonuses program, the work that Schick had put into the *Star Frontiers* project now looked like it would yield no royalties. Furious, Schick resigned, and there was talk of legal action. Work on *Star Frontiers* would continue as a staff project, but it would now be late entering a marketplace that SPI planned to assault with its forthcoming game *Universe*. Morale among the design staff declined across the board, and this led to more departures. Staffers from the West Coast who were seen as unruly, like Paul Reiche and Evan Robinson, were let go.

A post-termination resignation letter—of the "you can't fire me 'cause I quit" variety—hastily written by Kevin Hendryx that summer gives an understandably bitter take on the matter: "TSR claims that it cares about and values its employees, and that it wants all employees to be happy in their jobs; yet any who become unhappy are considered to have 'bad attitudes' (a currently very popular euphemism), and rather than investigate the causes of employee discontent, TSR prefers to take the simplistic view that such persons are malcontents and that mass terminations are the best solution." It also calls out "rampant nepotism and cronyism," a growing concern among employees as the ranks of Gygax and Blume family members in the company swelled.

When *Random Events* resumed in May, the very first article it ran addressed "Recent Personnel Changes" and insisted "there is no 'purge' or any implied threat to our employee population" as, among the many people let go, "there was no common reason in any of the situations, each was an event unique to the individuals and work arrangements involved." But disgruntled exiles made sure the message spread far and wide: "Rumor says that TSR has fired a dozen or so employees for 'bad attitude,'" as *Different Worlds* reported, wondering "does this presage a corporate shift of emphasis?" But as quickly as TSR issued pink slips, they brought in replacements; the cover of the June *Random Events* alone lists seventeen new hires. Within that issue, those new staffers could read a limerick:

> There was a young fellow named Gary
> Whose face was decidedly hairy
> His passion for games
> and weird thought-up names
> provided the jobs—and we're merry.

Whatever motivated the reductions in staff, it was not want of cash. In order to report results at a time of year closer to when rivals like Avalon Hill and SPI did, TSR planned to close its 1981 fiscal year at the end of the second quarter in June, rather than the end of the third quarter in September as it had since its founding. As such, the fiscal year 1981 earnings for TSR Hobbies stood at around $9.7 million, which might seem like only a marginal increase over the previous year's take of $8.3 million. But that is because it only counted three quarters of sales—and what would have been their fourth quarter was a dramatic one, grossing $6 million. For this reason, most of the bar graphs used to chart the company's growth over the years mark a $16 million total for 1981. TSR Hobbies had sold 750,000 copies of the *Basic Set* over the twelve months leading up to June, at $12 each—which would become their most widely repeated media brag.

With that kind of income, the obligations of the settlement with Arneson proved eminently manageable. TSR Hobbies booked an operating charge for 1981 of $600,000, reflecting the minimum royalty payments it would owe to Arneson over the next four years. While this figure would have bankrupted the company back in 1979, now TSR could absorb it easily. Even factoring it in, TSR made over $1 million profit in 1981, slightly above the year before.

As for how the revenue tally situated TSR in the adventure games industry of the time, we can go back to Howard Barasch's annual scoreboard in *Strategy & Tactics*. Ignoring their abbreviated nine-month fiscal calendar, he gave TSR's 1981 figure as $17 million, out of a total industry income of $31 million. TSR's take thus exceeded that of all other adventure game businesses combined. Around half of all consumer spending on adventure games was on role-playing titles, which led to a 78 percent boost over the year before. Barasch pegged Avalon Hill's income from adventure gaming at $5.2 million and SPI's at $2.1 million. A handful of companies came in at or over $1 million, including Game Designers' Workshop and Yaquinto. The Judges Guild take, with its agreements with TSR still in place, was measured at $770,000. Barasch had the revenue of prominent firms like the Chaosium and Steve Jackson Games under $200,000 dollars each. Companies like Flying Buffalo—and Adventure Games—were not individually listed, but instead grouped into an "Other" category that Barasch valued at less than a half-million dollars total. TSR thus wielded a clout in the industry unknown since Avalon Hill's heyday in the early 1970s.

The insatiable appetite for adventure games came to the hobby from a fresh demographic: in 1981, a full 60 percent of TSR products would be purchased by or for consumers ages 10 to 14. That youthening of the player base had implications for how the public weighed the potential impact of the game. *Discover* magazine had covered the "*Dungeons & Dragons* Craze" in their January issue with a balance of perspectives, but when it came to Egbert, it suggested that "his disappearance was never fully explained" but that "many people thought his death was related to the reality-bending quality of the game." It also referenced the Heber City incident the year before, which is described as one where parents "exorcised *Dungeons & Dragons* from the after-school program amid charges that it was antireligious, too heavy with symbols of witchcraft and demonology." Throughout the year, the success of *D&D* attracted increasing scrutiny from evangelical pundits. Christian Life Ministries, an independent church in Sacramento, California, began circulating crude tracts pointing to "direct violations of God's Holy Word" in *D&D* that would furnish "several reasons why Christians cannot play this game." Many of these arguments come across as nit-picking: For instance, because some promotional text in *Players Handbook* calls the game "mind-unleashing," it must be forbidden, as "Christians are to be constantly in control of their thoughts." Or because the rulebooks state that in the fantasy of the game "even the gods themselves may enter your character's life," and the very plural "gods" implies pantheism, it violates a biblical commandment, regardless of whether anyone believed those gods were real.

Christian Life Ministries reached most of its following through a radio show featuring the evangelist John Torell. Torell was the sort who crusaded against the celebration of Halloween and believed Sacramento to be home to a thousand witches. *D&D* became a focus of his broadcasts, and one listener, a church directory salesman, and was alarmed to discover that the Rancho Cordova Park and Recreation District on the east side of Sacramento had scheduled two *D&D* sessions at its facilities for the summer of 1981. Apparently twenty students had signed up to participate. So, a challenge was brought before the park and recreation board, demanding the *D&D* sessions be canceled. Torell's argument was that *D&D* "is religion in the guise of a game," and therefore scheduling the game violated the separation of church and state under the constitution: the district would be encouraging a particular religion in the twenty students who had signed up for the sessions. The board was told matter-of-factly, "This game teaches witchcraft and demon worship and that leads to Satan Worship." In the court of public opinion, even *D&D* itself faced something of a crisis over its identity and nature: Was it just a game, or an introduction to dark magic?

On June 17, the Cordova Park and Recreation District Board voted in a 3-to-2 split to cancel the classes after ninety minutes of spirited debate. The teacher who was scheduled to lead the sessions could only remark, "I can't believe the board did what it did. It's unreal." One of the dissenting board members went on record to say, "I feel we've censored something we don't have authority to censor." But it would be misleading to represent that the vote hinged entirely on religious censorship. A board member who supported the cancelation justified it by explaining, "if a program is controversial, we shouldn't hold it in a public facility." Parks and recreation boards can be forgiven for being unwilling to take provocative stances. But another member who voted for the ban argued that since "the Supreme Court has already barred religious activity for public facilities," they were compelled to cancel the classes, as "*Dungeons & Dragons* is clearly religious in content." That same board member expressed no objection to playing the game in private, saying he would even "defend that right." This was exactly the argument fundamentalists had hoped would prevail, and buoyed by its success, the same line of argument came to the Folsom-Cordova School Board—there, however, it would be rejected.

Ultimately, the Rancho Cordova decision became yet another sound-bite of controversy that would be spliced with the steam tunnel incident and the Heber City decision by the media. Canceling a planned activity subsidized by public funds is not equivalent to setting a policy prohibiting that activity in a community, but this nuance would rarely be acknowledged. In its reporting about the Rancho Cordova controversy, the *Los Angeles Times* blithely asserted that "school officials in Heber City, Utah, have banned the game," which simply was not true. The understandable reluctance of parks and recreation board members to court controversy would similarly lose all nuance in subsequent reporting and become another community imposing a ban. "What are they going to do there in Sacramento?" *Different Worlds* breathlessly asked. "Are they really going to ban *D&D* from their recreational park programs? I can see it now . . . kids playing in closets, under the bed sheets, etc. Why don't those adults grow up?"

The summer convention season in 1981 was a game of musical chairs, as GenCon and Origins fought a proxy battle over smaller regional conventions. Origins would take place in the Bay Area, thanks to the winning bid by the team that had run GenCon West for TSR back in 1976 and 1977. So, there would be "Pacific Origins," but that left the East Coast potentially without a summer event. Two plans thus developed simultaneously: Avalon Hill aspired to run an "AtlantiCon" in Baltimore, but independently, the team that had had run Origins in 1979 and 1980 worked toward an "East Con" in Cherry Hill, New Jersey. TSR threw its full weight behind the latter plan, which was soon rebranded "GenCon East." The two events were scheduled for the same weekend, just a couple hours apart by car, and an outmaneuvered Avalon Hill ultimately scrapped its plans, moving its slate of AtlantiCon events to the GenCon East schedule.

Although in years past, the Avalon Hill *General* happily boasted about attendance figures for Origins, they were not eager to share numbers for Pacific Origins, which were surely well less than 4,000, possibly even a thousand less. Avalon Hill's coverage was very critical of the Pacificon team, both for lacking organization and for an emphasis on fantasy and role playing over wargaming. Indeed, as Tom Shaw of Avalon Hill would later fume in a letter to *Campaign*, "Pacific Origins rejected our offer to promote Origins in the manner in which we have supported all past Origins conventions." This was not lost on the attendees, one of whom remarked that "the organizers stressed *D&D* and FRP far too much for the type of con Origins should be." The Bay Area was the home turf of the Chaosium, and the convention

The TSR van gets a flat tire on the Indiana Tollway, en route to GenCon East in 1981. Photo courtesy of Merle and Jackie Rasmussen.

featured a heavy presence of West Coast fantasy luminaries, as well as a strong showing from the medieval reenactors in the Society for Creative Anachronism, but not much of the board wargaming that Origins had been created to promote.

At Pacific Origins, a unified "Origins Awards" system replaced the previous hodge-podge of the Charles S. Roberts Awards and H. G. Wells Awards. The year before, Howard Barasch established as its voting body an Academy of Adventure Gaming Arts & Design made up of creative professionals and contributing hobbyists in the industry, who would pay a modest $2 per year for membership. Around two hundred academy members were eligible to vote in the 1981 awards, under the supervision of a twenty-five-member awards committee who could vet nominations and categories to make the accolades defensible. The unintended consequence of this process was that Gary Gygax was voted into the Adventure Gaming Hall of Fame, the highest honor among the awards, previously reserved for the likes of Tom Shaw and Jim Dunnigan.

Arneson could not have been happy to see Gygax collect any further laurels, but his own plan to launch an International Fantasy Gaming Society as a competitor to the RPGA lost impetus with the founding of the Academy of Adventure Gaming Arts & Design, as well as the growing influence of a group called the Game Designer's Guild, which also gave a design award at Origins. Arneson had trouble persuading other key designers that yet another award—one given to designers, never publishers—was needed. He organized a meeting at Pacific Origins, but Ken St. Andre would afterward complain that it lacked any real agenda or direction; for the rest of the year, Arneson's IFGS concept languished. But his ambition to challenge TSR was not curbed: for the July issue of *Dragon*, Arneson took out a full-page advertisement for *Adventures in Fantasy* in which the logo of his Adventure Games company looms larger than the game's title.

TSR staged a modest display at Pacific Origins, largely attending in order to influence the site selection for Origins in 1983. To their chagrin, the winning bid came again from Metro Detroit Gamers, who had stolen GenCon's thunder in 1978. With that, Origins would return to direct Midwestern competition with GenCon two years hence. This was surely in retaliation for the heavy-handed way that GenCon East brushed aside Avalon Hill's proposed AtlantiCon, and the resulting bitterness led TSR to spurn Origins once again. But still, Avalon Hill had to admit "GenCon East was more of an Origins than Pacific Origins in everything save the name." Contemporaneous reports suggested that about 4,600 gamers came to Cherry Hill, New Jersey, in the last weekend of July to attend.

Although Gary Gygax was advertised as a guest of honor at a special dinner at GenCon East, he reportedly took ill at the last minute, and attendees never laid eyes on him there. But Gygax would never miss the main GenCon, where attendance at Parkside came in at 5,100, a healthy lead on Origins. The main *D&D* release for the convention would be the long-awaited *Fiend Folio*. Due to various legal issues surrounding the disassociation of Games Workshop with TSR early in 1980, the *Fiend Folio* had, as its editor Don Turnbull would explain, languished "in a sort of legal limbo—untouched and untouchable—for nearly two years after completion." It exited that plane in

February 1981, but the volume would not make it into the hands of gamers until that summer, marking the fifth consecutive year that TSR had published a hardcover *Advanced Dungeons & Dragons* book.

Gygax himself delivered a GenCon seminar, one that was scheduled at the last minute via the "Daily News" updates circulated on site and given a two-hour slot just after lunch on Thursday. The topic was the "D&D Game System vs. the AD&D Game System." Gygax still hoped to litigate in the court of public opinion the legal matter that had been settled earlier in the year. But GenCon was more focused on the future of the game than its history: the inside cover of the program advertised the location of Mattel's booth in the exhibit hall, and Mattel took out a full-page advertisement in *Dragon* for the *Computer Labyrinth Game* in the July issue. "We've taken the *Dungeons & Dragons* game out of the Dark Ages," the ad copy playfully reads; at the time, electronic games posed no apparent threat to tabletop *D&D*, so it read as a lighthearted jest. This would be the summer, incidentally, that *Donkey Kong* would introduce the character of Mario to the world, a perilous time to neglect the surging popularity of electronic games.

GenCon always had a way of reenergizing Gary Gygax. "At GenCon XIV," he related in the pages of *Dragon* soon thereafter, "I had the opportunity to talk with many of you good folks again, and a message came out loud and clear. It is high time that I got busy and finished the *Temple of Elemental Evil* module and started producing regular information regarding the *World of Greyhawk* Fantasy World Setting." Whatever decisions he had made about dedicating his energies toward business, game design was simply part of his identity. Gygax even invited TSR staff over to Dragonlands for a party on the second Saturday in September, a gesture demonstrating his return from self-imposed exile after the difficulties of the past twelve months.

As Gygax returned to creative work at TSR, he became increasingly protective of his ideas. He circulated a memo in August forbidding "anyone [from] designing material, including information on the politics, religions, or anything else" associated with his world of Greyhawk: "This is my creation," Gygax insisted, "and any development involved will be done either by myself or by those who are familiar with my campaign and way of thinking." Greyhawk, like GenCon, was a property that Gygax retained a personal stake in, something he treasured above any copyrights or trademarks assigned to TSR that were now worked by its design staff.

There were a lot of cooks in the *D&D* kitchen by this point, and it was getting crowded—to the point where TSR had trailer offices brought in and parked out back behind the LRP building to house more employees. The only realistic solution would be to acquire a much larger building that could serve as a corporate headquarters, with room to grow, which would include facilities suitable for manufacturing as well as office space. This would mean creating a significant number of local jobs, so TSR wielded its leverage to secure financial support from local government. In June, TSR reached a preliminary agreement with the nearby town of Elkhorn to build a facility there, bankrolled with a $1.5 million industrial revenue bond from the city. But this provoked outrage in Lake Geneva, and a scathing editorial in the *Lake Geneva Regional News* about the business-hostile attitude of the city government. Before the end of July, TSR had a better offer, closer to home: a $3 million bond from Lake Geneva.

Gygax could already share with Steve Marsh in July that "we have made arrangements to acquire a large building near to us to which we plan to move this year. It has over 30,000 square feet, and we should be able to devote all of it to offices and conference rooms." That would be 201 Sheridan Springs Road, just up the street from the LRP building, which in comparison spanned just a meager 17,500 square feet. As the new facility was the former home of a medical supply company called Torrent, employees would call it the Torrent building, but it would acquire its own identity as TSR's headquarters once the extensive renovations permitted staff to start moving in. With the city's bond, Gygax explained to Marsh, they would not only acquire this office but also "build a manufacturing plant." The planned construction of a two-story manufacturing facility connected to the Torrent building, which would itself be granted a partial second floor, made the total projected footprint of the headquarters around 96,000 square feet. The *Regional News* called it "the largest industrial expansion program in Lake Geneva history." The town of Lake Geneva had placed a large bet on the future of its most unlikely success story.

As with the previous purchase of the Hotel Clair, and before that 723 Williams Street, TSR Hobbies itself would not buy the Torrent building: instead, a real estate partnership comprising the company's directors would own the facility. Now that the directors included Kevin, the new partnership G, B, & B Investments was formed for this purpose. As before, TSR's assets would guarantee the debt, and TSR would pay G, B, & B rent on the building, which the partnership then used to pay off principal and interest on the financing of the construction, bonds that would be held by the American National Bank of Chicago. Kevin Blume in October could share with employees that they expected to close the deal for the Torrent building within weeks. As a tribute to the triumvirate now running TSR, at the company Founders Day party that month, the cake served at the Red Eye Inn now depicted three jolly faces: Gary, Brian, and Kevin.

Real estate expansion was far from the company's most ambitious plan. TSR spent much of 1981 in negotiations with Twentieth-Century Fox for a film deal, though delays resulting from the writers' strike declared in April made progress slow. Ultimately, they broke off talks "because we did not believe that the studio would be willing to produce the sort of top-notch movie we must have," as Gygax wrote in September. In another contemporaneous interview, Gygax stressed that "we didn't want to end up with the rather disastrous type of movie that Tolkien's ring trilogy ended up with," referring to the recent animated features. Instead, a *D&D* movie would need to be "based on the *Dungeons & Dragons* game—with imagination, and creativity, and excitement, and adventure, and not some sort of a Hollywood epic which takes the name and then perverts everything else." Gygax hinted within TSR that "three studios are very interested in a movie based on *D&D* gaming or *AD&D* gaming." We can be forgiven for wondering how that distinction might translate to the screen. He also disclosed to TSR staffers that "we have an Oscar-winning screen writer lined up to handle the script." That would be James Goldman, famous for *The Lion in Winter*.

But the mass-media narrative of *D&D* was not entirely TSR's to dictate. The power of the steam tunnel myth truly became apparent in the advanced notices preceding the September release of a novel, an inevitable novel, Rona Jaffe's *Mazes and Monsters*. The *Los Angeles Times* explained in mid-August that "the game to which both Jaffe and the book's title refer is one played by college students with such devotion that it leads to a participant's mysterious disappearance. There was a real-life situation in which a Michigan State student wound up missing after playing *Dungeons & Dragons*." Jaffe averred that the story is totally fictional, as is the game it represents, but that would not stop reviewers from linking it to a supposedly true story. A review in the *St. Petersburg Times* only remembered that "Neither Egbert's parents nor the private investigator who found him ever confirmed or denied that Egbert got carried away with *Dungeons & Dragons* and was playing the game during his disappearance"—though of course Egbert's parents had denied exactly that. If Dear still harbored the ambition to sell the story, Jaffe had handily beaten him to that market—and to the bestseller lists.

Fiction could provide TSR with another opportunity for diversification. In September, its product review board vetted concept briefs developed by Rose Estes for a series of "multi-adventure books" intended to introduce younger readers to the themes of *D&D*. Jim Ward provided a thorough analysis of how these books would be superior to the popular Bantam "Choose Your Own Adventure" series, which included the four highest-selling juvenile books for 1979–1980. The planned Estes books, to be called the "Endless Quest" series, would be longer, with fewer endings, less violence, a more concrete setting, and a greater literary sophistication. By this point, product marketing needed to conduct research before an investment into a new area like this could be justified: outreach to juvenile library groups, public schools, and so on would be needed. Ultimately, the project would be greenlit for the New Year.

Much of this professional approach to product development was driven by Kevin Blume. In September 1981, at the height of TSR's boom, Melvin Blume transferred his 200 shares of stock to Kevin—previously Kevin held only 5 shares. Now that Kevin was a director of the company, it made sense to give him incentives to increase shareholder value. But this might be a problematic transaction: under the shareholder agreement, no stock owner had the right to sell or transfer shares without first offering them for sale to TSR, and then for sale to the other shareholders on a pro rata basis. Nevertheless, Kevin was issued a certificate, and he then became the third-largest shareholder. A similar interest in motivating employees led to the expansion of the TSR profit-sharing plan, which began acquiring treasury stock; by October, it was already the fourth-largest shareholder, with 130 shares. From a corporate governance perspective, those shares could effectively be voted by the board of directors. This all served to further cement corporate governance under the Blume family and Gygax.

The company expected to hire some sixty employees over the next year, raising payroll to around $3 million, which required more executive messaging about the intended corporate culture. The October *Random Events* directed the attention of employees to the new TSR Mission Statement signed by all three directors, which boldly begins: "TSR Hobbies Inc., its divisions and subsidiaries, will create, acquire and manufacture, distribute and license select adult, family and children home oriented leisure time products and services to selected customers worldwide and maximize utilization of assets for the purpose of maximizing shareholders wealth and of promoting the growth of the company." It was replete with vacuous promises, such as "All Management of the Corporation will operate positively and innovatively." This was indeed the sort of company TSR was becoming.

As a token of this new professionalism, Mike Carr's role was recast from General Manager into executive vice president of the manufacturing division. He still reported to Kevin Blume in that position, but his direct reports included Steve Witt as well as Sloan *père et fils*, Bob and Jack, which sandwiched Carr uncomfortably between Kevin and various in-laws. Carr had serious responsibilities in this role, including the construction of the new manufacturing facility on Sheridan Springs Road over the next six months. "The building itself is 54,000 square feet overall, with 51,000 square feet devoted to warehouse, assembling and storage areas and the rest being office and work areas," Carr related to the November *Random Events*. Carr notes that the renovations to the Torrent building were being managed by Kevin and his brother-in-law Steve, so "talk to Steve if you'd like to see the plans." Again, if anyone whispered about nepotism, Gary Gygax would not be one to point fingers: he then elevated his son Ernie to head the consumer services division, which comprised administration of the RPGA— Frank Mentzer now reported to Ernie—GenCon events, and the Dungeon Hobby Shop. By December, the RPGA could claim about 1,800 members, a bit fewer than TSR had hoped to attract in its first year; Gygax had written that "we will be doing well if we get 2,000 initial members."

To live up to the expectations for growth, TSR needed to cast a wider net, for example with television advertising. To further connect with the younger market, TSR updated the company mascot, "Morley the Wizard," to look even more cartoonish and affable than before. In support of the new version of Dave Megarry's classic *Dungeon!* board game, TSR would spend $800,000 on a media buy that covered twenty-five cities as the holidays approached. TSR now looked ever harder at the traditional board game market: they had poached Mike Gray from Milton Bradley to help shepherd board game efforts. Having bested competitors the likes of Avalon Hill, they now looked upward to bigger game.

Reaching that lofty market would be easier if TSR improved the public image of *D&D*. A revised *Deities & Demigods* shipped toward the end of

RANDOM EVENTS

The Unofficial Voice of TSR Hobbies, Inc.

November 15, 1981

The Inner Sanctum

By *Mike Carr*

The TSR Manufacturing Division encompasses the areas of Operations (Steve Witt), Pre-Press Services (Pat Price), Traffic (Kathy Lynch), Physical Plant (Dan Matheson), Shipping (Ken Reek) and Inventory Purchasing (Bob and Jack Sloan). These people and their able staffs keep things rolling.

The centerpiece of the Division's plans is the new manufacturing building planned for construction in the next 6 months. The specific timetable for construction depends upon the final go-ahead from our bankers and attorneys, but once we get the green light our architects and contractors are ready to go. If we can get the cement slab in place before the weather gets nasty, the building can go up in a couple of months. Steve Witt and Gary Welsh(of Crispell-Snyder ,our architect) have been coordinating the plans for the new structure, and took a quick trip to Oklahoma last month to visit the company constructing the building. The building will be shipped here in several pieces and assembled when the slab is in place.

The building itself is 54,000 square feet overall, with 51,000 square feet devoted to warehouse, assembly and storage areas and the rest being offices and work areas. We'll start out by storing and assembling the individual parts to many of our products. This will have several advantages, all of which will help us increase our profitability:

Flexibility—We can make up batches of finished products as we need them, using the Hewlett-Packard computer and its software systems to maximize efficiency.

Ease of Storage—Pieces and parts can be stored flat, taking up much less space than finished products (when boxed games are stored, they include a lot of air and take up a lot of room!).

Financial Benefits—Storing parts and materials rather than finished goods is benficial from an accounting and tax standpoint.

As time goes on, we expect to move beyond assembly and into other production-related areas if they prove feasible and cost-effective. The land TSR is acquiring has room for further expansion, so our options are open.

The former Torrent building and its renovation are an integral part of the corporate plans, and will mean a nice new setting for most of us. Steve Witt, Kevin Blume, and others have been working on a final floor plan for the new offices. Talk to Steve if you'd like to see the plans, as he has a copy of the drawings.

As you can see, the future for the Manufacturing Division is bright. Our quality people have been responsible for our past accomplishments, and will continue to help us move toward future successes. Our "Can Do!" philosophy is a reflection of the challenges that lie ahead and our willingness to meet them. We're a proud part of the TSR team!

Mike Carr

Introducing the "New" Morley

As promised at last month's employee meeting, we are running a picture of Advertisings's new concept of "Morley the Wizard", TSR's animated spokesman.

RANDOM EVENTS is neither a trademark owned by anyone nor copy-righted. No Rights Reserved.

1

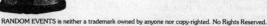

First page of the November 15, 1981, issue of *Random Events*, where Mike Carr details the plan for the new manufacturing facility, and the canonical rendering of "Morley the Wizard" first appears.

the year removed a few demonic elements, but there is some irony that a company trying to rid itself of troublesome optics about real-world religion would cut from its theology a pair of fictional pantheons—the Cthulhu and Melnibonéan mythos—rather than any of the ones corresponding to real-world religions. The chorus of Christian voices condemning *D&D* had become louder and more strident: now instead of fringe preachers hollering into radios, we can find a more considered treatment like the article in the December issue of *Eternity* magazine, which reviewed the "pervasive occultic overtones" in the game and claimed that "*D&D* perverts the biblical concept of resurrection." Because for a Christian "to dismiss the occult ties of *D&D* as mere fantasy is naïve," the author concluded, "to retain these materials in our homes is at best a poor example and at worst an abomination."

But TSR flourished nonetheless. In November, *Inc.* magazine informed TSR Hobbies that in its December issue the company would be numbered among "an elite group of 100 of the fastest growing enterprises in the United States." *Inc.* rated companies on how much sales growth they had demonstrated in the past five years, between 1976 and 1980: they counted TSR showing a 5,233 percent increase over that period, which ranked them sixth on the list. Management joyously circulated a photocopy of *Inc.*'s congratulatory letter, adorning it with another of the *Peanuts* comics that were a signature element of Kevin Blume memos: this one showed Sally Brown exclaiming, "A Good Grade!"

While *Inc.* apparently based its model on TSR's 1981 revenue rather than its 1980 figures, it still shows the very impressive arc that elevated the valuation of the company. Reviewing the $16 million in 1981 revenue at the shareholder meeting in November, roughly double the year before, the new book value of TSR stock doubled over the previous year to $2,000. Had TSR waited until now to settle with Arneson, this would have doubled the payout to buy his shares. The Blume family stake in TSR of 990 shares was now worth nearly $2 million. But that was only part of the story: the 1976 option for 700 shares held by Brian Blume, and the identical one held by Gary Gygax, each had a further worth of $1.4 million, if either of them invested the $70,000 to exercise the shares. Even Will Niebling's option for 500 shares, purchasable at $62,500, would be worth a cool million. Of those three executives, only Gygax, thanks to his royalty income, had the disposable income to exercise the shares—but he was in no hurry to do so; the option would not expire for five more years, and things could only go up from here.

When interviewed by the *Milwaukee Sentinel* for its November 6 edition, Brian Blume denied that *D&D* was a fad and predicted growth would continue. "Milton Bradley is probably the largest producer of adult-level games in the world right now," Blume explained. "We probably have about one-fourth of the sales that Milton Bradley does and, at the rate we are going, we are going to catch them in just a few years." Milton Bradley had just recently entered the market with its *Dark Tower* electronic game, which their own executives openly acknowledged as a simplification of *D&D*, though it perhaps competed most directly with Mattel's computer labyrinth adaptation. But it is not clear which metric led Blume to construe TSR's sales as approximately a quarter of Milton Bradley's game business—Milton Bradley revenues came in over $380 million for the 1981 fiscal year. The companies simply existed on a different scale: TSR had about 135 employees at the time, and Milton Bradley had well over 4,000. A venerable mainstay, Milton Bradley was estimated to hold about 25 percent of the board game market at the time, and its flagship product was still the *Game of Life* first marketed back in the 1860s. The toy industry remained far larger than a niche hobby like TSR's: in 1981, the Rubik's Cube alone brought in some $50 million. The largest toy and game company, Mattel, broke through the billion-dollar barrier in 1981, with sales of $1.13 billion—a substantial chunk of that derived from one million sales of their Intellivision video game console, creating a vast potential audience for its forthcoming *D&D* cartridges. The licensing fees such a titan paid to TSR were, in light of its broader finances, table scraps. The gold-generating magic that Gygax and his partners had unearthed in the steam tunnels in 1979, when put in the broader perspective of the world of business, just conjured pocket change.

TSR only looked like a big fish swimming in the tank with its peers in the adventure games industry; released into the wilds of the broader hobby, it would pose little threat. Gygax estimated for the *Milwaukee Sentinel* that TSR's revenue would grow to somewhere from $25 million to $30 million for the next fiscal year. The reporter, being careful to note that professionalism had not made the company stolid, commented on the lack of a dress code and that "the company allows many employees to create their own work schedules." Mostly the reporter was captivated by the backstory of Gygax's heroic-inventor character, how "he quit his job as an insurance underwriter and formed his partnership with Kaye" after many years of "trying unsuccessfully to interest companies in producing" the fantasy adventure games he designed. "Brian and I sat down in 1975 and said we were going to grow into a multimillion-dollar corporation," Gygax now recalled.

Perhaps TSR also looked big because the tank it shared with the likes of SPI and Heritage had now sprung a leak: many wargaming firms failed to adapt themselves to the changing market. It was a recession year for the American economy, and while adventure games were growing, most of the growth was in role-playing games. On December 30, 1981—remembered by SPI staffers as "Black Wednesday"—SPI management announced a 25

LAKE GENEVA - Jubilation was the word, last week as the TSR board of directors shovel the last spades full of dirt onto the grave of the soon to be late game designer, Dave Arneson. Arneson, who was not available for comment, has long insisted that he be a part of the TSR operation. In compliance with his wishes, Dave was buried alive with a cask of Italian wine, under the foundation of the new 3.5 million dollar headquarters.

TSR office humor circa 1981 reinterprets a photograph of the groundbreaking ceremony for TSR's new manufacturing facility as an involuntary burial for Dave Arneson.

percent staff reduction and a very uncertain path forward. And back in October the gossip column in *Different Worlds* had asked "Is Heritage bankrupt?" before reporting a month later, "Rumor from Texas has it that Duke Seifried may quit Heritage before January," depriving the company of its president. Following the lapse of its *AD&D* license, the Judges Guild was barely subsisting doing playing aids for *Traveller* and *Tunnels & Trolls*. It was not clear who would survive another year.

The groundbreaking ceremony for the new TSR manufacturing facility took place on November 23. A ceremonial photograph of the occasion shows Gygax and the Blume brothers on site, all bundled up for winter, shoveling the first parcels of earth from the lightly frosted ground. The mayor of Lake Geneva and various other dignitaries look on with approval. But inevitably, the mischievous scamps at TSR repurposed this image for office humor: their caption explains that this image actually shows the moment when "the TSR board of directors shovel the last spades full of dirt onto the grave of the soon to be late game designer, Dave Arneson." Even with the lawsuit settled, the "great War" that Arneson had long desired would now come to pass, with TSR squaring off against the remainder of the industry. In this struggle, however, TSR needed no adversary: it would prove to be its own worst enemy.

TSR Turn Results for 1981

Revenue: $9.7M (for 3 quarters, $16M annual),
profit $1M
Employees: 120
Stock Valuation: $2,000
GenCon attendance vs. Origins: 5,100 vs. 3–4,000
Value of Arneson settlement: $1.2M+

Supposed Number of Witches in Sacramento: 1,000+

1982: Extravagance

In the fall of 1981, Doug Blume and his brother-in-law Steve Witt had attended a city council meeting where Geneva Lake divers announced they had discovered the remains of a famous sunken ship and requested financing to raise it. Nothing better exemplifies the attitude of TSR at its height than the company's resolve to bankroll the recovery of the *Lucius Newberry*, which had caught fire and plummeted beneath the waves in 1891. Under the rubric of "building community relations," TSR gave the divers an initial $10,000 to continue the work, and promised another $50,000 at least.

Scry ahead to September 27, 1982, when this herculean undertaking drew a crowd to the Geneva Lake riviera. Divers then attempted to levitate parts of the *Lucius Newberry*, as the 115-foot vessel could not return to the surface intact. Eyewitnesses reported that the 30,000-pound engine reached land and was then hoisted onto a flatbed, which navigated the precarious journey to Sheridan Springs two miles away under police escort. Asked if the *Lucius Newberry* would become a new game, a TSR spokesperson could only reply, "I don't think so." *Random Events* went a bit further, proposing that "if the engine and boiler were not severely damaged that they could be made operable. Perhaps someday the Lucius Newberry will sail Geneva Lake again." Ultimately, TSR would donate the massive boiler to the Smithsonian.

If that sounds ancillary to their core business, consider that in January, TSR announced it would be sponsoring the US Olympic Bobsled Team. It would be a year of lavish gestures like this, of a company spinning virtually out of control. Events piled on events so rapidly that its management structures simply had no way to manage them. It was a year of great expectations and missed omens, and it ensured the foundering of the company Gygax and Blume had created in 1975.

Will Niebling was interviewed by the *Game Designer's Guild Newsletter* at the beginning of the year at the annual Manhattan Toy Fair. When asked whether "TSR feels *Dungeons & Dragons* has peaked," Niebling denied it incredulously. "We are expecting sales of close to $45 million this year." If those numbers sound grand, they were nothing compared to what people at TSR were projecting internally. In the first *Random Events* of 1982, Gygax laid out his "crystal ball" vision for the company as follows: "During 1981 we approximately doubled in gross income. It is projected that this will continue as our 1982 growth curve. A safe estimate for 1983 places TSR's growth rate at 150% of the preceding year—let's say $75,000,000." Even that, he said, might be conservative: "volume could grow beyond that because of several factors which are as yet too nebulous to judge." A February *Janesville Gazette* article relayed the logical conclusion that "if present trends continue, company officials project TSR will be a $280 million operation annually by 1985." At those revenue levels, someone might justifiably claim that TSR rivaled Milton Bradley's take.

Everyone now wanted to tell TSR's story. In an interview the board of directors gave to *Inc.* magazine for its February issue, following their admittance to the magazine's "Fastest Growing Private Companies" list a few months before, Kevin Blume elaborated that the growth TSR expected was attributable to *D&D* sales: "We figure that the game is still well below the halfway point on its growth curve." The interviewer took careful note of the lack of traditional management or business experience at TSR—but with half an echo of the steam tunnel incident, the article suggested that "at TSR, the line between playing the game and running the business is sometimes blurred." Playing *D&D* is "a lot like business," according to Gygax, who continued, "I'd like to think that it teaches our employees to analyze and cooperate. Game players have to learn to look beyond the obvious and see the number of variables they have to deal with." Asked by the *Inc.* reporter if he missed playing games, Kevin Blume—who had never really been much of a gamer—replied, "I love to play, but it wasn't that difficult to forego. Now I'm playing a much larger game called business. That's why we're intuitively good businessmen—because games are a great way to learn."

Like the *Forbes* article two years before, *Inc.* paints the executives of TSR Hobbies as adventurers navigating a labyrinth of business: "Behind any door, you might find a lucrative licensing agreement with a major manufacturer, an exciting movie deal with a Hollywood studio, or a new distribution avenue with a well-established publisher. Behind the same door, though, you may find a bottomless pit into which you will watch your capital drain sickeningly or a menacing black dragon that will snap up your untested employees and spit them out in the blink of an eye."

Many doors in that dark maze were about to open. In the February *Random Events*, Kevin Blume predicted that the company would grow from its current seven divisions, not counting the TSR UK subsidiary, into twelve new divisions before the end of the year. He could see nineteen divisions and five foreign subsidiaries on the distant horizon. One forthcoming division briefly mentioned was "GNW," short for Greenfield Needlewomen. This was the name of a Greenfield, Indiana, firm TSR had just acquired which made needlework kits sold in crafts stores. They were known for offerings like the "Forest Treasure Drawer Sachets," pouches that could be filled with fragrant herbs and spices. Gygax had hinted at this forthcoming deal in the first *Random Events* of the year when he foretold, "We will certainly enter the craft field this year." TSR's relationship with Greenfield began with some management consulting done as a favor to the owners, but as they were looking for just such an entry into the space, TSR bought the company. Only later would it come out that owners, the Stano family, were, inevitably, related to the Blume brothers: Connie Stano's mother Helen was the sister of Kevin and Brian's mother.

Greenfield Needlewoman was just the first in a spate of acquisitions and new ventures that TSR launched before April. TSR had long neglected the potential revenue of making their own miniatures—a roughly $6 million market in 1982—so they lured Duke Seifried away from Heritage to oversee plans for "white metal" miniatures and a toy line. Not that Seifried's former employer was a viable business anymore: Howard Barasch would take Seifried's place as Heritage's president, but all he would preside over was the inevitable decline of the firm into insolvency. And TSR acquired *Amazing Stories*, the oldest science-fiction magazine, hiring the legendary George Scithers to take over as its editor. This dovetailed into a broader TSR plan to diversify into the fiction market: in March, Gygax could also share with Steve Marsh that "there are four 'Endless Quest' paperback books," referring to the Rose Estes gamebook project, "due out in a few months, and after that we'll take a look at regular book publishing." Then of course there was the merchandising—there had to be merchandising alongside such a broad media strategy. In April, TSR hired Andy Levison, an attorney with a soft spot for licensed collectibles, who manned TSR's East Coast office in the Toy Center in New York. Under deals he managed, there were *D&D*-themed T-shirts, beach towels, bath sheets, party favors, and dozens more licenses that fed income into TSR—including a license with the LJN company to produce plastic *D&D* toys.

When Gygax reported on the hiring of Seifried and Scithers to Marsh, he had to add "and who knows who else" because by this point there was no keeping track. Gygax continued to Marsh, "We are negotiating with several firms to acquire them." One of those firms, it turned out, was SPI. SPI was a sacred institution of the wargaming community, but the market for its *Strategy & Tactics* magazine had long since peaked, and its attempts to branch outside of wargaming had only led to an enormous debt load. The venture capital they needed to stay solvent could only be gotten in exchange for the collateralization of all of SPI's assets. When they could no longer afford to print their flagship magazine, they briefly explored selling the entire business to Avalon Hill, before reluctantly turning to TSR. Based on a preliminary understanding of the strengths and weaknesses of the business, TSR loaned SPI roughly $425,000, most of which was paid to the venture capital group, in a deal secured by SPI's assets.

The remainder of the hobby games industry watched with abject horror as the SPI situation played out. Every move taken by TSR, SPI, and Avalon Hill was subject to intense and immediate scrutiny, and since so many key industry figures were involved, the volume of rumor and commentary was unprecedented. As publication of *Strategy & Tactics* had halted, Howard Barasch could no longer use its gossip column to share his side of the story—so he founded a new, independent newsletter called *The Insider* to keep pace with unfolding events. But the gist was that on the last day of March, SPI announced their loan agreement with TSR, which gave TSR voting proxies for the primary SPI shareholders—thus Kevin Blume was summarily voted president of SPI. After a closer examination of their books, as one staffer explained it, "TSR found that the debts were far more than anticipated and the assets amounted to less than had been expected," and thus "the security granted to TSR began to appear inadequate." Barasch reported that it might require double the initial loan to make SPI solvent. So, effectively, the TSR-controlled SPI defaulted on its debt to TSR, at which point TSR took possession of SPI's assets and left the rest of SPI to die. All this caused great consternation in SPI's remaining staff—and created an opening for Eric Dott, who ran Avalon Hill, to lure them over to his side. The design team resigned en masse on April 7, leaving a panicked Kevin Blume with the shell of what SPI had once been. At the time, incidentally, Gary Gygax was in London, where he would be the guest of honor at GamesFair 1982, held the first weekend of April.

Avalon Hill scored quite a coup at TSR's expense, but the dissolution of SPI must have alarmed them—if SPI could not make it as a board wargame company, how viable was the very industry? Avalon Hill had diversified already into the computer games market with its Microcomputer Games brand, but this remained a minor part of its overall income, and they faced fierce competition there from companies like Automated Simulations—Jon Freeman's firm—and Strategic Simulations, Inc. It was essential at this point that Avalon Hill capture a significant share of the role-playing game market: in the SPI design team, soon to be rebranded as Victory Games, they had acquired a staff that could compete in the role-playing market. But they were not content to put all their eggs in that basket; they too had to invest in further acquisitions of freelance titles and development talent.

Dave Arneson's old friend Richard Snider was hired by Avalon Hill at the start of 1982. Naturally, when he arrived at Avalon Hill, Arneson urged him to get the company to publish the second edition of *Adventures in Fantasy*. Snider responded to Arneson that he pitched the proposal and that "initially there was support for going with *Adventures in Fantasy*," but that it was "destroyed" for two reasons: first, that "in a published lifetime of over two years *Adventures in Fantasy* has done diddly," and second that Arneson's request for a 6 percent royalty was met by Eric Dott with the response "not a chance." Thus Snider had to relay that "Avalon Hill is not interested in acquiring the rights to *Adventures in Fantasy* now, or ever." He had a few suggestions for how Arneson might complete the work, but realistically, without Snider taking the pen, the second edition would never see the light of day. Effectively, this marked the end of *Adventures in Fantasy*, and of Arneson's effort to supplant *D&D* with his own rewrite. From this point forward, Arneson would refocus his creative efforts on getting Blackmoor campaign scenarios into print—something that would be difficult to arrange without TSR's cooperation.

Arneson moreover increasingly promoted his Adventure Games brand. After all of his complaints about publishers receiving awards instead of game designers, there could be no greater irony than seeing a beaming Dave Arneson at the 1982 HIA show accept the Creative Excellence Award plaque for the board game *Rails through the Rockies*—as the publisher Adventure Games, for a game designed by an outside freelancer.

When *Inc.* magazine had reported on TSR at the beginning of the year, its piece noted the loose and consensual governance model at the top, which required the unanimity of Gygax and both the Blume brothers to move forward on any new venture. "We have an unwritten working arrangement where we sit down and thrash out major issues," Brian Blume affirmed. Doug Blume, in his capacity as vice president of human resources, elaborated in the March *Random Events* that the operation of the "Presidential Office" in TSR was quite unique, in that "the office is actually held by three individuals: Gary, Brian and Kevin (the Senior Executive Officers)." As such, "the Presidential Office is a triumvirate, and all have equal power and share all responsibilities of the Office." The group operated, Doug explained, on the basis of unanimity: "They agree or no decision is made. All votes are equal, no two can be a majority."

Doug Blume's article could be read to imply that Gary Gygax no longer ran TSR Hobbies. The April issue of *Random Events* dedicated its front page to a piece written by Gygax that effectively constituted a rebuttal. Gygax carefully delineated the responsibilities of the three-man board of directors from the everyday administration and operation of the company. Although he acknowledged that there are "three officers who are technically considered as serving in a presidential function," he insisted that "decision making at the senior exec level is not by consensus, however." He clarified, "the Presidential office is at the top," and "next is the office of Brian, the Senior Executive Officer. Then comes Kevin as Chief Operating Officer." Gygax parenthetically adds to his description of Kevin's position the denigrating epithet "the dirty end of the stick?"

Gygax signaled in that article that they planned to restructure TSR into a holding company managing independent subsidiaries. "When corporate reorganization is completed . . . each separate subsidiary operation will be organized to have its own corps of officers, with President, Vice Presidents, etc." While those new operations could mimic the structure of TSR Hobbies with "a multi-personed group to head them up," he felt that "they might function more efficiently with a single head." Gygax had to concede that at present, "we have a rather unique manner of functioning, and the new structure will allow for expansion and growth." Surely we should read into this, and the open dispute between Gygax and the Blume family in the employee newsletter, that Gygax now felt the strain of the triumvirate structure—that it would not be sustainable forever.

Being the titular head of TSR meant touting the successful business decisions and rationalizing the failures. Already in May, Gygax had to take to the front page of *Random Events* to justify the spate of acquisitions that had opened the year. He defended the Greenfield Needlewomen move as a necessary expansion from the hobby business into the adjacent crafts business: "There is no question that crafts is a larger field than hobbies," and he charts a trajectory where "GNW will develop a growing line of products within the next few years, so that its share of the gross income of TSR will be around 20% of the total." With *Amazing Stories* in the fold, Gygax hoped to shift TSR closer to the fiction publishing market, especially for fantasy fiction. When it came to SPI, even as the cheerleader Gygax had to concede "SPI was good news and bad." Having lost the bulk of their design staff in the transition was a serious problem, but he promised to reboot SPI's magazines and get new wargames into print. "In all, we aim to revitalize SPI," he vowed. All three ventures, he assured readers, "will fit into our operation without undue difficulties."

Gygax also shared his personal interests, largely around his film project. "Sometime this year we should have a script," he predicted, formally announcing that they had at this point engaged the famous James Goldman as the screenwriter. That sort of talent did not come cheap. "Film making is not a matter of weeks and months, it is more a matter of years," he lamented, and so the end of 1984 was the earliest anyone could hope for a completed project. He also spoke to his intention to recruit a division head to manage media opportunities, as well as other ideas in progress like a "syndicated radio series," an expensive idea championed by Dave Dimery and Frank Mentzer. They made a pilot for a radio show, and although that project never took off, the overall media division would become part of the new, more modular corporate structure as the reorganization progressed.

But was running a business like this really what Gygax wanted out of life? When Frank Mentzer wrote to Gygax in May 1982 complaining about how he was being railroaded into tasks other than creative work, Gygax retorted, "Do you think I wish to be President of this outfit? Bullshit! I could be loafing, enjoying myself, and writing when I felt like it." Gygax still felt that he had an obligation to the company, that it depended on his leadership, and his job was therefore doing whatever was "best for TSR," even if it was not always enjoyable. "TSR pays you, and as long as you take Morley's gold piece, you'll go where duty sends you," Gygax advised Mentzer.

At the end of that letter to Mentzer, Gygax portrayed Kevin Blume's path to success in the company as an example for an ambitious young man—and Mentzer certainly was that. "Kevin started as an accountant, bookkeeper, and stop-gap measure. Through his own hard work, dedication, devotion to TSR, performance, and desire he was first made an officer, then a board member." Gygax downplays the obvious family connection, claiming, "It wasn't because he was Brian's bro—take my word on that!" In his correspondence of the time, Gygax defended the Blume brothers, even in letters to people who did not work for TSR. As Gygax wrote in response to concerns expressed by Steve Marsh, "Do give Brian the benefit of the doubt—he is both forgetful at times and also pretty difficult, but he is overall one heck of a good fellow."

Some defense was required because the Blume family inspired increasing distrust among TSR staff. One incident involved Rose Estes, author of the "Endless Quest" books, and her unsuccessful attempt to exercise a stock option. As Mentzer detailed it in his May letter to Gygax, word of this incident had made the rounds of TSR staff: "a documentable breach of promise occurred . . . when Rose paid for promised stock, had her check cashed (when it stated on it that it was stock), and then was told no go." Mentzer was well aware that there were "extenuating circumstances, B^2 promised what he couldn't deliver, tighter stock control, etc.," but this could hardly instill confidence in Blume family management.

For all of the company's talk about eschewing traditional management structures, as the staff ramped up, the lack of the administrative expertise needed for a medium-sized business became a problem that had to be addressed. They contracted with communications consultants, a firm called IIIC, who tried to make it easier to pass information through TSR's fast-growing ranks. They began hiring experienced corporate veterans, like John Ricketts, who came on board in April as executive vice president of the games division, with almost two decades of experience in retail and marketing in the hobby business. TSR sponsored continuing education in management for eligible employees: Dave Sutherland entered a program at the Lake Forest

School of Management then, as did Kevin Blume's wife's brother, Jack Sloan. The change that was most visible externally was the hiring of Dieter Sturm to handle public relations; he had previously worked at the Playboy Resort in Lake Geneva, which had itself fallen on hard times and would shortly come under new ownership. Sturm was notorious in Lake Geneva that year for his "snow shark" public installations, plastic fins jutting out of snow banks, which were part of a running joke with a local radio station. He sold shark repellant in bottles, and he knew how to make a splash.

The week of June 7, TSR Hobbies held its first-ever corporate strategy planning session, and from that exercise they emerged with a "Philosophy & Creed" that they promulgated through *Random Events*. The governing structure that followed created the "Year of the Three Presidents," as it was remembered. A midyear organizational chart has Gygax as the president of TSR Hobbies with only three direct reports: the president of the TSR Fun Group, Brian Blume, who had all games, publishing, and entertainment media; the president of the TSR Services Group, Kevin Blume, who had manufacturing, human resources, and sales; and then a "Special Projects" team headed by Duke Seifried. But of the ten divisions and two subsidiaries of TSR, six were under Kevin and six under Brian; legal and marketing reported to Kevin, whereas the licensing work Andy Levison was doing, as well as trademarks, reported to Brian. As of June 22, all TSR purchase orders, even for the smallest amounts, had to be personally initialed by Kevin for approval. This structure freed Gygax to follow his creative interests in motion pictures and other ventures; it also increasingly removed him from daily operations and from direct control over how the business would be run.

Gygax did some continuing work on *AD&D*, which he published through *Dragon*, including installments toward a second volume of the *Monster Manual* and new work toward an expansion of the main system, but as for when those might turn into products, he could only cry, "Please don't ask me when!" The time for *D&D* to invade Hollywood was nigh: *E.T.*, a June 1982 release, showed a group of boys playing a fantasy role-playing game around their suburban kitchen table. Conversely, the release of *Conan the Barbarian* provided Gygax with an opportunity to explain everything that a fantasy film should not be. "If you have any respect for Conan as presented by Howard, then I suggest you stay away from the theater or else be prepared for great disappointment." He knew he could do better. "I promise all of you," Gygax wrote in the July issue of *Dragon*, "that if the *D&D* film isn't of the quality of *Star Wars* and *Raiders of the Lost Ark*, I will not only blast it . . . but I will apologize to you as well."

For the 1982 fiscal year ending June 30, TSR brought in $20.8 million in net revenue, for a profit of $1.8 million—its most profitable year to date. But TSR's communications about their growth started to become a bit murky at this point. They did not double their revenue over their often-claimed $16.5 million for the previous year—yet because TSR had an abbreviated nine-month fiscal year in 1981, during which time they actually logged just under $10 million, technically they could claim the 1982 figure of $20.8 million was double that. But no matter how they spun it, growth was lower than projected—albeit TSR was still larger than everyone else in their sector put together. Avalon Hill amassed perhaps $8 million in sales for the year, but much of that was in their computer games and sports games; only about $5.5 million fit unambiguously into the adventure games space. SPI had died. GDW and Yaquinto held steady at around $1 million in sales each. Companies like the Chaosium or Flying Buffalo made roughly a half million dollars. An upstart like Mayfair Games came in at $170,000. Arneson's Adventure Games is pegged at around $75,000 in sales for 1982.

Howard Barasch's scoreboard of the fiscal health of the industry—now appearing in *The Insider*, as *Strategy & Tactics* was defunct—reveals a sobering trend. As he charts it, the entire industry grew from earnings of $36.5 million in 1981 to just $41 million in 1982. From this he extrapolates that consumer spending increased by only 12.6 percent, at a time when inflation was 11.8 percent: spending on games was effectively flat. This put a sudden stop to year-after-year industry doubling since 1978. America had entered a recession at the end of 1981, which lingered until 1983, and now video games claimed a serious part of the entertainment market. So, 1981 really had marked a ceiling for tabletop adventure games.

Regardless of what they told the world, TSR knew the reality on the ground. Sales of the flagship *Basic Set* were down 16 percent in 1982 from the year before, and without a new hardcover *AD&D* book, *Advanced Dungeons & Dragons* book sales were down 25 percent. In a July letter to Will Niebling, Gygax freely conceded that "sales of the *D&D* Basic Set are decreasing." The burning question was not if they were decreasing, but why, and what could be done about it. True to its new corporate identity, TSR organized a

"Task Force to Extend Product Life Cycle of D&D and AD&D Product Lines and to Diversify New Product Appeal to Broader Market Segments." But Gygax basically dismissed its analysis, blaming slow sales on the economy, on poor product placement in retail outlets, and TSR's "failure to produce new products." Gygax even pushed back on the threat of computer games, which "represent no threat to our games at the current time," because they offer "no social interaction, no exchange of ideas." TSR had half-heartedly released a trio of internally developed computer games this year, including an adaptation of Megarry's *Dungeon!* board game, but Gygax still saw this as a marginal side-business.

Gygax's solution to the problem was simple: "Frank Mentzer will be joining me for training soon. Frank will be in charge of the work necessary in both D&D and AD&D products." Gygax believed that he and Mentzer had a firmer grasp on the needs of the market than TSR's marketing people. "For some time," Gygax related with exasperation, "I have stated exactly what these product lines needed, and this has been ignored. I have taken steps to correct it. I will see that it is taken care of." In this widely circulated memo, which also went to the Blume brothers, Duke Seifried, and others, Gygax very conspicuously placed his bet that Mentzer would rescue the *Basic Set.*

Another suspected factor in stagnant sales was the evangelical chorus loudly proclaiming *D&D* irreligious. TSR thus organized a large task force to develop a religious persecution response, divided into various "action plans" coded as RPR. Fundamentalist newsletters had begun to promulgate rumors that *D&D* led children to self-harm. For example, John Torell claimed he had spoken the previous September to a Seattle doctor who "is treating a policeman for severe depression brought on by the suicide of his sixteen-year-old son. The son, who had been heavily involved in *D&D* for two years, shot himself in the head with his father's service revolver. The doctor went on to say that so far in this country during 1981, 60 suicides have been directly attributed to *D&D*." Who knows where that number came from, but the figure quickly became a talking point for fundamentalists, as it inevitably would following Egbert's suicide in 1980. This was not a problem that would go away: it would only get worse. Simultaneous with the RPR process, on June 9, 1982, a young man named Irving "Bink" Pulling II committed suicide at his home in Montpelier, Virginia, in a case that would soon be linked to *D&D* as the "Satanic Panic" gained momentum.

In the RPR project, Gygax saw a tough job that Duke Seifried could dependably tackle from under the rubric of his Special Projects division. It was Mentzer who lobbied Seifried in May for a multipronged approach, beginning, "we MUST redesign all game covers (Basic Sets and hardbacks) to convey a wholesome image, and completely avoid the demonic or angelic references objectionable even to reasonable religious groups." He counseled the same path for advertising, and further advocated that TSR get some outside help in managing public relations from someone prominent who moved in religious circles, or perhaps a psychologist. By the summer, TSR had retained Dr. Joyce Brothers as a spokesperson who could talk up the beneficial impact of role-playing games. She wrote her own essay about *D&D* filled with positive statements such as, "The *Dungeons & Dragons* game provides an especially safe way for young people to meet their needs for excitement and adventure."

As a part of the RPR process, the task force reviewed some religious pamphlets criticizing *D&D*. Groups like the Christian Life Ministries had gone page-by-page through the core *D&D* books and isolated phrases they believed expressed the true intentions behind the game: teaching a religion, namely that of witchcraft. TSR staff thus went through its own deep read of the *D&D* books under action plan RPR03, which would extend throughout the summer. Looking at the sections on demons and devils in the *Monster Manual*, RPR03 came up with a list of possible approaches for mitigating any religious concern, which ranged from moving demons and devils into an appendix to deleting them entirely. The review of *Deities & Demigods* almost had to begin, "a new title might help defuse this volume as a source of material used against the company." Given it contained text such as "Serving a deity is a significant part of *D&D*, and all player characters should have a patron god," internal changes would be required as well. TSR moreover created a set of guidelines for new product content "designed to create a wholesome yet interesting impression on the public. We do not wish to be offensive to our potential customers yet by the same token we do not need to eliminate the spark that intrigues the buyer." They based these guidelines on the "comics code," the self-imposed restrictions on the content of comic books in place since the 1950s.

Codes and standards became necessary when the design staff expanded beyond just a handful of gamers: Why not hire as many as you can, if limitless growth was just around the corner? TSR added Doug Niles to the design department at the beginning of the year, then Tracy Hickman not long thereafter, and then Merle Rasmussen and Jeff Grubb both turned up as spring went into summer, and Carl Smith shortly thereafter. Most designers were tasked with the development of modules, which sold well enough—popular ones could move 100,000 copies a year—that they helped TSR believe *D&D* revenue would continue to grow. The swelling design staff needed to find a bigger home than the Hotel Clair, and plans were underway to migrate their department over to the spacious new headquarters on Sheridan Springs Road.

As the summer convention season approached, the annual sparring over venues between TSR and Avalon Hill had broken into an open war. Just a year earlier, Don Greenwood of Avalon Hill had graciously agreed to withdraw his AtlantiCon from the convention schedule so that GenCon East would not suffer from attendance drain. In deference to Greenwood, the group that had then run GenCon East decided to cancel their 1982 event, scheduled just four weeks before Origins returned to Baltimore. But this was utterly unacceptable to TSR, who had their outside counsel send a blunt demand to reverse its cancelation and step aside so TSR could run GenCon East, justifying this aggressive move as a defense of the GenCon trademark. TSR stunned the industry by teleporting forty-five of their Lake Geneva staff to Cherry Hill, New Jersey, to run the convention themselves, recklessly disrupting ordinary operations. TSR was so flush with cash that they could afford to indulge extravagant whims that would best have been suppressed.

The confrontational way that TSR brought about a GenCon East in 1982 was only a taste of their coming assault on Origins, scheduled for the last week of July. Already on February 9, TSR had sent the Origins committee at GAMA a notice on "Prohibited Use of TSR Trademarks and Copyrighted Games," which effectively barred Origins from running any *D&D* events. As soon as it gained control of SPI's assets, TSR also canceled all SPI events at Origins. So, as news spread of Heritage's deteriorating situation and Duke Seifried's jump to TSR, Rick Loomis of Flying Buffalo saw a pattern in TSR's activities: a concerted attack on Origins and GAMA. "It begins to look as if TSR will go to any lengths to destroy GAMA," Loomis began, in the May issue of his *Wargamer's Information*, "with my tongue in cheek, of course, but only partially." He went on to review how TSR had mistreated GAMA in the past, but homed in on Gygax in particular and the way he leveraged

TSR to lord over the rest of the industry. TSR's immense size and resources meant "that all the rest of us ought to do everything the way Gary wants," he charged, "happily picking up whatever crumbs he grandly allows us to have." Loomis concluded by noting that GAMA was driven by the energies of Avalon Hill, SPI, and Heritage—and TSR, by decapitating Heritage and shuttering SPI, had stilled the last two. TSR's response came from legal counsel, demanding that Loomis "immediately correct the misstatements in your article."

TSR did not deign to exhibit at Origins, but they did send a few emissaries, including Will Niebling, who distributed a bombshell press release announcing that TSR would no longer honor lifetime subscriptions to SPI's *Strategy & Tactics*. While it is doubtful the magazine could have remained viable otherwise, it would be difficult to exaggerate how poorly this announcement was received by the community. Don Lowry was swamped with angry letters to *Campaign* magazine; he published one—incidentally, in the last issue of that venerable successor to *Panzerfaust*—that called it "a facile and legally dubious maneuver" and an "act of piracy" to declare existing magazine subscriptions invalid. Lowry affixed an editorial note to this missive clarifying that "it is the calmest of a number of similar letters received." In the *American Wargamer*, there was even talk of trying to launch a class-action lawsuit against TSR.

Origins thus became something of a wake for SPI. Reportedly, a number of people wore buttons reading "SPI died for our sins." But Avalon Hill choreographed the launch of its new Victory Games division as the resurrection of SPI incarnate. As *The Insider* reported, "Declaring themselves the former SPI R&D department, and telling of their accomplishments in SPI products, they are trying to rally SPI grognards under their banner before TSR can get into gear. After observing the number of people congregated around their booth at Origins, wishing them luck and attending their seminar, Victory seems to be way out in front."

Origins in 1982 would claim a respectable attendance of perhaps 4,000 or 4,500—but turnout was surely lessened by GenCon East, and the absence of *D&D* events. *The Insider* put a brave face on the matter by welcoming a respite from *D&D*-obsessed teenagers. The Judges Guild failed to appear entirely, and rumor had it they were near collapse. Their advertisements now emphasized supplements approved for use with *Dragonquest*, the SPI fantasy role-playing game—but now that too had become a TSR property, which returned Judges Guild to a desperate situation.

Dave Arneson must have been thrilled to see the Adventure Games title *Harpoon* win the H. G. Wells Award for Best Miniatures Game at Origins. The game even attracted the attention of an unpublished author named Tom Clancy, who would use the miniature rules in *Harpoon* to track the action of submarines in his work toward his 1984 debut novel, *The Hunt for Red October*. Wondering when and if Arneson would deliver on his many game design works in progress, *Different Worlds* snarkily listed under the "what is not happening department" how "Dave Arneson keeps repeating his 'these things take time' line."

A few weeks later, GenCon in 1982 would take on something of a carnival atmosphere as it endeavored to make gaming accessible to all. TSR dispatched Joyce Brothers to Chicago early in August to promote both GenCon and new products like TSR's *Fantasy Forest* children's board game designed by Mike Gray. Dieter Sturm devised a "First Time Gamers" partnership with local radio stations. Arrivals to the convention were greeted with a fifteen-minute welcome show, including a live musical performance by "Uncle Duke and the Dragons," a quartet fronted by Duke Seifried. NBC's *Today Show* aired excerpts of that musical number, which secured it one of the highest honors that TSR bestowed on its efforts, the Kevin Blume Snoopy Award for outstanding performance. A roving robot named Denby extolled the virtues of the newly released *Star Frontiers* to anyone within earshot. At this point, GenCon truly had become a promotional event for TSR products.

Yet the absence of any new *D&D* core rules release was palpable. A module called *The Forgotten Temple of Tharizdun* sold best at TSR's booth, outshining even *Star Frontiers*. The byline of *Star Frontiers* moreover raised a few eyebrows in the industry. "The design credits for *Star Frontiers* are listed as 'TSR Staff,'" *Different Worlds* shrewdly noted. "Why no names? I heard that Lawrence Schick, now of Coleco, is primarily responsible." The account in *Dragon* magazine begged to differ, but this became another industry talking point about TSR cheating designers of credit and royalties. And although TSR showed off its computer game projects, none of them were *D&D* products—because TSR had fielded out the electronic rights for *D&D* to Mattel. As a reminder of just how substantial that market might be, Mattel erected a large booth at GenCon to show its first Intellivision *D&D* cartridge in action.

The media blitz was certainly a success, as attendance for GenCon in August came in at a record 6,985, with 600 scheduled events. Amidst all of this splendor and bustle, how must Gygax have felt, to witness the humble gathering he had founded in 1968 rise to such heights? Mike Carr in *Random Events* said afterward, "It must really please him now to see that many people enjoying themselves." No doubt it did, but the issue of *Dragon* magazine distributed at the convention carried an exhaustive "Guest Editorial" by Gygax that painted a more fraught picture: "The lines are drawn, and they are drawn just where they have always been. Aside from one or two companies who have always supported efforts to bring fun to hobbyists, the lines are between TSR and the remainder of the industry," and "The contest is intensifying. It is time that someone spoke about it." Gygax reiterated once again the story of how GenCon and Origins became rivals, of how Avalon Hill tried to represent Origins as "the national convention" instead of GenCon. He vented years of bitterness, stemming from when Avalon Hill and SPI laughed at TSR as "the strange fellows who thought fantasy was more fun than wargames," and then as "the 'lucky' nobodies riding a fluke which would soon burn out." But now virtually everyone was imitating *D&D*, and instead of being dismissed, "TSR is envied and sniped at."

"In my opinion," Gygax summarized, "Origins and its supporters see conventions as a battleground, a place to 'stamp out' TSR once and for all." Even if we grant that, TSR accepted that invitation to battle long ago. Back in TSR's infancy when, as Don Greenwood put it, "GenCon is what got TSR off and running," the unveiling of Origins was an existential threat to the young company. Because Gygax believed GAMA was bent on the destruction of TSR, naturally "TSR does not think that GAMA serves the adventure gaming industry." So Gygax used the bully pulpit of *Dragon* to call for a boycott: "Let the other side in this dispute know your displeasure with their commercial attitude by staying away from Origins." This issue was read with some small interest by GAMA members at their booths at GenCon that year, all of whom knew well that it would very soon be seen by the magazine's 70,000 or so subscribers.

Nor did Gygax stop there: in the very next issue of *Dragon*, he turned his attention to Loomis's earlier accusations about TSR, representing that they had only now come to his attention. "If you seriously believe that TSR would spend hundreds of thousands of dollars merely to 'go to any length to destroy GAMA,' you are, in my opinion, either irrational or suffering from paranoia," Gygax fumed. Loomis had, incidentally, made it clear that he was not entirely serious. More materially, Gygax attacked the hypocrisy he saw in Loomis complaining about the scheduling of GenCon East to compete against Origins, when Origins had been scheduled in the Midwest to compete with GenCon in 1983. Ultimately, answering the accusation that he merely left crumbs for the rest of the industry to feed on, Gygax had to ask: "Who leads the Adventure Gaming industry? Who publishes cheap imitations of TSR games?" This was perhaps as close as Gygax could come to acknowledging the existence of *Tunnels & Trolls*. "Where would the whole industry be if it wasn't for TSR leading the way?"

"I can hardly believe it," Loomis responded in the next issue of his *Wargamer's Information*. "After all these years of ignoring Flying Buffalo and *Tunnels & Trolls*, the *Dragon* magazine has finally mentioned us." As he rebutted Gygax's various claims, Loomis got down to the fundamental question of whether Gygax and TSR were worthy of leading the hobby games industry. He recommended that Gygax take after someone who "treats the other people in the industry as friends instead of enemies or dirt under your feet," and then offhandedly remarked that "the designer of *Tunnels & Trolls* is still a friend of mine, and he didn't have to sue me to collect his royalties."

Loomis paints TSR's current treatment of the industry, and Gygax's past treatment of Arneson, as manifestations of the same problematic behavior, and in that light, it is plain to see why the industry effectively rallied around Arneson: out of a shared sense of grievance. It scarcely mattered who did which work back in 1973, Gygax infuriated everyone else into taking Arneson's side. Loomis had been present at the initial GAMA meeting in 1978, and became the organization's first leader: How would he feel about Gygax calling for a boycott on Origins? And regardless of what role Gygax personally played in the botched SPI situation, it was still TSR's doing, and TSR was Gygax's company. To industry insiders—the sorts of people who read *The Insider*—Gygax came across in such a poor light that of course it made sense that Arneson did all the work, that Gary merely "edited" and published the game before seizing all the money and all the credit. Gygax's *Dragon* rants showed a man trying to dominate the entire industry. For trolling Gygax into punching down, Loomis received widespread plaudits from the community. In the pages of *Alarums & Excursions*, one commentator put it bluntly: "As a matter of public relations, Gary could not have done worse . . . and nobody at TSR had the nerve to tell Gary not to publish that editorial because it would be bad public relations."

If Gygax comes across to us as insecure, lashing out at Loomis and other enemies real or imagined, he had ample reason to be so. He had risen from utter destitution to a level of wealth he surely had no idea how to manage. He wrote to Steve Marsh in August that his cash reserves were "at a low ebb right now," as he had apparently underpaid his 1981 taxes by $120,000, which required him to borrow money. "I have a large payroll, heavy indebtedness in mortgages and time payments on businesses, and I'm still paying horrendous taxes." But this did not exactly mean that Gygax was living frugally: less than a week later, he reported in another letter that his Dragonlands ranch was "almost at thirty head of horses now, and the stable being completed in November will come none too soon." He was building a third story onto his house, too.

Gygax's personal financial situation mirrored that of TSR itself. In the middle of the year, Steve Witt gave an update on the status of the many TSR Hobbies properties in the pages of *Random Events*. As the manufacturing facility construction neared completion, Witt confirmed that TSR would imminently acquire more land next to the Torrent building for further construction in the future. They hoped to move all of employees in creative, the designers and artists still cooped up in the deteriorating Hotel Clair, as well as the Dragon Publications staff at 723 Williams Street, to the Torrent building before the end of June—but that date would slip by nearly six months. After that consolidation, the little grey house at 723 Williams "will be vacant, pending a corporate decision as to its future." But Witt reported that TSR had something else in mind, something very extravagant, for the building they would be vacating at 772 Main Street: "The goal of the corporation is to renovate the building into a restored version of the Old Clair Hotel." That was a bit more prosaic than the proposal Gygax had floated the year before: that after they moved all warehoused product out of the basement of the Hotel Clair "we intend to construct a large museum-like area and an actual (simulated) dungeon labyrinth." But with *D&D* sales flat at best, if not declining, how realistic were any of these lavish plans?

All but lost in the bustle of this extravagance, malaise was growing at TSR. Back in December 1981, Gygax had sent a memo to Mike Carr expressing concern about some of the decisions being made in product engineering, which fell under Carr's remit as head of manufacturing. The dice that had been inserted into the latest revision of Dave Megarry's *Dungeon!* board game were TSR's own numeral six-sided dice, rather than standard pipped dice. Being slightly

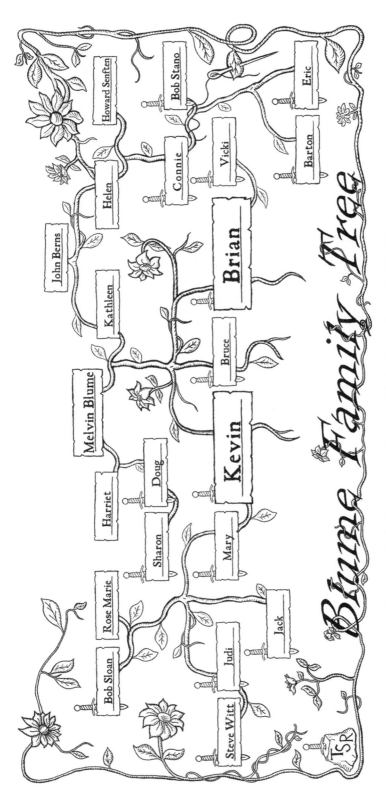

A family tree showing the various relatives, marked with daggers, of Brian and Kevin Blume who worked for TSR.

cheaper, pipped dice were the de facto standard for mass-market board games; the sales organization strongly opposed using TSR's dice in that market segment. The problem was only spotted after about 140,000 units had shipped.

The person responsible for this decision was Jack Sloan, Mary Blume's brother, and thus a brother-in-law to Kevin and by extension Brian. Sloan defended himself by arguing that when TSR went to the expense of creating its own dice molds back in 1980, "at that time it was decided that we would try to use TSR dice for all of our needs." Gygax had received contrary information, and replied on January 21 that, "it seems as if there has been some prevarication at worst, or perhaps very bad communications at best." This placed Jack Sloan under a bit more scrutiny. Mike Carr was painfully aware that he was sandwiched into a layer of management between Sloan and his brother-in-law Kevin Blume, so Carr did the most sensible thing one can do in such circumstances: he kept a detailed paper trail of Sloan's activities. But he could not cut off the line of communication between brothers-in-law, which led to a farcical moment when Kevin Blume widely circulated a memo to himself, from himself, warning himself against "failing to follow chain of command" by allowing Sloan to circumvent his supervisor. But this was half mea culpa and half tacit threat that anyone going over Kevin's head to Gygax would be guilty of a serious violation.

Then, in the summer of 1982, when another crisis struck related to the *Fantasy Forest* game boards, no one was surprised to find Jack Sloan in the middle of it. The purchase order for *Fantasy Forest* boxes had been submitted with the *Dungeon!* board as a prototype. A problem arose because the vendor incorrectly recorded how the hinges on the board worked, and because of the different dimensions of the folded board, the *Fantasy Forest* board would not fit into the boxes that TSR had purchased. By this point, a blunder of this magnitude could not be kept secret from the sleepless vigilance of the hostile industry. *Different Worlds* already could report in its August issue: "I wonder whose head will roll in Lake Geneva for this one! The entire first print run of playing boards (90,000!) for TSR's new children's game, *Fantasy Forest*, was misfolded and will not fit into its box." Sloan blamed the vendor, and while TSR would have to absorb some of the cost, he struck a deal that would let them break even after a half-million sales of *Fantasy Forest*.

Once news of this mishap made the rounds, Gary Gygax asked Duke Seifried to quietly look into the matter. Seifried deputized Bryce Knorr, who worked in the Special Projects group, as an inconspicuous surrogate. As Seifried and Knorr started putting the pieces of the puzzle together, the optics of the situation quickly worsened. It turned out that Jack Sloan was spending quite a bit of time outside the office. He had been at a baseball game the day that the *Fantasy Forest* gameboards problem came to light, and had to be paged. Sloan apparently logged a lot of time golfing, especially with representatives from the vendor who published *Dragon* magazine—not just locally, but in the dead of winter, in Florida. He left to golf with vendors on both July 22 and 23, when Knorr conducted interviews.

As TSR staff learned about the investigation, the floodgates opened. John Ricketts, who ran the games division, wrote to Seifried to say that one of the company's more serious problems was the purchasing department, which was "inadequately staffed to do research of new and unique parts" and "does not continuously obtain competitive quotes for materials now in use." Ricketts shared these thoughts with Seifried in the deepest confidence, as he knew well that "management may not be willing to listen to reason in regard to critiques of the purchasing department." One piece of typed feedback sent to Seifried with a plea to "disguise the source of information" levies an open accusation at the purchasing department, and at Jack Sloan and his father in particular, that "these guys are costing the company hundreds of thousands of dollars and because they are relatives, nothing happens except they get promoted and praised." It also blames Sloan for "saddling the company with crayon dice below even the standard of inked Hong Kong dice."

Discontent had mounted to a point where something had to be done. First, a new company policy regarding gifts from outside vendors would be forthcoming. Then, on August 17, Jack Sloan received a formal letter from the company stating that he was suspended pending an investigation—yet inevitably, that letter came from Doug Blume, Sloan's brother-in-law. There must have been some token investigation by the human resources department, effectively controlled by the Blume family, but whatever the outcome, Sloan was restored to his position on September 1. Furious, Carr sent a letter the next day to both Kevin and Doug Blume: "I would like to go on record in stating that I feel your decision to bring Jack Sloan back to work with so many questions unresolved was premature" and "extremely damaging to morale company-wide." As Carr bluntly wrote, he "would prefer that Jack not be a part of this division."

By September 7, a crisis was at hand, and apparently everyone at TSR had a pretty good idea what was going on. Two employees under the Sloans in the purchasing department—persons not related to the Blume family—sent an open memorandum to senior management that day stating, "It is impossible to work under the existing circumstances with the present supervisory management." Affidavits giving particulars they had witnessed firsthand accompanied the memo, which pledged, "In the absence of the current management we will give you 110% effort and help the company get through this difficult situation." Knorr had spoken to an eyewitness who believed that Jack and Bob Sloan had both been in the office the past Saturday, in the company of Mary Blume, going through purchasing records and possibly tampering with them.

Knorr appealed to Seifried, "Can the company stand another week of this affair?" Carr pleaded with Gygax to intervene, so Gygax put an "Important Message!" right below the masthead in the September 15 issue of *Random Events*: "In order to assure both positive mental attitude and free lines of communication, please remember that you should copy the Office of the President of TSR Hobbies, Inc. on any matter which you believe is of importance to the company. No one can tell you otherwise, as restricted information flow in this regard violates my direct policy." No one—presumably including Kevin Blume.

Knorr urged putting an abrupt end to the situation. Of the four options he proposed, all involved Jack Sloan exiting the company, varying only in the degree of dignity that would accompany him. But in the end, Jack Sloan stayed on in the purchasing department. Instead, Mike Carr quietly left his position as the executive vice president of the manufacturing division and accepted a role as a worker bee in the education department writing "Endless Quest" books. *Dragon* editor Jake Jaquet resigned, reportedly disgusted by the situation with the Sloans and, as *Space Gamer* reported in its gossip column, exasperated by the obligation of publishing Gygax's futile broadsides against GAMA. Many others lingered in utter demoralization.

TSR held its 1982 Founders Day celebration on October 1 at the main house of the sprawling Loramoor estate, until recently a Franciscan friary, among the largest mansions on Geneva Lake—second only to the imposing Stone Mansion. In its extravagance, TSR hired a top chef to cater a multicourse meal for the event, at which employees could luxuriate on docks or the shady lawn. In 1980, just sixty-five employees had been on payroll for the first Founders Day party. This year found TSR "with an employee population of 250, with two newly acquired office buildings, a 'built from scratch' Manufacturing Building, progressive modular furnishings, 36 newly delivered HP 125 terminals and 55 new products in process." Who could have

imagined they would end up here, when TSR Hobbies hired its first employees seven years ago? Mary Gygax, circulating through the crowd, awed
newcomers with her 1976 business card, which read, "The Woman at TSR
Hobbies." She was soon to become a grandmother: Elise Gygax, who married earlier in the year, would have a son in November.

The November 1982 shareholder meeting would set a book value for
TSR stock of $3,000. This made the large option agreements held by Gygax,
Brian Blume, and Will Niebling ever more valuable. But if Niebling exercised his option for 500 shares, then he and Gygax would possess combined
assets sufficient to outvote the Blumes at a shareholder meeting. He was a
risk. Niebling for his part had begun expressing concerns about TSR's willingness to honor his option agreement, especially in light of the treatment
Rose Estes had received earlier in the year.

Kevin Blume preemptively asked Niebling for his resignation on November 11. *The Insider* would later suggest that this was inevitable: it observed
that Niebling "has been a side-kick of E. Gary for many years. With the acquisition of Duke Seifried this situation was not to remain unchanged." Gygax's
increasing reliance on Seifried, a consummate salesperson, may be one reason he did not intervene. Lagging sales of the *D&D* product line surely also
put Niebling in the crosshairs. Blume offered to buy Niebling's 5 shares, and
the 5 held by his wife, at their face value sum of $30,000, but in exchange
for his stock option, now valued at $1.5 million, Blume presented Niebling
with an agreement effectively worth $100,000. Niebling instead decided to
exercise his option on the spot, and after passing around the hat and borrowing a bit from some fellow executives, offered the $62,500 necessary for the
exercise. But TSR declined to honor his stock exercise, and he was dismissed
immediately. Rather than wait for Niebling to sue TSR, TSR sued Niebling
in December to declare the option invalid. But this did not exactly obstruct
legal action in the opposing direction.

It was a fresh public relations disaster. Niebling's lawyers would send copies of his complaint to TSR's critics in the hobby community, like Rick Loomis, who happily printed excerpts in his *Wargamer's Information*, and Howard
Barasch, who made it front page news in *The Insider*. Niebling's attorney told
Loomis that back on May 12, 1979, because Brian Blume signed the option
agreement at his own wedding reception, TSR attorneys insisted that "the
option was not valid because they claim he may have been intoxicated at the
time," and that Blume had no memory of executing the agreement. Niebling's
legal team easily found other ex-TSR employees—and even Mike Carr—willing

to testify that they too had faced rejection when attempting to exercise stock options, so they could represent this as a pattern of behavior. If his option was not to be honored, Niebling sought $10 million in personal damages from Gygax and Brian Blume.

A massive lawsuit was just another thing Gygax lacked the time to manage, between travel and Hollywood ambitions. TSR had entered into development work with a few potential partners toward a *D&D* animated cartoon series, and in September Gygax reviewed show bible drafts from Hanna-Barbera. Then Gygax had spent three days with James Goldman in the third week of September, working on the script—bear in mind, this was in the throes of the Sloan crisis, the week after his note in *Random Events* encouraged employees to communicate directly with the president's office. In November, Gygax gave readers of *Dragon* their first report on the film project. Progress came slowly due to his "resolve to maintain as much control over the *D&D* movie as humanly possible." But this meant that another project related to *D&D*, one over which he had no control, would hit the screens first: *Rona Jaffe's Mazes and Monsters*, scheduled for a television premiere on CBS on December 28. The Egbert character in the story would be played by a young Tom Hanks, who had already earned some measure of fame with two year's work on the sitcom *Bosom Buddies*. Hanks told an interviewer from the *Detroit Free Press* the day before *Mazes* aired that he was aware of the Egbert story as it unfolded. "I remember reading about the disappearance with some interest. When I was in college, I played *Dungeons & Dragons* too."

Gygax wrote piecemeal extensions to *D&D* when he could, but he also made his delegation of design work a matter of public record in *Dragon*: "Most of you are not aware that soon I will retire from the position of 'sole authority' regarding the *D&D* game system. Frank Mentzer has 'volunteered' to assume a new trainee position where he will work with me directly." Although the planned *Monster Manual II* slated for a 1983 release would bear Gygax's name, he left Mentzer to generate its index of all *AD&D* monsters. Mentzer agonized over the difficulty of taking over *D&D* development, and frequently groused about compensation and corporate support, but Gygax urged him to just get the work done. "The fact is," Gygax wrote in a December 17 letter to Mentzer, right before leaving for France, "the game system is pretty good as it stands. The holes are trivial. Our competitors peck away, but they are like flies trying to bite an elephant. Why are you worried? Your work to date is excellent. Just keep turning it out. I will make certain that both Kevin and Brian do whatever they can to make sure that our best selling products are delivered in a timely fashion." Gygax had sketched Mentzer a roadmap that would eventually promote him to "Vice President of Fantasy Role-Playing Games."

Any company that spent so extravagantly, in the face of stagnant sales, will find itself in need of a line of credit. By the end of the year, thanks to rampant gossip about the purchasing department and a decided increase in belt-tightening measures, *Random Events* had to address the "cash flow problem" that TSR Hobbies was experiencing, blaming it mostly on the long delay between settling with vendors and receiving payments from retailers. "While TSR has a sizable line of credit with our banks, we have not had to borrow any money during this time when the whole economy is struggling." Just in case, TSR had secured a $10.8 million line of credit with the American National Bank, more money than they were likely to need in the short term. It was, as they say in the finance industry, a revolving credit line, one where the amount TSR could borrow would fluctuate based on the company's assets, its inventory and receivables. But taking on any sort of debt would put TSR into new territory. Kevin Blume found himself saddled with the responsibility of negotiating that credit arrangement, even though this was not exactly in anyone's remit: "I was the best there was in the company," he would say in an interview the following year, "but I wasn't the right person."

Where two years ago, Brian Blume and Gary Gygax had cautiously explored paths to expand the company, this year TSR recklessly tried everything: moving into computer games, movies, radio, toys, miniatures, fiction publishing, needlecraft, and even underwater salvage. It had nothing like the structures in place necessary to impose discipline on that mess. And worse still, they attempted all this in a year when the market was contracting. The price of their extravagance was about to become clear.

TSR Turn Results for 1982

Revenue: $20.8M, profit $1.8M
Employees: 180
Stock Valuation: $3,000
GenCon attendance vs. Origins: 7,000 vs. 4,000+
Number of Presidents of TSR: 3

Players Eliminated: SPI

IV Disjunction

1983: Splitting the Party

In the first week of 1983, the *Wall Street Journal* published a favorable but cautious article about TSR called *"Dungeons & Dragons* Game Propels Firm to Success, but Growing Pains Lie Ahead." In the estimation of the *Journal*, TSR controlled around half of the entire market for adventure games—they reckoned this made up 5 percent of the total market for non-electronic games. TSR boldly promised the *Journal* that "sales will continue to almost double in each of the next two years."

The growing pains came in when the *Journal* interviewed former *Dragon* editor Jake Jaquet. He had left TSR because, as he put it, "the inexperience and nepotism were making it difficult for things to function smoothly." He cited the problems with the *Fantasy Forest* board, all but naming Jack Sloan. Jaquet told the *Journal* that TSR Hobbies employed twenty relatives of Brian Blume; Gygax put the number at ten, and denied that the sprawling Blume family network posed a problem for the company. Given all the Blumes, Sloans, Witts, and Stanos, the number was certainly at least fifteen.

With *D&D* sales leveling off, revenue would presumably double through diversification. The *Journal* did commend the success of the "Endless Quest" series, remarking that "the four books, introduced last summer, rank first, second, fourth and fifth on the list of juvenile best sellers compiled by B. Dalton Bookseller." This article was also one of the first places that TSR publicly telegraphed the extent of its media ambitions: in addition to the radio-show pilot and the planned film, TSR "may produce cartoons for Saturday morning television." To cast such a wide net, they needed people, and Gygax predicted TSR would recruit up to 150 more in the next year or so. All this did begin to sound rather expensive. As the *Journal* noted, "TSR plans to continue its rapid expansion, and to do that may borrow substantial sums for the first time."

TSR signaled its move into new markets at the start of the year with a revised corporate logo, one that no longer depicted wizards or lizards but instead just the stylized outline of the letters "TSR" in a diagonal descent that only hinted at a dungeon map's geometry. On the back of their annual dealer catalog, Kevin Blume—in his capacity as president of the TSR Service Group—announced that the company had chosen as its motto for the year "New Directions For a Proven Leader." He stressed diversification measures like the craft products of Greenfield Needlewomen, concluding, "Let us together make 1983 a banner year for games, toys, hobbies, and crafts."

Although 1983 would be a banner year for games, it would not be in the way TSR had hoped. The entire industry was upended by a single new title, an import from Canada that traded at an obscene price point of up to $40. Released domestically in March 1983, *Trivial Pursuit* would soon flood the American retail game marketplace, invading the shelf space in K-Marts and bookstores where *D&D* might otherwise have connected with customers, bringing in some $70 million by the year's end. Its meteoric rise made TSR's year-over-year growth for the past decade seem plodding. There was no small irony that *Trivial Pursuit* contained a "Sports & Leisure" category question "Who invented *Dungeons & Dragons*?" The answer, inevitably, listed only one name: "Gary Gygax."

As they planned to enter the toy market aggressively, TSR had to hit all of the early trade shows of 1983 where hobby stores made purchasing decisions—and spend lavishly to stand out from the crowd. TSR shipped twenty-six employees to the HIA show in Anaheim at the end of January, some of whom stayed for twelve days for the construction and dismantling of their forty-by-eighty foot castle booth. Not content with keeping their assault limited to the realm of business, Mayfair Games famously erected "a small wooden catapult with accompanying styrofoam rocks" so they could bombard the walls of TSR's castle. "No," *The Insider* reported with disappointment, "TSR never did sally forth to attack the besiegers."

TSR's fortifications protected its ambitions. Within their walls, you might meet Larry Elmore, the cover artist for Mentzer's revised *Basic Rules*, who sat in front of a huge reproduction of that iconic image. Gary Gygax and Kevin Blume posed for pictures holding copies of re-skinned *Advanced Dungeons & Dragons* rulebooks, with less demonic art furnished by Jeff Easley. Connie Stano would represent the Greenfield Needlewomen, who would "be exhibiting in a newly designed booth, which will also be a real attention-getter," as

Random Events promised. Having a strong crafts showing was a necessity at the HIA, as "the Association's convention coordinators placed a heavy emphasis on crafts." Of the more than six hundred exhibitors spread out over 1,300 booths at the HIA show, only about fifty were from companies in the Adventure Gaming category. The hobby and crafts industry—which accommodated effectively all leisure products sold by hobby retailers, from model airplanes to yarn to computer games—represented roughly a $3.5 billion market at the time. At about 1 percent of that total, adventuring gaming remained a slender slice of the pie, and role-playing games just a sliver of that.

The Insider noted that "no new TSR role playing games were presented" at the HIA event, but its rival "Avalon Hill announced its soon-to-be-released *Powers & Perils*, its first fantasy role-playing game," spearheaded by Richard Snider. Given reports that Avalon Hill's analog game sales were down 15 percent from the previous year—and with the demise of SPI fresh in everyone's mind—*Powers & Perils* would be only one front in Avalon Hill's bid for the role-playing game market. They had also acquired ex-TSR designer Tom Moldvay's *Lords of Creation*, a project that had gained little traction with his former employer, but now reportedly commanded a $10,000 advance. They even whispered to *The Insider* of a new gangster RPG called "Machine Gun Kelly" by Dave Arneson—though *Different Worlds* gossip would soon clarify the project was "mostly designed by Steve Lortz, but I hear that Dave Arneson's name is on it to promote sales." All this just built up to the big news: Avalon Hill had secured the rights from the Chaosium to publish a new edition of *Runequest*, one of the most respected competitors to *D&D* in the fantasy role-playing game space. And then Victory Games, the former SPI design team at Avalon Hill, had aspirations in role playing as well. If these plans came to fruition, Avalon Hill would be mounting a direct, multipronged assault on TSR's core business.

There was no Heritage booth at the HIA show, as about five weeks prior, their bank had called in hopeless debts and shuttered the operation. Beforehand, Heritage had been entertaining suitors for a potential acquisition: since Duke Seifried was still a substantial shareholder, he had no small interest in seeing the company make a graceful landing. Kevin Blume had flown down to Dallas to discuss a purchase—but no deal resulted. Naturally, after the fiasco with SPI the year before, the exact role TSR played in the demise of Heritage, another of the cornerstones of GAMA, became the subject of some dark rumors. *Space Gamer* had previously reported that Blume and Seifried had never even spoken to the principals at Heritage during their purported scouting expedition.

Kevin Blume had started to take a more public-facing role at TSR, so at the HIA show, he summoned that reporter, John Rankin, to clarify TSR's ambitions in the miniatures space. *Space Gamer* had also covered the imminent expiration of the Grenadier license, and the hardball tactics TSR had employed, unsuccessfully, to force Grenadier into a lopsided partnership. Rankin would secure a more in-depth follow-up interview with Blume, who "described himself as a 'cold fish' in the business sense, and yet he's as pleasant a fellow as you could ever hope to meet—charming, in fact, in a reserved sort of way."

Rankin could not resist asking Blume about rumors of a potential split of TSR, including one provocative story that Gary Gygax planned to exit the company, possibly with Duke Seifried in tow, to develop Greyhawk as an intellectual property, and that Kevin and Brian Blume planned to sell TSR's remaining assets to Mattel. Rankin suggested "there were three or four versions of this story floating around the HIA show." Blume shrugged off those tall tales. When pressed about any schism in the management, Blume preached unity: "Brian and Gary and I run this company as a triad, and obviously we don't have 100% unanimity. But to date we have always been able to find an agreeable position among the three of us. We have never had the types of problems one would normally associate with a triad. We counterbalance each other amazingly well."

The *Wall Street Journal* article had mentioned that Gygax "concedes that he lacks management expertise," as did his partners the Blumes, which they hoped to address "by taking a few management courses." TSR had the year before begun working with the American Management Association (AMA), an educational group that supported corporations with various training programs, seminars, and accreditations. At the beginning of the year, TSR began offering AMA courses like "Essentials of Management" to employees— apparently some sixty staffers participated in that course, at a cost to the company of around $20,000. The human resources organization made it clear in the February *Random Events* that these programs "are actual, measurable indicators of the company's interest in promoting organizational development." Gygax and his co-president Blumes would travel to attend the AMA's

"Management Course for Presidents," and all vice presidents would take the "Top Management Briefing," an in-house equivalent.

But the most glaring deficiencies in their management could not be repaired with incidental training courses. TSR thus engaged a firm headed by the industrial psychologist Robert Thompson to provide guidance on improving performance at the senior executive level. Thompson recommended that Judi Witt, Kevin Blume's sister-in-law and then executive vice president of business information services, should obtain a bachelor's degree at least. The company therefore agreed that she would take a sabbatical and enter Lake Forest as a student in the fall semester. TSR would cover her tuition, fees, and any other expenses, providing her as well an annual stipend. The reality that TSR would soon be paying a direct relative of the Blume family not to work at the company could only redouble concerns about nepotism.

Still, these expenditures would not make or break a company of TSR's size: investments in mainstream media advertisements had now reached a point where they dwarfed this sort of petty cash. The $1 million worth of consumer print ads they projected for 1983 paled beside the $2.1 million they would spend on television, with a further half million earmarked for radio spots. Comparatively, they budgeted only $200,000 for industry and trade press: they wanted to reach consumers, not retailers. Almost exclusively, these ads promoted two titles: *D&D* and *Star Frontiers*. While there was some grousing internally about promoting *Star Frontiers*, the forthcoming May 1983 conclusion of the Star Wars trilogy, *Return of the Jedi*, made a space opera role-playing game look like a sensible bet.

Visiting the GamesFair convention in the UK in March, Gygax had much to say about the movie business, including how he hoped to be an adviser on the forthcoming 1984 Conan sequel, as TSR was now in negotiations to license the Conan property for modules and possibly "Endless Quest" books. He waxed rhapsodically about the screenplay for the *D&D* movie, reiterating his frequent promise that it would fall "between *Star Wars* and *E.T.*" By the end of April, media observers had already begun signaling that Marvel Comics was working on an animated series based on *D&D*. With this would come an agreement between TSR and Marvel to license the characters and properties of the animated series for coloring books and related children's products, and the possibility of a Marvel-themed superhero game—if TSR could persuade Marvel to partner with them, rather than the well-funded Mayfair.

In pursuit of these media interests, Gygax spent a good amount of time in Hollywood, as he wrote in *Dragon* late in the spring, announcing what was then called the *"Dungeons & Dragons Children's Show,"* the promised Saturday morning cartoon. Not that it was all business: Gygax also "sat in the fabled Polo Lounge and quaffed foaming jacks of scotch and soda or beakers of silver bullets." But that was all part of networking in California to build contacts for television and film properties, including making the acquaintance of "the worthy Buck Rogers man, Flint Dille." Dille was a young writer who was already working on Saturday morning cartoons like the *Mister T* series, and would soon have credits for *G. I. Joe* and *The Transformers*, who also happened to be the grandson of the original publisher of Buck Rogers. Gygax and Dille had begun collaborating toward a sword-and-sorcery television series. "With a bit of luck," Gygax added wistfully, "I'll be returning to sunny California soon to turn outlines into scripts and scripts into films."

A February notice in the *Lake Geneva Regional News* forecasted that "this month TSR will complete construction of its $3,500,000 addition to the company's international corporate headquarters on Sheridan Springs Road." They needed the space, given the pace of hiring. The year before, each issue of *Random Events* might introduce eight or twelve new hires, with headshots and a paragraph of explanatory text. Now, the March 1983 *Random Events* alone fit 25 headshots onto a single page—and then an additional 24 on another page, the latest of 312 total TSR Hobbies employees, with perhaps another 25 or so attached to the TSR UK subsidiary. Hiring was simply out of control. Between staffing, facilities, advertising, and diversification, the company was spending a staggering amount of money.

In the spring, TSR's human resources department ran a service called "Direct Line" permitting staffers to submit anonymous questions to senior management through a drop box. Employees were well aware that TSR was going into debt. One bold soul asked, "If TSR needs money, why borrow it from banks instead of allowing investors to buy shares?" Many employees would gladly have purchased equity in the company; the closest they could get was investing in the TSR profit sharing plan. The response was, "TSR is not, in general, currently making its stock available for sale. One of the main reasons for this is that we have had a number of incidents which ended in a person who is unfriendly toward the Company controlling some of our stock." Now that did not just hint at the likes of Arneson and Megarry, but

TSR designers pulling their weight, from right to left: Tracy Hickman, Jeff Grubb, David "Zeb" Cook, Carl Smith; Smith again (in foreground), Bruce Heard, Merle Rasmussen, and Jim Ward. Taken at the TSR family picnic at Delavan Township beach, June 18, 1983, six days before TSR's restructuring. Photo courtesy of Merle and Jackie Rasmussen.

Niebling as well. Echoing sentiments that Gygax had expressed as far back as 1975, the "Direct Line" response went on to declare: "Selling to outsiders would cause us to eventually give up control over our own destiny."

TSR could have managed its debt if sales had followed the curve projected the year before. And indeed, in early April, Gygax told the press that "he's approached almost daily by corporate suitors to go public with a stock issue or to sell out to a conglomerate," boasting that "the company's rather cautious sales projection for 1983 is $35 million"—a far cry from the $75 million he had predicted the year before, but this too would turn out to be naively optimistic. TSR had been in the business long enough to know that the first quarter of a calendar year would be slow, following the holidays, and the company often took a loss for those months. But when a rebound failed to manifest by April, and then into May, the senior executive team realized that sales were drastically below the worst-case estimates, nothing like the doubling they had promised the *Wall Street Journal* just months earlier.

The issue of *Random Events* released in mid-June would turn out to be the last. Its front page displayed two stories, each with a picture of its author: one by Gygax called "Innovation: Where We Came From—Where We Are Going," and the other by Brian Blume, titled "TSR Means Innovation." Both of them tell the origin story of the company, with ample deference to one another, though Gygax focused more on where they came from than where they were going. Blume wrote optimistically of the future Greenfield Needlewomen product line, and boasted, "For years, bankers have been amazed that we could grow to our current size without borrowing their money. All it required was a little innovative financing." And looking back to the close of, say, the 1981 fiscal year, it was remarkable: TSR held no bank notes, and perhaps had $230,000 in long-term debt, of which only $64,000 would come due by 1982.

But as the 1983 fiscal year closed in June, TSR's debt situation had changed dramatically. The company had borrowed roughly $4 million from banks by this point and owed a further $2 million in accounts payable to vendors and service companies. At this point, the company was borrowing against its line of credit with the American National Bank just to make payroll. The bank was alarmed by this situation, and had considerable influence it could exert over the company, which it now began to exercise. A look at the fundamentals for the 1983 fiscal year explains why an intervention was necessary: where sales were strongest, they were flat. TSR revenue nominally grew this year, up to $26.7 million, a modest improvement on the $22 million they booked the year before. But a big chunk of that income, $4.3 million, is attributable to the growing publishing business, that is Rose Estes's "Endless Quest" novels, which had by the middle of the year sold around two million copies—albeit it did not augur well that Estes, still furious over the rejection of her stock exercise, quit the company around this time after an unsuccessful attempt to negotiate better compensation for her efforts. TSR's licenses for third-party products brought in a further $1.8 million: Andy Levison, TSR's New York–based licensing director, had secured a dozen new licenses over the past year.

But considering only revenue from games, 1983 figures were basically flat over the year before. And this would be the first year that TSR had to book significant interest payments on the money that they were borrowing—more than $600,000. They scraped up cash where they could, including with the sale of the little gray house at 723 Williams Street, their first office and the original home of the Dungeon Hobby Shop. It was moreover obvious by this point that Greenfield Needlewomen had no prospect of growing into a fifth of the total income of TSR Hobbies now or ever, and that the business should simply be discontinued: TSR would write off $504,702 for shuttering it as they closed out the 1983 fiscal year. As a result, the company took a narrow loss, audited at $69,410.

Long before they announced these figures, the triumvirate at the top of TSR knew well that meaningful changes had to be made. When a formerly profitable company takes a loss, an executive reshuffle will often follow. What TSR Hobbies needed was an organizational structure that would isolate the steady games business from riskier diversification measures like the craft needlework business, or their substantial gamble on media properties. Moreover, if they were going to make a serious entry into international markets, they could minimize the tax consequences by keeping money from international sales offshore—there was talk of millions connected to the toy business tied up in Hong Kong. But perhaps most of all, TSR needed to curtail areas of overexpansion.

So the directors did what gamers call "splitting the party": they divided the company in four. A note to the division heads went out on June 13, announcing that the board of directors intended to change the name of the company from "TSR Hobbies, Inc." to simply "TSR, Inc." With that, TSR Hobbies would cease to exist, eight years after its founding, and with it went the position of president of TSR Hobbies, formerly occupied by Gygax, now unoccupiable. Gygax would lead all film and television projects under a TSR Media company. The lucrative licensing business would go to Brian Blume, who would manage Andy Levison and his team as TSR Ventures. All international business, including the TSR UK subsidiary, would be organized under a new TSR Worldwide umbrella, run by Andre Moullin. Everything that remained—the original business in games, publishing, miniatures, and so on—would fall under TSR, Inc. That company would be headed by Kevin Blume, and rather than being organized under an ever-growing set of unwieldy divisions, now there would be only six clean divisions reporting to Kevin. Where Brian Blume had been chairman of the board of TSR Hobbies, Inc., now Gygax would now be chairman of the board of TSR, Inc.

This eliminated the problem of having three presidents for one company: Gygax could run his own company, Brian Blume another, and Kevin Blume yet another. But with the presidents of all four companies reporting to a board of directors composed of those three, the situation seemed likely to reignite the same disputes that arose in the TSR Hobbies triumvirate. Or, maybe it would work better, and it was worth trying. There was just one more process they had to execute, which the bank demanded: immediate staff reductions to offset the reckless hiring over the past twelve months, which had grown total payroll to nearly four hundred.

The plan went into effect on the morning of Friday, June 24. The chosen leaders of the consolidated six divisions of TSR, Inc. were summoned to a ten-thirty meeting that described the new structure; others who would be moved under those six vice presidents, including Ernie Gygax, were similarly debriefed then. By eleven o'clock, the bulk of the leadership team was sequestered at the Shore Club, in a hotel a few miles south from downtown Lake Geneva, on the other side of Buttons Bay. Over the next several hours, the staff reductions were executed at Sheridan Springs, with nearly sixty persons removed from the payroll. Some of the layoffs reflected the elimination or consolidation of positions, while others targeted underperforming employees. Everyone received a week or two of severance, and many were eligible for placement services, as well as extensions on health insurance and similar benefits. Dick Gleason, the head of human resources, remained at headquarters to handle any disgruntled employees, and reportedly tensions ran high enough that Gleason's life was threatened.

June 24 was a day of reckoning for many key players at TSR, and a culling of unsuccessful or risky ventures. While it was unsurprising to see the managers of Greenfield Needlewomen leave the company after TSR wrote off the acquisition, it was also the last day of many other relations of the Blumes, including Bob Sloan and his controversial son Jack. Steve Witt had received his last paycheck earlier in June—and Judi Witt would simply enter her "sabbatical" at Lake Forest, under an increasingly dubious arrangement that would later devolve into a fresh scandal. Duke Seifried, head of special projects for Gygax, left the company, and with him much of TSR's hope for dominating the miniatures and toy business. A few major initiatives were shuttered in the process: TSR walked away from mass-market board games like *Fantasy Forest*, which were expensive to produce yet returned low sales figures. They also pulled the plug on their computer games business after their brief foray the year before, leaving this entirely to partners like Mattel—and of course to competitors, ranging from Avalon Hill to newcomers like Electronic Arts, a group that had already recruited designers the likes of Jon Freeman and former TSR staffer Paul Reiche.

Both Gygax and the Blumes did protect their immediate family from the purge. Doug Blume would now report directly to Brian Blume at TSR Ventures. And Ernie Gygax would remain in consumer services through the summer to oversee the conventions, before relocating to his father's media business. Despite his ostensible withdrawal from game design, Gary Gygax moreover retained Frank Mentzer and François Mercela-Froideval as direct reports working on special projects, including Mentzer's ongoing revisions to the Basic *Dungeons & Dragons* game. Mentzer became "Creative Aide to the Chairman of the Board."

In external publicity, TSR put a brave face on the changes: the wily Dieter Sturm would not confirm any link between the reorganization and financial setbacks, insisting, "More or less, what you're looking at is money coming into the company from sales and not focused properly." But every last detail of TSR's difficulties was consumed ecstatically by the hobby zines of the day. The best contemporary coverage came from *The Insider*—though it must be noted that June 23 had marked the final closure of Heritage, when their last assets were auctioned off, so Barasch probably found TSR's comparatively minor problems a welcome distraction from his own sad situation.

In Barasch's estimation, in the power struggle over TSR, "Gygax had deserted the battlefield to others, retreating to California to become a movie writer/producer/star or whatever to work out some type of deal or deals concerning a D&D movie or series." He judged, not unfairly, that "Gygax had pretty much separated himself from the TSR daily operation and found greater personal satisfaction in other pursuits also in the name of *D&D*." So, Barasch reasoned, "the Blumes offered a position of prestige as chairman of the board and a company of his own that appealed to his current interests." Gygax could hardly refuse.

As Barasch counts himself "not one to indulge in street gossip," he somewhat delicately skimmed over how "it had been mentioned by several people that Mr. Gygax had found other female companionship which eventually led to the break-up of his marriage." It is true that Gygax had separated from his wife Mary in March, just a few months before this corporate reorganization took effect. Barasch thus deduced, "The emotional trauma stemming from a separation and divorce plus the intense interest in working with mass entertainment had set the stage for Gary's receptiveness to a major change." It surely also reflects the culmination of ambivalence that Gygax had expressed since the summer of 1980, in places like his "Who Am I?" essay, about serving as the company's chief executive. Changes in his personal life perhaps made it easier to plot a change in his career.

Gossip about Gygax's divorce spread quickly among industry insiders, to no small degree propelled by how inflammatory Gygax's past jeremiads had been. In the course of Gygax's pointless flame war the previous year with Rick Loomis, Loomis had at one point mused that due to his own commitment to quality products, "I guess I'll never have a mansion on a 5-acre estate, or 29 Arabian horses, or a chauffeured limousine." This apparently prompted Gygax to send a rash personal letter to Loomis in response with a postscript bragging: "Estate is c. 23 acres. Herd numbers c. 30 head but is kept on farm, not estate, for most part." So now, in mid-1983, Loomis could poisonously mention in his newsletter, "It is unfortunate indeed that the current gossip is that Gary is splitting with his wife, and moving to the west coast with his girlfriend. I was told the wife was going to keep the estate." So much bad blood had been spilled in the industry that few insiders felt sorry for Gygax. Fortunately, most fans of *D&D*, who read little but *Dragon* by way of industry news, were effectively isolated from these restructurings and scandals.

The process of decoupling the licensing, media, and international businesses from the parent company TSR, Inc., would not be a trivial one. The day before the split was announced, Gygax wrote to Kevin and Brian to recommend that his new company operate in Hollywood under the name "Dungeons & Dragon Entertainment, a Division of TSR, Inc." He felt that having *Dungeons & Dragons* in the name was "absolutely required" in order to sell to the media market. Although there was considerable pressure to separate this new entity from the parent company, within a week Gygax had to concede that "it does not seem feasible to establish the new corporation as an effective entity prior to August 1." In part this was because they lacked any plan to transition the many employees he would poach: the Dungeons & Dragons Entertainment Corporation (DDEC) needed Gygax's son Ernie, TSR's media head John Beebe, his old friend Dave Dimery, longstanding presidential aide Jim Johnson, and a number of other members of support staff. Moving them off of the TSR payroll onto checks cut by a newly founded DDEC would take time.

The TSR Hobbies games division weathered the transformation into TSR, Inc. without any significant staff reductions. John Ricketts continued at its helm, and indeed on June 24 had invited the other division heads to his place for drinks when their vigil at the Shore Club became too tense. The Monday after, first thing in the morning, Ricketts held an all-hands meeting that opened with a round of applause from the team. "Thank you for giving me the clap," Ricketts deadpanned. From there, he mostly tried to bolster the group's confidence in the company's continuing viability. As Kevin Blume now had a more intuitive structure reporting to him, and no further distractions resulting from the "three presidents" arrangement, he would have more time to focus his on executive responsibilities. Ricketts felt that Blume was already delegating more and giving the division heads the power to make meaningful decisions. One caveat Ricketts had to make was that Gygax and Mentzer would still oversee the *D&D* product line—so perhaps some demarcations would not be so stark. Nonetheless, Ricketts expressed confidence that TSR would make $40 million in sales over the next fiscal year.

But Ricketts would not remain at the company long enough to see that prediction falsified. A second round of layoffs would come in July, and Ricketts would be out. The bank insisted on a 30 percent staff reduction, and the June layoffs had only been the first installment—the second round cut staff down to just shy of 260 souls. Now Mike Cook, publisher of *Dragon*, would assume the position of vice president of R&D Products, a division that would encompass toys, hobbies, games, and periodicals. This reflects in no small part the enormous power of *Dragon* as a platform for TSR, one that now reached more than 100,000 subscribers.

Among those who exited in the July round of lay-offs was Mike Carr. After the Sloan family debacle, Carr had spent the last nine months in the education department working on books, including his *Robbers and Robots* (1983), a book in the "Endless Quest" series that sold a quarter million copies. But we can only feel so bad for Carr. Not only did he manage to sell back his 108 shares to TSR, then valued at $3,000 a piece, but a few weeks later he applied for a job as a commodities broker in Chicago, which turned out to be with the much-storied "Turtles" group, famous for their radical successes in the early 1980s.

The purchase of Mike Carr's 108 shares further bolstered TSR's treasury stock holdings. As of June 30, auditing records show that TSR owned 400 of its own shares. Since they needed cash quite urgently, it is perhaps unsurprising that in July they sold treasury stock to the TSR profit sharing plan: 120 shares in exchange for $360,000. Removing that much liquidity from the fund, however, made it difficult for long-term employees to claim the benefits they had been promised from it, a source of further disputes with exiting staffers.

After Carr's departure, only one member of the original 1976 Twin Cities coalition remained at TSR: Dave Sutherland, the company's first staff artist. Following this reorganization, Sutherland would continue to work in the research and development organization, this time tasked with helping build three-dimensional models for miniature figures. The miniatures business was one diversification effort that TSR continued to push in the summer of 1983. Later, as a cartographer for modules, Sutherland would continue to work at TSR well into the 1990s.

With its newfound austerity, TSR would no longer indulge in gestures like the bizarre intervention it had staged for GenCon East the year before. So, this summer, the initiative in the combat phase went to its opponents. In 1983, Origins returned to Detroit, in July, just weeks before GenCon, replaying the confrontation of 1978. Metro Detroit Gamers reported an attendance of 4,500, but disappointed exhibitors grumbled that the count was more like 3,000.

Avalon Hill founder Charles S. Roberts resurfaced for Origins in 1983 to celebrate the company's twenty-fifth anniversary. One member of the chattering class reported in *Alarums & Excursions* that "Charles Roberts received a plaque naming him the Father of Board Wargaming," and that "Dave Arneson received a plaque naming him the Father of Role-Playing Games." Everyone knew that "this will undoubtedly cause fury in Lake Geneva as an attack on TSR by GAMA." But by this point, a narrative had taken hold in the minds of fans: "As I understand the history of D&D," the commentator in *A&E* explained, "Arneson wrote the rules and Gygax published them the first time around, and if this is true then the award was deserved." While Arneson was perhaps the last person who would champion the "simple" job of writing rules, such historical nuance would not have much bearing on the decision made at Origins, as Gygax "can hardly expect to receive an award by an organization he declared war against."

Roberts for his part viewed the title with "faint amusement," as he had "no thought, let alone premonition, of founding a company, avocation, or industry" when he designed *Tactics*, the first modern board wargame, adding, "May I note that I would rather be known for something that was the result of deliberate effort." But for Arneson, these sorts of ceremonial appearances now defined his role in the community; his name was a battle standard around which those wronged by TSR could rally. When Grenadier lost the *D&D* license, they immediately secured Arneson's endorsement for their new "Fantasy Lords" series of generic miniatures. While he still managed his modest Adventure Games business, manning its booth at Origins to showcase Dave Megarry's new *Pentantastar* game, Arneson produced effectively nothing for Adventure Games himself. Instead, he could be found working on a few pages for an anthology project, similar to the Chaosium *Thieves' World*, that Rick Loomis planned for his *Cityblade* series. No doubt Loomis was delighted to throw a bit of business to the true "Father of Role-Playing Games." As for Arneson's "Machine Gun Kelly" project with Steve Lortz, no mention would be made of it again.

The combatants who attended the summer conventions in 1983 perhaps suffered from a bit of battle fatigue. Conspicuously absent at Origins was Avalon Hill's promised foray into role-playing games. They had heavily promoted *Powers & Perils* at earlier trade shows, but one Origins attendee reported "people would walk by an empty room where a *P&P* demonstration was scheduled, peer in, and walk away." When Eric Dott and Tom Shaw of Avalon Hill gamely posed for a picture with the Chaosium crowd to commemorate their *Runequest* acquisition, they still held up the Chaosium edition of the game, as their new edition was still pending. The former SPI staffers at Victory Games, under the Avalon Hill umbrella, brought their new role-playing game *James Bond 007* to demonstrate only, promising a September release. This would compete directly with the TSR game *Top Secret*, with the benefit of the popular film franchise license that TSR had sought in 1980 but had been unable to secure.

TSR made no official showing at Origins—but they did launch a clandestine mission suitable for an espionage game. Many had read Kevin Blume's favorable remarks about GAMA in the *Space Gamer* earlier in the year, and learned that Kevin "was at Origins Sunday to discuss healing the rift between TSR and GAMA." But whispers at Origins about TSR's staff reductions and reorganization just weeks before had spawned conspiracy theories that were, as the chattering class put it, bordering on "paranoia." A gossiper explained how "one GAMA member told me he suspects that the TSR reorganization has as one of its motivations to create smoke screens under which old offenses can be concealed as the Blumes take over GAMA from within, now that the attack from outside has failed."

It was no doubt easier for Kevin Blume to repair TSR's relationship with Origins while Gygax ramped up his company on the West Coast, headquartered at a Hollywood Hills ranch that once was owned by the movie producer King Vidor. It served as both a home and an office, and immediately became known as Dragonlands West. It had living space enough for Gygax and his son Ernie, as well as a guest bedroom for John Beebe, and another for Jim Johnson, and even quarters for entertaining the occasional traveling dignitary. The best part of this arrangement was that the rent on the property could be treated as a business expense. At a time when TSR was culling its employees, the projected annual rent on Dragonlands West came to $120,000.

Within the bubble of Hollywood, the extravagance of TSR's past lived on and even intensified. "Some of the most beautiful women I've ever seen were around," Flint Dille would recall, and for Gygax, "it was a time for him to enjoy the profits of his enterprise," filling the mansion with gaming tables and staging lavish parties. "We were like a bunch of multi-millionaire 12-year-olds." By July, they also had on staff at DDEC Donna Yukevich, who worked as a project coordinator for the office—but it was no secret that she was more than just an employee to Gygax.

Even Hollywood could not keep Gygax away from GenCon. He returned to personally address the Strategist's Club banquet, apologizing for his absence in California. *The Insider* could not resist a snarky aside: "Who was that crazy fellow in the front table at the Strategist Club banquet at GenCon. I understand he cracked-up, spewing food everywhere when Gary Gygax told the audience that he has been out of sight for a while in California 'doing other things.' Sometimes it could be embarrassing to be too much of an insider." In 1983, GenCon began to pull decisively ahead of Origins, with a turnstile attendance reported at over 8,000, probably at least twice the number that gathered in Detroit. It had begun to outgrow the campus facilities at Parkside, and now had to branch out into satellite venues. Gygax ran a Sunday seminar on "Adventure Entertainment" about the forthcoming mass-media depictions of *D&D*. This year GenCon brought something sorely missed the year before: a new *Advanced Dungeons & Dragons* hardcover, in the form of the *Monster Manual II*, which included the many monsters Gygax had socialized in his *Dragon* column over the past year. It was featured alongside the new *Basic* and *Expert Rules* edited by Frank Mentzer, and the new "white metal" fantasy miniature boxed sets, the final legacy of Duke Seifried's brief tenure at the company.

Right after GenCon, Gygax had to dart to California to manage the launch of DDEC's great hope: the *Dungeons & Dragons Animated Series*. On September 17, the *D&D* Saturday morning cartoon show debuted on CBS—and another event timed to coincide with it forced Gygax to hairpin back to Wisconsin. That evening, there was a grand company party in Lake Geneva: in lieu of the traditional Founders Day celebration marking the formation of TSR Hobbies—a company that no longer existed—this year they commemorated the ten-year anniversary of the establishment of the original Tactical Studies Rules partnership. Gary Gygax and Brian Blume co-hosted the event, a more formal affair held at the Americana Lake Geneva Resort, the property that was formerly the Playboy Resort, and thus the venue for the tenth GenCon back in 1977. The pair of them had taken drastic measures this summer to stabilize the company to which they had dedicated a decade of their lives. Would they succeed?

For all their talk about dividing TSR into four separate companies, the plan proved hard to implement in practice. DDEC had to maintain offices in the Sheridan Springs headquarters in Lake Geneva: while Beebe was projected to spend 75 percent of his time in Beverly Hills, Dimery was only expected to spend 25 percent of his time there. Donna Yukevich was the project coordinator at Dragonlands West, but Joy McCoskey remained in Lake Geneva to coordinate matters there. During this transitional phase, DDEC staff who needed frequent access to TSR's payroll or procurement services simply had to work at the Torrent building—like Gail Carpenter, a recent hire who was appointed accounting manager for DDEC in the last week of September.

The thin walls between the companies made separating them a tricky proposition. Due to the difficulties disentangling DDEC from TSR, Inc., Marvel was sending its royalty checks to the parent corporation, further confusing the supposed split between the two. Over at TSR Ventures in New York, Andy Levison persuaded LJN to sell figures based on characters like Uni and Tiamat from the *Animated Series*—but would that count as revenue for TSR Ventures or DDEC? If they were to split the proceeds, what would be fair shares? Measuring the impact of the cartoon show on the bottom line of the games business also had its challenges. A memo at the time by Dimery suggested that "a production such as the Saturday Morning Children's show is, in effect, a 30-minute commercial" for *D&D*. Would it not then be natural that "some percentage of compensation should be given to DDEC for sales increases which are obviously due to the exposure of the children's show"? And moreover, as TSR's design department began working on a board game based on the children's show, how should the revenue from its sales be shared? Even at the end of October, the most optimistic projections suggested that DDEC would not be able to pay salaries out of its own bank account until the New Year, so it effectively operated as a Hollywood branch of TSR, Inc.

The *D&D* animated series came in with decent ratings: it had a 26 share Nielsen rating for its first weekend, for an overall rank of 9 out of the 36 Saturday morning cartoon shows; and then a 24 share, dropping to a rank of 10, for its second weekend. In both cases it nudged ahead of *Pac-Man* on ABC but fell behind *The Smurfs* on NBC, which was then aired in a domineering ninety-minute, three-episode block. Although pleased with the reception of the show, DDEC staffers fretted over the cursory advertising CBS had done for it—DDEC had no budget to advertise independently. The show also faced some production problems; *The Insider* spread rumors that "some of the adventures had excessive violence and needed to be yanked." CBS insisted that Marvel had failed to produce episodes; Marvel retorted that CBS held fresh episodes in reserve to make sure they would not have to air a rerun for the November sweeps. Instead CBS aired reruns for two weekends in October, to everyone's disappointment.

After all of Gygax's enthusiasm for the Goldman feature film script the year before, there seemed to be little energy at DDEC to pursue it as an opportunity. Instead, there was talk of doing a series of "low-budget, swashbuckling, sword, and sorcery type movies" set in the World of Greyhawk. The film project with the most momentum was a treatment written by Gary Gygax and Flint Dille to be called the "Scepter of Seven Souls." Another proposal you can find listed on their project sheets at the time was called "Gord the Rogue." But these projects competed for attention with a variety of other computer, radio, and television projects. Ernie Gygax spent some time developing whimsical animated cartoon proposals for ideas like "Smallest Samurai," and "Cyborg Commando Champions."

Sometimes, it felt like the disparate ideas around media properties and games just might snap into alignment. Looking only at the numbers, the acquisition of *Amazing Stories* the year before had failed to deliver much of a return: despite the makeover by TSR's art department and a superior distribution network, the venerable progenitor of science-fiction magazines continued to drop in circulation. But near the end of 1983, TSR was contacted by Universal Studios, who wanted to license *Amazing Stories* for a potential television program. It turned out that behind Universal was Steven Spielberg, who intended to use the brand as a vehicle for a new anthology series—not that TSR knew this at the time they agreed to license the title. Such a high-profile media property necessarily created opportunities for TSR and DDEC alike—but to realize these opportunities, the companies needed an interface that worked.

The lavish lifestyle and grand ideas in Beverly Hills were on a collision course with the sobering reality of declining revenue at the home office. Near the end of the year, with no financial relief in sight, TSR's bank insisted on more significant restructuring within the company, in addition to further staff reductions. TSR relied heavily on its business consultant, Robert Thompson, to oversee this reorganization. Thompson recruited a new vice president of finance and corporate secretary, Wilbur J. Scott, an executive who formerly held senior positions at Sta-Rite, a Wisconsin manufacturer. Scott began introducing a bit of fiscal discipline on all parts of the operation. Furthermore, Thompson identified three local executives to serve on the board as outsider directors to show the bank that TSR was committed to accepting more seasoned guidance from the very top.

The outside directors were Wesley Sommer, president of the E. F. Brewer company, a medical equipment firm; James Huber, a partner at Foley and Lardner, the law firm that represented Gygax in his divorce proceedings; and Robert Kidon, the human resources vice president at Rexnord, another manufacturing firm. Thompson held meetings at his office to introduce them to Kevin Blume, and at the November shareholder meeting, they were dutifully voted on to the board. All had a safe reputation for traditional expertise in managing companies. Through spokesman Dieter Sturm, TSR now issued platitudinous corporate press releases marking these sorts of changes: Kevin was quoted as saying, "The addition of the new members is intended to strengthen the company by injecting into its control and planning systems the expertise and demonstrated accomplishments of these directors." That same shareholder meeting, incidentally, held the value of TSR stock steady at $3,000.

It is a fitting bookend to 1983 that, in the final weeks of the year, the *Wall Street Journal* wrote a follow-up piece to its January article about TSR, titled, "After Success of *Dungeons & Dragons*, TSR Fights Poor Management, Uneven Growth." The grinning portrait of Gary Gygax below the headline draws the eye to that "poor management" quip. The article reviews the various lay-offs, the "eccentric new ventures into diversification" that never panned out, and of course "the write-off of one company," Greenfield Needlewomen, that "gave TSR a loss." Under Kevin Blume's administration, the

Journal was pleased to see, more experienced and traditional managers were entering the company, including Wilbur Scott and the three new outside directors. But of the new managers, the *Journal* astutely noted, "None, however, have experience with the tricky game industry and its fads." Much rested on the success of the Dungeons & Dragons Entertainment Company: "Now the company is placing most of its hope for greater sales of the game in the new *Dungeons & Dragons* cartoon show." It did not escape the attention of the *Journal* that the show was trailing *The Smurfs* in its time slot. At the end of the *Journal* article, Kevin Blume implied that TSR was an attractive acquisition target, but that surrender was not in the cards: "We're having far too much fun, and we make far too much money."

For the time being, that money overwhelmingly came from *D&D* sales, and Gygax still held control over *D&D*. The design staff cranked out modules, but Gygax jealously guarded the core products in the *Basic* and *Advanced Dungeons & Dragons* lines, carefully shepherding all work toward them. As Mentzer developed the *Companion Rules* throughout the year, Gygax found the time to read the drafts, injecting pedantic corrections about matters like the range of weapons. Moreover, the pair began collaborating on future *D&D* products, including work toward Gygax's long-delayed *Temple of Elemental Evil* and the new *Book of Marvelous Magic* that would be published with both their bylines. This inspired Gygax to leverage fractions of his 2.5 percent contractual royalty as an unofficial "creative bonuses" program. In a note to Mentzer he wrote, "I propose you get 80% of the royalties for the *D&D* game supplemental book of magic items as you conceived of and did that much of the work." Gygax had long been grooming Frank Mentzer to take over a revision of *Advanced Dungeons & Dragons*: in a memo, Gygax invited Mentzer to notify him when he was ready "to begin this immense project," promising, "I will then schedule the creative meetings and direct the outlining of the changes to be made, time schedule, and personnel to be used." That memo went out with a carbon copy to Mike Cook, the executive in charge of the games division, as if it were a mere formality to let Cook know how things were going to go.

After all, Gygax was chairman of the board of TSR, Inc. He had been the steward of *Dungeons & Dragons* since its publication, to the great success of the company. Who would ignore his guidance? As a member all of the boards of directors of the nascent companies, Gygax still worked closely with the Blumes. All three traveled to attend in person the December 1983 board meeting at the Mill, the offices of TSR UK. There was necessarily friction between them, as there had been when the "three presidents" structure was first announced. In theory, giving each of the three their own company would give them each a personal area of direct responsibility. In practice, however, the party did not split cleanly—a reality that had stultifying consequences for the business.

TSR Turn Results for 1983

Revenue: $26.7M, losses $69K

Employees: 400

Stock Valuation: $3,000

GenCon attendance vs. Origins: 8,000 vs. 3,000–4,000

Nielsen Rating of D&D Cartoon debut: 26 share

Players Eliminated: Heritage

1984: Cursed

The less said about 1984 the better. *Dungeons & Dragons* turned ten years old at the beginning of the year, and to the outside world the product had become a fixture of modern culture—but for Gygax, the anniversary could hardly feel like a celebration. It was a year when things trended from bad to terrible.

As of a January 4 staff meeting of DDEC in Beverly Hills, Gygax's media business still had not weaned itself from its corporate parent. The meeting minutes actually put on record the statement: "We are making every effort to establish an agreement with TSR to allow us the freedom to generate revenue and run a smooth operation, with profits." Dire warnings about cost control pervaded the discussion, to the point where there was talk of subletting the King Vidor ranch during the upcoming Los Angeles Summer Olympics to get some cash in their coffers. And although "a proposal from Columbia Pictures T.V. pertaining to an 'Endless Quest' series was made," in the current situation "no decision can be reached until the agreement between DDEC and TSR is finalized." There was similar grumbling about lack of access to the TSR Ventures licensing agreements for the *D&D Animated Series*. Gygax closed the meeting on a hopeful note: "We will become a viable operation with a sound return," he promised.

That lack of separation affected Lake Geneva staff as well. Frank Mentzer, as he tried to support the various activities required for *D&D*, found himself separately tabulating the hours he dedicated to TSR Worldwide, TSR Ventures, DDEC, and TSR, Inc. This naturally led to a glut of paperwork. And as Mentzer reminded Mike Cook on January 24, "Part of my job description is to review all products for the *D&D* and *AD&D* games," and if he did not have the opportunity to review modules and related products, then "costly second-printing repairs may be required." Gygax had his back on this matter: in a follow-up memo, which Gygax pointedly copied to Cook and Kevin Blume, he instructed Frank to "please let me know if the system is somehow breaking down," in which case Gygax, in his capacity as Chairman of the Board, "will see that matters are rectified at that point."

In the broader industry, things had begun to trend decidedly downward from the peak of 1981. *The Insider* reported that "adventuring gaming" had a scarce showing at the 1984 Hobby Industry of America show early in February, with only half the firms who attended the year before. TSR there telegraphed numerous releases to come, including a dozen related modules for an *AD&D* campaign to be called Dragonlance: hazy plans were also announced for Dragonlance to have its own calendar, miniatures, and board games, an ambitious transmedia play that would pave a new direction for TSR. Media properties became a focus of TSR investment, as they heavily promoted a new slate of licensed products like Conan modules, the long-expected *Marvel Super Heroes* game, and, in a February 7 press release, a coming *Adventures of Indiana Jones* game. The only worrisome messaging for TSR at the HIA show came from Avalon Hill, who finally surfaced in the role-playing space with *Powers & Perils*, as well as Tom Moldvay's *Lords of Creation*, and finally their new boxed set of *Runequest*, slated for a spring release. Avalon Hill still bet its future on its Microcomputer Games division, with titles like its recent *Telengard* bringing it into the computer fantasy role-playing game market, a space TSR had elected to abandon. With all of its other woes, the last thing TSR needed was a concerted attack from its largest rival and further splintering of consumer spending.

What TSR needed most was experienced management. Wilbur Scott, a seasoned professional who had joined TSR at the end of the previous year to oversee finance and became corporate secretary, quickly repented of his folly and returned to his consulting business. So, toward the end of February the company hired Richard T. Koenings, a lawyer who had been an assistant corporate secretary at Schlitz up until 1982. The newly instated outside directors found in Koenings something of a kindred spirit: he was a veteran businessman, not an adventurer. Koenings was quickly elevated by the board to the corporate secretary position at TSR, where he began to wield significant influence over operations. It was the beginning of an era when a rotating cast of unfamiliar faces would begin to steer the company. Although the presidency of TSR had been a stable institution from the death of Don Kaye up to 1983, its occupancy now resembled the more turbulent periods in the annals of imperial Rome, when a succession of fleeting emperors proved insufficiently wary of the next usurper.

Increasing desperation about costs meant the exit of more employees—at first, those tied to failed ventures like the "white metal" miniatures project, and then at long last, deep cuts in TSR's games division that came on April 4, which corporate records would call a "day that will live in infamy." François Froideval, Gygax's anointed co-successor in the design of *D&D* alongside Frank Mentzer, was no longer on staff. But Froideval was someone who had little impact on TSR sales: the departure of a breadwinner like Jim Ward was simply stunning. In all, fifty-six employees then exited the firm. Off of DDEC's payroll went some of Gygax's closest allies: his bodyguard and chauffeur Jim Johnson and his longtime friend Dave Dimery. Even Donna Yukevich, his love interest of the previous year, and her sister Penny did not survive that cut—perhaps this reflected the growing influence of Gail Carpenter, who now traveled with Gygax to Beverly Hills as his companion.

Kevin Blume's job, ably assisted by Dieter Sturm, was to explain any misfortune as a positive step. The April layoffs, for instance, were portrayed as "a planned move to upgrade the focus of management's directions and efforts, in addition to further reducing operating expenses to meet the cash flow needs of the company." Payroll would fall to around 170—but that was still far more staff than they needed, given the current scope of the business. Some crucial staffers, wary that TSR was circling the drain, left of their own accord: Mike Gray fled back to Milton Bradley; Marc Acres, Carl Smith, and Steve Sullivan joined John Ricketts at Pacesetter Games. Gradual staff reductions became the norm throughout the year. TSR published a four-column single-page telephone directory on a monthly basis, and from March onward, its columns slowly shortened, and its typeface enlarged, until there were three columns, and then only two.

The week of the April cuts, Gygax could be found in the United Kingdom, once again as the guest of honor at TSR's GamesFair. In pictures from the event, Gygax looked slender, as if California agreed with him—perhaps his reportedly wild lifestyle at the King Vidor ranch had a slimming effect. It would be Gygax's third trip to Europe since just December, reflecting a life now spent largely on the road. Gygax split his downtime between Wisconsin and the Hollywood Hills: when living in Lake Geneva, he had taken up residence at Stone Manor, the grandest old estate on the lake, now divided into condominiums. It is difficult to overstate what it must have meant to Gygax, who had gazed across at Lake Geneva's grandest mansion from its shores since he was a child, to now call it his home. In a personal note to Steve Marsh, he described the travel as wearisome and was grateful for the chance to spend most of the summer of 1984 in his home town; Stone Manor had a rooftop garden suitable for entertaining, so he and his partner Gail Carpenter hosted a "Summer's Eve" party there on June 20. Chairman of the board though he was, Gygax left the "dirty end of the stick" work of reducing staff to Kevin Blume and continued to live extravagantly.

Meanwhile, accusations that *D&D* inspired occultism still trickled through school boards, but at least no one had sued TSR over it—until now. In June, Patricia Pulling filed a $10 million suit against TSR for negligence in the 1982 suicide of her son Irving L. "Bink" Pulling II. This followed her failed $1 million lawsuit against the principal of Patrick Henry High School in Ashland, Virginia, where Irving Pulling had played *D&D*. The suit had claimed negligence because the principal allowed the game to be played when he had to be aware of its "potential dangers." How could he not be aware? After all, that school in Heber City, Utah, had banned the game because of those exact dangers, as had the district board of Rancho Cordova—and that young man who had been driven into the steam tunnels by the game, he later committed suicide. All of these events had been so widely publicized, would a principal not have to be negligent to tolerate the game on school grounds?

The suit against the high school had promptly been dismissed, and likely a suit against TSR would fare no better—but whether Pulling won or lost, it generated publicity for her cause, and dragged down *D&D*. As a focus for those activities, Pulling incorporated the informal group she had begun assembling the year before as a nonprofit called Bothered About Dungeons & Dragons (BADD), which circulated pamphlets and press releases compiling incidents of murder and suicide putatively linked to *D&D*. Her activities formed a major branch of the growing "Satanic Panic" reaction against supposedly anti-Christian youth culture.

Pulling's case caught the attention of Pat Robertson's Christian Broadcast Network, which now took up its own crusade against *D&D*. Robertson himself appeared on camera describing "news reports of murders, suicides, fantasy mental changes. Young people who are going totally crazy as a result of this game." CBN dispatched a correspondent to the Pulling home to interview Patricia, who spoke to the inherent evil of the game. If there was any silver lining for TSR in this continuous religious assault, it was that mainstream journalism began to push back against its excesses. Ron

Powers, on the CBS show *Sunday Morning*, judged that the CBN story about *D&D* "was not slanted; it was almost vertical."

TSR had enough problems without the censure of televangelists. After digging through corporate governance documents, Richard Koenings, in his capacity as corporate secretary, reached out to board member James Huber for a legal opinion about the manner in which Kevin Blume had acquired Melvin Blume's shares at the end of 1981. The idea had been that Melvin would sell his 200 shares to TSR for their original valuation of $100 each, and Kevin would purchase them at the same price—but Huber knew it did not transpire that way in practice. Although Melvin signed over his stock to TSR, and Kevin received the shares, no money seems to have changed hands between Kevin and TSR, and there existed no written agreement on the matter between any of the parties. "It would appear," Huber wrote, "that there is a potential claim by the other shareholders that there was an actual or constructive transfer of stock from Melvin Blume to Kevin Blume." That would be a problem, because the 1975 shareholder agreement required that anyone dispensing with shares must formally offer them first to TSR, and in the case that TSR refused, existing shareholders would have the opportunity to buy them on a pro rata basis, meaning proportionately to the amount of stock they already held—with the intended effect of preventing majority shareholder stakes from diluting. Prior to the transaction, Kevin Blume held only 5 shares.

Will Niebling's ongoing law suit over his negated option for 500 shares made this a pressing matter. Niebling had long doubted the legality of the 1981 Blume family transfer, and now his counsel argued that Melvin Blume's 200 shares should be offered to the other shareholders—but that Gygax and Brian Blume should be excluded from purchasing them, since by consenting to the transfer in the first place, they had effectively waived their pro rata rights to purchase the stock under the shareholder agreement. This could let minority shareholders like Niebling acquire a larger stake in the company.

There were not many good options for how to fix the situation. Huber saw a significant risk of a minority shareholder lawsuit if matters stayed as they were. Any attempt to rectify things by retroactively exchanging money would face similar vulnerabilities and could potentially have tax implications for both Kevin and his father, given the $1,000 valuation of the stock in 1981, let alone its current $3,000 book value. Perhaps the least bad option was to simply rescind the 1981 transfer entirely. But the whole point of the exchange had been to give Kevin the financial incentive that accompanies a major stock position—and now he served as TSR's president. Many documents from this period list the holder of those 200 shares as "Kevin B. Blume/Melvin Blume." This controversy necessarily weakened Kevin's position with the outside directors on the board—but not as much as TSR's failure to recover financially.

Despite cascading layoffs, TSR ended the 1984 fiscal year worse off than it had been twelve months earlier. Games revenue superficially looked flat: it went from $22.5 million in 1983 to $23.7 million in 1984. But adjusting for inflation and returns, the games business likely contracted for the first time. Licensing revenue as well rose below the inflation point, up around $150,000 to $1.8 million. Publishing remained a bright spot, increasing slightly from $4.3 million the year before to $5.5 million in 1984, but that had to weigh against a number of startling offsets. Despite its efforts to downsize operations, TSR's cost of revenue rose from $5.7 million to $8.7 million, so any increase in profits would need to exceed that. Its debt to the bank had increased from $4 million in 1983 to $5.3 million, and $600,000 of it would come due over the next year. Setting up the TSR International firm apparently cost an additional few hundred thousand dollars, as did the West Coast operation. In a stern rebuke to Gygax's Hollywood ambitions, TSR gave up on the huge investment it had made in the James Goldman script, and took an accounting charge of a half million dollars in costs related to the planned feature film. In all, TSR booked a loss of around $750,000 for fiscal 1984.

After the earnings came in, Kevin Blume sent a letter to every TSR employee defending the company's future prospects. The situation could not be worse than things were when he joined back in 1976 and TSR "struggled for survival" on a daily basis, he reasoned. In 1984 TSR had to acknowledge, "We are now transitioning from our corporate youth to a maturity that will mean managed growth, stability and new opportunity." To help secure that stability, Blume hired Willard Martens, a veteran of the Main Hurdman firm that did TSR's auditing, to once again attempt to enforce discipline in the company's financial management. Blume telegraphed confidence that "teamwork and dedication" will let the group "meet the challenges of the future and take TSR to even greater heights."

Kevin Blume had never condoned the tedious grudge that Gygax held against Origins and GAMA, and one of the accomplishments of his tenure was mending that relationship. TSR rejoined GAMA, and would exhibit at the tenth

Origins in Dallas in 1984. "It's ridiculous when the leader of the industry is not a member of the organization devoted to that industry," Blume told *Dragon*. "A situation like that removes legitimacy from both sides." Although he blamed the aggressive scheduling of Origins in Detroit the year before for the feud, he hoped that "TSR and GAMA can stop wasting their efforts battling each other." Blume conceded that "there probably were a few GAMA members who did want to burn TSR," but he optimistically supposed "this was a minority position."

Even Origins seemed cursed in 1984. After the Texas university originally scheduled to host it jacked up fees, the convention had to change its venue at the last minute to the Dallas Market Center, where local hotels were already booked to capacity, so people needed to be shuttled in. No one associated with Origins would dare to propose an attendance figure. One long-time attendee remarked, "The unofficial consensus estimate of the total attendance was 1600–1900, while it seemed like the same 50 or 100 people went through the dealer room over and over, with few new faces showing up." Two faces you could find in the dealer room belonged to Zeb Cook and Kevin Blume, gamely manning TSR's modest exhibitor booth. Blume deigned to schedule one of TSR's summer releases for Origins, the *Marvel Super Heroes* role-playing game, and also held an "Ask TSR" session to offer a more conciliatory message than was heard there from TSR back in 1977.

At Origins, Dave Arneson was elected to the Adventure Gaming Hall of Fame. In the wake of that proclamation, which reiterated the previous year's honorific that he was "the father of fantasy role-playing," it was announced that Arneson "is re-writing his famous *Blackmoor* supplement for publication by Blade, a division of Flying Buffalo." And so a project he had pitched first to Judges Guild in 1977, and then relocated to the Chaosium, had yet another promised home. This betokened a deepening relationship between Flying Buffalo and Adventure Games, one where Rick Loomis's firm would take over marketing and distribution for Arneson's existing Adventure Games titles. There were several reasons for this: because Arneson had recently married, and because he planned in 1985 to go on a religious mission for the Way International to San Francisco, both of which left him little time to oversee a game company. But in the end analysis, the Flying Buffalo arrangement amounted to a quiet way of shuttering the Adventure Games business, and with it Arneson's ambition to compete against TSR.

After the fiasco that was Origins, there could be no doubt that GenCon would dominate the summer convention scene. But when Gygax came to GenCon in August, he felt like a stranger in his own home. He was indignant that TSR had not scheduled any speaking events for him: "being the best known personality in TSR, the lack of utilization of my usefulness was appalling," he wrote in a memo circulated to much of TSR's leadership. He walked the halls like just another one of the reported 8,600 attendees. Mentzer and the RPGA scrambled to secure him an emergency audience of gamers, but it was a sobering experience. Two other attendees, incidentally, were Gygax's Hollywood writing partner, Flint Dille, and his sister Lorraine Dille Williams, whom Gygax met briefly, and fatefully, that weekend.

Surely Gygax's feelings of alienation stemmed partly from the lack of his own work on display at GenCon: it foretold what a post-Gygax TSR might look like. Among TSR's top new sellers at the convention was the *Marvel Super Heroes* game, designed by Jeff Grubb and written by Steve Winter, and its associated miniatures. Zeb Cook's *Indiana Jones* was also heavily promoted. Ed Greenwood ran a ten-player adventure called "Into the Forgotten Realms" set in his personal campaign world. Tracy Hickman and Margaret Weis, with a cast of TSR luminaries including Harold Johnson and others, held their "Dragonlance Interactive Theater" event, a teaser for the novels set in that world, which were set to be published in the fall. The *Companion Rules* would be the first chunk of *D&D* core system that Frank Mentzer furnished himself, as opposed to his reimagining of Tom Moldvay's revision to Eric Holmes's edit of the original *D&D* rules. It was a slate of offerings that felt substantial enough to support a game company without a Gygax at its helm.

But GenCon also reminded hobbyists that TSR would face ever more aggressive competition, as a full-page advertisement in the program heralded the revenge of Games Workshop: the game *Warhammer*, which had been released in Britain the year before, had now landed a major American invasion. The *Dragon* had to call it "the most coherent blend of wargaming and fantasy role-playing available." Bolstered by a full figure line by Citadel Miniatures, the Games Workshop house forge, it epitomized the fusion of rules with lucrative miniature sales that TSR had belatedly sought, but let slip through its fingers.

Finally, 1984 would be the year that GenCon bid farewell to Parkside, as a scheduling conflict for 1985 helped TSR decide on a relocation to the Milwaukee Exposition Convention Center and Arena—known as MECCA—where they hoped the larger venue would let them grow to 12,000 attendees. Provided that TSR would survive to host it.

Ordinarily, TSR would be thrilled to see a major book release with the words "Dungeon Master" in the title, but they were less so for the autumn 1984 release of *The Dungeon Master: The Disappearance of James Dallas Egbert III*. Despairing of monetizing the film rights to the Egbert story, William Dear cashed out his own version of events in prose. His book jacket photograph shows him brandishing a machine gun, and the contents live up to that level of self-promotion and posturing. Dear heaps blame on Michigan State University and, shamelessly, Egbert's parents—in his telling, it was only through Dear's heroic intervention that Egbert overcame his ordeal.

The release of Dear's book earned him a victory lap of appearances on television shows, including *Good Morning America* at the end of October. It also earned him the scorn of Egbert's parents: his mother would complain to the press, "It is totally inaccurate—dates, places, times, everything. He prints conversations with my husband and me in Lansing when we weren't even there. I hate to see him making a profit from it." Ferman Badgley of the MSU police—who back in 1979 called Dear's confident pronouncements to the press about games and steam tunnels "merely speculation"—now had the opportunity to dismiss Dear's entire book as "malarkey." But it once again brought this story, and purported role of *D&D* in it, back to the popular imagination, in the most negative of lights—which meant that *D&D* would surely be supposed the cause of more tragedies. A murder-suicide in Lafayette, Colorado, on November 2, yielded a fresh crop of new headlines like "Deaths Linked to Fantasy Game" that would be assiduously collected by people like Patricia Pulling. And these came in the midst of an expensive television advertising blitz from TSR, spearheaded by top New York agency BBDO, promising that their role-playing games would "Unleash the Power of your Imagination."

The continuing scrutiny of religious groups motivated TSR to follow through on one of the RPR03 recommendations from 1982 and reissue *Deities & Demigods* under the more innocuous title *Legends & Lore*, at the same time replacing its psychedelic Erol Otus cover with a high fantasy painting of Odin by Jeff Easley. The title substitution was made with so little fanfare that some suggested TSR was trying to trick consumers into buying the same book twice. A commentator in the November issue of *Alarums & Excursions* remarked that TSR had "bowed to the Moral Majority." This in part reflected the political climate of the Reagan era, which gave new influence to Christian fundamentalists: "With Jerry Falwell now whispering in Ronny's ear, we might be seeing more of this. Stay tuned." Gygax himself would condemn the "recently retitled *Legends & Lore* . . . as a sop, or bowing to pressure from those who don't buy our products anyway." But by this point, a deeper desperation had taken hold at TSR.

Kevin Blume sent another company-wide letter, an attempt to drive up morale, at the end of the third quarter. He acknowledged that "*Trivial Pursuit* sales have taken dollars away from us." That game would rack up sales of 20 million copies by the end of the year, bringing in an estimated $1.4 billion worldwide over a span of just thirty-six months; its creators could, with a blind eye to inflation, boast that their game had in that interval made more money than *Monopoly* and *Scrabble* combined over their history. *D&D* never looked smaller than it did in its shadow. Blume casts this as an opportunity, as TSR could "take advantage of the gaming audience it has helped create." But many now believed TSR would not recover under his leadership.

"TSR seems to be sinking fast," the gossip column in *Different Worlds* reported. "Latest rumor has it that their bank has placed an operations man right under President Kevin Blume, effectively cutting Kevin off any important corporate decision-making." At this point, Richard Koenings was calling the shots. But when it came to *D&D*, Koenings made it clear that he would continue the previous arrangement: he sent an October 16 note instructing Mike Cook, "pursuant to my conversation of last week with Gary Gygax and confirmation of Kevin Blume," that "all *D&D* and *AD&D* works, derivates or related items" must be "run past Frank Mentzer" in order to guarantee quality and consistency.

In his capacity as chairman of the board, Gygax issued a company-wide memo on October 26 to give his own perspective on TSR's situation, largely in an attempt quell the "many stories, tales, rumors and odd bits of misinformation floating around." Yes, he did acknowledge that *D&D* "has probably peaked, and there should now be a plateau developing." No longer would this be a growth market. He had reconciled himself to the reality that TSR was not about to rival the likes of Parker Brothers and Milton Bradley, conceding that "it isn't too likely we'll ever enter the Fortune 500 list."

"Certainly we've gotten off the track in the past," Gygax admitted. "Who doesn't make mistakes?"

A lack of new releases was one cause Gygax cited for their current troubles—1984 was, like 1982, a year without a new *Advanced D&D* hardcover release. After GenCon, Gygax resumed his "Sorcerer's Scroll" column in *Dragon*, where he informed the general public that François Froideval, working as a freelancer, was "now compiling what we devised for including Oriental characters in the game." He also shared that his protégé Frank Mentzer was "now nearing completion of part four of the *D&D* game system (the *Masters Set*) and he will thereafter go on to finish the fifth and final portion of the game proper (the *Immortals*)." But most telling in his column was his frustration with the prospects of his expedition to the Hollywood Hills. Gygax reported that, in addition to Goldman's script—the one TSR had just written off as a half-million dollar loss—there was "a treatment (by Gygax and Dille)" but "no studio has yet optioned either."

Gygax relayed to *Dragon* readers Hollywood's skepticism about a *D&D* movie: "At a recent meeting with some film executives, we stressed how solid a core of dedicated enthusiasts there is for a *D&D* game-based film. In a world where hype is expected, our statements were viewed as puffery, gross exaggerations made to sell an idea." He therefore called on the readership of *Dragon*, which now stood around 120,000, to mail back to DDEC a reply card expressing enthusiasm for the film project. "Finally, if you know any DMs or players who don't regularly get *Dragon* magazine, tell them about this effort and ask them to send in a postcard of their own containing all the information on the reply card." They needed every voice they could get.

In the end, TSR would achieve its media ambitions through another path. An October 18 press release announced the forthcoming *Dragons of Autumn Twilight*, the first full-length fantasy novel to be published by TSR, and the initial Dragonlance release. With it, and plans to release two more Dragonlance novels completing a trilogy in 1985, TSR entered the world of genre fiction publishing. Staff artist Larry Elmore painted the cover, and TSR could rely on Random House's distribution chain for its "Endless Quest" books—which had now sold over five million copies—to get copies of *Dragons of Autumn Twilight* in front of readers. The press release promised that "TSR is expanding its book publishing arm with entry into various new but closely related book categories in 1985." If the company showed any fresh promise in this difficult time, the move into fantasy novels, ones with tie-ins to the gaming portfolio, was probably it.

As if the year had not gone badly enough, Dave Arneson sued TSR, again, on November 14. Arneson had received $100,000 in royalties for the *Monster Manual II* since its publication the year before. But given the financial straits the company was in, eventually someone at TSR lighted on the attractive notion that the 1981 settlement with Arneson did not apply to the *Monster Manual II*. They soon learned that once you start paying royalties for a title, you can expect a lawsuit if they cease.

Arneson's latest dispute hinged on a fresh question, although reminiscent of the former ambiguity about language like the "game or game rules" in the 1975 *D&D* contract. The 1981 settlement, in the hopes of clarifying for which *Advanced Dungeons & Dragons* works Arneson would receive his 2.5 percent royalty, uniquely identifies their titles and product codes in a format like "the book currently published by TSR entitled *Advanced Dungeons & Dragons Monster Manual* (2009) and any revised edition or foreign language translation thereof." But what exactly constitutes a "revised edition" of a book like the *Monster Manual*? According to the 1981 settlement, a revised edition is "a printed work having a title the same as or similar to the related earlier work, revised to include changes or additions to the text, but continuing to include substantially the same rules and subject matter as contained in the earlier work." That surely seemed unambiguous at the time. For example, the Moldvay *Basic Set* was a "revised edition" of the Holmes *Basic Set* because the two comprise rules for the same thing: TSR discontinued the Holmes edition when Moldvay's appeared. Even though Frank Mentzer's *Basic Rules* boxed set had a slightly different title, it similarly revised and replaced Moldvay as it covered "substantially the same rules and subject matter."

But now take the *Monster Manual* and the *Monster Manual II*. The titles are not identical, but they are similar. We probably would not say that *Monster Manual II* revised the text of the *Monster Manual*—it did not redefine earlier monsters—though it was additive, piling on more of the same. Does the *Monster Manual II* "include substantially the same rules and subject matter" as the *Monster Manual*? Unlike the case of Holmes and Moldvay, the *Monster Manual II* did not replace the *Monster Manual*.

The case would not require years of legal maneuvering, it would resolve in just four months. This time, a judgment would be rendered with refreshing clarity, considering the many ambiguities incumbent on the 1981 settlement. The United States District Court in Minnesota ruled that "the substance of both these works is a listing and description of monsters to be used in playing *Advanced Dungeons & Dragons*. Both works are identical in their purpose and application." Indeed, the court deems them to be the same work: "the unifying basis of the two works, their essential idea, is that these parts make up a whole; an encyclopedia of creatures for the *Advanced Dungeons & Dragons* game." This impression was surely bolstered by the index that Mentzer had assembled at Gygax's request for the *Monster Manual II* giving the page numbers where monsters could be found—not just in that volume, but also in the original *Monster Manual* and the *Fiend Folio*. With this legal victory, Arneson would receive further royalties for the *Monster Manual II* as if it were the *Monster Manual* itself, at a time when TSR desperately needed money.

Inevitably, more ex-employees filed suits against TSR. It would not be until after the New Year that *Different Worlds* reported, "Rose Estes, author of many 'Endless Quest' books, is suing TSR for reneging on a stock purchase plan." Estes had quit the year before in a dispute with management over compensation; now, as Niebling's lawsuit progressed over a far larger rejected exercise, her more modest ask seemed like something easy to satisfy. And from his new home in Connecticut working for Coleco, Lawrence Schick sued TSR as well, over the creative bonuses that had been canceled for *Star Frontiers*, which had made enough money to be worth legal action.

If there was any consolation to be had in a year of financial disasters, it was that the rest of the industry suffered equally. Even the venerable Milton Bradley announced at the beginning of the year that it had taken a loss in 1983 of $18.7 million—its first loss since 1948—largely due to an expensive attempt to diversify into the video game space. No doubt they also felt the pressure of *Trivial Pursuit*. This made the company an acquisition target: at its September shareholder meeting, Milton Bradley approved a $360 million takeover bid by Hasbro.

Having bestowed its flagship *Runequest* on Avalon Hill, the Chaosium radically downsized, shedding *Runequest* designer Steve Perrin and even selling off *Different Worlds* magazine, which would go on hiatus for the first half of the next year. *Fire & Movement* magazine, which had sidled into the former niche of SPI's *Strategy & Tactics*, ran into its own problems in the spring of 1984, and did not manage to print another issue until right before the New Year. When it resumed, Howard Barasch shared his industry insights in its pages, including the tidbit that Monarch Avalon's Avalon Hill division posted a $225,000 loss for the final quarter of 1984, on sales down some 30 percent—much of that attributed to difficulties in the MicroComputer Games division. At least *Runequest* served Avalon Hill well: Chaosium reported that *Runequest* sales surpassed the combined annual sales of *Powers & Perils* and *Lords of Creation* in just two months. And Flying Buffalo had severely overextended with its new products in the first half of 1984, which led to staff reductions and low morale. With that, the prospect of Arneson publishing Blackmoor adventures through Flying Buffalo evaporated: Arneson once again migrated that project to a new publisher, this time to Mayfair, who expected to print them in April 1985.

When *Inc.* magazine checked in again with TSR near the end of 1984, the magazine still described the company as "a business fantasy come true." But they had to admit that the yearly doubling or even quadrupling of sales that first brought TSR to their attention was over: now "annual company revenues have crept forward cautiously." Beyond Gygax's mass media efforts, they also inquired with Kevin Blume about new games under development: to the end of a diverse product roadmap, Blume appended, "very possibly even a game that role plays growing a business." But the era when business would be a game to the small group of adventurers who banded together to run TSR was ending. After a year of trying, they managed to sell the dilapidated Hotel Clair in November, which apart from warehouse space reduced their presence in Lake Geneva to the headquarters at Sheridan Springs. By the last month of the year, it had become clear that more stringent measures would be needed to stop the bleeding.

A memo circulated December 7 reduced salaries for all employees: most lost a quarter of their paychecks, though some officers took only a 10 percent hit. Management promised that this was merely a deferral, and that the wages garnished by this policy would be repaid to employees in 1985 as a bonus—no later than in September of that year. But this blatantly signaled a dire financial situation for the company, so any assurances would be contingent on TSR's survival, which was far from a certain matter.

With these demoralizing steps came a dramatic change at the helm of the company. The last straw was likely when Koenings learned, in a November 30 letter, the terms of the "sabbatical" taken by Judi Witt, Kevin's sister-in law. Her ongoing agreement with TSR to sponsor her college education not only included, as she put it, "tuition and fees at any accredited school of my choice, books, supplies, lab costs, equipment, transportation, application and transfer fees, and any other expenses," but also her $25,000 annual stipend, and retention of her full benefits as a TSR employee. This highly dubious drain of TSR funds during a time of immense financial pressure, combined with the dangerous bungling of the stock transfer from Melvin Blume to Kevin, on top of TSR's continuing failure to stop hemorrhaging money, made it crystal clear to Koenings that Kevin had to go.

"Effective last Friday," Richard Koenings wrote in a memo to all employees on Tuesday, December 18, "I am the Chief Executive Officer of TSR, reporting directly to the Board of Directors. All functions of the company," and he underlined "all," "are now under my sole authority and responsibility. As of the same date, owner/employees are solely acting in a consulting capacity to me."

Dieter Sturm, TSR's spokesman, would tell the media that Kevin Blume had "removed himself." Koenings pushed for this move, but Wesley Sommer would explain it was not his idea alone: "I think that all the directors felt that it would be good for the company, and I think the Blumes felt it would be good." But it is no small matter to sideline an employee like Kevin Blume because of his family's large stake in the company. Their proportion of shares was close enough to half that they would need only a modest coalition to reshape the board entirely. By this point, however, shares mattered less than debt, and TSR's creditors pressured the company to take steps that Kevin Blume did not have the stomach for. This was a company he had worked for since the end of 1976; Koenings had only been there about ten months, and he never saw TSR in its prime—since the moment of his arrival, the company had known only perpetual crisis, and he was looking for any way to steady the ship.

If there was one thing that TSR and its primary creditor, the American National Bank, could agree on at the end of the year, it was that the company could not remain viable going forward without an infusion of capital. That could come from outside investment—or, if necessary, from the sale of assets. From his time in Beverly Hills, Gygax was moving in circles where people had the sort of money and interests to bail TSR out. Only one question remained: What price they would have to pay to lift the curse?

TSR Turn Results for 1984

Revenue: $29.6M, losses $750K
Employees: 167
Stock Valuation: $2,500
GenCon attendance vs. Origins: 8,600 vs. 1,600+(?)

Players Eliminated: Adventure Games

1985: The Ambush at Sheridan Springs

In the new year, the hobby trade press salivated over rumors of TSR's impending demise. *Different Worlds* reported that Kevin Blume was out as president. It went on to gossip: "The company is up for sale: asking price $6 million and dropping. Their magazine, *The Dragon*, is also for sale at $1 million. Lorimar, Norman Lear's production company, is interested in TSR if Gary Gygax stays to run the company." Gygax however dismissed these reports as "absolutely untrue. We (TSR, Inc.) are looking for an investor willing to acquire an interest in the company. Lorimar Productions wants to option properties. We're (TSR, Inc.) working on the options."

Gygax had lined up potential investors by the beginning of February: more rumors swirled after TSR public relations staff announced that a Beverly Hills investment group had filed a letter of intent to "acquire a major position" in TSR, Inc., though TSR concealed the identity of this bidder. Even within the company, there was considerable secrecy about this three-person consortium, whom they internally called the Foreman group. But no plan to steady TSR could work without resolving the lingering question of the Blumes and their ownership position. Following Kevin's removal as president, the board attempted to negotiate a severance agreement with both Blumes, but the brothers made acceptance of any such agreement contingent on the buyback of their stock—otherwise, they reasoned, they must remain active in the company to protect their substantial investment. Holding nearly half of TSR shares, their family could not be ignored.

The obvious way for an investor to "acquire a major position" in TSR would thus be through buying out the Blumes, which is exactly what the Foreman group proposed to do. Under their plan, the Blumes would depart, and Gygax would continue as an officer at the company, at his current level of compensation, for the next five years. There was just one hitch: the control provisions in TSR's shareholder agreement precluded selling stock to an outsider, in keeping with Gygax's vow of a decade ago. To satisfy the Foreman group, the company would need to amend its shareholder agreement to abolish the preemptive right of majority shareholders to purchase stock pro rata, thereby opening the door to an outside group gaining controlling interest. A special February meeting of the shareholders was thus scheduled and, a resolution waiving preemptive rights passed on March 1. It might be said that the text was excised from the document hastily, in a way that might cause problems if the shareholder agreement became the object of any legal challenge.

But the Foreman group lowered their offer as they delved deeper into TSR's troubled finances: the company projected revenue would be down for 1985, perhaps as low as $24 million. Thus at that same February shareholder meeting, TSR lowered the value of its stock from the $2,500 set last November to just $300, the price the Foreman proposal offered the Blume brothers and their spouses. That figure reflected "recent performance" and anticipated a looming crisis. It was just a tenth of the share value six months before—and, we might recall, also the maximum amount anyone thought *D&D* might be worth, back in the beginning of 1974. And even that low stock price was contingent upon a positive resolution of the Niebling law suit—if Niebling won, the value of TSR shares would be diluted by an off-putting 19.5 percent to just $240. Incidentally, the corporate profit-sharing plan, which was heavily invested in company stock, lost 75 percent of its value thanks to this precipitous drop, crushing any lingering morale in the employee base.

TSR's humbler estimation of its own value required fresh belt-tightening measures. Another round of layoffs came on March 8, as Koenings trimmed thirty-six more TSR employees. It was in this round that the final remnants of the Blume family left TSR's payroll, including Doug Blume and Vicki Blume. Even the eternally chipper spin doctor Dieter Sturm had to attribute the company's downsizing to a "continuation of decline in sales volume." He conceded that this was possibly due to market saturation, especially as low sales of Mentzer's *Basic Rules* implied that the product was not attracting new customers. Module and accessory sales, however, remained strong, so TSR planned to refocus its marketing on existing hobbyists.

Gygax still believed fresh *D&D* product would help TSR recover, so he drove the anthologization of his recent *Dragon* articles into *Unearthed Arcana*, a book for players who had absorbed his *Players Handbook* and wanted more. But Gygax had no time to do this personally, and Frank Mentzer was

4. If the Company is not able as a matter of law to purchase all or any number of the Decedent's Shares or if for any reason the Company elects not to purchase the Option Shares, then the surviving Shareholders or the remaining Shareholders , as the case may be, shall have the option to purchase such stock at the same price and upon the same terms and conditions as provided hereinabove for the purchase by the Company, and each such Shareholder shall be entitled to purchase such Decedent's shares or Option Shares in the proportion which the number of shares of the Company shock owned by him bears to the number of shares of the Company stock owned by all other Shareholders who elect to purchase, unless otherwise agreed among themselves.

4. If the Company is not able as a matter of law to purchase all or any number of the Decedent's Shares or if for any reason the Company elects not to purchase the Option Shares, then the ~~surviving Shareholders or the remaining Shareholders , as the case may be, shall have the option to purchase such stock at the same price and upon the same terms and conditions as provided hereinabove for the purchase by the Company~~, and ~~each such Shareholder shall be entitled to purchase such Decedent's shares or Option Shares in the proportion which the number of shares of the Company stock owned by him bears to the number of shares of the Company stock owned by all other Shareholders who elect to purchase unless otherwise agreed among themselves~~.

The original pro rata clause of the TSR Hobbies August 1, 1975, Stock Agreement plan (above), and the version after modification on March 1, 1985 (below). "Decedent's Shares" refer to the stock holdings of a deceased person; "Option Shares" refer to shares that a living person chooses to divest.

understandably preoccupied with his *Master* and *Immortal Rules*, so Gygax tapped Jeff Grubb from Mike Cook's staff to consult on the design. It was a time for conciliatory gestures on Gygax's part: he invited Arneson to publish his Blackmoor modules under TSR's imprint, rather than pushing them through Mayfair. Under the heading "Let's Bury the Hatchet," Gygax even had some magnanimous words to say in *Dragon* about his long-time nemesis, the Origins convention. After its humiliating attendance drop the year before, Origins posed no immediate threat, so Gygax formally rescinded his three-year-old call for a boycott on the convention, now urging gamers "to support and attend all conventions—Origins, the GenCon event, and all other good events whenever and wherever they are held." TSR generously authorized a *D&D* tournament at Origins, though they would not attend as an exhibitor.

It might have appeared that Gygax was tying up loose ends. In fact, he was on the cusp of taking a bold step to rescue TSR. But he would set in motion a series of events that was as deterministic as the endgame on a chessboard: there were only so many moves to be made, and observers might foresee an inevitable conclusion. Unlike much of what transpired to date, this final battle would be little observed by the broader industry. Instead, it was fought behind the closed doors of board meetings, a terrain where Gygax might easily be outflanked. It is there that we will find the conclusion of his adventure at TSR.

At the end of March, TSR suddenly announced that it would be "restructuring itself financially" using current resources, and that "any negotiations with outside investment groups are void." This reflected the events of a board meeting on March 18, 1985, where Gygax revealed that he had exercised his July 1976 option for 700 shares of TSR, Inc. stock at a cost of $100 each. This raised his total holdings to 1,371 shares, which fell just slightly below half (49.6 percent) of outstanding TSR shares, then numbering 2,761. But the 40 shares owned by Gygax's son Ernie, when combined with his father's holdings, would suffice to secure controlling interest (51 percent) in TSR. Immediately, Gygax pushed to "nix" the Foreman deal, according to the raw notes taken by Willard Martens at that board meeting; Gygax had found a path, he believed, that would keep control of TSR away from outsiders. So, on March 29, the board named Gygax president and chief executive officer of TSR, Inc., in addition to his current position as chairman of the board.

Koenings scheduled an all-hands meeting for April 1, "to report on the status generally of the Company and specifically on the positive rebuilding and capital expansion efforts planned and underway." By the time they held that meeting, in the shipping area of the Torrent building, only about 95 employees were left to witness the transition in leadership back to Gygax, just a quarter of peak staffing in mid-1983. As for Koenings, his services were no longer required; Willard Martens would now become the board's secretary, in addition to his continuing responsibilities as vice president of finance, and treasurer. Martens at this point wielded much of the power over corporate spending once held by the Blume brothers.

Gygax's decision to exercise his 1976 option might look reckless: there would be no point in owning any shares in TSR if the company collapsed for want of operating capital, and exercising these shares would turn only a modest profit considering their abrupt decline in value. But it was a ten-year option, due to expire in 1986: time was running out, and those shares might be as valuable now as they would ever be. Moreover, Gygax did not actually write TSR a check: ever starved for liquidity, TSR owed him a far greater sum than that in royalties at the time, and Gygax merely forgave $70,000 of company debt to him in exchange for those shares, debt that might never be paid if the company went under.

If TSR would no longer seek an infusion of cash from the Foreman group, how did Gygax plan to continue operating? The answer was that he had found someone else to invest in TSR, whom he hoped would join the company, someone Gygax had met briefly at GenCon the year before: Lorraine Williams, sister to Flint Dille, Gygax's Hollywood writing partner.

Around the first of March, Gygax had related to Dille how he was trying to find investors and potentially reorganize TSR at the time. So, when Dille next spoke to Williams, he casually asked her if she had any "loose change" she might invest in TSR, and when she suggested she might, he urged her to call Gygax. The brief conversation that followed convinced her that it warranted a closer look. As she lived relatively close by, in a Gold Coast townhouse in Chicago, she made the drive up to Lake Geneva a few mornings later and met with Gygax in his study at Stone Manor, where he explained the history and situation of the company. As TSR required a substantial investment, Williams wanted access to hard data about its prospects. After lunch, Gygax arranged for the pair of them to visit the Sheridan Springs office to let her review the company's books along with Koenings and Martens. She sensed some wariness—TSR had courted a number of investors fruitlessly—but she won them over. At the end of the first day, she recalled that Gygax looked at her and judged, "You're impressive."

Williams was about thirty-five at the time, and her educational background was in medieval European history rather than business. Before coming to TSR, she had worked primarily on licensing the intellectual property and trademarks associated with Buck Rogers. She had the "loose change" to invest in TSR because she and her brother came from money: their grandfather John F. Dille published the original Buck Rogers comics, and the Dille family owned the rights to the character and controlled a trust collecting the resulting royalties. The success of the *Star Wars* franchise had helped propel Buck Rogers back into popular culture: the *Buck Rogers in the 25th Century* television show, for example, had aired on NBC from 1979 to 1981.

Gygax invited Williams to join TSR as a vice president of administration in an offer letter, dated April 1, which included several stipulations relating to investment. First, Williams's employment agreement deferred a third of her salary of $90,000 per year into stock purchases, so effectively she

Lorraine

would make $60,000—Gygax's salary as president was now set at $120,000, incidentally. It furthermore required her to immediately purchase $50,000 worth of TSR stock upon accepting the agreement, and to buy a further $100,000 worth of stock in the 1986 calendar year. Given TSR's precarious financial situation, this represented a significant cash infusion, but also a substantial risk to Williams as an investor. Gygax wrote in her offer letter of her "commitment to TSR" as evidenced by her "determination to acquire a substantial holding in the corporation," though the amount in question fell far short of a controlling interest—Gygax remained cautious about outsider control. Gygax made hiring Williams a high priority: consider that the board voted him president and CEO on a Friday afternoon, and her offer letter dates to the following Monday. Indeed, he thought highly enough of her that the offer letter concludes, "I am placing your name before the Board for election to a Directorship."

A new infusion of capital could go a long way toward solving one of TSR's most pressing problems. At the March 29 board meeting that had voted Gygax into the presidency, the board also agreed to purchase all of the Blume family stock, including Brian's unexercised option for 700 shares (minus the strike price), at a valuation of $340.87 per share, for a total of

$506,070.30. No one expected it would come as a lump sum: various install-ment plans were considered, paying it out over the course of four years or so, with accrued interest added. That, accompanied by an attractive sever-ance package, reflected a significant improvement on what the Foreman group had offered the Blumes, and a way of finally securing their exit from the company.

But the board of directors no longer controlled TSR's purse. Almost immediately after Gygax took control of TSR, the American National Bank cut TSR's line of credit from the original $10.8 million down to $5 million. Martens would later state "with Mr. Gygax in majority control, that the bank perceived a real difficulty in being able to control expenditures and control ultimately their line of credit and their collateral."

In an attempt to assuage their doubts, Gygax went in to meet with the bank on April 3. But he also came with his hat in his hands: TSR needed an additional $500,000 at a minimum to continue operating. Gygax fur-thermore had to raise with the bank the recent board vote to purchase the Blumes's stock. But capital was scarce at the time, and lenders behaved conservatively, as the American financial industry began to reel under the throes of the savings and loan crisis that toppled several prominent Mid-western banks. In a letter to Gygax dated April 9, the American National Bank made it clear that they believed Gygax underestimated just how much money TSR owed to its vendors and service providers. The $500,000 in cash for operations that Gygax requested was flatly denied. As the letter explained, "The Bank's interest in advancing funds beyond its lending for-mulas would in any circumstances be limited to the amount of new cash equity contributed to TSR." Furthermore, on the matter of TSR acquiring the Blume family stock, the Bank deemed "such a transaction inappropriate for TSR given its financial condition and consequently the Bank will not consent to the buy back."

This put TSR's board in an increasingly difficult situation. They scheduled a meeting for April 16 at the headquarters of Rexnord, west of Milwaukee in Bishop's Woods, bright and early at quarter after nine in the morning. As they would be discussing Lorraine Williams's employee agreement, she arranged to be present, but for only part of the meeting—she introduced herself to the board, and listened to some of the discussion about a response to the bank. In a private conference, the board did confirm Williams into her position as vice president of administration and grant her a six-month option to purchase 50 shares at $300; identical option grants were simultaneously bestowed upon executives of the TSR games, international, and media business: Mike Cook, Andre Moullin, and John Beebe, respectively. The stock grant that Williams received fell far short of the broad investment Gygax had sought. When Gygax raised with the board the possibility of adding a seventh director—that is, Williams—the matter was postponed for further discussion. "I got a vote of no confidence," Williams recalled, adding that Gygax told her, "we'll talk about it later."

When the Blumes learned at this meeting that the bank had blocked the acquisition of their stock, they once again expressed reluctance about signing any severance agreement with TSR. What happened next is a matter of some dispute. During a recess in the meeting, Gygax met with Kevin and Brian Blume privately in a second-floor solarium in the Rexnord facility. According to the Blumes, they offered their shares to Gygax, who agreed to purchase them personally with his own funds. Gygax later refuted this claim, but as the discussion happened behind closed doors, it is no simple matter to ascertain the truth of it.

The Blumes left the meeting confident that their exit path was clear. Two days later, they sent a formal notice to TSR of their intent to sell their shares, presumably to Gygax. Then on May 6, they finally signed a severance agreement with TSR. Under it, both brothers would receive a year of pay: $8,333 per month for Brian, and $7,500 a month for Kevin. Kevin's reduced share reflected a penalty for subsidizing his sister-in-law Judi Witt's "sabbatical," under a separate settlement that would be signed a few days later. It let the Blumes retain their TSR benefits program, and even gave Kevin the right to purchase the company car he used. In return, the agreement secured their continuing support in some of the legal challenges against TSR: Kevin Blume would be deposed in Rose Estes's lawsuit on May 12. The G, B, & B Investment real estate partnership which owned the Torrent building could not close immediately due to the complexities of the bank's involvement, but the severance agreement promised "that TSR Inc. shall use its continuing best efforts . . . to effect a transaction whereby TSR, Inc. acquires all assets and liabilities of the partnership." The Saturday after signing the agreement, Brian and Kevin hosted a "retirement party," inviting TSR staff over to Brian's modest home on Miller Road in Lake Geneva. "We have had a lot of good times working with you," the invitation read, "but now it is time for us to say goodbye. Come party with us to celebrate new futures."

As vice president of administration and chief operating officer under Gygax, we might say that Williams stepped into Kevin Blume's old shoes. She ended up performing those tasks which, as Gygax had once said of Blume's operational role, constituted "the dirty end of the stick." For example, Gygax did not sign TSR's severance agreement with Koenings, back on April 8; even though the blank on the form was labeled "E. Gary Gygax, President, TSR, Inc." the signature above it was Williams's. It is perhaps more striking that Gygax would not even sign the Blumes' severance agreement on May 6: Williams executed it in his place as well. Williams would describe Gygax as someone "not eager to have the day-to-day management of the company, but what he wanted to do was to be involved in the creative aspect of the company, and have someone else do the day-to-day management."

In so far as the creative work involved game design, Gygax delegated much of that responsibility as well. Gygax effectively split the 2.5 percent royalty for his forthcoming *Oriental Adventures* between Zeb Cook and François Froideval; his name would grace the cover, but no one maintained much of a pretense that Gygax actually wrote the text. Where we do see Gygax exerting creative energy at the time is in writing fiction.

After frustrating years of being blocked by the gatekeepers of Hollywood from telling his stories, Gygax pivoted back to his original passion. Dragonlance had established TSR as book publisher, and Random House would handle distribution, so nothing could really stop him from achieving his longtime ambition of becoming a published fantasy author. Gygax asked the editor of *Dragon* early in April to telegraph that a novel set in Greyhawk, called *Saga of Old City*, would be forthcoming late in the year, pleading that he was "just too involved with corporate survival at the moment to be able to perform the task." But he did find the time to submit a teaser to the one-hundredth issue of *Dragon* for a story called "At Moonset Blackcat Comes," the long-delayed introduction of his character Gord—back in 1983, "Gord the Rogue" had been a planned film project for the DDEC, one shelved with the remainder of DDEC's plans. Now, thanks to TSR's growing fiction business, the character of Gord found another way to reach to public. Perhaps after his lengthy identity crisis, Gygax had at last started on a path to fulfillment.

In the spring, years of harsh cost-cutting measures at TSR finally began to have a salubrious effect: with less than a hundred persons on payroll, overhead had lessened to a point where the company's substantial games and publishing businesses could pay for themselves. After a seemingly endless stream of losses, TSR made a small profit for the months of April and May. On June 13, the salary deferrals imposed the previous December finally ended. "The current financial condition of the corporation is still in need of improvement," as Martens drily put it in a company-wide notice, "but because of the hard work and extra efforts you all have put forth during these past six months we are able to make this change."

But Martens had to urge everyone "to be cost conscious and work efficiently as possible." He knew well that the company was going to take one last hard hit before advancing on the road to recovery. In June, the end of the fiscal year, they needed to register some accounting charges: for that month alone, they took a $2 million loss. The year had been full of punishing financial obstacles. At the bank's behest, Williams and Martens had worked with a consulting service to reorganize TSR's massive unsecured debt to vendors and service providers; ultimately, they struck a deal where TSR would repay about $1.2 million to its minor creditors over the course of ten months. TSR took a further charge from the ongoing severance obligations the company incurred to part with the Blume brothers and with Koenings. They also had to write off costs related to the failed miniatures business and some losses in the international business, and an additional $1 million went to writing off excess and obsolete inventory, product that they now had no hope of selling.

The company's accounting firm judged that TSR took a total loss for the 1985 fiscal year of roughly $3.8 million, a number so damning it was immediately suppressed. TSR feared to release their audit for the year because their accounting firm would have been required to add an "ongoing concern" clause to the audit. As Williams would put it, such a red flag "would have lost us our sixty-day terms of credit with our vendors. Without those sixty day terms, we were out of business."

The financial crisis was exacerbated by the enormous overhead of the DDEC operation in Hollywood. The books of TSR, Inc. were never cleanly separated from the operations of the DDEC, and with Gygax back at the helm of TSR, the two effectively collapsed. The cost of renting the King Vidor ranch in the Hollywood Hills, around $10,000 a month, was of serious concern to the board, and having been informed that the bank specifically limited the amount of money that TSR could advance to DDEC, Gygax nonetheless signed a continuing lease for the King Vidor ranch on June 24. Apparently, the board learned about the lease only when James Huber contacted the rental company. Ultimately, Gygax agreed to pay the rent himself—Martens would withhold more than $50,000 from Gygax's royalties from July forward to cover expenses for the house. This did nothing to reassure the board that Gygax would manage the company in a way compatible with their obligations to their creditors.

Creditors were not the only uneasy parties dealing with TSR. Two months after the departure of the Blume brothers, neither Gygax nor TSR had made any movement to acquire their family stock position. The Blumes had sent TSR a fresh "Notice of Intent to Sell and Offer to Sell" on May 31, and then another on July 22, which declared their willingness to sell their entire stake at $500 per share. These notices asserted that TSR's inaction "releases these shares from the shareholders agreement," which would permit them to sell them to other shareholders, but they also included a complaint that TSR refused to furnish the Blumes with a shareholder list. This charge was met with silence; on July 23, Brian hand-delivered a copy to TSR to stimulate a response.

On August 15, the Blumes finally got their answer, from board member Jim Huber, which called into question any sale of Brian's unexercised 700-share option and raised again the murky situation of the 200 shares Kevin Blume had received from his father. Kevin then sent a mailing directly to Williams on August 25, with carbon copies to the TSR board, which expressed his "total disbelief" that there could be any confusion about the Blume shareholder position and stressed that their severance package "was accepted based on E. G. Gygax's offer to buy the Blumes's stock in TSR, Inc.'s stead." He concludes by demanding directly, "When can we expect to receive E. G. Gygax's offer?"

If you had wanted to ask Gygax something on August 25, you could have gone to Milwaukee, where he was signing autographs at the TSR booth at GenCon that Sunday morning from ten to noon. Gygax had taken his own advice from last year and scheduled himself prominent appearances on all four days of the convention. This was the first year GenCon relocated from its longstanding venue at the University of Wisconsin at Parkside to the large Milwaukee convention center known as MECCA. The character of the event necessarily changed as it transitioned from a university environment, where games could be scheduled for intimate classrooms, to the cavernous halls of a convention center, with their thundering din, dividing up space with curtained avenues bearing names like Dice Drive and Barbarian

Boulevard. "One of the big promotional hypes this year was that Gygax was back," one attendee told *Alarums & Excursions*. "This seemed to create a stir among some of the attendees." Frank Mentzer was on hand to run a tournament based on *Temple of Elemental Evil*, "an excerpt from the long-awaited T2 module. Be the first in your group to play!" Though advance press suggested they hoped to draw 10,000 gamers, maybe even 12,000, early reports suggested attendance did not rise much over 6,000. Even an institution as longstanding as GenCon took a hit from such a transition.

A few days after GenCon was over, Gygax wrote back to Kevin Blume to flatly deny that he had ever agreed to purchase the Blume family position in TSR back in April. "No offer was ever made, as the individuals present at the Board meeting will state." He did concede that he promised he would try "to find a consortium of individuals willing and able to purchase Blume-held shares at the price promised, i.e., in the neighborhood of $350 per share." But Gygax then observed, "I understand that you have changed your position, now requiring a price of $500 per share. I must state that such a price is, to the best of my knowledge and belief, excessive and unreasonable." The shareholder agreement basically prevented TSR from acquiring shares at any price above the book value established by shareholder vote. Gygax would later claim that Williams advised him "that they had made some sort of an invalid offer; don't worry about it. Legal counsel was handling it." Indeed, Huber had already questioned the legality of the proposed sale. As there was no imminent risk that anyone would take the Blumes up on this offer—Gygax curtly told them it was "virtually impossible"—he turned his attention elsewhere. In an analysis of a game of chess, one might deem that a blunder.

Not that weightier matters did not demand Gygax's attention at that historical moment. The financial situation more or less hit rock bottom in the first week of September, when TSR exceeded a spending cap and the bank stopped advancing funds to the company altogether. They had lacked a signed agreement since the start of the New Year, and the bank demanded a meeting to negotiate a path forward. Although Gygax and Williams were both supposed to attend in the company of James Huber, Gygax apparently had other plans in Los Angeles that day. His cavalier attitude toward these matters further eroded the confidence of the remainder of the board.

And Gygax had external worries as well. Patricia Pulling continued to press her case against *D&D* in the court of public opinion, bolstered by the claims of Thomas Radecki, a campaigner against various mass-media influences on children. The pair had assembled a list of more than fifty murders or suicides they linked to *D&D*. Already at the beginning of the year there were rumors that *60 Minutes* would air an episode about "the public outcry against *Dungeons & Dragons*" as early as April or May. In fact, it did not surface until this moment of crisis in mid-September. It appeared right on the heels of a September 9 article in *Newsweek* called "Kids: The Deadliest Game," which effectively previewed the broadcast story. These two pieces generated the worst public relations week for *D&D* since the Egbert incident six years earlier.

Ed Bradley solemnly introduced *D&D* in the *60 Minutes* segment with the proposition that there are "a lot of adults who think it has been connected to a number of suicides and murders." Bradley gamely pronounced the name of eight adolescents whose deaths, or murders, Pulling and Radecki blamed on the game. After a brief profile of TSR, the piece turned its cameras on Gary Gygax, wearing an avuncular sweater, and TSR's spin doctor Dieter Sturm, decked out in a suit. "Gary Gygax owns the company, and invented the game," Bradley explained before he donned his spectacles to grill the pair of them over the cases tabulated by Pulling and Radecki. Sturm delivered a prepared TSR talking point: that with three or four million players, the suicide rates among players are within normal statistical averages for the teenage population. "I have yet to see one bit of valid, clinical evidence to show that this has been anything more than coincidental with a disturbed child," Gygax confirmed, concluding that Pulling's crusade was "nothing but a witch-hunt."

Bradley introduced Radecki as "a scientist who teaches at the University of Illinois medical school"—although as recently as August, the director of that medical campus had disavowed Radecki's credentials to the press, reporting that instead Radecki had briefly held an unpaid appointment for some time in 1983 and that he "has had essentially no contact with students and no role in the college of medicine" since then. On camera, an excited Radecki told Ed Bradley that of twenty-eight cases he had studied of deaths linked in *D&D*, "in some of those it was clearly the decisive element," and in others merely a "major element," insisting it was "not coincidence." Radecki also related with a straight face an account of parents who witnessed their child "summon a *Dungeons & Dragons* demon into his room before he killed himself." Through the magic of television, Gygax and Pulling then engaged in a back-and-forth dispute. Gygax in one shot insisted *D&D* was make believe, like

Monopoly, where at the end of a game no one has lost any money; the next shot cut to Pulling, who countered that "it is not like *Monopoly*, there is no board, it is role-playing, which is typically used for behavior modification."

Those *Newsweek* and *60 Minutes* stories opened the gates to more of the same. On September 20, Pulling appeared in Connecticut at Putnam High School for a 500-person "information session" about *D&D*, following the board of education's unanimous decision not to ban the game, despite a local petition circulated by the Christian Information Council. She was joined there by William Dear, still hawking his book *The Dungeon Master* and eagerly warning about the dangers of *D&D*. Ever one for a dramatic touch, Dear played a cassette tape he had recorded during the Egbert investigation of an interview with a young fan in the throes of *D&D* "addiction."

This spate of sensational publicity was a very unwelcome distraction at a critical time for the fate of TSR, and it could not have steadied the nerves of creditors concerned about the repayment of TSR's loans. The bank at this point demanded additional collateral to continue TSR's line of credit: beyond a claim on the facilities on Sheridan Spring Road, they requested trademarks and service marks, including those for GenCon and Greyhawk. Gygax curtly informed TSR that it did not own those trademarks. In an October 4 memo to the legal department, Gygax insisted that "any work bearing my name as a creator or co-creator is to be done under my copyright, not that of TSR," and that moreover "trademarks created by me are likewise my sole and exclusive property." No doubt there was some sensitivity about Greyhawk in particular as Gygax's forthcoming novel in that setting, called *Saga of Old City*, would prominently feature the "Greyhawk Adventures" trade dress. Gygax thus made an ultimatum: "All material is submitted only under this express consideration. Unless TSR agrees to this condition, you may not publish my work." By now, the remainder of the board had come to believe that Gygax's financial interests in his creative activities for the company conflicted with his responsibilities as its chief executive, and that this had to be resolved before TSR could move forward.

Lorraine Williams started to intervene on Monday, October 7, while Gygax was out of town to address the Washington School of Psychiatry, followed by three days of meetings with publishers in New York. Everything had to be carefully choreographed from this point forward. She called Kevin

Blume and asked if they could meet soon, somewhere off TSR premises, and discovered that he was eager to get together that very day. Brian was easily persuaded to join them. She secured a conference room at the Hilton Hotel by Geneva Lake where she and the Blume brothers could meet at seven that evening, bringing with her both Martens and a draft agreement to purchase the Blume family stock. Then, the day after, Williams had lunch with Kevin at Fazio's restaurant, where she set the wheels in motion by handing over a check, made out to Brian, for $70,000—to cover the exercise of Blume's 1976 stock option, the twin of the one Gygax had exercised in March. Right after that lunch, the Blumes dispatched a notice to TSR and its shareholders of their "intent to sell all of the 990 shares of TSR, Inc. held by the undersigned and 700 shares to be obtained by Brian J. Blume upon the exercise of his option to purchase such shares, for $350.00 per share, a total of $591,500.00." The letter stipulated a ten-day clock for the process: if and when TSR refused to buy the shares, any other shareholders then had ten days to write to Blume to exercise their option to purchase his stock. By not doing so, the shareholders collectively would be expressing their "waiver of option to purchase or inability to purchase these shares."

The remaining shareholders in the corporation at this point are easily named. There were the immediate members of the Gygax family: Gary, his estranged wife Mary, their son Ernie and daughter Elise. Dave Wesely held the 1 share he had gotten from Dave Arneson, and Heritage Models, though now defunct, was still listed as the owner of 3 shares granted by Arneson in the TSR ledgers. Will Niebling and his wife Schar had 10 shares. A handful of current employees still held a few shares each: Frank Mentzer, Harold Johnson, Kathy Lynch, and Don Turnbull. A gamer named Mark Leymaster had long ago acquired a single share. The TSR profit-sharing plan also commanded close to 10 percent of the company's stock at this point, shares that could be voted by its trustees: effectively, the company's president and its corporate secretary. And while Williams could arrange to become a shareholder herself, thanks to the option the board had granted her in April, she elected to save that for the last possible minute, to not give away her plan.

So it transpired that Williams had resolved to acquire control of TSR. Why? Shortly after she came on board, the relationship between Gygax and Williams began to sour. The financial situation of the company remained very dire, and Williams did not approve of TSR's handling of the Blume family situation. If she were going to invest further in TSR, it would have to empower her to make real changes in the way the company was operating. Therefore, in October 1985, she saw no need to give Gygax any advance notice of her pending deal with the Blumes. "Gygax and I were not talking very much during that time because we had very fundamental differences," she would remark. Furthermore, informing Gygax that she intended to purchase the Blume family shares would be, as she put it, "an invitation for him to get in and just try to screw it up, and to once again try to thwart the ability of the Blumes to sell their stock and to get out and to go about their lives."

Williams could count on the support of Martens, who held on to the check that shortly came in from Brian Blume for the exercise of his 700-share option. Late in the day on October 10, Martens in his capacity as treasurer and secretary sent a letter to all TSR, Inc. shareholders and the board of directors, first acknowledging receipt of the Blumes' "intent to sell" and second announcing that TSR would not buy the stock, thus opening the door to other shareholders to purchase them. In fact, Martens explained that it would literally be illegal for TSR to purchase them, as a Wisconsin statute forbid an acquisition that "would exceed unreserved and unrestricted capital," and at the moment TSR stood on the verge of bankruptcy.

Gygax had returned to the office that Thursday, and must have seen the notice of the Blume family—and the immediate refusal from Martens. But Gygax had been receiving "intent to sell" notices from the Blumes for months now, many pressuring him to fulfill the promise they claim he had made. Although the Blumes's price had come down quite a bit from the initial ask, the position of TSR at the time was so precarious that anyone would hesitate before investing a half million dollars in it. Maybe the Blumes would go lower still? October 11 was a Friday, and then there was the weekend. No one expressed any interest in buying the Blume shares.

As the ten-day clock wound towards a close, Williams got ready. Before she could buy the shares from the Blumes, she needed to become a shareholder herself, or she would be in potential violation of the transfer provisions of the shareholder agreement. On October 16, Williams wrote a check to TSR for $15,000 to exercise the option for 50 shares the board had granted her in April—exactly six months after she had received the option, and the very day it would expire. She delivered the check to Martens by hand, and sweetly asked, "In how many seconds am I going to get my certificate?" She and Martens had a strong relationship, and little jokes like this were typical of their exchanges. Martens decided to tease her a little bit, replying, "If you ask for it too fast, it might be really slow." He had not

A photocopy of TSR, Inc. Stock Certificate no. 104, issued to Lorraine Williams on October 16, 1985, where Williams has signed as president.

yet issued Blume's certificate—there were some technical problems clearing Williams's $70,000 check to Blume, so Martens could not deposit Blume's check until those resolved. Well past the point of no return, executing a plan that required punctuality, Williams suggested impatiently, "Well, you know, I hope you don't hold mine for a couple of weeks." Seeing the expression on her face, Martens ventured, "I think I'll get up and do it."

Her stock certificate was signed by Martens, in his capacity as board secretary, and Williams signed for the slot marked "president"—as she had many times before when wielding the "dirty end of the stick" for severance agreements and similar functions. The pair would sign another certificate two days later, on Friday, October 18, this one in the amount of 700 shares assigned to Brian Blume for his option exercise. Lorraine met with the Blumes for lunch at the Lake Lawn Lodge—at a bit of remove from the office, in nearby Delavan, where Kevin resided—along with Martens and an attorney who would oversee the escrow agreement they were about to sign. Brian dutifully endorsed all his shares to Williams and deposited them into the escrow along with his wife's. Kevin and his wife would do the same, though because of the controversy surrounding 200 of their shares, Melvin Blume was also party to the agreement—Kevin executed it on his father's behalf, after securing permission over the telephone. Under the terms of the escrow, on the last day of 1986, and each December 31 thereafter for the following four years, Williams would deposit $104,300 plus interest (calculated at 13 percent annually) in exchange for these shares.

With that, Williams secured the Blume family stake in TSR. Another weekend passed, and then on Monday, Martens and Williams would sign yet another fateful stock certificate, number 107, which assigned all 1,690 Blume family shares to Williams. This made her the majority shareholder of the company. While the past days' events were playing out, Gygax's fiancée Gail Carpenter's mother passed away, and the pair of them drove to Kentucky for the funeral. Gygax did not return until late in the evening of October 20.

Upon his return, Gygax continued to feud with the board of directors over royalties, trademarks, and copyrights. He seemed to believe that with his controlling interest in the company, he could dictate terms to the board, even reshaping it if necessary. On October 21, he sent them a memo with the following blatant threat: "After thoughtful consideration, I am convinced that it is in the best interest of TSR, Inc., and thus its shareholders to ask that the Board be reduced from its current maximum of seven members to a maximum of three directors." Those directors who remained would receive no further compensation for their work on the board; at the time, directors received $12,000 a year and a further $500 for each meeting they attended. Gygax intended to implement these measures as of the next shareholder meeting, coming up on November 12.

The board requested a meeting for the following day. Gygax came ready for a fight, but woefully unprepared for what was to come. On the evening of October 22, 1985, at the Sheridan Springs office, when Martens began to spill the beans, Gygax must have immediately recognized that the exercise of the Blume option for 700 shares had diluted his own stake below half of the outstanding stock in the company. But Martens did not volunteer who would control these newly issued shares.

Since these events played out in real time, Gygax had little opportunity to reflect—Wesley Sommer formally requested that Gygax tender his resignation. No doubt still grappling with his new circumstances, he refused. Sommer therefore proposed the following to the TSR board for a vote: "Resolved that, in the best interests of the corporation, E. Gary Gygax be terminated as President and Chief Executive Officer and Chairman and that TSR and Mr. Gygax negotiate and seek to enter into an agreement whereby Mr. Gygax would continue to do creative work and the Company continue to utilize his creative talent." This last clause no doubt related to the royalty issue previously under discussion. James Huber seconded this motion. The motion passed with three directors in favor, one opposed (Gygax), and one abstaining (Huber).

While this stunning turn of events might seem momentous enough for one meeting, the board then turned its attention to the newly created vacancies in TSR's senior management. Immediately, the Blumes put forward Sommer to succeed Gygax as chairman of the board. This passed easily. But then Sommer advanced another proposition: that Lorraine Williams should replace Gygax as interim president and CEO of TSR. Blindsided, Gygax pushed back against this proposal—Williams had only worked at TSR for six months, and had no background in games. But Sommer championed Williams on the grounds that she previously had acted as president in Gygax's absence; she would transition into the role with the least disruption to the company. Gygax counter-proposed bestowing the position on Willard Martens, who, in addition to acting as secretary for the board, was finance vice president of TSR, but Martens demurred, ostensibly due to his other responsibilities.

After a short discussion, the board approved the motion to appoint Lorraine Williams president and CEO, overriding Gygax's strenuous objections. Surely Gygax would not have bothered to contest the appointment had he understood the true situation, the critical piece of information everyone else in the room was privy to that he lacked. Gygax had missed the warning signs: he overlooked how immediately prior to the board meeting, several of the other directors, including Sommer, Huber, and Kevin Blume, had congregated in Williams's office. In that private conference, those parties agreed not to reveal the extent of the changes in shareholder positions to Gygax. It could not have been hard to persuade the board, who had tired of Gygax's posturing over his rights and compensation, that this was the prudent path.

So, on October 22, Gary Gygax walked into an ambush. Ignorant of Williams's newfound stake in TSR, he could only watch in amazement as the board stripped him of his job and appointed Williams his successor. As the final action of the meeting, the board moved to grant Gygax a severance package "consistent with what has been done in the past," presumably a reference to the package extended to the Blumes. Kevin Blume seconded this motion. The severance package was approved by the board, and the meeting adjourned at quarter of seven. In only ninety minutes, Gygax, utterly baffled, watched control of TSR transfer to an outsider, a non-gamer, someone who had no connection to *D&D*.

After the board meeting, but before he made his way out of the building, Gygax dropped a note in Martens's office requesting a current list of TSR shareholders. As Gygax was no longer an employee, and no longer chairman of the board, Martens referred his request to Jim Huber, since the policy of the company precluded distributing that list unless it were covered by a protective order in connection with litigation, as the Blumes had discovered not long ago. Gygax was totally in the dark as to what had just happened.

Word of these cataclysmic events immediately spread through the game community, but at first blush, no one discerned that Williams was behind it. Likely thanks to Wesely's single share of stock, word had already reached Arneson in his apartment near Golden Gate Park in San Francisco by October 24, but like Gygax, he thought the Blumes were behind it. Arneson wrote to Dave Megarry, "Biggest news around here is that Gary has been removed from being President at TSR and in all likelihood next month's shareholder meeting will see the Blumes back in the saddle again. Disaster, I am told, will shortly follow as the bank will 'call the note' or the company will be run into the ground." For the first time in a long while, Arneson had some personal stake in TSR's roadmap: "Needless to say my planned module series is probably deader than the proverbial doornail. I am told that such is not the case. I will have to wait and see." A Blackmoor module series and the income it promised was of particular interest to him as the 1981 settlement agreement had run its course, and Arneson's royalty payments would now dry up; rumors in the hobby fanzines suggested that the old offices of Adventure Games in the Twin Cities had been padlocked by creditors.

In advance of the shareholder meeting scheduled for the week of November 12, Gygax took forceful but ultimately futile steps to undo the damage—attempting a bit of retroactive continuity, as gamers would say. He felt the best path would be simply to exercise his rights under the shareholder agreement by sending Brian Blume, on November 5, an unsolicited cashier's check for \$113,750, as a 50 percent down payment to secure 650 of the Blume family's shares. The \$350 per share price "was perhaps high under the circumstances," as Gygax would remark a few days later, "but certainly worth paying for control of the corporation." This move complied with the terms of the shareholder agreement, as there was no precedent for any "ten-day clock" in that document: it allows the company thirty days to purchase offered shares, and then states that if another shareholder buys them, then "one-half of such purchase price shall be paid in cash within ninety (90) days." Hence Gygax's presumptuous check simply ignored the possibility that the shares were already spoken for. Those 650 shares would have restored control of TSR to Gygax by a comfortable margin.

But from the moment the Blumes had signed their agreement with Williams on October 18, their shares resided in legal escrow, so Brian was in no position to accept such an offer, as he somewhat cryptically explained to Gygax over the phone. Ironically, had the board not dispensed with the pro rata clause of the stock agreement back in March to clear the way for the Foreman deal, Gygax could have relied on that, as it would have permitted Williams to purchase only a number of shares proportionate to her own holdings, which could amount to no more than 50 shares. With such a poison pill, a hostile takeover is virtually impossible; without it, an outsider assuming control was all too plausible.

Gygax's unsolicited check was not the only challenge to Williams's transaction. Don Turnbull, a shareholder loyal to Gygax, sent a letter on October 28 to Brian Blume that made its gradual way overseas from Britain stating that he had not received the "intent to sell" notice until well after the ten-day clock had expired, and politely asked if Brian and Kevin would care to reset the clock until mid-November to give him time to consider it. A similar notice came by registered mail from Ernie Gygax, who still resided in Hollywood.

On November 11, the day before the shareholder meeting, the situation began to become clear. Gygax spoke to Kevin that morning about the mysterious agreement that barred him from acquiring the Blume family stake, and while Kevin initially proposed to drive in to Lake Geneva to share a copy with Gygax, he had to apologize when his legal counsel barred that. "I'm sorry too," Gygax replied, and then took the matter to the courts, demanding an emergency restraining order against the Blumes, Williams, Martens, the escrow attorney, and TSR itself, to effectively prevent any stock transfer until the dispute could be resolved. In his desperation, at around five o'clock in the afternoon, Gygax drove over to Brian Blume's house and hand-delivered a supplement to his earlier stock exercise offer, which promised he was ready, willing, and able to purchase as many Blume shares as necessary to regain control of the company, even if that meant all of them. Subpoenas went out the next morning, and the shareholder meeting was indefinitely postponed.

A judge could not review the matter until November 14. In his initial pleading, Gygax's attorney summed up the circumstances as he saw them: "The situation, notwithstanding the hypertechnical arguments, is a very simple one. It's a man who is the co-founder and large shareholder in this company, who had clear rights under a shareholder agreement to control, in the event that the Blumes's interest decided to sell out. They did so decide. He exercised his right and now comes a newcomer to the company, with a deal with the Blumes and is attempting to seize control and may de facto, subject to the power of the court, have already done so." Based on a couple days of initial investigation, the court agreed that the matter was worth looking into, and a temporary injunction was put in place barring TSR from allowing share transfers until the legal situation could be resolved.

The resulting battle stretched into the second half of 1986, during which time Williams remained interim president and Gygax was now merely a shareholder and outside director. The court reviewed TSR's 1985 upheavals and concluded that the Blumes had satisfied the obligations of the shareholder agreement by providing TSR, and Gygax personally, with ample notice of their intention to sell, as well as numerous opportunities to purchase their shares, dating back to April 18, 1985. When the bank constrained TSR from purchasing the Blume stock, the remaining shareholders had an option to buy the shares as the agreement stipulates, but Gygax "sat on his rights," the court decided. When no one stepped forward, the Blumes were "thereafter free to sell their stock to anyone they chose at any price; thus, their subsequent sale to Williams did not violate the shareholders' agreement." The court also considered the question of whether Gygax had promised to buy the Blume family position in the solarium at Rexnord on April 16, and finally ruled on the basis of testimony from the independent board members that Gygax had "agreed to buy their stock, and the Blumes and [Gygax] reported that commitment . . . to the other directors." The court upheld the sale to Williams, lifting all injunctions, on August 28, 1986.

Faced with the prospect of holding a minority stake in a TSR, Inc. run by Williams, Gygax elected to walk away from the company, resigning all positions in October 1986 and selling his shares to Williams. As he put it in a farewell note to *Dragon*, "The shape and direction of the *Dungeons & Dragons* game system . . . or that of the *AD&D* game system, are now entirely in the hands of others." At the bitter end, his parting shot still maintained that the *Advanced* system was not the same game as the original. But the long battle he had fought to retain control of *Dungeons & Dragons* against a succession of challengers had ended.

TSR Turn Results for 1985

Revenue: $24M, losses $3.8M

Employees: 96

Stock Valuation: $300

GenCon attendance vs. Origins: 6,000 vs. ?1,200+

Players Eliminated: Gary Gygax

Gary

Epilogue: Endgame

Gygax thus found himself, at the end of 1986, in the same position Arneson had a decade earlier: on the outside of *Dungeons & Dragons* looking in. Should we be astonished to find Gygax following in Arneson's footsteps with such fidelity that he endorsed a new edition of the *City State of the Invincible Overlord*—now published by Mayfair, not the Judges Guild—and that TSR had to sue over it? Like Arneson, Gygax quickly formed his own rival games company, though his efforts tread too close to *D&D* intellectual property, resulting in further litigation, and ultimately, a lucrative settlement for Gygax that rid TSR of his interference. But despite his best efforts, Gygax, like Arneson, never came close to having another *D&D*.

Gygax had spent so long shaping the history of TSR while he ran it, he was hardly going to stop when he left, or ignore his final chapter. Because Gygax's years at TSR ended in disappointment, the narrative of TSR he now told was a tragedy: his new character was the hero betrayed by perfidious business partners. In his 1986 farewell piece in *Dragon*, he had said nothing about his ouster from TSR apart from that "the Board of Directors of the corporation saw fit to remove me as the company's President and Chairman of the Board." But in the fall of 1988, he opened up in an essay called "A Funny Thing Happened on the Way to the Board Room" for a small gaming magazine called *The Familiar*.

With just two years' worth of dust settled on the lawsuit that severed him from TSR, Gygax had enough self-awareness to recognize he could not reflect on his ouster dispassionately. "Is there bitterness?" he asked himself in *The Familiar*. "Could such be avoided considering the conditions?" But that bitterness took its toll on the fidelity of his account, in claims about TSR's finances like "I began to see an inkling of trouble in the fall of 1984," which neglects the catastrophic situation TSR found itself in after its overextension by mid-1983, during which Gygax, as president, had no small inkling of trouble when the bank demanded they lay off a third of TSR's workforce after two years of substantial declines in core *D&D* sales. His timeline of events laid all of the blame at the feet of the Blume family, casting himself as a victim of their financial indiscipline, and later, when they sold their shares to Williams, of their vengeance.

Gygax, ultimately, turned out to be a man who had a disinterest, sometimes bordering on contempt, for running a business—but who could not bring himself to relinquish the business either. This is not a desirable quality in a chief executive, and it created the need for corporate structures where others made the day-to-day decisions about running TSR, often only to face second-guessing from Gygax. He viewed the job as a sacrifice, something he had never sought, but instead had thrust upon him. He discharged its duties well enough when TSR remained at the hobby level, but once it grew beyond a "low-level-character sort of company," he found the controls of its apparatus maddening, and turned his attention elsewhere.

While Gygax conceded to *The Familiar* that he was recording only his subjective impressions, he felt confident that "with added years will come a better perspective." Instead, his bitterness intensified over time as his new ventures languished, making it ever harder to align the historical facts of his tenure at TSR with his later claims. An interview with Gygax that appeared in *The Gamer* in 1992 thus began with a warning that "if Gygax says it, someone will disagree, contradict, or deride." By that point, Gygax's story about the Blumes had drastically magnified their malfeasance: for instance, he claimed of TSR that by 1984 "there were 600 on payroll and 100 were related by marriage or blood" to the Blumes, where neither of those figures could withstand a cursory fact check.

"Little about the creator of the role-playing game is straightforward or undisputed—including his status as the creator of the role-playing game," *The Gamer* article continued. As time passed, and the stature of *D&D* in popular culture solidified, the question of who has the right to claim that status far overshadowed any disputes about the financial troubles of TSR in the mid-1980s. The article quotes Gygax asserting, "*D&D*, I wrote every word of that. Even my co-author admits that." But *The Gamer* had access to Arneson as well, and it summarized: "Arneson admits nothing of the kind, but won't say much because of a court settlement with Gygax and TSR." By saying little, Arneson could hint that a great secret, one quite unfavorable to Gygax, had been suppressed by legal measures. Yet back in April 1981, when the ink of their settlement was barely dry, Arneson did not seem to feel any impediment to detailing Gygax's part in the authoring of the original game in words like: "At the time, they had a lot more spare time than I did and they had a lot of ideas, so they came up with their own version of the rules. They sent theirs to us and we fooled around with them for a while." Arneson's later reticence masked his own ambivalence toward productizing *D&D* in 1973 and then working at TSR in 1975, both of which Gygax was at some pains to overcome. It might not be unfair to say that Arneson only became energized about the prospects of *D&D* when he felt it was something taken away from him, when there was a "great War" to wage.

Weaponized rhetoric, which was originally forged during the battle for *Dungeons & Dragons* in the first decade of its existence, lays strewn throughout the historical record like unexploded ordinance. The testimony of the game's creators naturally formed the basis for the first attempts to compile an origin story of *D&D*. It has led many people—myself included—on wild-goose chases, trying to substantiate later claims that turn out to be will-o'-wisps born of the conflict. These statements were not engineered impartially, and it is hard to wield them without inheriting their bias: as with any claims crafted since the summer of 1977, when Gygax first ventured that "*D&D* was not Dave's game system by any form or measure," they are implements that have to be understood within the context of the battle, not statements that should be taken at face value—like *Diplomacy* propaganda, or perhaps like the contemporary claims that *D&D* killed children after first luring them into Satanism.

It was the primary aim of this book to show, to the extent possible, the baseline events that all this rhetoric has obscured. In the 1970s, Gygax and Arneson collaborated on *D&D* without any notion of what it would turn into, or what it could mean for their lives or legacies. From the moment the game enjoyed even a modest success, they were always scrambling to keep up, to position themselves and each other as they struggled to understand how their unexpected windfall had come to pass—and how to hold on to it. Their relationship, as hobbyists and collaborators, could not survive the transition to a workplace, let alone an industry. Nor ultimately could Gygax's partnership with his fellow hobbyist Brian Blume, when it became clear that business beyond a certain level could not be pursued like an adventure. As Gygax directed the product's marketing over its first decade, it is unsurprising that his name is more associated with the game of *D&D* than any other. Or maybe the name Gygax is just the more memorable one.

A history like this one can never resolve all the uncertainties around the story: some are ambiguities built into the history itself. Did the 1975 contract language about the "set of game rules or game entitled *Dungeons & Dragons*" apply to the entirety of the Holmes *Basic Set*, or to revisions like the *Advanced* game? This question has no definitive answer: the legal language was written before anyone imagined such derivative works might someday exist. And the harder you look at the circumstances surrounding Gygax's ouster from TSR in 1985, the less easy it is to say who was in the right. Even questions that seem relatively straightforward—like whether Arneson quit his job at TSR or was terminated—turn out to be matters that do not admit of tidy resolution. But the nuance of these circumstances does not prevent us from understanding what happened, provided we can accept its unresolvability and the role it played in setting the parameters of the battle for *D&D*. Real life is messy, unlike the alluring narratives we spin as we try to make sense of it all; real people are messier than the characters they adopt for themselves or project onto each other.

In their lifetimes, Gygax and Arneson never saw *D&D* regain the pinnacle of success it had enjoyed during the height of their battle. Lorraine Williams ran TSR for a decade or so—about as long as Gygax had—largely profiting from the strategies on display at GenCon in 1984, campaign settings like Dragonlance and the Forgotten Realms. She still had to manage the fallout of the previous decade, like the $1.4 million the courts determined TSR had to pay Will Niebling for wrongly invalidating his stock option; Gygax was cleared of any personal culpability, but the Blumes were fined $50,000 in punitive damages. Under her tenure, GenCon and Origins would finally be held jointly in 1988. But toward the end of the 1990s, TSR once again fell on hard times. The industry had begun to change: while the second edition *Players Handbook* outsold the *D&D* computer adaptation *Pool of Radiance* in 1989, by the time *Baldur's Gate* came around in 1997, that would sell ten times more copies than a hardcover *D&D* manual. Looking at sales alone, it seemed the world had passed *D&D* by.

After Williams sold the struggling TSR to Wizards of the Coast, Wizards' founder Peter Adkison made it a priority to mend the rift in the industry, and invited both Gygax and Arneson to help unveil the third edition of *D&D* in 2000. He also promptly did away with the conceit that there existed some separate "advanced" version of *D&D*. It was an era where Gygax would make a cameo appearance on *Futurama* and Arneson would appear as a wizard in the *Dungeons & Dragons* live-action film. Although a community of retro gamers remained dedicated to the original game, for most, it was an object of nostalgia. But the flagships of fantasy gaming in the 2000s, computers games like *World of Warcraft*, knew their profound debt to *D&D*—when Gygax passed away, the makers of that game made a public statement that "*D&D* was an inspiration to us in many ways and helped spark our passion for creating games of our own." They even added a little flavor text to the game invoking the name of Gygax.

Throughout the last decade of his life, the ever-gregarious Gygax dedicated considerable time to online forums, answering all manner of questions, and could still be found in Lake Geneva, running games at smaller shows, up to the end. Arneson taught game design at a Florida university, but remained a more reclusive figure. Neither would live to see an era when GenCon—which now takes place in Indianapolis—regularly draws more than 60,000 attendees. A spike in attendance coincided with the development of the fifth edition of *D&D* and a huge resurgence of interest in tabletop games.

Back in 1980, a reporter who asked if *D&D* was only a passing fad learned that "Gygax and Blume think not. *D&D*, they say, will last fifty years or more." As unlikely as it was in the 1970s that this esoteric offshoot of the wargaming hobby might become a pop-culture phenomenon, it is just as unlikely that in 2021 the game would be more popular than ever. As a new generation grows up playing the game, it may be that the true impact of *Dungeons & Dragons* has yet to be felt.

Sources and Acknowledgments

This book grew out of, or perhaps accreted within, an essay I wrote in 2014 called "The Ambush at Sheridan Springs," which I retained as the title of the concluding chapter. Some stray passages and sequences from the original "Ambush" survive here, which I hope will not be regarded as self-plagiarism.

As a guiding principle, I made every effort to let Gygax, Arneson, and their contemporaries explain themselves as they did at the time these events occurred. Many of the direct quotations in this piece are thus taken from their correspondence; as these letters today are held in a variety of private collections, their citations below may not be of immediate value to scholars, but, in time, circumstances will surely improve. The same might be said for many fanzines cited below, though digital archives of those swell every day. Digitized or not, fanzines are notoriously hard to work with: there are difficulties with dating, paginating, and attributing many contributions to them, so their citations may contain gaps or variances from conventional formats. Some spelling, grammar, and dating errors have been silently corrected in transcribing from these letters and zines.

This book talks a great deal about conventions, especially GenCon and Origins, and the primary record for scheduled happenings at those conventions comes from their printed programs. It must be said that tabulating convention attendance in this era was more of an art than a science—reporting sources made little meaningful distinction between paid attendance, unpaid attendance and turnstile attendance, and figures were often intentionally inflated or suppressed—so where not otherwise attributed, numbers given for convention attendance follow my best estimate from an aggregate of data sources. For nearly all of these events, reliable and definitive figures simply do not exist.

Much of the story of TSR told here derives from documents created between 1973 and 1986 that were saved by employees or preserved in court records. These include corporate newsletters (notably *Random Events*), various internal corporate correspondence and memos, quarterly or monthly sales reports, annual audits, meeting minutes (board, shareholder, and staff), contracts, stock certificates, legal filings, employee handbooks and directories, profit-sharing plan documents, internal reports, business cards, press releases, corporate retrospectives, and period photographs from the era. These documents too may lack clear dates or attribution that would ordinarily flesh out a citation, so some are more likely to be characterized in the body text than cited below. For the "Turn Results" at chapter ends, TSR employee headcount tallies represent documented peaks and valleys during the calendar year, rather than exact figures for December 31.

Beyond internal TSR records copied for legal cases, some details come to this story from testimony or documents generated for legal purposes. Accounting data prior to 1977, and statements of royalties paid and salaries, relies on exhibits, affidavits, and correspondence from Minnesota case *Arneson v. TSR et al., Civ. No. 4-79-109* (for the earliest royalties and sales, John Beard's letter to Michael Hirsch, September 7, 1978, is of special value). Mid-1980s accounting data and sales details similarly follow the testimony and affidavits of Walworth County, Wisconsin, Circuit Court case *Gygax v. TSR et al., 85-CV-907*.

Where not otherwise noted, more general hobby industry financials including annual revenue and unit sales follow SPI and Howard Barasch's annual rankings in *Strategy & Tactics* no. 33 (1964–1972), no. 42 (limited 1972–73 figures), no. 47 (1973–74), no. 54 (1974–75), no. 60 (1975–76), no. 66 (1976–77), no. 71 (1977–78), no. 76 (1978–79), no. 83 (1979–80), and no. 89 (1980–81), concluding with *Insider* no. 6 (1981–82). Revenue figures for TSR, which largely follow their audited financial reports, give net sales after returns and allowances (where available); TSR's external communications often massaged these numbers heavily.

It is only by assembling disparate fragments of information from a multitude of sources that a history like this can develop a coherent picture—but inevitably not a complete one. Should these events prove of continuing interest to posterity, there remains far more work to be done, for which the present study, I hope, might serve as a reliable baseline.

Illustrations in this book, including maps, woodblocks, and a family tree, were furnished by my co-conspirator Drew Meger of Corey Press. The miniatures depicted on the cover are the work of Jim Wampler of Mud-puppy Games.

This book is the result of around seven years of research into the corporate history of TSR. I need to thank Frank Mentzer, Tim Kask, Mike Carr, Bill Mein-hardt, Scott Brand, Allan Grohe, Victor Raymond, Bill Hoyt, Dave Megarry, Merle Rasmussen, Matt Shoemaker, Marc Miller, Lewis Pulsipher, and George Phillies for helping to provide documentary sources for this project, and for talking through the particulars. This project would not have been possible without the many interviews and conversations I've had with people who were there are at the time, including: Terry Kuntz, Greg Bell, Ernie Gygax, Jim Ward, Jeff Perren, Dave Wesely, Tim Jones, Al Hammack, Diesel LaForce, Lawrence Schick, Zeb Cook, Harold Johnson, Steve Marsh, Steve Winter, Jeff Grubb, Erol Otus, Kevin and Mary Hendryx, Jeff Easley, Bruce Nesmith, Mike Gray, Flint Dille—and, some years ago now, Gary Gygax and Dave Arneson. I'd also like to thank Noah Springer, Elizabeth Agresta, Mary Bagg, Yasuyo Iguchi, Mary Reilly, Jim Mitchell, and Helen Weldon at the MIT Press for their help getting this into shape. Jason Begy put the index together and caught many errors in the text. Finally, I'd like to thank Mike Witwer, Mark Greenberg, Bill Meinhardt, and Mike Carr for thoughts on the work in progress, and give special thanks to JLP.

Part I

The narrative in this opener is a composite of court testimony of Gary Gygax (November 14, 1985, and January 29, 1986), Wesley Sommer (November 15, 1985), and Willard Martens (June 19, 1986) in Walworth County, Wisconsin, Circuit Court case no. 85-CV-907, as well as minutes from the October 22, 1985, meeting of the board of directors of TSR, Inc.

Opening Moves

6   **Monopoly alone then traded:** Edward J. Doherty, "Monopoly Is Forty Year Favorite," *Xenogogic* 6, no. 1 (1973): 7–8.

6   **It took Roberts four years:** see Don G. Campbell, "'Thought' Games Proven Salable," *Indianapolis Star*, December 6, 1960. Sales figures follow the July 1983 Charles S. Roberts Auction catalog; and see *Silver Jubilee: Avalon Hill's First 25 Years in Review* (Baltimore: Avalon Hill, 1983), 5, for Roberts's ouster.

8   **"Cardboard counters can never":** Gary Gygax, "Counsels of War," *Wargamer's Newsletter* no. 108 (1971): 5.

8   **"first successful attempt at uniting":** Tom Shaw, *Avalon Hill General (AHG)* 4, no. 3 (1968): 2.

9   "Newport of the West": Ann Wolfmeyer and Mary Burns Gage, *Lake Geneva: Newport of the West* (Lake Geneva, WI: Lake Geneva Historical Society, 1976).

10   "well-mannered, well-dressed intellects": Ray Py, "War—Is the Name of the Game," *Beloit Daily State News*, August 26, 1968.

11   only eight people: Don Greenwood, "Wargamer of the Month: Gary Gygax," *Panzerfaust (PZF)* 2, no. 8 (1968): 3.

11   yielded around $50: *International Wargamer Quarterly* 1, no. 6 (1968): 3. Same for *Arbela* sales and Gystaff advertisement.

12   "family, religion, . . . work and sex": Gary Gygax letter to *Kipple* no. 162 (1968).

13   three hours each day to wargaming: Greenwood, *PZF* 2, no. 8.

14   "What got to me": Gary Gygax letter to Bill Speer, November 4, 1968.

14   "When I was forced": Gary Gygax letter to *PZF* 3 no. 5 (1969): 6.

Gygax and Arneson

15   Some met up with Gygax: John Mansfield, "Lake Geneva 1969," *Canadian Wargamer* no. 13 (1969): 2–8.

15   "a Chicago insurance executive": George Harmon, "War Buffs Gather to Argue 'What Ifs,'" syndicated in *Pittsburg Press*, July 30, 1969.

16   "the 1:1200 model sailing ships": Greenwood, "The Second Time Around," *PZF* 4, no. 6 (1969): 19.

16   "rules in co-operation with Gary Gygax": Dave Arneson, "Club News" supplement to *Corner of the Table*, undated (October 1969?).

17   "I've resigned from IFW": Gygax letter to George Phillies, September 18, 1969.

17   Lake Geneva Tactical Studies Association: Gygax, May 10, 1974, letter to *Great Plains Game Players Newsletter* (GPGPN) no. 9 (1974): 6.

17   LGTSA Medieval Miniatures Rules: *Domesday Book* no. 5 (1970): 3–10.

18   "I can't stand this job": Gygax letter to Lewis Pulsipher, June 19, 1970.

18   "I lost my job": Gygax/Phillies, December 13, 1970.

18   "work around Lake Geneva": Gygax, "The American Scene," *Wargamer's Newsletter* (WGN) no. 112 (1971): 17.

19   "During this temporary (forced) vacation": Gygax, *WGN* no. 112.

19   Lowry pushing a rule book called *Fast Rules*: *International Wargamer* 3, no. 7 (1970): 16.

20   **"Lowry says that he'll soon be publishing"**: Gygax letter to Arneson, March 22, 1971.

21   **also offered the *Frappe!* rules**: *International Wargamer* 3, no. 10 (1970): 16.

21   **taxonomy of different-colored dragons**: Gygax, "Grayte Wourmes," *Thangorodrim* no. 3–9 (1969–1970).

21   **earlier ideas on Tolkien**: Leonard Patt, "Rules for Middle-Earth," *Courier* 2, no. 7 (1970): 12–13.

22   **"somewhat foolish"**: Greenwood, "Thumbnail Analysis," *PZF* no. 48 (1971): 14.

22   **"play-tested various prototypes"**: Greenwood, "Interview: Guidon Games," *PZF* no. 47 (1971): 13–15.

23   **"sales of *Alex* & *Dunkirk* are pretty slow"**: Gygax/Phillies, July 22, 1971.

23   **"very impressed with Gary Gygax"**: Kevin Slimak letter to Phillies, July 30, 1971.

23   **"garden for survival"**: "Games of Fantasy Spell Success for Gygax Family," *Clinton Topper*, 1980 [newspaper clipping without a date or any author listed].

23   **"employment in this area is low"**: Gygax/Phillies, July 22, 1971.

24   **"training as a shoe repairman"**: Gygax/Phillies, September 7, 1971.

24   **"so busy trying to learn"**: Gygax/Arneson, September 9, 1971.

24   **"I have to get back to shoe repairing"**: Gygax/Phillies, December 31, 1971.

24   **serialized a draft**: Gygax and Arneson, "Don't Give Up the Ship," *International Wargamer* 4, no. 6–10 (1971).

24   **"I'll do a preface also"**: Gygax/Arneson, September 9, 1971.

24   **"royalties should run"**: Gygax/Arneson, January 2, 1972.

24   **sum Lowry paid Gygax . . . in 1971**: Gygax's 1971 1040 tax form.

25   **"bring in something like $20/month"**: Gygax/Arneson, January 2, 1972.

25   **"We won't get rich"**: Gygax/Arneson, January 2, 1972.

25   **"fish him into preparing a final copy"**: Gygax/Arneson, December 11, 1971.

25   **"Too bad if Carr"**: Gygax/Arneson, August 14, 1972.

26   **"I'm quitting all wargaming"**: Gygax/Arneson, March 6, 1972.

27   **"I've felt more like reading"**: Gygax/Pulsipher, undated (late June 1972?).

27   **"Hope Lowry will send"**: Gygax/Arneson, September 30, 1972.

27   "will write to Lowry": Gygax/Arneson, September 9, 1972.

27   "The explanation of why the checks": Gygax/Arneson, December 15, 1972.

28   "I still have not heard from Lowry": Arneson/Gygax, December 12 (misdated, after 15), 1972.

28   "the brightest hope": Gygax/Arneson, February 1, 1973.

29   "give you credit + free set": Gygax/Arneson, December 15, 1972.

29   "fairly minor": Arneson/Gygax, December 12 (misdated, after 15), 1972.

29   had begun shopping: Parker Brothers letter to Dave Megarry, December 28, 1972.

30   "I'll whip out a booklet": Gygax/Arneson, April 5, 1973.

30   "Trust you'd like to split": Gygax/Arneson, April 15, 1973.

31   "I have been offered the number two spot": Gygax/Arneson, February 13, 1973.

31   "If we get going": Gygax/Arneson, May 3, 1973.

31   Adventures Unlimited: Dave Megarry letter to Dave Arneson, February 5, 1974.

31   "Don is overextended": Gygax/Arneson, undated (summer 1973).

32   "Lowry, as far as I can personally see": Gary Gygax letter to Dave Megarry, August 2, 1973.

The $300 Idea

33   "Some of us here are getting": Gygax/Megarry, August 2, 1973.

33   Lowry reported in *Panzerfaust*: Lowry, "G2 Reports," *PZF* no. 60 (1973): 47.

34   "an outstanding success": Greenwood, "Infiltrator's Report," *AHG* 10, no. 3 (1973): 23.

34   "We're getting ready to roll": Gygax/Arneson, September 4, 1973.

34   "trifling": Jeff Perren and Gary Gygax, *Cavaliers and Roundheads* (Lake Geneva, WI: TSR, 1973): 5.

35   "is taking an initial 100": Gygax/Arneson, September 27, 1973.

35   "Depending on how well": Gygax/Arneson, September 27, 1973.

35   "the whole triad": Don Lowry, "Line of Communication," *PZF* no. 60 (1973): 4.

36   "I don't promise it": Gygax/Arneson, December 30, 1973.

36 **"I thought you'd do a better job"**: Gygax/Arneson, May 3, 1973.

36 **"We do want a set of rules"**: Gygax/Arneson, December 27, 1973.

38 **"this is going to cost"**: Gygax/Arneson, January 13, 1974.

38 **"watching a lathe"**: Brian Blume autobiography, *Strategic Review* (*SR*) 1, no. 5 (1975): 8.

38 **"wise and noble president"**: Gygax May 10, 1974, letter to *GPGPN* no. 9 (1974): 5.

40 **"eventual return"**: Gygax/Arneson, January 13, 1974.

40 its sales **"had really slowed"**: Gygax/Arneson, June 2, 1974.

41 landlord intended to sell the house: Gygax/Arneson, March 13, 1974.

42 **"wee hovel"**: Gygax/Arneson, May 19, 1974.

42 **"I was all black and blue"**: Gygax/Arneson, May 19, 1974.

42 **"Don isn't about to come up with any more loot"** and **"Gad!"**: Gygax/Arneson, July 3, 1974.

42 **"Don's a nice guy"**: Gygax/Arneson, May 19, 1974.

43 **"simply to help TSR along"**: Gygax/Arneson, November 24, 1974.

43 **"if Mike will finance"**: Gygax/Arneson, June 2, 1974.

43 **"It costs about $40"**: Gygax/Arneson, December 30, 1973.

43 **"It doesn't pay to advertise"**: Gygax/Arneson, July 3, 1974.

44 **"ridiculous (I mean miserly!!!)"**: Gygax/Megarry, March 6, 1975.

44 **"ultra-confidential"** and **"it'll take some time to raise $12"**: Gygax/Arneson, June 2, 1974.

45 **"Oden wanted TSR to do those ERB rules"**: Gygax/Arneson, August 11, 1974.

45 **"jealous orcs"** and **"Why is it"**: Gygax/Arneson, May 19/20, 1974.

46 **"theirs was the best exhibit"**: Jim Lurvey, "Wargamer's Diary," *GPGPN* no. 12 (1974): 13.

46 an informal poll: "Lake Geneva," *La Vivandière* 1, no. 4 (1974): 11.

46 **"This year's convention"**: Bill Hoyer, "GenCon VII Report," *American Wargamer* 2, no. 2 (1974): 3.

46 **"the hit of the convention"**: Hoyer, "Lake Geneva Convention," *Signal* no. 65 (1974): 3.

46   "GenCon date is dictated": Gygax/Arneson, November 24, 1974.

47   "a certain amount of communication breakdown": Scott Rich letter October 9, 1974, to *GPGPN* no. 15 (1975): 19.

48   "Gary Gygax recognized me": Joe Angiolillo letter to Kevin Slimak, September 16, 1974.

48   "is now willing to look at *Dungeon*": Gygax/Megarry, September 10, 1974.

48   "we are still working on funding": Gygax/Megarry, December 1, 1974.

48   "to partake in the activities": Greenwood mass-mailing November 13, 1974.

48   "fantasy trips through *Dungeons & Dragons*": Origins advertisement, *AHG* 11, no. 4 (1974): 31.

49   "Although we don't make much": Gygax/Arneson, November 24, 1974.

50   "Our lawyer said" and "What I really regretted": Gygax/Arneson, December 19, 1974.

50   "I do not wish to touch the Barker deal": Arneson/Gygax, December 31, 1974.

50   "Heritage is still our best customer": Gygax/Arneson, November 24, 1974.

51   "Once we get big enough": Gygax/Arneson, June 19, 1974.

51   "Said he would get back to me": Arneson/Gygax, December 31, 1974.

Part II

1975: Sage Street, Goodbye

55   "Had a very nasty blow": Gygax letter to Alan Lucien, February 6, 1975. See also "Donald Kaye Dies at 36," *Lake Geneva Regional News* (*LGRN*), February 6, 1975.

55   "Mrs. Kaye is very capable": Gygax/Lucien, February 6, 1975.

56   "*Chainmail* this week": Gygax/Arneson, February 12, 1975.

56   "hard at work": Arneson/Gygax, January 29, 1975.

56   "Keep plugging there, Dave": Gygax/Arneson, January 28, 1975.

58   "We will never allow TSR": Gygax/Megarry, March 6, 1975.

58   "Further to what I said": Gygax/Arneson, February 19, 1975.

58   "Even if MiniFigs carries your ships": Gygax/Arneson, March 3, 1975.

59   "I am certainly not in the most desirable" and "I am always ready, willing and able": Arneson letter to Tony Bath, February 7, 1975.

59 "is thoroughly sick of his job" and "No question that you wouldn't": Gygax/
    Arneson, March 3, 1975.

60 "save us about $300": Gygax/Arneson, March 14, 1975.

60 "provide Jim with from 100 to 250": Gygax/Arneson, March 3, 1975.

60 "Tell Carr that this will mean": Gygax/Arneson, March 3, 1975.

60 "TSR will absolutely dominate": Gygax/Arneson, March 14, 1975.

61 "much demand for D&D supplements": Gygax/Arneson, April 21, 1975.

61 "I have been occupied writing": Arneson, *Corner of the Table* August 5, 1975.

63 "*Panzerfaust* interviews TSR": *PZF* no. 69 (1975): 14–17.

63 "two-faced shaft-master": Gygax/Megarry, March 6, 1975.

63 "Lowry was once a nice guy": Gygax/Arneson, January 28, 1975.

63 "Dave Sutherland's a really excellent artist": Gygax letter to Bill Hoyt, June
    16, 1975.

64 salary of $80 per week: Gygax, "Who Am I?" *Space Gamer (SG)* no. 41
    (1981): 5.

65 "hell hole, which has no air conditioning": Greg Costikyan, "A Convention
    Dirge," *GIGO* no. 4 (1975): 26.

66 "the man who started it all": "The First National Wargaming Convention,"
    AHG 12 no. 3 (1975): 2.

66 He told the *Washington Post*: William Gildea, "Complex Sophisticated War
    Games Obsess Passionate Players," syndicated in *Anderson Indiana Herald*,
    August 10, 1975.

66 Howard Barasch of SPI was the unofficial scorekeeper: See "Sources and
    Acknowledgments" for citations of Barasch's industry tracking.

67 "Gygax is a kind of heroic figure": John Sherwood, "Lovers of War Games Let
    Nothing Bar Play," syndicated in *Newport News Daily Press*, July 28, 1975.

67 "no figure manufacturers were present": Arneson/Bath, August 8, 1975.

68 "D&D is too important": Mark Swanson, "Kyth Interstellar Bulletin," *Alarums
    & Excursions (A&E)* no. 1 (Los Angeles, 1975).

69 "role-playing": Rich Berg, "Shrapnel," *Moves* no. 23 (1975): 26.

69 "the big trend in wargaming today": Jim Creighton, "From Hussars to Hip-
    pogriffs," *St. Louis Post Dispatch*, August 31, 1975.

70   "Origins had a larger attendance": Gygax, "Out on a Limb," *SR* 2, no. 2 (1976): 14.

72   TSR Hobbies accepted a substantial investment: Exhibits read into Gygax testimony, 85-CV-907, January 29, 1986.

74   "Tim will also do some design work": *SR* 1, no. 5 (1975): 1.

74   "within the next three months": Arneson, *Corner of the Table*, August 5, 1975.

75   "We were very surprised": Brian Blume letter to Arneson, October 18, 1975.

76   "much of the mutual misunderstanding": Gygax/Arneson, October 21, 1975.

76   "We ask that we have permission" and "now the fourth largest": Gygax/Arneson, November 12, 1975.

77   "I would not recommend": Gygax/Megarry, December 29, 1975.

78   "The shop is going slowly": Gygax/Arneson, November 12, 1975.

78   "I hate to be pouty": Arneson/Gygax, November 18, 1975.

1976: Stab

79   "Williams is actually Broad St.": Gygax letter to *Gamelog* (formerly *GPGPN*) no. 22, April 19, 1976.

79   "My work here in Lake Geneva": Arneson to "Eleanor and Bob," February 2, 1976.

80   "It has been remodeled": Gygax, *Gamelog* no. 22, 1976.

80   credible circulation of around 1,500: Gygax/Phillies, January 13, 1976.

81   "The game *Dungeons & Dragons* and the title": David A. Lenon letter to Robert E. Ruppert, March 5, 1976.

82   "from the Arctic of Minnesota": Arneson, *Corner of the Table*, March 1976.

83   drove to nearby Racine for "fellowshipping": Arneson letter to Connie Samet, March 10, 1976.

86   "readying a small fantasy campaign": Gygax, *Gamelog* no. 22, 1976.

89   "a thing called *Dungeons & Dragons*": J. E. Pournelle, "Promises and a Potpourri," *Galaxy* 38, no.1 (1977): 119.

90   teeming throng of 2,500 persons: Lowry, "Line of Communications," *Campaign* (formerly *Panzerfaust*) no. 76 (1976): 37. See also *AHG* 13, no. 2 (1977): 2.

90   "Gygax and TSR will probably be admitted": Don Greenwood to George Phillies, August 18, 1976.

90 **"Paid attendance was in the vicinity"**: "GenCon IX Final Update," *DR* no. 3 (1977): 30.

90 **"he has created some excellent"**: "GenCon IX Address: Fritz Leiber," *Gamelog* no. 26 (1977): 4.

90 **"a mustached man of youthful middle years"**: Fritz Leiber, "Wargames—Fierce Battles Fought on Mapboards," *San Francisco Examiner*, September 5, 1976.

90 **principals of Games Workshop:** Ian Livingstone, "Gen Con IX," *Owl & Weasel* no. 18 (London: Games Workshop, 1976): 6.

91 **matter went to the courts:** Heritage Models, Inc. v. TSR Hobbies, Inc. and E. Gary Gygax, United States District Court, Northern District of Texas, 3-77-0495-G.

91 **"personal thanks to Dave Megarry"**: "Acknowledgments," *Judges Guild Journal*, Installment I (1976).

92 **"writing a complimentary commentary"**: "Tips from the Tower," *Judges Guild Journal* Installment K (1977).

92 **"somewhat similar to the intriguing fantasy booklets"**: Merle Rasmussen letter to Gygax, October 22, 1976.

93 **"concerned with shipping"**: Arneson letter to John and Richard Snider and Steve Rocheford, November 19, 1976.

93 **"The night life around Lake Geneva"**: Arneson letter to John Snider, October 7, 1976.

93 **"forlorn love life"**: Arneson letter to Steve Rocheford, September 20, 1976.

93 **"there is a chance that TSR will open"**: Arneson letter to Richard Snider, October 7, 1976.

94 **Most afternoons after lunch:** Arneson/John Arneson, November 17, 1976. See also Arneson testimony to the Wisconsin Labor and Industry Review Commission, March 24, 1977, 3.

94 **"a set of role playing rules for medieval Japan"**: Arneson/John Snider, October 7, 1976.

94 **"by special permission"**: TSR shareholder meeting minutes, November 3, 1976.

95 **Heated words were then exchanged:** Arneson/John Snider, Richard Snider, and Rocheford, November 19, 1976.

99 **"he turned livid"**: Gygax letter to Wisconsin Labor and Industry Review Commission, May 31, 1977.

99   **Arneson made his way:** Arneson/Gygax, November 19, 1976 (unsent).

100 **"I have no future plans":** Arneson/John Snider, Richard Snider, and Rocheford, November 19, 1976.

101 **"I will be starting a company here":** Arneson/John Snider, November 30, 1976.

1977: The Great War

103 **"TSR asks that you not go ahead":** Mike Carr letter to Arneson, January 5, 1977.

104 **"avoid any TSR copyright infringements":** Arneson/Carr, January 8, 1977 (misdated 1976).

104 **"a line of role-playing game booklet":** Arneson/John Snider, November 30, 1976.

104 **"Dave's weakness seems to be":** Mike Carr recommendation letter, December 7, 1976.

104 **"Have you been bad mouthing TSR":** Rob Kuntz letter to Arneson, January 21, 1977.

105 **"overcome a lot of bad P.R.":** Arneson letter to Ken Shepro, April 21, 1978.

106 **"it may seem":** Arneson to Duke Seifried, January 18, 1977 (misdated 1976).

106 **"as publisher and author TSR":** Arneson to Jim Oden, January 19, 1977 (misdated 1976).

108 **"Gary 'pulled me' into his office,":** Dave Sutherland to Arneson, (undated, early 1977).

108 **"By the end of the year":** Arneson/John Snider, April 20, 1977.

109 **"TSR Hobbies, Inc., may well have failed to fulfill":** Arneson to TSR Hobbies (undated, early April 1977).

110 **"the Blackmoor dungeon will probably remain":** Arneson/Oden, April 26, 1977.

111 **"Blackmoor by Judges Guild is fine with us":** Oden/Arneson, April 30, 1977.

111 **"I think we could do a good job for you":** Bill Owen letter to Arneson, April 18, 1977.

111 **"unpolished gem":** Dave Arneson, *First Fantasy Campaign* (Decatur, IL: Judges Guild, 1977): 1.

111 **Intent to sell seven shares:** Arneson/Megarry, March 24, 1977.

112 **"Origins of the Game":** Gygax, "Gary Gygax on *Dungeons & Dragons*," *DR* no. 7 (1977): 7.

113 **"more than welcome to submit":** Tim Kask letter to Arneson, June 22 (?) 1977.

113 **"I am at a loss":** Arneson/Kask, July 12, 1977.

113 **"Roots of *D&D*":** Arneson, "The Roots of *Dungeons & Dragons*," *Wargaming* no. 4 (1979): 47–48.

114 **none of the other panelists:** John T. Sapienza, "Alberich's Ring No. 8," *A&E* no. 26 (1977).

114 **"excommunicated from TSR":** Alex Murocmew, "Rant Ravings," *A&E* no. 27 (1977).

114 **"his original rules (which TSR edited to death)":** Paul Keyser, "A Submission from Nimolee," *Wild Hunt* (*WH*) no. 21 (1977).

115 **"a trial balloon":** Keyser, *WH* no. 21 (1977).

115 **"pave the way for greatly expanded":** Dave Arneson, *Dungeonmaster's Index* (St. Paul, MN: 1977), Foreword.

115 **"You thought you hated Kask":** Bill Seligman, "I Would Have Made a Great Platinum Dragon #10," *A&E* no. 25 (1977).

115 **"trash":** Murocmew, *A&E* no. 27 (1977).

115 **"If you see a fantasy game":** Seligman, *A&E* no. 25 (1977).

115 **"We will go after anyone":** Keyser, *WH* no. 21 (1977).

115 **"Overall, it appears as if Tim":** Murocmew, *A&E* no. 27 (1977).

116 **"Politically, the rapidly widening schism":** Bill Herdle, "From the Other End of the Circle," *A&E* no. 26 (1977).

116 **opened the fourth iteration of Origins:** Al Macintyre, "Origins '78 in Michigan—How the Site was Chosen," *Campaign* no. 83 (1978): 29. See also John Prados, "The Evolution of Origins," *Moves* no. 45 (1979): 7.

117 **"pretty well butchered by TSR":** John Snider/Arneson, July 23, 1977.

117 **"raise as big a fuss as you dare":** Arneson/John Snider, undated (August 10, 1977?).

117 **"my voluntary associate":** Kask, "Dragon Rumbles," *DR* no. 5 (1977): 3.

117 **Although Jaquet reported:** "RPGA Interview with 'Jake' Jaquet," *Polyhedron* no. 4 (1980): 7–8. See also *DR* no. 8 (1977).

117   **meeting with an "accident" in Lake Geneva:** Arneson/John Snider, undated (August 10, 1977?).

118   **"All close servants of the Egg":** Arneson, *First Fantasy Campaign*, 18.

119   **"It is clear to me":** Ed Simbalist to Arneson, September 26, 1977.

119   **"Arneson is reputed to have left TSR":** George Phillies, "Murdered Master Mage," *WH* no. 19 (1977).

119   **"Generally, they do not know":** Arneson/John Snider, undated (August 10, 1977?).

119   **"game mechanics, combat, and most":** Richard L. Snider, "The Making of Adventures in Fantasy (and Other Such Nonsense)," undated.

121   **Blume jotted down on a piece of paper:** Ken Shepro letter to Brian Blume, January 16, 1978.

122   **unable to travel:** Arneson letter to Duke Seifried, December 13, 1977.

122   **"October, minus six":** Oden/Arneson, February 22, 1978.

122   **Arneson would fume to Megarry:** Arneson/Megarry, March 15, 1978.

123   **TSR admitted it had "misappropriated":** "TSR Achieves Compromise in Legal Suit," *LGRN*, December 15, 1977.

123   **"'Basic' D&D was the first step":** Gygax, "View From the Telescope Wondering Which End is Which," *DR* no. 11 (1977): 5–6.

1978: Stolen Glory

125   **Arneson's lawyers sent a letter:** Shepro/Blume, January 16, 1978.

126   **"gives no credit to any":** Arneson/Shepro, February 8, 1978.

126   **"all new monsters are strictly":** Gygax, *Monster Manual* (Lake Geneva, MI: TSR, 1977): 4.

126   **"author Gary Gygax, in his":** Kask, "Editor's Library," *DR* no. 12 (1978): 22.

126   **"What a bunch of clods":** Arneson/Megarry, March 15, 1978.

127   **"fancy Chicago lawyers":** Arneson/Oden, January 9, 1978.

127   **"I would not really care to see":** Oden/Arneson, February 22, 1978.

127   **"apparently there is some misunderstanding":** Tom Shaw to Arneson, January 23, 1978.

128   **"All the stuff I was planning":** Arneson/Oden, February 28, 1978.

129   **"without D&D they would not exist":** Arneson/Shepro, April 21, 1978.

130 **"So it is no longer *Dungeons & Dragons*":** Ken St. Andre, *Tunnels & Trolls* (Phoenix, AZ: Cosmic Circle, 1975): 4.

131 **"This item," Arneson posited, "clearly consists":** Arneson letter to TSR, June 28, 1978.

131 **"Simply put," Beard responded:** John Beard letter to Arneson, July 6, 1978.

132 **"16 young, imaginative employees":** David Autry, "Childish Fantasies Booming Business," *Racine Journal Times*, March 19, 1978.

132 **"buy the downtown bowling alley":** Arneson/Megarry, March 15, 1978.

134 **"by Dave Arneson, edited by Gary Gygax":** P. E .I. Bonewits, *Authentic Thaumaturgy* (Albany, CA: Chaosium, 1978): 6.

134 **"the 'Fantasy Supplement' to *Chainmail*":** Gygax, "Sorceror's Scroll," *DR* no. 16 (1978).

134 **"GenCon is what got TSR off and running":** Greenwood, "Economics of Origins," *Campaign* no. 83 (1978): 28.

134 **"those that have communicated their desires":** Gygax, letter to *Campaign* no. 86 (1978): 43.

135 **"a grossly fat and thoroughly despicable":** Gygax, *Steading of the Hill Giant Chief* (G1) (Lake Geneva, WI: TSR, 1978): 2.

136 **"I was informed that traditionally all awards":** Arneson, "An Open Letter to Metro Detroit Gamers," *Campaign* no. 89 (1978): 41.

136 **"We do not agree with Mr. Arneson":** Greenwood letter to Arneson and Metro Detroit Gamers, September 14, 1978.

137 **"In cases of doubt as to who designed":** John Mansfield letter to Arneson and Metro Detroit Gamers, September 26, 1978.

138 **"we're expecting between 4,000 and 6,000":** Autry, *Racine Journal Times*, March 19, 1978.

138 **"we figure that we lost some 500":** Kask, "Dragon Rumbles," *DR* no. 19 (1978): 2.

138 **"some nasty people in Lake Geneva":** Gygax, "MDG Shows Origins (and GenCon) How to Run a Convention," *DR* no. 19 (1978): 2.

138 **"Authoring these works means":** Gygax, *Players Handbook* (Lake Geneva, WI: TSR, 1978): 5.

138 **"The manner in which persons":** Howard Mahler, "Babyl-On #19," *A&E* no. 46 (1979).

139   **Nine-thirty Sunday night:** David A. Feldt, "Hobby/Industry News," *Ann Arbor Wargamer* no. 20 (1978).

139   **"Grand Opening Week Celebration":** *DR* no. 16 (1978), inside back cover.

139   **"Our new building is quite large":** Gygax, "TSR News," *Campaign* no. 89 (1978): 38.

140   **"exercise his right as a shareholder":** J. Michael Hirsch letter to Brian Blume, October 11, 1978.

142   **"I cannot make a unilateral decision":** Gygax/Hoyt, March 18, 1978.

143   **Blog the Cro-Magnon:** unpublished Arneson holograph.

144   **"had a major role in the creation":** Howard Thompson, "An Interview with Dave Arneson," *SG* no. 21 (Austin: Metagaming, 1979): 5–7.

145   **"began with only the basic monsters":** Arneson, *First Fantasy Campaign*, 2.

Part III

1979: Treasure in the Steam Tunnels

153   **"Dave Arneson is suing TSR":** Gigi D'Arn [alias], "A Letter from Gigi," *Different Worlds (DW)* no. 2 (1979): 36. Note that the figure $300,000 likely derives from a misreading of the complaint, which demands both $50,000 in pecuniary damages and $50,000 in punitive damages from the "Defendants and each of them," where three defendants are named: TSR Hobbies, the Tactical Studies Rules partnership, and Gary Gygax. That would not, however, entail that each of those three defendants had to individually pay $50,000 twice to Arneson (adding up to $300,000), but instead that the requested $100,000 come from whichever of those three defendants is in a position to pay it. See the language in the complaint that similarly demands the 5 percent royalty on *D&D* from the "Defendants and each of them," which does not mean that Arneson sought a 15 percent royalty, with 5 percent of that paid personally by Gygax.

153   **a new long-form piece:** Gygax, "*Dungeons & Dragons*: What It Is and Where It Is Going", *DR* no. 22 (1979): 29–30.

153   **"a method to get you":** Rich Berg, "Briefings," *Strategy & Tactics (S&T)* no. 71 (1978): 20.

154   **"Dave Arneson apparently tore":** D'Arn, *DW* no. 2 (1979).

154   **"privately financed":** Gigi D'Arn, "A Letter from Gigi," *DW* no. 5 (1979): 37.

154   **Brian Blume . . . signed a stock option:** Robert G. Dowling letter to *WI* no. 42 (1983): 1. See also *TSR, Inc. v. Niebling*, No. 87–0393, Court of Appeals Wisconsin, District Two, April 12, 1988, decision.

155 **buy a fourteen-room stately manse:** "Games of Fantasy Spell Success for Gygax Family," *Clinton Topper*, 1980.

155 **submitted a number of articles:** Lawrence Schick, "Choir Practice at the First Church," *DR* no. 24 (1979): 34. See also Gygax, *DR* no. 24 (1979): 19.

156 **"to handle combat at first":** Arneson, "My Life and Role-Playing," *DW* no. 3 (1979): 6–8.

157 **"Following *Chainmail's* advice":** Gygax, "Sorceror's Scroll," *DR* no. 26 (1979): 29.

157 **A ruling from the United States District Court:** Judgment of Edward J. Devitt, Civ. No. 4-79-109, July 25, 1979.

158 **"burgeoning subculture":** Beth Ann Krier, "Fantasy Life in a Game Without End," *Los Angeles Times*, July 11, 1979.

158 **"appallingly addictive":** Jon Freeman, *The Winner's Guide to Board Games* (Chicago: Playboy Press, 1979), 280–281.

158 **appointed Gygax its president:** Gygax letter to Steve Marsh, August 8, 1979.

158 **"The corporation employs":** "White Dwarf Interviews Gary Gygax," *White Dwarf (WD)* no. 14 (1979): 23.

159 **competing title like *Chivalry & Sorcery*:** Ed Simbalist letter to Arneson, February 1, 1978. See also "Interview with Gary Gygax," *Gryphon* no. 1 (1980): 18.

159 **double the sales of:** Dave Hargrave, "New Arduin Chronicles #6," *A&E* no. 51 (1979), gives *Runequest* figures; internal GDW figures show *Traveller* sales of around 2,000 copies per quarter.

159 **the release of 44,000 copies:** Rose Estes, "GenCon XII," *Model Retailer*, November 1979, 52.

161 **"slow, fat, clumsy, and placid":** Gygax, *Village of Hommlet* (T1) (Lake Geneva, WI: TSR, 1979): 4.

161 **"Arneson was handing out":** Dale M. Staley, "Ironbridge Chronicles," *A&E* no. 54 (1980).

162 **"What boy?":** Estes, "GenCon XII."

162 **Newspapers for Egbert incident:** All are identified by name and day published. The few left unattributed either cite headlines alone, or statements syndicated by the AP, UPI, Gannett and Knight Ridder services.

167 **"detective hired by the parents":** Tim Kask, "Dragon Rumbles," *DR* no. 30 (1979): 1.

167   **"was a relatively obscure pastime"**: "Dungeons-Dragons Grows in Popularity," *Green Bay Press Gazette*, September 30, 1979.

167   **"important gains in distribution"**: Gygax/Marsh, September 18, 1979.

168   **"Isn't it true that this is really"**: Neesa Sweet, "Dungeons & Dragons," *Fantastic Films*, September 1980: 59.

168   **"Predictably, he didn't mention"**: Gigi D'Arn, "A Letter from Gigi," *DW* no. 6 (1979): 39.

169   **"It's getting pretty hard to guess"**: "Interview with Gary Gygax," *Gryphon* no. 1 (1980): 17.

169   **"I would also to like to interview"**: Rudy Kraft letter to Arneson, November 8, 1979.

171   **"What happened to Dave Arneson?"**: David P. Joiner, "Shadowcrafter of Arestle #2," *A&E* no. 51 (1979).

171   **"Rumors had been circulating"**: "News and Plugs," *SG* no. 25 (1979): 19.

171   **"One night Duke was complaining"**: Gigi D'Arn, "A Letter from Gigi," *DW* no. 5 (1979): 36.

172   **The separation of TSR from Games Workshop:** Don Turnbull, "Apologies—and Arguments," *DR* no. 55 (1981): 10.

1980: The Spotlight

175   **"Ever since *D&D*"**: Barbara Kleban Mills, "If Students' Tails Are Dragon and Their Minds in the Dungeon Lately, Blame Gamesman Gary Gygax," *People* January 14, 1980, 64–65.

176   **"Without a doubt"**: Barasch, "Gossip," *S&T* no. 79 (1980): 35.

176   **"TSR Hobbies will emerge"**: Thompson, "Metagaming Report," *SG* no. 27 (1980): 4.

176   **"Had he and co-designer Richard"**: Ronald Pehr, "Featured Review: *Adventures in Fantasy*," *SG* no. 30 (1980): 23.

176   **"hopelessly unplayable"**: Jon Pickens, "The Castlemere Gazette," *A&E* no. 60 (1980).

176   **"a real turkey"**: Sean Summers, "Tales from the Year of the Horse," *A&E* no. 60 (1980).

176   **"The price is high"**: Eric Goldberg, "Games," *Ares* no. 4 (New York: SPI, 1980): 36. Goldberg does add that if "some of the burdensome rules" are streamlined, then, "when played, the game is a lot of fun."

177   **"hatchet job"**: Dennis P. O'Leary letter to *SG* no. 32 (1980): 30.

177   **ranked second-to-last overall:** "Errata: 1980 Game Survey" *SG* no. 39 (1981): 39.

177   **"Arneson is plugging away"**: Gigi D'Arn, "A Letter from Gigi," *DW* no. 8 (1980): 47.

177   **TSR announced in the pages:** Advertisement, *White Dwarf* no. 18 (1980): 4.

177   **"the British Empire Strikes Back"**: Advertisement, *White Dwarf* no. 20 (1980): 35.

178   **"The game will have a labyrinth-type"**: *Random Events* 1, no. 3 (1980): 9–10.

178   **Schick would fly to Nassau:** *Random Events* 1, no. 1 (1980): 2.

178   **a film based on D&D was in the works:** Syndicated in "Dick Clark Joins Film World," *Asbury Park Press*, June 6, 1980.

180   **led the FBI to the Hotel Clair:** Stan Carter, "It's Just a Game, but Try Telling That to the FBI," *Omaha Sun*, October 30, 1980.

180   **news from Wasatch Middle School:** David Hampshire, "Wasatch Kids Are Playing *Dungeons and Dragons* and More Than Monsters Are Breathing Fire," *The Newspaper*, April 17, 1980.

181   **"We finished out the cycle"**: "Dungeons & Dragons, Other Disputes: Proper Issues for State School Board?" *The Newspaper*, July 3, 1980.

181   **"is very definitely antireligious"**: Molly Ivins, "Mormons Halt the Devil's Game," syndicated in *Press Democrat*, May 4, 1980.

181   **Satanic Panic:** See Joseph P. Laycock, *Dangerous Games: What the Moral Panic over Role-Playing Games Says about Play, Religion, and Imagined Worlds* (Oakland: University of California Press, 2015).

181   **"They should raise a foundation"**: Moira Johnston, "It's Only a Game—Or is It?" *New West*, August 25, 1980.

182   **"I've weighed it very heavily"**: Diane Gentile and Robert France, "Detective Won't Tell about Egbert," *Journal Herald*, August 18, 1980.

182   **"the mystery of his whereabouts"**: UPI, "Teen Computer Genius Apparently Shoots Self," *Indiana polis Star*, August 12, 1980.

182   **"at the urging of a flamboyant private detective"**: William Robbins, "A Brilliant Student's Troubled Life and Early Death," *New York Times*, August 25, 1980.

183   **a curt announcement:** Jake Jaquet, "Dragon Rumbles," *DR* no. 37 (1980): 2.

183   **proposal to form an association:** Jake Jaquet, "Proposal to Form an Association for D&D and AD&D Players," (undated).

184   **"By comparison . . . the Black Hole of Calcutta":** *Random Events* 1, no. 3 (1980): 7.

184   **"impassioned plea to the historical":** Terry Alan Baney, "Mr. Smith Goes to Chester," *Campaign* no. 99 (1980): 12.

185   **"autographed copies would be collectors' items":** Jeff Seiken, "A Game Buyers' Paradise," *Campaign* no. 99 (1980): 15.

186   **"a little known territory":** Gygax, *World of Greyhawk* (Lake Geneva, WI: TSR, 1980): 9.

186   **"Special thanks are also given to Chaosium":** James M. Ward with Robert J. Kuntz, *Deities & Demigods* (second printing, Lake Geneva, WI: TSR, 1980): 4.

187   **"the two shows are highly competitive":** Ted Rakstis, "Adventure Gamers Invade GenCon," *Playthings* November 1980: 46.

187   **A few pictures from the day:** *Random Events* 1, no. 6 (1980): 8–9.

187   **"Is *Dungeons & Dragons* the Hula-Hoop":** Geoffrey Smith, "Dungeons and Dollars," *Forbes*, September 15, 1980: 137.

189   **"in charge of the people who create":** *Random Events* 1, no. 5 (1980): 2.

189   **"used to work for Doug":** *Random Events* 1, no. 8 (1980).

190   **"I was stricken with a strange illness":** Gygax/Marsh, September 30, 1980.

190   **"to postpone full recovery":** Gygax/Marsh, October 29, 1980.

190   **Gary pretending to cut the cake:** *Random Events* 1, no. 7 (1980).

192   **"I expected my mother to live":** Gygax/Marsh, November 24, 1980.

192   **"Ever sat for an hour":** Arneson letter to Greg Stafford, November 8, 1980 (misdated).

193   **"Dave Arneson has been disappointed":** Barasch, "Gossip," *S&T* no. 84 (1981): 54.

193   **"if authors A and B":** *Nimmer on Copyright, supra* note 57, § 6.07.

194   **Arneson's legal team held up:** Arneson legal team brief "What Is the Law Regarding the Rights of a Co-Author of Intellectual Property" (undated), 8. See also "Donna v. Dodd, Mead & Co.," 374 F. Supp. 429 (S.D.N.Y f974).

194   **"Dave Arneson didn't write a word":** Johnston, *New West*, August 25, 1980: 40.

196   **"There is nothing of any consequence":** Freeman deposition, JF-6.

196   **"I would also appreciate":** Stephen F. Peters letter to Michael Hirsch, November 13, 1980.

197   "a pickup of the three": Gygax, *Polyhedron* no. 2 (1981): 6.

197   "co-write (or at worst, ghost write)": Gygax/Marsh, December 18, 1980.

197   "He's the Top Dungeon Master": *DR.* no 43 (1980): 14.

197   "We live in a turbulent time": Frank Mentzer memo to Gygax, December 23, 1980.

1981: Identity Crisis

199   "an elaborate B-grade movie set": Barasch, "Gossip," *S&T* no. 85 (1981): 16.

200   "The terms of the settlement": "Press Release," *Pegasus* no. 1 (Decatur: Judges Guild, 1981): 78.

200   the terms were far more modest: TSR 1981 Financial audit, "Commitments," 10. See also "Arneson vs. TSR," District Court of Minnesota, Fourth Division, Civil No. 4-84-1180.

200   "I bet that if you put five zeroes": Gigi D'Arn, "A Letter from Gigi," *DW* no. 12 (1981): 46.

201   "At the time, they had a lot more": "An Interview with Dave Arneson," *Pegasus* no. 1 (1981): 5.

202   "not much magical ink": Gygax, "Sorceror's Scroll," *DR* no. 55 (1981): 17.

202   "it is the same thing that struck": Gygax/Marsh, June 12, 1981.

202   "I probably will not get back": Gygax/Marsh, June 30, 1981.

202   "In 1976 came an identity crisis": Gygax, "Who Am I?" *SG* no. 41 (1981): 5.

204   "fallacy exemplified by another 'so-called'": Arneson mass-mailing, June 8, 1981.

205   "knocked off quite a few": Gygax/Marsh June 12, 1981.

205   the time when Erol Otus: *Twenty Years of TSR* (TSR: 1995): 19.

206   the prolific artist Otus departed: *Random Events*, September 1981.

206   Furious, Schick resigned, and there was talk of legal action: "Schick v. TSR," United States District Court for the District of Connecticut, Civil no. H-84–975.

206   "TSR claims that it cares": Kevin Hendryx resignation letter, August 28, 1981.

207   "Rumor says that TSR has fired": D'Arn, "A Letter from Gigi," *DW* no. 12 (1981): 46.

208   "direct violation of God's Holy Word": Transcript of James R. Cotter, "Dungeons & Dragons Lecture," September 16, 1980, distributed by Christian Life Ministries.

209   **believed Sacramento to be home:** Ronald B. Taylor, "Fight over Game: Play or Worship of Devil?" *Los Angeles Times*, June 24, 1981.

209   **"This game teaches witchcraft":** UPI, "'Dungeons and Dragons' Loses to Fundamentalists," *Honolulu Advertiser*, June 13, 1981.

210   **"What are they going to do there":** D'Arn, "A Letter from Gigi," *DW* no. 14 (1981): 44.

210   **"Pacific Origins rejected our offer":** Tom Shaw letter to *Campaign* no. 106 (1981): 42.

210   **"the organizers stressed D&D":** Sean Summers, "Sacrificial Sentiments," *A&E* no. 74 (1981).

211   **a unified "Origins Award":** Bill Somers, "The Origins Awards: Going Through Some Changes," *Adventure Gaming* 1, no. 2 (1981): 18.

212   **Gary Gygax was voted:** "Infiltrator's Report," *AHG* 18, no. 2 (1981): 47.

212   **"GenCon East was more of an Origins":** "Origins Past and Present," *AHG* 18, no. 3 (1981): 41.

212   **"in a sort of legal limbo":** Turnbull, "Apologies—and Arguments," *DR* no. 55 (1981): 10.

213   **"At GenCon XIV":** Gygax, "Sorceror's Scroll," *DR* no. 55 (1981): 17.

213   **"anyone designing material":** Gygax memo to Dave Sutherland, August 24, 1981.

214   **TSR reached a preliminary agreement:** "Another Industrial Loss," *LGRN*, June 11, 1981.

214   **TSR had a better offer:** "TSR Plans $3 Million Project," *LGRN*, July 7, 1981.

214   **"we have made arrangements":** Gygax/Marsh, July 27, 1981.

214   **"the largest industrial expansion":** "TSR to Break Ground on $3.5 Million Project," *LGRN*, November 19, 1981.

215   **Kevin Blume in October could share:** Kevin Blume, "Inner Sanctum: Part Two," *Random Events*, October 15, 1981: 1.

215   **"because we did not believe":** Gygax, "Inner Sanctum," *Random Events*, September 1981.

215   **"we didn't want to end up":** "RPGA Interview with E. Gary Gygax," *Polyhedron* no. 2 (1981): 5.

215   **"the game to which":** Dick Lochte, "Book Notes," *Los Angeles Times*, August 16, 1981.

215   **"Neither Egbert's parents":** Kelly Scott, "A Cliché at Every Twist and Turn," *St. Petersburg Times*, September 27, 1981.

216   **product review board vetted:** Gordon Gile, TSR memo, "Product Review Board Report of September 16, 1981 Meeting."

217   **"we will be doing well":** Gygax memo to Brian Blume, et al., May 27, 1980.

219   **"pervasive occultic overtones":** Ronald M. Enroth, "Fantasy Games: Is There an Occult Connection?" *Eternity*, December 1981, 36.

219   **"an elite group":** Bradford W. Ketchum Jr. letter to Gygax, November 10, 1981. Circulated in *Random Events*, December 15, 1981.

220   **"Milton Bradley is probably the largest":** Larry Engel, "Game Producer Sees Treasure on Dungeons & Dragons Road," *Milwaukee Sentinel*, November 6, 1981.

221   **Black Wednesday:** Michael Moore, "Catching Up," *S&T* no. 91 (1983): 16.

222   **"Is Heritage bankrupt?":** D'Arn, "A Letter from Gigi," *DW* no. 15 (1981): 47. See also D'Arn, *DW* no. 16, 45.

1982: Extravagance

223   **The recovery of the *Lucius Newberry*:** "TSR to Raise the City of Lake Geneva," *Random Events*, October 15, 1981: 3.

223   **Scry ahead:** Brian Pitzer, "Lucius Newberry Salvaged by TSR Hobbies," *Random Events*, October 20, 1982: 3. See also "Newberry Rescued," *LGRN*, September, 30 1982.

223   **Smithsonian:** "Museum Plans Feb. 24 Program on Newberry," *LGRN*, February 14, 1985.

223   **US Olympic Bobsled Team:** "TSR Sponsors US Bobsledder," *LGRN*, January 28, 1982.

224   **"TSR feels *Dungeons & Dragons*":** *Game Designers Guild Newsletter* no. 10 (1982): 4.

224   **"if present trends continue":** Helen Chase, "TSR: 'No Limit to Imagination,'" *Janesville Gazette*, February 11, 1982.

224   **"We figure that the game":** Stewart Alsop II, "TSR Hobbies Mixes Fact and Fantasy," *Inc.*, February 1, 1982.

225   **Greenfield Needlewomen:** Martens testimony, 85-CV-907, November 15, 1985.

225   **TSR acquired *Amazing Stories*:** George H. Scithers, "The Observatory," *Amazing*, November 1982: 162.

225   **"there are four 'Endless Quest' paperback":** Gygax/Marsh, March 22, 1982.

226   **One of those firms . . . was SPI:** Barasch, *Insider* no. 1–2 (1982).

226   **"TSR found that the debts":** Michael Moore, "Catching Up," *S&T* no. 91 (1983): 16. See Also Jaquet, "Dragon Rumbles," *DR* no. 64 (1982): 2.

227   **created an opening for Eric Dott:** Barasch, *Insider* no. 1 (1982).

227   **"initially there was support":** Richard Snider letter to Arneson, January 18, 1982.

229   **"Do you think I wish to be President?":** Gygax/Mentzer, May 13, 1982.

230   **"Do give Brian the benefit":** Gygax/Marsh, March 22, 1982.

230   **"a documentable breach of promise":** Mentzer/Gygax, May 12 (misdated 15), 1982.

230   **a firm called IIIC:** Kathy Yih, "Introducing IIIC," *Random Events*, January 1982.

230   **Dave Sutherland entered a management program:** "TSR People in Management Programs," *Random Events*, February 1982.

231   **"snow shark":** "The Chatterbox," *LGRN*, January 21, 1982.

231   **"Philosophy & Creed":** *Random Events*, August 16, 1982.

231   **"Please don't ask me when!":** Gygax, "Everything you never knew about spell books," *DR* no. 62 (1982): 14.

231   **"If you have any respect for Conan":** Gygax, "A Couple of Fantastic Flops," *DR* no. 63 (1982): 72.

232   **"sales of the *D&D* Basic Set are decreasing":** Gygax to Will Niebling, July 12, 1982.

233   **John Torell claimed:** Christian Life Ministries, "Answers to Common Questions about Dungeons and Dragons," November 1981, 7.

234   **"we MUST redesign all game covers":** Mentzer letter to Duke Seifried, May 5, 1982.

234   **Joyce Brothers:** Joyce Brothers, "Games . . . *Dungeons & Dragons* Role-Playing Game and Game Play" (1982?).

234   **"a new title":** TSR RPR03 Final Report, draft September 27, 1982.

234   **"designed to create a wholesome":** Seifried to TSR staff, June 7, 1982.

235   **outside counsel send a blunt demand:** John Beard letter to Shawn Carroll, (undated, responding to letter of January 30) 1982. See *DW* no. 18–20, Gigi D'Arn for hobby community confusion about GenCon East.

235 **"It begins to look as if TSR":** Rick Loomis, *Wargamer's Information* (*WI*) no. 39 (1982): 1.

236 **"immediately correct the misstatements":** Letter from Robert J. Johannes, *WI* no. 40 (1982): 4.

236 **"a facile and legally dubious maneuver":** *Campaign* no. 111 (1982): 44.

236 **"SPI died for our sins":** D'Arn, "A Letter from Gigi," *DW* no. 24 (1982): 46.

236 **"Declaring themselves the former SPI":** Barasch, *Insider* no. 2.

237 **Clancy, who would use the miniature rules:** "Game News," *Game News* no. 4 (1985): 3.

237 **"these things take time":** D'Arn, "A Letter from Gigi," *DW* no. 23 (1982): 54.

237 **TSR dispatched Joyce Brothers:** Duke Seifried, "Special First Time Gamers and Visitors Program for the Gen Con Show," *Random Events*, August 16, 1982: 9.

237 **Kevin Blume Snoopy Award:** "The Greatest Game Convention in the Land," *Random Events*, September 15, 1982: 5.

237 **"The design credit for *Star Frontiers*":** D'Arn, "A Letter from Gigi," *DW* no. 25 (1982): 46.

238 **"It must really please him":** *Random Events*, September 15, 1982: 5.

238 **"The lines are drawn":** "Guest Editorial," *DR* no. 65 (1982): 6.

238 **"If you seriously believe":** "Open Letter to Rick Loomis," *DR* no. 66 (1982): 71.

239 **"I can hardly believe it":** Rick Loomis, *WI* no. 40 (1982): 1.

239 **"As a matter of public relations":** John T. Sapienza, "The Golden Dragon 47," *A&E* no. 88 (1982).

240 **"at a low ebb right now":** Gygax/Marsh, August 12, 1982.

240 **"almost at thirty head of horses":** Gygax/Marsh, August 18, 1982.

240 **"will be vacant, pending":** "Interview with Steve Witt," *Random Events*, June 15, 1982.

240 **"we intend to construct a large museum-like":** Gygax/Marsh, August 12, 1981.

240 **Gygax had sent a memo:** Gygax memo to Mike Carr, December 29, 1981.

242 **"at that time it was decided":** Jack Sloan memo to Carr, January 13, 1982.

242 **"failing to follow chain of command":** Kevin Blume to himself, undated (refers to May 14, 1982).

242 **"I wonder whose head will roll"**: D'Arn, "A Letter from Gigi," *DW* no. 23 (1982): 54.

243 **"inadequately staffed to do research"**: John Ricketts to Seifried, July 27, 1982.

243 **Two employees working under the Sloans**: names withheld, September 7, 1982.

244 **"Can the company stand another week"**: Bryce Knorr to Seifried, September 7, 1982.

244 **Jake Jaquet resigned**: "Scanner," *SG* no. 57 (1982): 40. See also *Wall Street Journal*, January 7, 1983, 19.

244 **TSR held its 1982 Founders Day**: "Friary for Founders Day Fete," *Random Events*, October 20, 1982.

245 **"has been a side-kick of E. Gary"**: Barasch, *Insider*, no. 4 (1982).

245 **Blume presented Niebling with an agreement**: Barasch, *Insider*, no. 9 (1983).

245 **"the option was not valid"**: Robert G. Dowling (attorney for Niebling), *WI* no. 42 (1983): 1.

246 **three days with James Goldman**: Gygax/Marsh, September 14, 1982.

246 **"resolve to maintain as much control"**: Gygax, "A Couple of Fantastic Flops."

246 **"I remember reading about"**: "'Bosom Buddies' Star Tom Hanks Moves from Comic to Tragic Role," *Detroit Free Press*, December 27, 1982.

246 **"Most of you are not aware"**: Gygax, "Sorceror's Scroll," *DR* no. 65 (1982): 10.

247 **"cash flow problem"**: Ann Huck, "Cash Flow," *Random Events*, December 15, 1982, 10.

247 **"I was the best there was"**: Heywood Klein, "After Success of Dungeons & Dragons, TSR Fights Poor Management, Uneven Growth," *Wall Street Journal*, November 25, 1983: 15.

Part IV

1983: Splitting the Party
251 **"sales will continue to almost double"**: Paul B. Carroll, "Dungeons and Dragons Game Propels Firm to Success, but Growing Pains Lie Ahead," *Wall Street Journal*, January 7, 1983: 19.

252 *Trivial Pursuit* **would soon flood**: Andrea Pawlyna, "Toys for Grown-Ups Are Popular, Too" syndicated in *The Annistar Star*, December 22, 1983.

252 **"Who invented Dungeons & Dragons?"**: Susan Buchsbaum, "TSR Profile," *Inc.*, December 1, 1984.

252   "a small wooden catapult": "The HIA Show," Howard Barasch, *Insider* no. 5 (1983).

252   "be exhibiting in a newly design booth": Eileen Lucas, "The New Year's Trade Show Season," *Random Events*, January 19, 1983: 1.

253   "the Association's convention coordinators": Jim Johnson, "HIA Convention: Hard Work But Worth It," *Random Events*, March 1983: 2.

253   a $3.5 billion market at the time: "Strong Showing for Games at HIA Show," *GamePlay* no. 2 (1983): 30.

253   "mostly designed by Steve Lortz,": D'Arn, "Gossip," *DW* no. 28 (1983): 54.

253   Kevin Blume had flown down to Dallas: John Rankin, "Metal," *SG* no. 60 (1983): 34.

254   "described himself as a 'cold fish'": Rankin, "Metal," *SG* no. 63 (1983): 12.

254   working with the American Management Association: Joe Slezak and Doug Blume, "Organizational Development and Training Update," *Random Events*, April 1983: 7.

255   Thompson recommended that Judi Witt: Judi Witt letter to Richard Koenings, November 30, 1984.

255   investments in mainstream media: TSR internal "Direct Line," May 2, 1983.

255   "between *Star Wars* and *E.T.*": Paul Cockburn "GamesFair '83," *Imagine* no. 2 (1984): 12.

255   media observers had already begun signaling: Dave Bianculli, "Television," *Acron Beacon*, April 21 1983: B9.

256   "sat in the fabled Polo Lounge": Gygax, "Sorceror's Scroll," *Dragon* no. 74 (1983): 6.

256   "this month TSR will complete": "TSR Hobbies' Expansion Among Fastest in Country," *LGRN*, February 3, 1983: 4.

256   "If TSR needs money": "Direct Line," May 9, 1983.

257   "he's approached almost daily": "Game maker living out his fantasy," *Green Bay Press Gazette*, April 5, 1983.

257   rebound failed to manifest by April: "Notes taken by Merle M. Rasmussen during [TSR] Games Division Meeting conducted by John Ricketts on June 27, 1983, 9:30 a.m.," 4.

259   divided the company in four: "TSR Reorganizes," *LGRN*, June 30, 1983: 1.

260   The plan went into effect: "Notes taken by Rasmussen," June 27, 1983: 1.

261   **"More or less":** "TSR Hobbies Reorganizes," *SG* no. 65 (1983): 40.

261   **"Gygax had deserted the battlefield":** Howard Barasch, *Insider* no. 7 (1983).

262   **"I guess I'll never have a mansion":** Loomis, *WI* no. 40 (1982): 4.

262   **"Estate is c. 23 acres":** Gygax, *WI* no. 41 (1983): 1.

262   **"It is unfortunate":** Loomis, *WI* no. 41 (1983): 1.

262   **"it does not seem feasible":** Gygax letter to TSR board, June 27, 1983.

262   **"Thank you for giving me":** "Notes taken by Rasmussen," June 27, 1983: 1.

263   **bank insisted on a 30 percent staff reduction:** Rasmussen meeting notes, undated (July 1983?).

263   **the much-storied "Turtles":** Curtis Faith, *Way of the Turtle* (2007).

263   **in July they sold treasury stock:** TSR, Inc. v. Niebling, no. 87–0393, Court of Appeals Wisconsin, District Two, April 12, 1988, decision.

264   **Metro Detroit Gamers reported:** Barasch, "Origins," *Insider* no. 8 (1983).

264   **"Charles Roberts received a plaque":** John T. Sapienza, "Golden Dragon 54," *A&E* no. 98 (1983).

264   **"faint amusement":** Charles Roberts, *Silver Jubilee* (1983): 6.

265   **"people would walk by an empty room":** Matthew J. Costello, "Featured Review: *Powers & Perils*," *Fantasy Gamer* no. 6 (1984): 24.

265   **Kevin "was at Origins":** Sapienza, *A&E* no. 98.

266   **projected annual rent:** "Estimated Expense Analysis for 1984 Budget," DDEC internal document, under "Calif. Manse" expenditures.

266   **"Some of the most beautiful women":** Steven J. Engelbert, "Gary Gygax," *The Gamer*, March/April 1992: 29.

266   **"Who was that crazy fellow":** Barasch, *Insider* no. 8 (1983).

267   **Beebe was projected to spend 75 percent:** John Beebe letter to Gygax, September 7, 1983.

267   **"a production such as the Saturday Morning":** Dave Dimery letter to Gygax, October 6, 1983.

268   **it had a 26 share Nielsen rating:** DDEC monthly meeting minutes, September 29, 1983.

268   **"some of the adventures":** Barasch, *Insider* no. 9 (1983).

268   **CBS insisted that Marvel:** DDEC monthly meeting minutes, October 28, 1983.

268   **TSR was contacted by Universal:** Roger Moore, "Now That It's Over," *Polyhedron* no. 20 (1984): 27. See also George H. Scithers, "The Observatory," *Amazing*, January 1985: 115.

269   **TSR relied heavily on its business consultant:** 85-CV-907 testimony by Wesley Sommer (November 15, 1985; June 20, 1986).

269   **"The addition of the new":** "TSR Names Directors," *LGRN*, January 19, 1984: 5.

269   **"the eccentric new ventures":** *Wall Street Journal*, November 25, 1983: 15.

270   **"I propose you get 80%":** Gygax/Mentzer, November 8, 1983.

270   **"to begin this immense project":** Gygax/Mentzer, November 29, 1983.

1984: Cursed

273   **"Part of my job description":** Mentzer letter to Mike Cook, January 24, 1984.

273   **"please let me know if the system":** Gygax/Mentzer, February 17, 1984.

274   *The Insider* **reported:** Barasch, *Insider* no. 11 (1984).

275   **"a day that will live in infamy":** *Twenty Years of TSR* (Lake Geneva, WI: TSR, 1995): 9.

275   **"a planned move":** "TSR Reduces Work Force," *LGRN*, April 12, 1984.

275   **Gygax looked slender:** Paul Cockburn, "Gamesfair '84," *Imagine* no. 15 (1984): 3.

276   **spend most of the summer:** Gygax/Marsh, October 11, 1984.

276   **Patricia Pulling filed at $10M suit:** "Around the Region," *Washington Post*, June 16, 1984: B2.

276   **her failed $1M lawsuit:** Eve Zibart, "Judge Rejects Suit Typing Suicide to Fantasy Game," *Washington Post*, October 27, 1983: B7. Also See "Suit Filed in Suicide over Game," *Fort Lauderdale News*, August 11, 1983: 3A.

276   **Bothered About Dungeons & Dragons:** "Parents of Teenage Suicide Victims Battle Dungeons & Dragons," *Clarion Ledger*, October 15, 1985.

276   **"news reports of murders, suicides":** *Sunday Morning*, CBS, June 17, 1984 (from transcript).

277   **"It would appear":** James Huber letter to Richard Koenings, June 26, 1984.

278   **"struggled for survival":** Kevin Blume to all TSR employees, July 31, 1984.

278   **Blume hired Willard Martens:** "Appointment to Martens," *LGRN*, July 12, 1984.

279   "It's ridiculous": "TSR and GAMA Are Back Together Again" *DR* no. 85
       (1984): 90.

279   **One long-time attendee:** Dave Nalle, "Offerings to the Lord of 1000 Blades,"
       A&E no. 110 (1984).

279   **Arneson "is rewriting his famous Blackmoor":** "News Briefs," *Fantasy Gamer*
       no. 6 (1984): 36.

280   **"being the best known personality":** Gygax letter to TSR staff, September 25,
       1984.

280   **Dragonlance Interactive Theater:** Roger Moore, "Now That It's Over," *Polyhe-
       dron* no. 20 (1984): 27.

280   **"the most coherent blend":** Ken Rolston, "Advanced Hack-and-Slash," *DR* no.
       85 (1984): 64.

281   **"It is totally inaccurate":** Jennifer Harsha, "A Tragic Tale of Fact and Fantasy,"
       Lansing State Journal, October 28, 1984: 1D. See also Harsha, "Dear Defends
       Motives," *Lansing State Journal*, November 2, 1984.

281   **New York agency BBDO:** Kevin Blume memo "Update from the President to
       TSR Employees," November 1984. See also untitled TSR newsletter, September
       1984.

281   **"bowed to the Moral Majority":** Martin Wixted, "The Dark Ages Pages #22,"
       A&E no. 112 (1984).

282   **"a sop":** Gygax, "Sorceror's Scroll," *DR* no. 103 (1985): 8.

282   ***Trivial Pursuit* sales":** Kevin Blume memo "Update from the President to TSR
       Employees," November 1984.

282   **bringing in an estimated:** Don Oldenberg, "Stakes Getting Higher for Next
       Trivial Pursuit," syndicated in *Fort Worth Star Telegram*, November 23, 1986.

282   **"TSR seems to be sinking":** D'Arn, "Gossip," *DW* no. 37 (1984): 46.

283   **"now compiling what we devised":** Gygax, "Sorceror's Scroll," *DR* no. 90
       (1984): 16.

283   **"At a recent meeting":** Gygax, "Would You Go to See a D&D film?" *DR* no. 93
       (1985): 4.

283   **"TSR is expanding its book publishing":** Dragonlance press release, October 18,
       1984.

283   **Arneson sued TSR, again:** District Court of Minnesota, Fourth Division, Civil
       no. 4-84-1180.

285 **"Rose Estes . . . is suing TSR":** D'Arn, "A Letter from Gigi," *DW* no. 39 (1985): 46.

285 **Schick sued TSR:** District Court of Connecticut, Civil no. H-84–975.

285 **venerable Milton Bradley:** "Hasbro to Acquire Milton Bradley," *Los Angeles Times*, May 5, 1984. See also Desiree French, "Shea Resigns Hasbro Position," *Boston Globe*, September 27, 1984.

285 **Chaosium radically downsized:** "Big Changes at Chaosium," *SG* no. 73 (1985): 46.

285 *Fire & Movement* **magazine:** *F&M* hiatus began with no. 42.

285 **tidbit that Monarch Avalon:** Barasch, "Firing Line," *F&M* no. 43 (1985): 11.

286 **"a business fantasy come true":** Buchsbaum, "TSR Profile," *Inc.*, December 1, 1984.

286 **"tuition and fees":** Judi Witt letter to Richard Koenings, November 30, 1984.

287 **"removed himself":** "Scanner," *SG* no. 74 (1985): 47.

287 **"I think that all the directors":** Wesley Sommer testimony, 85-CV-907, June 20, 1986. See also Gygax letter to Kevin Blume, August 29, 1985, "Richard Koenings, then CEO of TSR, Inc., had already removed you from the positions with the corporation, and the majority of the Directory upheld this decision and action, as you must recall."

1985: The Ambush at Sheridan Springs

289 **"The company is up for sale":** D'Arn, "A Letter from Gigi," *DW* no. 39 (1985): 46.

289 **"absolutely untrue":** Anne F. Jaffe, "Maximize the Fun," *Game News* no. 2 (1985): 10.

289 **"acquire a major position":** "TSR Sale Pending?" *LGRN*, February 14, 1985.

289 **the Foreman group:** Exhibits filed in 85-CV-907 reference it as "Foreman" or "Forman". Various drafts of severance agreements for the Blumes are filed as exhibits.

290 **Another round of layoffs:** "TSR Lays Off 36 Employees," *LGRN*, March 14, 1985.

290 **"continuation of decline":** "Scanner," *SG* no. 74 (1985): 47.

291 **"Let's Bury the Hatchet":** Gygax, "Sorceror's Scroll," *DR* no. 95 (1985): 10.

291 **"restructuring itself financially":** "TSR Not Sold After All," *SG* no. 75 (1985): 46. See also "Group Won't Buy TSR," *LGRN*, April 11, 1985.

291 **"to report on the status"**: Koenings letter to all TSR employees, March 27, 1985.

293 **Gygax merely forgave:** Gygax testimony, 85-CV-907, January 29, 1986.

293 **"loose change"**: Williams testimony, 85-CV-907, June 20, 1986.

295 **"with Mr. Gygax in majority control"**: Martens testimony, 85-CV-907, November 15, 1985.

296 **"I got a vote of no confidence"**: Williams testimony, 85-CV-907, June 20, 1986. Also see TSR board meeting minutes for April 16.

296 **What happened next:** Kevin Blume testimony, 85-CV-907, June 19, 1986.

297 **"not eager to have"**: Williams testimony, 85-CV-907, June 20, 1986.

297 **Gygax effectively split the 2.5 percent:** Gygax letter to Zeb Cook, May 9, 1985.

297 **"I'm just too involved with corporate survival"**: Gygax letter to Kim Mohan, April 7, 1985.

298 **a small profit for the months:** Martens testimony, 85-CV-907, November 15, 1985. $11,000 for April, $21,000 for May.

298 **"The current financial condition"**: Martens memo to TSR employees, June 13, 1985.

298 **struck a deal where TSR would repay:** Martens testimony, 85-CV-907, November 15, 1985.

298 **"would have lost us our sixty-day"**: Williams testimony, 85-CV-907, June 20, 1986.

299 **only when James Huber:** Martens testimony, 85-CV-907, June 19, 1986.

300 **"One of the big promotional"**: Kate Gehrke, "Walkabout No. 3," *A&E* no. 124 (1985).

300 **"No offer was ever made"**: Gygax letter to Kevin Blume, August 29, 1985.

300 **"that they had made some sort of an invalid offer"**: Gygax testimony, 85-CV-907, January 29, 1986.

300 **TSR exceeded a spending cap** Williams testimony, 85-CV-907, June 20, 1986.

300 **other plans in Los Angeles:** Sommer testimony, 85-CV-907, November 15, 1985.

301 **"the public outcry"**: "Scanner," *SG* no. 74 (1985): 47.

301 **disavowed Radecki's credentials:** Robert Lee Zimmer, "Critic of TV Violence Has His Own Critics," *Rapid City Journal*, August 24, 1985.

302   **Pulling appeared in Connecticut:** Lisa Catanese, "Experts Call Game Harmful," *Hartford Courant*, September 21, 1985.

302   **Lorraine Williams started to intervene:** Williams testimony, 85-CV-907, June 20, 1986.

304   **"Gygax and I were not talking":** Williams testimony, 85-CV-907, June 20, 1986.

304   **"In how many seconds":** Williams testimony, 85-CV-907, June 20, 1986. See also Martens testimony, June 19, 1986.

305   **Lorraine met with the Blumes:** Williams testimony, 85-CV-907, June 20, 1986.

306   **"After thoughtful consideration":** Gygax letter to the TSR board, October 21, 1985. Read into Sommer testimony, 85-CV-907, June 20, 1986.

307   **"Resolved that":** TSR board meeting minutes, October 22, 1985.

308   **Gygax dropped a note:** Martens testimony, 85-CV-907, February 10, 1986.

308   **rumors in the hobby fanzines:** Lee Gold shared the rumor about Adventure Games being padlocked in *A&E* no. 115.

309   **"was perhaps high":** Gygax testimony, 85-CV-907, November 14, 1985 (morning).

309   **"I'm sorry too":** Gygax testimony, 85-CV-907, November 14, 1985 (afternoon).

310   **"The situation, notwithstanding the hypertechnical arguments":** Bruce Kaplan, attorney for Gygax, 85-CV-907, November 14, 1985 (morning).

310   **"sat on his rights":** Judgment of Robert D. Read, Circuit Judge, August 28, 1986.

311   **"The shape and direction":** *DR* no. 122 (1987): 40.

Epilogue: Endgame

313   **Gygax following in Arneson's footstep:** *TSR, Inc. v. Mayfair Games, Inc.*, Northern Illinois District Court, 91 C 0417, gives a July 9, 1987, date for the agreement that its *City-State* product cover would attribute its introduction to "E. Gary Gygax, creator of *Advanced Dungeons & Dragons*."

313   **"the Board of Directors saw fit":** *DR* no. 122 (1987): 40.

313   **"Is there bitterness?":** Gygax, "A Funny Thing Happened," *Familiar* no. 2 (1988): 14.

314   **"low-level-character sort of company":** Gary Gygax, *Dragon* (*DR*) no. 35 (1980).

314   **"if Gygax says it"**: Steven J. Engelbert, "Gary Gygax," *The Gamer*, March/April 1992, 24.

317   **"*D&D* was an inspiration to us"**: *War of Warcraft* 2.4.0 patch note, March 25, 2008.

317   **"Gygax and Blume think not"**: Geoffrey Smith, "Dungeons and Dollars," *Forbes*, September 15, 1980: 139.

Index